Spanish Cinema

The Auteurist Tradition

EDITED BY

Peter William Evans

OXFORD
UNIVERSITY PRESS

OXFORD
UNIVERSITY PRESS

Great Clarendon Street, Oxford OX2 6DP

Oxford University Press is a department of the University of Oxford.
It furthers the University's objective of excellence in research, scholarship,
and education by publishing worldwide in

Oxford New York

Athens Auckland Bangkok Bogotá Buenos Aires Calcutta
Cape Town Chennai Dar es Salaam Delhi Florence Hong Kong Istanbul
Karachi Kuala Lumpur Madrid Melbourne Mexico City Mumbai
Nairobi Paris São Paulo Singapore Taipei Tokyo Toronto Warsaw

with associated companies in Berlin Ibadan

Oxford is a registered trade mark of Oxford University Press
in the UK and in certain other countries

Published in the United States
by Oxford University Press Inc., New York

British Library Cataloguing in Publication Data
Data available

Library of Congress Cataloging in Publication Data

ISBN 0-19-818415-8
ISBN 0-19-818414-X (Pbk.)

1 3 5 7 9 10 8 6 4 2

Typeset in Sabon
by Cambrian Typesetters, Frimley, Surrey
Printed in Great Britain
on acid-free paper by
Biddles Ltd,
Guildford and King's Lynn

14 - 99

099554

61649

2 FE
3 0 JAN

Acknowledgements

I should like to thank the Research Committee of the School of Modern Languages, Queen Mary and Westfield College, University of London, for help with expenses incurred in the publication of this volume. Thanks are also due to the Filmoteca, Madrid (especially Marga Lobo). Stills by kind permission of José Luis Borau, El Imén, Pedro Almodóvar, El Deseo; Jet Films; Víctor Erice, Elías Querejeta; Juan José, Bigas Luna; Julio Medem; Carlos Saura, Magna Productions. I would also like to thank Matthew Hollis and Sophie Goldsworthy at OUP for their help and encouragement throughout this project.

Contents

List of Contributors

BERNARD P. E. BENTLEY is Chairman of Department and lecturer in Spanish at the University of St Andrews. He teaches Spanish cinema and has edited *The Film as Text*, and published 'The Credit Sequence of *La mitad del cielo*', *Forum for Modern Language Studies* (1995).

JOSÉ LUIS BORAU is the dirctor of major films in the recent history of Spanish cinema, including *Hay que matar a B* (1964), *Furtivos* (1975), *La Sabina* (1979), *Río abajo* (1984), *Tata mía* (1986), and *Niño nadie* (1997). He has also co-scripted various films, including *Mi querida señorita* (1971) and *Camada negra* (1977).

CELESTINO DELEYTO teaches English literature and film at the University of Zaragoza. He has published articles on Saura, Almodóvar, and Erice, and he is co-editor of *Terms of Endearment: Hollywood Romantic Comedy of the 1980s and 1990s* (Edinburgh University Press, 1998).

MARIA DELGADO is a lecturer in the School of English and Drama at Queen Mary and Westfield College, University of London. She is co-editor of *In Contact with the Gods? Directors Talk Theatre* (Manchester University Press, 1996, 1999) and editor of *Valle-Inclán Plays: One* (Methuen, 1993, 1996). She has written widely on film, and is an advisor to the London Film Festival.

XON DE ROS is a lecturer in Modern Spanish Studies at King's College, University of London. She has published in film, modern literature, and cultural studies, and has interests in comparative literature and film studies.

MARVIN D'LUGO is Director of the Screen Studies Program at Clark University, where he teaches courses on Spanish and Latin American cinemas. His *Guide to the Cinema of Spain* was published in 1997 (Greenwood Press), and he is currently completing a co-authored volume, *Theories of National Cinema* (Routledge).

PETER WILLIAM EVANS is Professor of Hispanic Studies at Queen Mary and Westfield College, University of London. His recent publications include

The Films of Luis Buñuel: Subjectivity and Desire (Oxford University Press, 1995), and Women on the Verge of a Nervous Breakdown (BFI, 1996).

ROBIN FIDDIAN is Fellow and Tutor in Spanish at Wadham College, Oxford, where he is also University Reader in Spanish. His publications have centred on modern Spanish American writing and twentieth-century Spanish literature and cinema. His publications on film include his co-authored book Challenges to Authority: Fiction and Film in Contemporary Spain (Tamesis, 1988), and the co-edited volume Sound on Vision: The Oxford Spanish Film Event 1997–98 (BHS, 1999).

JOHN HOPEWELL has written two books on the Spanish cinema, Out of the Past: Spanish Cinema after Franco (BFI, 1985), and El cine español después de Franco (Arquero, 1989). He is the Bureau Chief of Variety and Moving Pictures International in Spain.

BARRY JORDAN is Professor of Hispanic Studies at De Montfort University, Leicester. He has published work on post-war Spanish literature, drama, and, more recently, Spanish film. His books include Writing and Politics in Franco's Spain and Carmen Laforet . . . Nada (1993), and he has co-authored Contemporary Spanish Cinema (1998).

DOMINIC KEOWN is a Fellow of Fitzwilliam College and a lecturer in Catalan and Spanish at the University of Cambridge. He has written widely on the interface between culture and politics in contemporary Catalonia but also retains a keen interest in Iberian cinema of the post-war period, especially the films of Luis García Berlanga.

MARSHA KINDER is Professor of Critical Studies in the School of Cinema-Television at the University of Southern California. Her books on Spanish cinema include Blood Cinema: Reconstructing National Identity in Spain (University of California Press, 1993), with a companion bilingual CD-ROM, Refiguring Spain: Cinema/Media/Culture (Duke University Press, 1977), and Buñuel's The Discreet Charm of the Bourgeoisie (Cambridge University Press, 1998). She is a member of the board of Film Quarterly.

JO LABANYI is Professor of Modern Spanish Literature and Cultural Studies at Birkbeck College, University of London, and Director of the Institute of Romance Studies, University of London. Her publications on film include articles on Spanish cinema in the early Franco period (in Screen, 38/3 (1997), and in Heroines without Heroes: Female Identities in Post-war European Cinema 1945–51, ed. Ulrike Sieglohr, forthcoming).

SUSAN MARTIN-MÁRQUEZ teaches at Tulane University. She has written widely on Spanish cinema and has been completing a book on Feminist Discourse in the Spanish Cinema.

RIKKI MORGAN is Dean of the School of Languages and Social Sciences at Anglia Polytechnic University. She has written widely on Spanish cinema. Her latest publication is the co-authored book *Contemporary Spanish Cinema* (Manchester University Press, 1998).

CHRIS PERRIAM is Professor of Hispanic Studies and a member of the Centre for Research into Film at the University of Newcastle upon Tyne. He is working on film stars and masculinity in recent Spanish cinema, and has published on modern Chilean literature.

STEPHEN ROBERTS is a lecturer in Hispanic Studies at the University of Nottingham. His research interests include twentieth-century Spanish thought, literature, and film, and he has published widely on different aspects of the work of Miguel de Unamuno.

WENDY ROLPH is Professor of Spanish and Vice-Dean of the Faculty of Arts and Science at the University of Toronto. Her publications on Spanish cinema include essays and chapters in *Anales de la literatura española contemporánea*, *Post-Franco, Postmodern: The Films of Pedro Almodóvar* (Greenwood, 1991), *Revista canadiense de estudios hispánicos*, *Scripta mediterránea*, and *Words and Moving Images*.

ISABEL C. SANTAOLALLA teaches at Roehampton Institute, London. She has written on Spanish, British, and Hollywood cinema. Her most recent publication on Spanish cinema is 'Close Encounters: Racial Otherness in Imanol Uribe's *Bwana*', in Robin Fiddian (ed.), *Sound on Vision* (BHS, 1999).

PAUL JULIAN SMITH is Professor of Spanish in the University of Cambridge. He has written ten books on Spanish and Latin American film and litera-ture, including *Laws of Desire: Questions of Homosexuality in Spanish Writing and Film* (Oxford University Press, 1992), *Desire Unlimited: The Cinema of Pedro Almodóvar* (Verso, 1994), and *Vision Machines: Cinema, Literature and Sexuality in Spain and Cuba* (Verso, 1996).

NÚRIA TRIANA-TORIBIO lectures in Spanish film and history at the University of Liverpool. Her publications include articles in *Film History* and the *Bulletin of Hispanic Studies*, a chapter on Ana Mariscal in *Heroines without Heroes: Female Identities in Post-war European Cinema*

1945–51 (ed. Ulrike Sieglohr, Cassel/BFI, forthcoming), and the *Encyclopedia of Contemporary Spanish Culture* (Routledge, forthcoming) and *Contemporary Spanish Culture Studies* (Arnold, forthcoming).

List of Illustrations

Prologue
The Long March of the Spanish Cinema towards Itself

JOSÉ LUIS BORAU

EVEN though the term 'auteur' is problematic, largely because it somewhat neglects the protean and varied origins of cinematographic images, it nevertheless adequately suits the purpose of Peter Evans and his contributors, whose aim is to articulate a truth about Spanish cinema: namely, that its success both qualitatively and quantitatively stems from the efforts of those film-makers who placed above all else the desire to produce a work of art expressing a personal vision.

Spanish cinema, among the oldest in Europe, a cinema that never lost its momentum—even during the Civil War feature films continued to be made—and which even from its beginnings reached reasonably high levels of production, only claimed the attention of international critics about twenty or so years ago, after the death of Franco. Arguably, even today it is still a cinema that, despite a few outstanding films by directors such as Saura, Almodóvar, Bigas Luna, de la Iglesia, or Amenábar, remains unknown to mass audiences; despite, too, the growing, often admiring attention of historians and scholars in universities and centres of audiovisual and cultural studies throughout the world.

Such names, along with others less familiar abroad, but equally important to our industry, can be considered to be auteurs, in the sense that French critics, led by Bazin and his influential *Cahiers du cinéma*, gave to the term. Our film industry parallels a situation common to all those seemingly exotic, but geographically neighbouring, national industries. Those too are known only through a few directors—their auteurs—and sometimes not even then, as world attention is attracted by just a few remarkable or fortunate films.

But there are two essential differences. The first, already

mentioned, is that the Spanish situation is not, at least not in continental terms, that of a minor industry, since during the second half
of the century its level of production, even in moments of crisis, did
not fall much under fifty films per annum. This figure has often
doubled in recent years. Nowadays eighty or ninety films are made
annually, a figure that places Spain at the forefront of film production in the European Union.

The second and most characteristic of these differences is that
the work of the auteurs is not the exceptional product of an industry characterized by commercial triumphs and local themes, as was
the case of the American cinema in its heyday or of France (and its
famous directors) in the 1930s. In Spain it was precisely the auteurs
who, above all after the first screening of ¡Bienvenido Mr Marshall!
in the spring of 1953, accepted responsibility for guiding and
redefining the film industry to which they belonged, trying to
endow it gradually—perhaps without too much collective
consciousness, but through personal effort and inspiration—with
themes, forms, and styles that replaced old practices and created
new guidelines, defining our film industry for audiences abroad
and—with greater difficulty—for home audiences, or at least those
sections that were most critical and demanding.

This is not to say that in the fifty years prior to Berlanga's
famous comedy excellent films had not been made in Spain. In fact
there were many which, re-viewed today, are better and more
appealing than memory records; they are even superior in some
ways to others being made elsewhere at the same time. This can be
said of certain films made by Florián Rey, Benito Perojo, Edgar
Neville, Sáenz de Heredia, Rafael Gil, or Juan Antonio Nieves
Conde, to name only a few important figures from the first phase
of sound. But they were, in general terms, films that were subjected
either directly or indirectly to certain constraints—social, cultural,
political—that both tied them down to various positions and
limited their aesthetic achievement to the demands, from a strictly
cinematic point of view, of alien interests.

Thus, among the aesthetic constraints, the country's literary and,
above all, dramatic heritage played a leading role in imposing
certain norms, almost always of an old-fashioned kind, in obedience to formulae ranging from the traditions of post-Romantic
melodrama, through the high comedy of Benavente and the sainete
or its zarzuela and folkloric derivatives. All of this often resulted in

exaggerated performances. If we add to all this an equally *fin-de-siècle mise-en-scène*, inspired by *costumbrista* aesthetics, it is easy to understand how the wretched Spanish film-goer often felt alienated by, if not actually hostile towards, a country and a society that existed only on screen, and which had become increasingly distant, and even antithetical, to everyday realities. Not even the arrival of the republic and renewed social and aesthetic concerns managed significantly to affect this state of affairs.

The dictatorship worsened the situation, exacerbating rather than eliminating these evils, as well as introducing new ones, especially of a political nature. The matter, however, is complex. Contrary to widely held notions, the Francoist authorities almost never imposed themes directly related to the Civil War and, in fact, in comparative terms, it is true to say that films inspired by the war, its origins, or its consequences were few in number. These enjoyed official support provided, of course, they did not undermine the sacrosanct values of those in power, namely the army, the Falange, or the Church. If they did they were immediately and summarily removed from exhibition, regardless of whether they had been passed by the censor. The intensity and despotism of the latter, especially in the advanced stages of the regime, continued even when new generations began increasingly to express their frustration at the prevailing ideology, and at the elimination of almost all traces of realism in the choice of material. Those who wanted to avoid the censor's eye developed a cryptic style of veiled allusion or clever innuendo that ultimately even eluded the grasp of audiences who, though opposed to the regime, were ill equipped to decipher its coded messages. A total economic dependence on a system of subventions pushed the producers, on the other hand, into favouring narratives that were not only innocuous but also concerned with topics that met the approval of successive Francoist governments: military heroism, Spain's grandiloquent history, a dated religiosity, revived anti-communism, or the golden-egg-laying goose of tourism.

As if that were not enough, the cinematic models routinely followed by certain ambitious directors were distant and inappropriate, something not perhaps surprising given the country's isolation. The order of the day was either zany Hollywood-style comedies, stilted imitations of Mexican melodramas, or hard-hitting neorealist narratives. Although the originals might have been admired—hence the reasons behind their imitation—their partial or total adaptation by a domestic director earned disapproval. And not only by the audience. Critics, too, were quick to denounce any sign of imitation, considering it denigrating if not actually anti-Spanish. All of these constraints—cultural, political, and even cinematographic—made it difficult for audiences to warm to these films. Among other reasons this was due to constraints resulting in narrative situations that were impossible to accept—or, more accurately, to swallow—even for the simple palates of average Spaniards, unwilling to sample delights supposedly prepared with their tastes in mind.

In other words, leaving aside, of course, the exceptions already mentioned, halfway through the century the Spanish cinema had still not found its way. Despite their excellent quality, the overall impact of Spanish films was limited. The disappearance of Franco and his regime—and with it, above all, censorship—did not alter the situation overnight, as was at first imagined or predicted. Even though over the previous twenty years the status quo had already begun to be undermined, new directors, graduates in the main of the Escuela Oficial de Cinematografía in Madrid, or of movements like the so-called Barcelona School—to the majority of whom the term 'auteur' could perfectly well be applied—were making films to which the public, in general terms, continued to react with indifference, largely remaining faithful to the diet of old formulae, tinged with references to issues of contemporary relevance, like the much-discussed *tercera vía* (Third Way) or beautiful girl-filled *destape* (nudity) films.

A generational change of outlook was needed with the appearance of more informed audiences, together with the irremediable disappearance of older ones now blindly and definitively hooked on TV. And, above all, the overthrow of the previously mentioned constraints was paramount so that the auteurs—allowing for the flexibility we are inclined to apply to the term—could impose their own new law: one that was never codified but whose first clause demanded acknowledgement of the country's realities, either in order to describe, engage, or even reconcile ourselves to those realities, or to indulge private fantasies, and not just of the sexual kind. A host of young directors, to a large extent inspired by the successes of the new pioneers—the trail blazed by Almodóvar and company—succeeded in bringing about change. Even though, following the closure of the old EOC, the majority had not had the opportunity to realize their projects in schools—simply because there were none, not official ones, anyway—they completed their apprenticeship by any means available through membership of professional collectives or by independently making the obligatory shorts.

All strangely pulling together in a Spanish milieu noted more for its individualistic and varied tendencies, they sought strictly to observe the first clause of that new law: to address a real country, avoiding circumlocutions and solemnity at all costs, stressing modernity—in the true sense of the word—and prioritizing cinematographic values over any desire to stamp their own personality on their work as auteurs.

An immediate consequence of such an attitude was that audiences instantly recognized the new landscape being presented to them onscreen, and that they more or less identified themselves with the characters that populated it, whose forms of speech, movement, and dress were, ultimately, their own. The young in particular responded enthusiastically to such a dramatic novelty. They excused technical deficiencies and approved of the actors used in these films, whose performances matched the sincerity of their directors and the inexperience of their audiences.

In all the largely positive features of recent statistics, attention should be drawn to something relatively novel in the history of our cinema: almost 70 per cent of spectators are under 30 years old, coming mainly from the more educated levels of society. In view of the deep-seated indifference, if not outright hostility, with which those same social groups or their equivalents had traditionally received our home-based films, this is an almost revolutionary development. It is not surprising, therefore, that people believe increasingly—though, admittedly, without necessarily knowing very much about the past—that Spanish cinema is going through its best period, at least from a creative point of view—that is to say from an auteurist perspective. This is an opinion shared by most of the press, as may be seen either in their summaries of the year's achievements or in remarks made at the Goya awards.

So much is this so that even at the risk of exaggeration it can be claimed nowadays that an auteurist film in principle almost guarantees success. And, conversely, success is harder to achieve if a film is considered merely commercial. 'If you want to lose money in

Spain today make one of "those" films,' a very well-known distrib-
utor and exhibitor in Madrid is often heard to remark, referring to
the fact that the old criteria of production and operation are no
longer relevant. Even though this is true, it would be important to
add—let's not fool ourselves—that with changes in audiences,
stories, and directors the attitude towards commercial cinema has
also altered, and has even affected the so-called auteurs. Clearly
this need not be something prejudicial to the evaluation of a film in
an industry like ours so dependent on its customers.

This was how, to borrow the English expression, the inmates—
that is to say the auteurs—ended up by taking over the asylum,
doing it with truly impressive decisiveness and authority, qualities
perhaps not much in evidence in similar situations elsewhere, even
though the acts of rebellion and conquest were a task that required
no less than half a century for its completion; a task whose history
provides the backbone to this welcome and insightful book. The
work of Peter Evans and his informed group of contributors, all
very familiar with the bumpy and shifting terrain of our cinema,
will be required reading for anyone interested in studying the
surprising changes of direction in its history brought about by its
auteurs, a history that could well eventually be called, maintaining
the imagery of conquest, the long march of the Spanish cinema
towards itself, or what really amounts to the same thing: towards
a cinema free of non-cinematic constraints, one that can be truly
said to be independent.

I

Introduction

PETER WILLIAM EVANS

DESPITE calls for greater effort in production, distribution, and exhibition, the Spanish cinema—still of course overshadowed by Hollywood which continues to earn by far the lion's share of box-office income—has been in recent years, through its own devices, but also sometimes helped by state or TV (especially Canal +) sponsorship, experiencing something of a boom.[1] The last year or so has seen the appearance of films as varied as *Cosas que dejé en la Habana* (Gutiérrez Aragón), *La buena estrella* (Ricardo Franco), *Abre los ojos* (Alejandro Amenábar), *Secretos del corazón* (Montxo Armendáriz), *La mirada del otro* (Vicente Aranda), *El abuelo* (José Luis Garci), and *Solas* (Benito Zambrano), providing evidence of a healthy balance between work by new and established directors, whose films are all characterized by a maturity of approach in form and content. The established directors mentioned above, Gutiérrez Aragón, Ricardo Franco, Vicente Aranda, Montxo Armendáriz, and José Luis Garci, continue to explore new avenues while remaining true to their known instincts: *Cosas que dejé en la Habana* forsakes the preoccupations of country life (so crucial to films like *Habla mudita* (1973), *El corazón del bosque* (1979), or *La mitad del cielo* (1986)) for the *mise-en-scène* of the city, but its focus on loneliness and the pain of human relationships unmistakably recalls the emotional ambience of those early films (not to mention a characteristic interest in food); *La buena estrella* abandons the *tremendista* aesthetics of a film like *Pascual Duarte* (1975), but its exploration of the brutalization of individuals neglected by an uncaring society continues to testify to its director's concern with

---

[1] For the history of state sponsorship and related matters, see García Fernández 1992.

the dehumanizing consequences of poverty and squalor; *La mirada del otro*, pushing to the limit Aranda's fascination with links between sexuality and identity, confirms him as one of the Spanish cinema's most provocative voices in the study of the overlapping territory between sex and gender; Montxo Armendáriz returns in *Secretos del corazón* to an abiding interest, the unravelling of the mysteries of childhood and adolescence; inspired by Galdós, José Luis Garci sensitively explores questions of paternity and family relationships. Of the new generation, Alejandro Amenábar is one of a host of young film-makers, including Julio Medem, Juanma Bajo Ulloa, Agustín Yanes, Gracia Querejeta, Icíar Bollaín, Azucena Rodríguez, and many others, whose work is beginning to attract critical attention not only in Spain but also abroad. Major festivals in Britain, the United States, and elsewhere have continued to exhibit Spanish films. While the reputation of Spanish cinema had to rely, at first, on the names of Buñuel and Saura, and then on Almodóvar, and perhaps to some extent Bigas Luna (with some individual films like *El verdugo* (1963), *El espíritu de la colmena* (1973), and *Furtivos* (1975) also making an impact in their own right), it now enjoys greater exposure largely thanks to a new 'New Spanish Cinema' of emerging talent. It may be that this has had a knock-on effect on the exhibition of Spanish films by foreign TV companies: in 1997, 75 Spanish films were shown in Germany, 89 in the USA, 17 in France, though still only 7 in Britain (*Boletín de la Academia de las Artes y las Ciencias Cinematográficas de España*, 32 (Feb. 1998): 4).

Significantly, the spectacular rise and development of Spanish cinema over the last twenty years or so has been largely associated with the work of directors who could loosely be said to belong to an auteurist as distinct from a popular tradition of film-making.[2] While overtly commercial or 'popular' cinema has continued to survive—enjoying sporadic box-office success with films like *Yo soy ésa* (Luis Sanz, 1990)—the real successes in terms of both quality and quantity have been auteur-based. The kind of genre-based films—musicals, thrillers, comedies, melodramas, epics, religious and child-based narratives, and so on—that very much characterized the greater output of the industry up to the mid-1970s have to

---

[2]   For definitions of the popular see Storey 1993. Here I use the term 'popular' as a definition of a more box-office-led cinema.

a large extent lost their audience not only, as ever, to Hollywood, but also to TV.

Equally, a gradual shift in the sociology of spectatorship for auteurist films is noticeable, for whereas the early work of Saura, Erice, and the rest appealed to minority audiences, it is clear that films by directors now working in that tradition are beginning to break box-office records. El Deseo, Almodóvar's production company, has of course led the way, earning more than anyone else in successive years from 1988 to 1991: 644,743,506 pesetas in 1988; 330,059,568 pesetas in 1989; 484,661,156 pesetas in 1990; and 739,108,326 pesetas in 1991 (García Fernández 1992: 156–7). But even El Imán, José Luis Borau's production company, appears in tenth place in 1980, having taken 79,125,084 pesetas. A list published in 1991 of the highest-earning films in Spanish history reads like a roll-call of work by the country's leading art-movie or auteurist directors: (1) *Mujeres al borde de un ataque de nervios* (1,158,933,832 pesetas); (2) *Tacones lejanos* (729,949,800 pesetas); (3) *La vaquilla* (527,459,739 pesetas); and (4) *Los santos inocentes* (523,904,485 pesetas) (García Fernández 1992: 140). In 1998, up to the time of writing, the top grossing films are *Airbag* with 1,180,000,000 pesetas, *Abre los ojos* with 936,646,039 pesetas, *Carne trémula* with 809,498,028 pesetas, *Secretos del corazón* with 492,679,736 pesetas, and *Perdita Durango* with 429,800,050 pesetas, all by major art-movie directors (*Boletín de la Academia de las Artes y las Ciencias Cinematográficas de España*, 32 (Feb. 1988): 13).

As well as the question of the complex relationship between films in this tradition made in the 1950s, 1960s, and early 1970s (to a certain extent including those, too, of the *tercera vía*, that group of films that sought to bridge the gap between the auteurist and popular traditions) and their modern variants, there are many other key issues involved in drawing up boundaries between different types of cinema. The art-movie tradition has increasingly attempted to achieve popularity on its own terms, not just through intertextual cross-fertilization with Hollywood, but by educating its audience into developing a taste for mature treatment of sophisticated material. Films like Almodóvar's *Mujeres al borde de un ataque de nervios* (1988) or Icíar Bollaín's *Hola ¿estás sola?* (1995) in turn depend on the audience's familiarity with commercial, studio-based films like *Johnny Guitar* (Nicholas Ray, 1954) and

Thelma and Louise (Ridley Scott, 1991), but in addition to both playing with audience expectation and acknowledging the vitality of mainstream popular cinema, these films incorporate elements of the popular in texts that transcend postmodernist abolition of aesthetic boundaries in their pursuit of more thorough treatment of subjects that in popular cinema often proved for various reasons— say, commercial or ideological—too difficult.

The decision to concentrate in this volume on the art-movie or auteurist tradition does not deny the importance of popular cinema in Spain. Indeed, a book concentrating not on Saura, Gutiérrez Aragón, and the rest, but on, say, a production company like CIFESA, stars like Sara Montiel or Marisol, and key genres as represented by comedies made by directors like Pedro Lazaga or melodramas by Rafael Gil, would provide an ideal companion volume. These topics are in their own way fascinating areas of enquiry, and no value judgement is implied in their exclusion here. This book simply concentrates on the former tradition, on films that despite all sorts of constraints, especially those associated with the Franco years, have managed more successfully to represent the personal vision of their creators. Even this objective, though, in deconstructionist times, is fraught with many difficulties. We are long past the age of 1950s and 1960s innocence when *Cahiers du cinéma*-inspired approaches to auteurist cinema could unproblematically declare the directors of such films to be the indisputable organizing presence of the work. Concentration here on auteurist films nevertheless reflects on their Janus-faced status as the mediators as well as the shapers and purveyors of meaning. This study takes as axiomatic the need to read each film within the contexts of Spanish history and sociology. Our aim has been as far as possible to balance attention to the chronological development of auteurist cinema in Spain since the 1950s with acknowledgement of representative work of some of the key directors from this period. Inevitably skating over some areas, the volume attempts to create in each chapter a proper balance between the intrinsic merits of the chosen film, the status of its director, and its problematization of key issues. This is obviously not something easily achieved. The choices here will not coincide with everyone else's; for every film privileged in this way many others have had to be neglected. We have concentrated on the last forty years or so, leading up to but not venturing too far into the 1990s because, for all their undisputed qualities, the films of the last few years have yet to endure the test of time, their long-term significance still undergoing a process of bedding down. Nevertheless, the boom in emerging directors, above all women directors like Chus Gutiérrez, Icíar Bollaín, Gracia Querejeta, Azucena Rodríguez, Isabel Coixet, augurs well for the future.

We begin in the early 1950s because a limit has to be placed somewhere, and the forty years or so since then have yielded some of the most stimulating and rewarding films produced by the Spanish film industry. To a large extent, too, this is the Spanish cinema that has found an audience abroad, despite what should be regarded as the undisputed merit of films like *Locura de amor* (Orduña, 1948), *Angustia* (Nieves Conde, 1947), *Bambú* (Sáenz de Heredia, 1945), and other pre-1950s productions.

In concentrating on individual films by key directors—though once again our choices have inevitably meant the sacrifice of others with good claims for inclusion—the volume aims to allow more space for sustained discussion of specific texts than has been possible in some of the excellent recent surveys—especially by John Hopewell, Marsha Kinder, Marvin D'Lugo, and Julio Pérez Perucha—that have appeared on this subject. The films initially discussed—*¡Bienvenido Mr Marshall!* (1952), *Calle mayor* (1956), *Los golfos* (1959), *Del rosa. . . al amarillo* (1963), *Tristana* (1970), *El espíritu de la colmena* (1973), and *Furtivos* (1975)—are all considered within the framework of the struggle against the political realities of dictatorship. During the course of these surveys major issues are touched on: Wendy Rolph in the chapter on *¡Bienvenido Mr Marshall!* looks at notions of Spanishness and relations between Spanish and other national cinemas; Stephen Roberts considers, among other matters, the links between *Calle Mayor* and its literary/film antecedents, refocusing, too, questions about the importance of Italian neo-realism during this period; Maria Delgado comments on questions of form (making connections with the French New Wave and Hollywood) and content, above all in relation to 1960s ideals of masculinity as represented and decoded in *Los golfos*; Susan Martin-Márquez explores in *Del rosa. . . al amarillo* the impact of popular culture on processes of socialization under Franco; Jo Labanyi, relying especially on Creed/Kristeva theories of the abject and the monstrous-feminine, considers *Tristana* from the point of view of film representations of gender; Paul Julian Smith raises questions of aesthetic and ideological significance in *El espíritu de la colmena*; Peter Evans relates *Furtivos* to a key moment in Spanish history and theorizes questions of gender through analysis of the film's disturbing treatment of incest.

These films were all made in difficult times. The remainder of those discussed in the volume reflect the greater ease with which film-makers could tackle their subjects after the two most decisive moments in recent Spanish film history: the death of Franco in 1975 and the abolition of censorship in 1977. The broader political context of the Transition comes under scrutiny in Marsha Kinder's reflections, in the chapter on *Cambio de sexo*, on gender issues, the uncertainties of the future in a post-Francoist Spain; and questions of regionalism and nationalism, as well as meditations on renewed interest in formal experiment, are all discussed by Dominic Keown, John Hopewell, Rikki Morgan, Xon de Ros, and Marvin D'Lugo in *Mi hija Hildegart, El corazón del bosque, Gary Cooper que estás en los cielos, Epílogo*, and *La muerte de Mikel* respectively.

In the last third of the volume, Núria Triana looks through *¿Qué he hecho yo para merecer esto?* at the Almodóvar phenomenon, Robin Fiddian through *La vida alegre* at Spanish political culture in a society not yet fully liberated from pre-democratic attitudes, Chris Perriam at questions of homosexuality and institutionalized homophobia through a discussion of *Las cosas del querer*, Isabel Santaolalla at notions of gendered and collective (Basque) identity as represented in *Vacas*, while Celestino Deleyto covers similar territory but focusing, through *Jamón jamón*, on traditions, rituals, and issues identified with other parts of the country. The volume concludes with chapters by Barry Jordan and Bernard Bentley containing discussions, respectively, of *Belle Époque*, a film that earned international recognition for its provocative treatment of subjectivity, and *Nadie hablará de nosotras cuando hayamos muerto*, a thriller that cuts across the boundaries of popular and auteurist cinema.

Through the perspectives of contemporary film and cultural theory, this volume surveys—in some cases for the first time in a sustained way—major landmarks in the Spanish cinema of the last forty years or so. The films under discussion here provide some of the most fruitful opportunities for revisiting and theorizing post-1950s Spain and its evolving, relatively recent cinema history.

REFERENCES

D'Lugo, Marvin (1997), *Guide to the Cinema of Spain*. Westport, Conn.: Greenwood Press.

García Fernández, Emilio C. (1992), *El cine español contemporáneo*. Barcelona: Art-Universitas.

Hopewell, John (1986), *Out of the Past: Spanish Cinema after Franco*. London: BFI.

Kinder, Marsha (1993), *Blood Cinema: The Reconstruction of National Identity in Spain*. Berkeley and Los Angeles: University of California Press.

Pérez Perucha, Julio (ed.) (1997), *Antología crítica del cine español 1906–1995*. Madrid: Cátedra/Filmoteca Española.

Storey, John (1993), *An Introductory Guide to Cultural Theory and Popular Culture*. London: Harvester/Wheatsheaf.

2

¡Bienvenido Mr Marshall!
(Berlanga, 1952)

WENDY ROLPH

OF the seventeen feature films which Luis García Berlanga has directed over a long and occasionally controversial career, *¡Bienvenido Mr Marshall!* (1952) remains the one which has most consistently been identified as marking a turning point in the history of Spanish cinema. Hence the appropriateness of its inclusion in this volume. Successive generations of writers on Spanish cinema, regardless of their theoretical grounding, historical perspectives, or critical approaches, have repeatedly reaffirmed the film's significance on both influential and qualitative terms. As a consequence, its reappearance continues to be virtually guaranteed on lists, surveys, and catalogues of the hundred, fifty, and even the ten 'best' films ever made in Spain.[1] A canonical text from a breakthrough decade, *¡Bienvenido Mr Marshall!* has been etched into collective memory for the decisiveness of its impact on the audiences of its era and the effectiveness with which it cracked open new possibilities for engagement with significant socio-political commentary within conventional comedic modes.[2] But the future of the film is becoming as interesting as its past. The iterations of its rerelease and distribution in subsequent decades through

---

[1] The fact that many of these manifestations of a pervasive contemporary trend are little more than journalistic opinion-polling exercises published in the popular press in no way detracts from their opinion-shaping effectiveness among the general public. As a consequence, such listings have become important tools for the commercialization and marketing of Spanish cinema as a phenomenon with a viable history. For a typical recent example, see Ballesteros 1995, where *¡Bienvenido Mr Marshall!* ends up ranked in sixth place.

[2] At 51 days, *¡Bienvenido Mr Marshall!* enjoyed the longest initial run of any film from 1952 but does not compare with Ladisao Varda's 1954 *Marcelino, pan y vino* (145 days) or Juan de Orduña's 1957 *El último cuplé* (325 days). For further statistical analysis, see Monterde 1995.

cineclub libraries, videotape rentals, and the current mass merchandizing of low-priced cassettes through commercial video retail outlets across much of urban Spain, while perhaps not always nor exclusively motivated by the film's solid historical and critical reputation, have nevertheless ensured that *¡Bienvenido Mr Marshall!* has become accessible to new generations of viewers, and thus available for re-evaluation of earlier assessments of its status as 'una obra que no ha perdido vigencia'.[3]

By providing an entertaining yet far from innocuous viewing experience, *¡Bienvenido Mr Marshall!* in its time quickly became both landmark and benchmark, demonstrating to other film-makers the richly provocative possibilities of film comedy as a means of outmanœuvring censorship and creating a climate of reception in which audiences might be encouraged to reflect on their own experience and to contemplate the extent of their cultural conditioning by ideologies which both informed and dominated their daily existence. It thus has routinely been cited as an early Spanish initiative in oppositional film-making, an important predecessor to the more audacious methodologies of dissent deployed in the 1960s and early 1970s by other film-makers who were increasingly concerned to push out the parameters of possibility of the New Spanish Cinema beyond those of its first phase. Yet, despite the frequency with which the wealth of clever comic moments of *¡Bienvenido Mr Marshall!* have been itemized and the consistency with which the film's prominence within the trajectory of Spanish cinema has been underscored, it is only relatively recently, as advances in technology have facilitated close critical analysis and as scholarly perspectives have been sharpened by a more generalized disengagement from narrowly auteurist approaches, that iconic celebration has given way to more systematic and detailed observation of this and other early landmark Spanish films. Eventually the question which must be asked, and which in a limited way the present discussion poses, is how well the Berlanga comedy classic

---

[3] Thus described by Diego Galán in an influential journal profile, his assessment coincided with an early surge of both popular and critical interest in the director's work in the mid-1970s. See Galán 1974. Subsequent monographic publications on Berlanga and his work have tended to appear in clusters, one such cluster at the beginning of the 1980s (Hernández Les and Hidalgo 1981; Pérez Perucha 1980–1) and a subsequent grouping in the 1990s (Gómez Rufo 1990; Cañeque and Grau 1993; Monterde 1995).

will continue to withstand such scrutiny in current and future
climates of reception both within and beyond the Spanish-speaking
sphere. My intervention into the dialogue over *¡Bienvenido Mr
Marshall!* assumes that the reader has not only access to a video
copy of the film but also a certain familiarity with the theoretical
perspectives within which recent critical commentary on the film
has been framed, especially by such scholars as Marsha Kinder and
Kathleen Vernon.[4] Much of my discussion will be shaped around a
few key elements of the comic rhetoric of exposition and performance through which it might be argued that the film is situating
itself as landmark. I shall, however, also conjecture briefly on some
of the possible consequences both of and for its status as landmark
in the reception which *¡Bienvenido Mr Marshall!* is currently positioned to receive as it is distributed by new institutions in various
formats, appropriated into divergent regional and global contexts,
and thus opened out to reinterpretation by a wider diversity of
viewers. How do the new structural mechanisms of the media
industries impose new controls on such consecrated texts?

Pues, señor, érase una vez un pueblo español, un pueblecito cualquiera. . .
Este pueblo no tiene nada de particular. . .

Frequently cited for the biting accuracy and post-war Spanish
specificity of its satirically humorous rendering of the 'hopes
raised/hopes dashed' moral fable, *¡Bienvenido Mr Marshall!*
narrates a few days in the life of a prototypical Castilian town,
Villar del Río. Yet even before the rendering of a series of incidents
and interpolations which resonate both to universal truths and to a
precisely contemporaneous inter- and extra-filmic moment in
history, the show-and-tell strategy of the 'once upon a time' opening sequence sets the stage by drawing together literary and cinematic traditions of 'beginnings' into an audiovisual overdetermination of ordinariness. There are, if one is prepared to
believe the voice-over narration, no unusual markers whatsoever to
distinguish either the film or its locus of action. Nor is there
anything other than the stereotypical in the typology of its relatively large cast of characters, nor, for that matter, in the diegetic

<hr/>

4 Both Kinder and Vernon approach the film as a case study within a broader
analysis and contextualization of Spanish cinema. See Kinder 1993; Vernon 1997:
35–64.

role which each performs. They represent the norms of village culture, collated to the standard spaces and places of village life, but sharpened and caricatured through the comic choreography of their interactions. The citizens of Villar del Río are galvanized by portentous arrivals: of a glamorous singing star to entertain them, and of a coterie of messengers bearing news of the imminence of yet another, even more significant arrival in the normally sleepy town. This latter arrival carries a dual promise: of rescue from the deprivations and hardships of the present, and of gratification of individual and collective desires and aspirations for the future. The villagers go to great lengths to prepare a worthy welcome for their eminent, powerful, and reputedly munificent guests but the pleasures, and their concomitant anxieties, turn out to be wholly in the anticipation rather than the actualization of the much-desired encounter. The visitors' vehicles rush noisily through town without so much as slowing down, and as the next day's rains fall both literally and figuratively on the aftermath of the citizens' elaborately choreographed parade the locals have little choice but to mop up, pay up, and get on with the routines of life as they have lived it before.

Simply yet slyly structured around a rhythmic alternation of arrivals and departures and the absurdly comic hyperactivity of reactions and preparations entailed by both, the cinematic narrative of *¡Bienvenido Mr Marshall!* highlights several kinds of rhetorical devices and formal and contextual linkages which, when followed through by the spectator and reassembled through an attentive reading of the film's explanations and qualifications and its audiovisual patterning of stops and starts and repetitions and reversals, have repeatedly been shown to radicalize the interpretative possibilities of the comedy while at the same time presenting a surface compliance with dominant ideological frameworks. Inscribed within tightly prescribed conventions and rituals of entertainment, *¡Bienvenido Mr Marshall!* nevertheless exposes the rules and roots of its own arsenal of artifice and in so doing interrogates both the origins and the intentionality of the very entertainment which it sets out to provide. Given the economic and intellectual context of Francoist Spain, especially in its early decades, the relatively narrow range of politically permissible notions of progress and prosperity would be especially unlikely to produce satisfactory and lasting solutions to that era's seemingly permanent crisis of impoverishment and lack. Thus most of the film's major moments, and the voice-over narration which threads them together, work cumulatively through the comedy to heighten awareness of a range of possible implications of the notion that, whatever the nature of individual human desire, events are bound both to distort its representation and to conspire against its gratification.

Os digo. . . que los americanos van a venir, y que el señor delegado ofrece un premio al que los reciba mejor. . . ah, pero no solamente mejor, sino más al gusto de los americanos. . .

That the anticipation of the poor Spanish citizens of Villar del Río arises as an inevitable consequence of the predicted visit by 'los americanos del norte, los del plan Marshall' grounds the film firmly in the historical moment of its production, the early 1950s when Spain's initial ineligibility for aid under the terms of the Marshall Plan had become ironically juxtaposed with the emerging strategic attractiveness of the Iberian peninsula to American foreign policy in the context of the Cold War. At the time of the film's release, Spain and the United States had already entered into negotiations through which, in exchange for various forms of aid, the United States would be permitted to establish a military presence in the country. In addition, the fact that the film's prototypical Castilian villagers enthusiastically prepare to welcome their American visitors by 'performing' their Spanishness as if they had all become participants in an Andalusian *meta-españolada* permits the overlay of further intertextual and socio-cultural dimensions onto *¡Bienvenido Mr Marshall!*, not only replicating contemporaneous attitudes and tendencies in the 1950s but also resonating over time to the interpretative issues raised by similar parodic devices in a number of other landmark films of the post-Franco years by filmmakers such as Almodóvar, Bigas Luna, and Carlos Saura. For individuals and collectivities, filmic or otherwise, to modify their behaviour to conform to internally driven (mis)perceptions of the expectations of others is nothing if not common, nor is it at all unusual to find instances of (mis)representation of cultural stereotypes driving various forms of popular and mass entertainment. Hence the general recognizability and universality of the interlinked conundrums of identity and authenticity underscored in and by the Berlanga film. Yet the historical and stylistic specificities to which the film owes both its original motivation and its formal elaboration remain foregrounded, not only as a consequence of the underscoring of these specificities in published studies on the film, but also through their appropriateness to an exposition of the central thematic preoccupation with the disguising of material reality in cliché as a double denunciation of inauthenticity in (Spanish) life and of falseness in (Spanish) film.[5]

That said, it would seem that the film goes somewhat further in probing sensitivities surrounding exactly what it is that powers representation. The cultural message to beam back to the American visitors is diegetically framed by the visitors' own distorted expectations of Spanishness, as conjectured by the distorting perspectives of the hosts. At the same time, and extra-diegetically, its potential impact on subsequent generations of viewers is set up to be transformed as new sets of—inevitably also distorted—expectations are brought to bear on the givens of the text. Such processes of redeployment, reversal, and retransmission underscore the fact that, indeed, it may well be that the reflected view and this view alone is the only viable, exportable image. If—as still seems sometimes to be the case—the visual manifestation of a desirably exotic Spanish specificity is most easily achieved, even for Spaniards, through the invocation of flamenco/torero/gitano typologies and false-front village topographies, it stands to reason that mapping an amalgam of Andalusian stereotypes and disguises onto the equally stereotypical Castilian pueblo—which itself has been 'created' cinematically not on a Cifesa backlot but through location shooting at Guadalix de la Sierra—not only multiplies the levels of exoticism but also ultimately explodes national and temporal specificities in its gentle spoofing of human gullibility when confronted with any kind of performance at all.

Throughout, the film's diegetic events both mirror and problematize the parallel activities of reception and interpretation, as—like the villagers within the text who initially misread the arrival of road crews decked out with American flags—the viewers are encouraged first to draw and then to revisit what may or may not turn out to be false conclusions based on circumstantial evidence

[5] Gómez Rufo (1990) is particularly insistent on this point, although the particular emphases which he places on this thematic focus as giving evidence both of the input of co-writer Juan Antonio Bardem and of the lingering echo of the moral and philosophical attitude of the Generation of '98 are tangential to the present study.

and the misarticulations of presence and absence. The question of absence becomes key to the interpretative possibilities of the text as cultural critique, especially of its performative components. For the film's double-edged strategies of intertextual representation of exoticism to work, and for its Hollywood and Reyes Magos/Santa Claus analogies to be permitted to play out fully, the Americans— like the real-life Mr Marshall—must be scripted never to arrive, in order that—like the cinematic phenomenon itself—they remain absent in their presence, essentially and necessarily both unreadable and unknowable. Thus they exist in *¡Bienvenido Mr Marshall!* only through the agency of the delegation which represents them, through the mediated projection of a No-Do documentary sequence, through the villagers' cinematically oneiric articulations of their innermost fantasies and fears—and through the (pre)conceptions of Americanness brought to the viewing of the film by the spectators themselves.

That the same process of falsification evident in the fabrication of a cartoon Andalusia is extended to a similarly exoticized America, both through the interpolated didactic documentary and through the expressionistic presentation of the villagers' dreams and nightmares, deepens the satire but also expands the range and complexity of issues open for discussion and debate. While appearing to celebrate the most facile and easily recognizable representations of both Spanishness and Americanness, the humour of *¡Bienvenido Mr Marshall!* repeatedly punches back, foregrounding the constructedness and superficiality of those representations in all of their facets and inviting criticism of the project as a collective (read national) cultural activity. In this sense, the readying of the clock-tower and the welcoming banners, the raising of the sets which recreate an Andalusian street scene, the coaxing of the live bull into a pseudo-taxidermic rendering of an illustrious taurine ancestor, and the rhymed sequences in the central square in which the townspeople are assembled, costumed, given instruction, and rehearsed in their roles by the impresario and the mayor, assume a special significance, first through their subversive invocation of other cinematic intertexts and second through the further underscoring of their falseness as they are rapidly dismantled, disassembled, or simply dissolved by the rain in the penultimate sequence of the film.

The nightmares of the citizenry are more than stylized satirical spoofs of cinematic genres both local (the historical epic) and international (American *noir* and western and Soviet social realism). Carefully matched to the obsessions and the predilections of the dreamers, oneiric extensions of the film's registers of performance, they permit the film-maker to 'move beyond the confines of an ahistorical formula film, the *españolada*, to project a critical vision of contemporary Spanish reality', as Kathleen Vernon has succinctly pointed out in the context of her close reading of the nightmare of the priest.[6] Read as a continuum, their cumulative effect produces a parodic double inversion of the delusive procedures of self-definition both within and beyond the text.

As hyperbolic conflations of metaphors it would seem that all four of the citizens' dreams participate to a greater or lesser extent in the bonding of socio-political and/or historical preoccupation with cinematic refabulation. Yet the individual stamp of each conceptual articulation and generically mediated elaboration in *¡Bienvenido Mr Marshall!* works against any single totalizing interpretation either of their thematic function or of their humorous and satirical effect. Perhaps more important, by juxtaposing the failure of history (both Spain's and America's) with the triumph of myth (Hollywood and the Reyes Magos), the dreams prepare the terrain for against-the-grain interpretations of the syncopated misalliance of sound and image in the film's coda, challenging and subverting any reading which would merely reinscribe the chastened and 'cleansed' citizens of Villar del Río within the dominant ideology of acquiescent resignation. In this, it is important to recognize the importance of the positioning of the disembodied voice of Fernando Rey within the film's hierarchy of knowledge, even though he is denied the visual iconicity his subsequent star status would later provide. The act of telling, especially at the beginning and the end of the film, is of course designed to script the viewer's interpretation(s). But it also works disingenuously in contradiction to that very scripting, enticing the viewer to play with the suggestion that there may turn out to be important, and interpretatively complex, limits to its applicability.[7] As well as engaging and

---

[6] Like Kinder, Vernon takes an essentially Althusserian approach to her study of 'politicized intertextuality' within the Berlanga film, tracing in considerable detail the interactions between its systems of representation and the material conditions of existence at the time of its production and initial exhibition. See Vernon 1997: 38–42.

[7] See the persuasive argument for the careful investigation of the interface between script and story made by David Herman (1997).

sustaining audience complicity in the villagers' desires, the voice-over provides a foil for analysis of those desires against logistical and ideological impediments to their gratification. But the voice-over also becomes subject both to self-contradiction and to qualification by the image track. Indeed much of the exquisitely funny tension in ¡Bienvenido Mr Marshall! between a not-so-innocent vision and visions of innocence plays out through slippages between script and story as well as the disjunctures between sight and sound. In the saga of opportunities missed, the possibility of improvement is offered, is withheld, but is never quite precluded, since the meaning of the ending—and through it the entire film—never quite manages completely to settle down into the resigned acceptance of the status quo which the overall movement of the narrative seems configured to suggest.

Bien pudiera ser que este cuento no tuviese final. En general las cosas nunca acaban del todo, ni tampoco salen como uno se había imaginado. . .

The cult status which ¡Bienvenido Mr Marshall! acquired as a precocious precursor of the New Spanish Cinema might have been expected to open it out over time to ranges of interpretation and categories of meaning transcendent of its articulated intentional and contextual specificities. But such has not happened, or at least not yet. The nuanced approaches to film analysis which have been so fruitfully deployed in the most recent studies have continued to frame it within the newly historicized and material specificities of its context of production. That context, of course, assumed pre-video conditions of viewing, conditions which have been virtually completely displaced by the technologies of television and the stoppable, rewindable tape. Rapid advances in technology have permitted scholars to reconsider latent and surface patternings of meaning, and to explore in greater detail the intertextual linkages between this film and others which it invokes. At the same time, video being potentially a much more nomadic medium than film, opportunities to see ¡Bienvenido Mr Marshall! are more randomly available than in the past, since exhibition is now neither exclusively dependent on theatrical rerelease nor programmatically locked in to film cycles and retrospectives. It is useful to consider the consequences of the shift from the range of predictabilities of relatively localized theatrical exhibition to the multiply unpredictable contexts of video reception in the widening spheres in which cultural goods are offered up for exchange. Even from the perspective of the micro-region, despite the assiduous efforts of cultural historians, the film's evocations of space, place, and circumstance resonate less and less to contemporary recognizabilities. The reality of the film's placement in the 'national classics' sections of video store shelves, well away from the highly trafficked areas where the most-in-demand titles are placed, codes it as being just one more among the many similarly jacketed rereleased video artefacts from a bygone era. The theme, script, and story of *¡Bienvenido Mr Marshall!* take as a given the complex web of relationships between economic dependency and cultural exchange. It would indeed be ironic if in future iterations that same interplay of economics and culture were to conspire against the markers of the film's difference, stripping it of its distinctiveness and levelling it within the cinematic landscape of the past. Such destiny for such a quirky film would be to the cultural impoverishment of all, since the humour of *¡Bienvenido Mr Marshall!* so clearly retains the capacity to resonate to the most universal of human truths.

REFERENCES

Ballesteros, Cecilia (1995), 'Cintas de oro: las 50 mejores películas del cine español', *Revista el mundo* (17 Dec.).

Cañeque, Carlos, and Grau, Maite (1993), *¡Bienvenido Mr Berlanga!* Barcelona: Destino.

Galán, Diego (1974), 'Luis G. Berlanga o el cine muerto de hambre', *Dirigido por*, 13 (May): 1–15.

Gómez Rufo, Antonio (1990), *Berlanga, contra el poder y la gloria: escenas de una vida*. Madrid: Ediciones Temas de Hoy.

Herman, David (1997), 'Scripts, Sequences, and Stories: Elements of a Postclassical Narratology', *PMLA* 112 (Oct.): 1046–59.

Hernández Les, Juan, and Hidalgo, Manuel (1981), *El último austrohúngaro: conversaciones con Berlanga*. Barcelona: Anagrama.

Kinder, Marsha (1993), *Blood Cinema: The Reconstruction of National Identity in Spain*. Berkeley and Los Angeles: University of California Press.

Monterde, José Enrique (1995), 'Continuismo y disidencia (1951–1962)', in Román Gubern, José Enrique Monterde, Julio Pérez Perucha, Esteve Riambau, and Casimirio Torreiro, *Historia del cine español*, Madrid: Cátedra.

Pérez Perucha, Julio (ed.) (1980–1), *En torno a Berlanga*. Valencia: Ayuntamiento.

Vernon, Kathleen M. (1997), 'Reading Hollywood in/and Spanish Cinema: From Trade Wars to Transculturation', in Marsha Kinder (ed.), *Refiguring Spain: Cinema/Media/Representation*, Durham, NC: Duke University Press: 35–64.

3

In Search of a New Spanish Realism: Bardem's *Calle Mayor* (1956)

STEPHEN ROBERTS

CALLE MAYOR (1956), Juan Antonio Bardem's story of a group of provincial louts (*gamberros*) who play a cruel joke upon a local spinster, had an eventful history. While it was being made, Bardem, a member of the clandestine Spanish Communist Party since 1943, a founder of the subversive film journal *Objetivo*, and an organizer of the 1955 Salamanca Film Congress which had been highly critical of the Francoist cinema, was arrested and briefly imprisoned.[1] The film itself was censored and an initial voice-over was added which attempted to take the sting out of the work's critical portrayal of Spanish provincial life by claiming that the events depicted could in fact take place in any small town in any country in the world. Upon the film's completion, it was smuggled out of Spain and, much to the Francoist authorities' chagrin, was shown at the 1956 Venice Mostra where it won the International Critics' Prize. This, together with the prestige that Bardem had already earned when his *Muerte de un ciclista* had been awarded the International Critics' Prize at the 1955 Cannes Festival, ensured the film a wide distribution throughout Europe and the New World.

And yet, despite this success and the fact that figures such as Cocteau, Clair, Resnais, Picasso, and Sartre had signed Jorge Semprún's letter of protest against Bardem's imprisonment, briefly turning him into the most visible symbol of resistance to Franco,[2] *Calle Mayor* received mixed reviews in the international press. Many critics located the film in the melodramatic tradition and called attention to the fine work of American actress Betsy Blair who, as the spinster Isabel, played a similar role to the one which

---

[1] See de Abajo de Pablos 1996: 46–50.
[2] The letter appeared in *Les Lettres françaises* (Paris) on 16 Feb. 1956.

had helped Delbert Mann's *Marty* win the official prize at the
Cannes Festival in 1955, but Derek Granger in the *Financial Times*
(23 Sept. 1957) wrote that he found it difficult to explain why 'the
appallingly tearful spectacle of a jilted spinster' had left him so
strangely unmoved. Other reviewers, like the anonymous film critic
in *The Times* (19 Sept. 1957), obviously impressed by the initial
voice-over, focused on what they saw as the universality of the film,
but Campbell Dixon in the *Daily Telegraph* (4 Sept. 1957) claimed
that its universal relevance was undermined by the absurd cruelty
of the joke played by the *gamberros*, for surely they would have
been deterred by a fear of legal and other consequences—'or has
Spain no penalties for breach of promise?' Almost every critic did
manage to agree, however, that the film had been deeply influenced
by Italian neorealist cinema in general and by Fellini's *I vitelloni*
(1953) in particular, although in France, as Marcel Oms has
pointed out, certain reviewers set out to prove that *Calle Mayor*
was nothing more than a copy of Fellini's film and of other works
by post-war Italian directors. Bardem, they said, should simply be
seen as a crude plagiarist.[3]

What one finds in all these reviews is a desire to explain the
significance of *Calle Mayor* through reference to universal bourgeois values or to foreign cinematic traditions, such as Italian
neorealism or Hollywood melodrama. There is little or no attempt
to understand the film in its own historical, political, and cultural
context or to gauge the ways in which it draws on, develops, or
creates a specifically Spanish cinematic style. The implication seems
to be that Spanish cinema, perhaps because of the tragic history
and circumstances of the country, was fundamentally and necessarily derivative.

And yet these critics were of course making serious points, especially as far as the film's neorealist credentials were concerned. This
can best be seen through a comparison of *Calle Mayor* and the film
it supposedly copies, *I vitelloni*. Fellini's film, like Bardem's, deals
with a group of bored young men in a small provincial town. Both
deliberately take the camera out of the studio in order to film in
real locations, in Fellini's case his home town of Rimini, in
Bardem's, Cuenca, Palencia, and Logroño, locations which are then
fused together to create the atmosphere of the unnamed provincial

---

3 See Oms 1962: 3.

town at the heart of the drama. By doing this, they are able to present the characters in their natural environment, the bars where they drink and play billiards and the gloomy and deserted streets and squares through which they wander after long nights of revelry. Both films also draw attention to the fact that, despite their often antisocial behaviour, the young men are very much a part and a product of their society. Fellini underlines his *vitelloni*'s fundamental conservatism by showing how the histrionic Alberto can carry on his life as a would-be Lothario and at the same time preach good Catholic morals to his sister Olga. Similarly, Bardem deliberately juxtaposes a scene in which the *gamberros* are drunk in a brothel with another in which two of them, dressed and behaving respectably, come out of Sunday mass in the company of their wives and children. To underline the characters' double standards, both directors include one earnest male character who stands somewhat apart from the activities of the rest. In *I vitelloni*, it is Moraldo, the only member of the group who finally realizes the young men's dream of escaping from the claustrophobic provincial town. In *Calle Mayor*, it is Federico, the Madrid intellectual and outsider who, like Moraldo, frowns upon the attitudes of the rest, especially their treatment of women.

In much of this, *Calle Mayor* would seem to conform to the classical definition of Italian neorealist films which, according to Peter Bondanella, plays up their use of real locations and asserts that 'they dealt with actual problems, that they employed contemporary stories, and that they focused on believable characters taken most frequently from [in their case] Italian daily life' (Bondanella 1996: 34). And yet, despite such similarities, there are also important differences between *Calle Mayor* and the neorealist tradition as a whole. Over the past decades, several critics have attempted to break down the notion that Italian neorealism was a school or a movement with basic precepts which were followed by all its practitioners. Bondanella, for example, underlines the differences, rather than the similarities, in the subject matter and style of the seminal neorealist films and also shows how directors such as Rossellini, Fellini, and Antonioni were already, by the early 1950s, leaving behind an interest in purely social and collective matters in order to create a more individualistic, introspective, and often poetic type of cinema (1996: chs. 2, 3, 4). Bondanella's perceptive study would not seem, however, to invalidate André Bazin's overarching definition of neorealism as a form of 'phenomenological realism'. For Bazin, neorealism did not signify solely a preoccupation with real events and people but also, and more importantly, a desire to capture on film the direct experience of reality itself, to express life-as-it-is-lived with 'its full force of vividness and detail'. In doing so, it 'never "adjusts" reality to meet the needs imposed by psychology or drama' but rather gives pride of place 'to the representation of reality at the expense of dramatic structures' (Bazin 1971: 87). As a result, films such as *I vitelloni* give priority to incident over plot and are therefore fundamentally episodic, with each episode existing by and for itself, 'unique and colourful as an event' (Bazin 1971: 86). Bondanella himself adds that the film's 'formless' plot and subjective camerawork allows Fellini to create an introspective work which concentrates on the limited and contrasting viewpoints of each character (Bondanella 1996: 125).

From this point of view, *Calle Mayor* would seem to belong to a very different tradition from neorealism. First, rather than being episodic and fragmented, the film is very much plot-driven and has an extremely tight narrative structure which shares some of the tragic inevitability of classical drama. Secondly, the film is as introspective in its own way as *I vitelloni* and yet we are made privy not to the inner turmoil of a whole series of characters, as in Fellini's film, but rather, as in a nineteenth-century novel or Hollywood melodrama, to that of the two central characters, Juan and Isabel, while the *gamberros* themselves are simply treated collectively as a group. Finally, Bardem is not content to broach social and moral questions in a more or less non-judgemental way, as Fellini seems to be, but has recourse to a number of devices which, as we shall see, enable the film to be openly moralistic and even didactic. But, as Bardem himself has pointed out, there is another, perhaps more fundamental difference between his film and *I vitelloni* (and, by extension, neorealist cinema). While always acknowledging his debt to Fellini's film,[4] he also pointed out in the Italian journal *Cinema nuovo* that Fellini's *vitelloni* are young men whose misdemeanours could be put down to their adolescent childishness while his own male characters 'sono delle persone "serie", sistemate, sono dei professionisti; e il loro comportamento, quindi, è, dal punto di vista umano e sociale, ancora piú grave' ('Tre domande a

---

4   See, for example, 'J. A. Bardem' 1957: 9.

Bardem' 1957: 328). They are in fact a group of professionals, a doctor, a lawyer, a bank clerk, a shopowner, and a journalist, obvious representatives of the social forces at work in their small provincial town and, indeed, their country. This seemingly insignificant distinction actually points to an essential cultural and historical difference between the two films. By chronicling the lives of a group of young men and their dreams of escaping to the big city, Fellini is able to study a mobile post-fascist country faced with the allure and problems of migration. Bardem, meanwhile, is portraying the forces at work in a society which, dominated by a dictatorship, is still fundamentally conservative and static. Given the very different realities that the two directors are dealing with, it should not therefore be surprising that *Calle Mayor*, while acknowledging its debt to neorealism, is actually rooted in different traditions and moving in a different direction: a direction which, this article claims, is essentially Spanish in nature.

A few reviewers of the time realized this and emphasized the specifically Spanish nature of the film, although most of these were film critics in the Spanish press who felt that they had a patriotic duty to play up the film's originality. J. M. García Escudero, for example, who had been Franco's Under-secretary of Cinema between September 1951 and February 1952, underlined that *Calle Mayor* should be seen as a work not of neorealism (a term with strong Italian associations) but rather of 'cine social' (García Escudero 1957: 29). But the most clear-sighted review of all came from a very different source, that of Guido Aristarco in *Cinema nuovo*. Aristarco, a Marxist critic and leading champion of Italian neorealism, had recently lived through Mussolini's regime, a fact which made him particularly sensitive to the context in which *Calle Mayor* had been made and the sorts of issues dealt with in the film. As a result, he was the first critic to emphasize that the film can only be fully understood in its own historical and cultural terms. Bardem's subject matter is his own country, a nation languishing under a dictatorship, and his film therefore has a language of its own (Aristarco 1956: 146–7). The question which we must ask ourselves now is: what exactly was this language, what traditions was Bardem drawing upon in *Calle Mayor*, what sort of cinema was he actually trying to create?

The best starting point for our enquiry is without doubt Bardem's own words. The director has almost always referred to himself simply as a realist,[5] and has often pointed out that he was first made aware of the potential of cinematic realism during the Italian film week which was held in Madrid in 1951.[6] His exposure at that time to the films of De Sica, Antonioni, and Visconti led him to realize that neorealism had managed to 'acercarnos al hombre, al prójimo, sin desarraigarle de su entorno y construir con él y sobre él el corazón palpitante del film' ('J. A. Bardem' 1957: 8). And yet Bardem has always emphasized that a truly realist cinema should act as a testimony to a specific historical moment, that its duty is to 'mostrar en un lenguaje de luces, imágenes, sonidos, la auténtica realidad de nuestro mundo, de nuestro ambiente cotidiano, "aquí y ahora", en el lugar donde vivimos hoy' (Bardem 1962: 6–7). It is a 'testimonio de un momento humano en un instante dado y en un determinado espacio' ('J. A. Bardem' 1957: 8) and, for Bardem, that instant and that space are very much 'el mundo español hoy' ('Entrevista con J. A. Bardem' 1962: 17). It is for this reason that Bardem made a clear distinction in 1957 between 'el neorrealismo italiano' and 'ese realismo español que algunos y yo pretendemos hacer' ('J. A. Bardem' 1957: 8). The implication would seem to be clear: Spanish film-makers have to find Spanish ways of dealing with Spanish reality.

All this Bardem made patently clear in his talk at the First National Film Congress held at Salamanca in May 1955, a talk which is of particular relevance to us as it was delivered as Bardem was preparing himself to write the screenplay for *Calle Mayor*. Bardem's speech is rightly remembered for its brave attack on the Francoist cinema which he claimed to be 'políticamente ineficaz, socialmente falso, intelectualmente ínfimo, estéticamente nulo, industrialmente raquítico'.[7] However, his main point is that the officially sanctioned films of the 1940s and 1950s—the military and religious dramas, the historical epics, and the folkloric musicals[8]—have turned their backs on reality with the result that the Spanish cinema 'no ha sido aún capaz de mostrarnos el verdadero rostro de los problemas, las tierras y los hombres de España' (Egido 1983: 50–1). What Spain now needs,

---

5 See, for example, Alonso Dobz 1988: 53–9.
6 For more details on this film week, see Kinder 1993: 451–2.
7 Bardem's talk is reproduced in Egido 1983: 50.
8 For an overview of the Francoist films of this period, see Hopewell 1986: 33–43.

he goes on to say, is a realist and socially committed cinema which can reflect and reflect upon the nature of Spanish reality. This would be a truly national cinema, 'nuestro cine, el cine español' (Egido 1983: 52). And Bardem indirectly suggests a way in which such a cinema can be created when he passionately defends 'la estupenda tradición realista de nuestra novela' which he claims has been betrayed by the anti-realist escapism of Francoist films (Egido 1983: 50). What Bardem seems to be implying, therefore, is that Spain's new cinema can be built upon a past, and essentially literary, tradition. This is a view which he restated in his *Cinema nuovo* interview of 1957 when, after yet again declaring his belief in the testimonial power of realism, he explained that: 'Usando questa parola [realismo], penso al cinema neorealistico italiano, che è probabilmente la forma italiana del realismo, e penso, di piú, alla tradizione artistica spagnola, richissima, dalla letteratura alla pittura, di opere realistiche' ('Tre domande a Bardem' 1957: 328).

If we now turn once again to *Calle Mayor*, we can see that Bardem's starting point for his recuperation of lost Spanish traditions in this film was his use of Carlos Arniches's comic farce *La señorita de Trevélez* (1916). That Bardem should decide to base his film on this classic of the early twentieth-century Spanish theatre should come as no surprise. For one thing, Arniches's dramatic work was well known for its popular realism, for its treatment of everyday themes through the use of typical, and often stereotypical, characters. For another, he was without doubt the most successful dramatist of the first decades of this century and his plays appealed to a wide cross-section of the Spanish public who found their own concerns reflected in the humorous events depicted on stage. Finally, several directors of the 1920s and 1930s had already translated his works from stage to screen and one of the most successful of these adaptations had been the Spanish director Edgar Neville's 1936 version of *La señorita de Trevélez* itself, a film which used the original play almost as freely as Bardem would. It is interesting, therefore, to compare and contrast these three versions and also to see to what degree they reflect the cultural and historical moment of their making (1916, 1936, and 1956).

La señorita de Trevélez marked a turning point in Arniches's career as a dramatist. It retains many elements of the *sainete* or *género chico*, the genre which Arniches had helped to perfect,[9] especially in its use of stock characters, farcical situations, and complicated plot. At the heart of the story is the joke which Picavea and his chums in the so-called 'Guasa club' play on Numeriano Galán, Picavea's rival in love. Picavea sends a forged marriage proposal from Galán to Flora de Trevélez, the local spinster, thereby compromising him in the eyes of Flora, her over-protective brother Gonzalo, and the whole provincial town. Most of the play is taken up with showing how Galán and Picavea try to escape from their predicaments, only to find themselves slipping ever deeper into the mire, and a great deal of comic mileage is extracted from the ridiculous situations that they are placed in. But much of the humour in the play comes from the characters themselves, especially Gonzalo, the middle-aged man who tries to dress and act as if he were twenty years younger, and Flora, whose ridiculous attire and exaggerated sentimentality have been learnt directly from the American films that she loves to watch. And yet, as the acts go by, other, more serious notes start to enter the play. For one thing, when he finally discovers the truth of the joke, Gonzalo reveals that he has spent his life deliberately dressing and acting young in order to hide from Flora the fact that the years are passing them both by. This sudden shift in tone from the burlesque to the tragicomic caused the novelist Pérez de Ayala to comment that the work was 'una de las comedias de costumbres más serias, más humanas y más cautivadoras de la reciente dramaturgia humana' (Pérez de Ayala 1966: 323), praise which helped to establish Arniches's reputation as a 'serious' dramatist. Many commentators were also impressed by the final speeches in the play where Marcelino, a secondary character, not only criticizes the actions of the 'Guasa club' but also indicts the 'ambiente de envidia, de ocio, de miseria moral' of provincial life and indeed 'el espíritu de la raza, cruel, agresivo, burlón, que no ríe de su propia alegría, sino del dolor ajeno'. These words, and Marcelino's claim that the only remedy for this lamentable national situation is 'difundiendo la cultura',[10] serve to give the play a 'regenerationist' note similar to that found in the works of Unamuno, Machado, and others, authors who were bitterly

---

[9] On the genealogy of the *sainete*, see McKay 1972: 28–47.
[10] Arniches, *La señorita de Trevélez*, III. viii; in Arniches 1994: 200–1.

obsessed with the social and political stagnancy of Restoration Spain.[11]

When Edgar Neville came to make his film version of *La señorita de Trevélez* in 1936, he discovered that the play was too short and so decided, with Arniches's approval, to amplify it.[12] He therefore added a whole series of slapstick scenes, reminiscent of Hollywood silent and 1930s comedies, and made the original *enredo* even more complex by introducing the character of Araceli, Galán's true love. But his most radical change is found just before the climax of the film, where Neville produces a dramatic reversal which undermines the spectator's expectations every bit as much as the original play had done. Neville's Flora, unlike Arniches's, ultimately discovers the truth behind the joke and, in a powerfully moving scene, suddenly appears not in the ridiculous flowered clothes and make-up which she had worn earlier but rather in the austere black which is expected of an ageing spinster. It is her character, therefore, and not Gonzalo, who is forced to confront reality and who introduces a note of tragicomic pathos into the film. In this way, Neville redirects the social criticism of Arniches's work by making the feminist point that, in a society such as the one shown in the film, women are the ultimate victims of men's schemes and lies.

By contrasting Arniches's and Neville's *La señorita de Trevélez* with *Calle Mayor*, we can see more clearly how Bardem recuperates an earlier theatrical and cinematic tradition and transmutes it into something both more realistic and more tragic. First, and at the most basic level, *Calle Mayor* retains the central story-line of its predecessors, the film being built around the joke played on the principal female character, Isabel, by the male pranksters. And yet the film is far from being a comedy or a tragicomedy since we are never invited to enjoy the *enredo* or to laugh with or even at the activities of the *gamberros*. Right from the very first moment that we see them together as a group, celebrating the intellectual's reaction on receiving the coffin at his home, we are repulsed by their grotesque laughter and behaviour. Bardem therefore shifts our attention from the development of the joke—which is used simply to give the story-line a sense of tragic inevitability—and focuses

---

[11] For a regenerationist reading of Arniches's play, see Monleón 1975: 141–61.
[12] See *Edgar Neville en el cine* 1977: 17.

instead on the implications and consequences of his characters' actions. Secondly, the film, just like the two earlier works, makes full use of types. The four main *gamberros*, Luis, Calvo, Luciano, and the doctor, are not endowed with any inner life but are rather portrayed through their stereotypically, and even exaggeratedly, loutish behaviour, while Isabel's mother (played by María Gámez, the actress who had portrayed Flora in Neville's film) and her household maid (played by Matilde Muñoz Sampedro, Bardem's own mother and star of the 1940s stage) could belong in any Spanish *costumbrista* or popular drama. In this, they provide a striking contrast with the main protagonists, Isabel, Juan, and Federico, whose moral dilemmas are treated with great depth and sensitivity.

But the main difference between the three versions lies in the prominent role which Bardem gives to the social setting in *Calle Mayor*. Arniches's play and Neville's film take place in the local casino and in the Trevélez household, although Neville does use a few location shots at the onset to point to the wider context of his story. Bardem, however, as the very title of his film implies, allows his provincial town to become his main protagonist. In doing this, he draws on another Spanish literary tradition, 'la estupenda tradición realista de nuestra novela' which he had spoken about in his Salamanca talk. From this point of view, *Calle Mayor* can be seen to contain deliberate echoes of a whole series of Spanish novels, from Galdós to Baroja. Chief amongst these is without doubt Clarín's *La Regenta* (1884), Spain's greatest nineteenth-century novel of provincial life. From the very beginning of his novel, Clarín is intent on providing the reader with a clear idea of the personality of his fictional town, Vetusta, and does so by carefully describing its different quarters in turn—the old aristocratic centre, the new middle-class area to the north-west, and the dirty working-class district further out—each of which will have an important role to play in the drama.[13] In a similar fashion, Bardem too carefully outlines the topography of his setting, his camera visiting the bustling commercial area around the Calle Mayor, the older quarter from the Cathedral to the brothel, and the new housing estate being built in the outskirts. Both works also go out of their way to show their characters in their 'natural' setting—the men in the

---

[13]   See Clarín 1981: 15–21.

casino, the women in church, the whole town congregating for the daily *paseo*—in a deliberate attempt to call attention to the influence that social ambience has on character. In this, *Calle Mayor* is very much an heir to the deterministic view of life which lies at the heart of *La Regenta*, and indeed of the realist and naturalist novel in general, but, in its depiction of the stifling atmosphere of provincial Spain, it also directly recalls the novels of the early twentieth-century regenerationist writers such as José Martínez Ruiz. Both *Calle Mayor* and Martínez Ruiz's *La voluntad* (1902) show how the pettiness and conventionality of small-town life leads to the moral destruction of their central characters and it is no coincidence that both stories are told to the inescapable rhythm of the Cathedral bells.

Through drawing on this novelistic tradition, *Calle Mayor* is able to turn what had been a tragicomic *sainete* in the hands of Arniches and Neville into a work of social or critical realism. And yet the film is not simply an abstract social realist drama since, within its realist framework, there is also a melodrama: the story of Isabel. Over the past few decades, there has been a concerted effort on the part of film theorists to present melodrama as a subject worthy of close academic attention, after centuries during which it was treated dismissively as a sentimental, popular, or 'woman's' genre.[14] Critical to this development was an essay by Thomas Elsaesser who, through a close study of the films of Hollywood director Douglas Sirk, revealed clearly how melodrama could 'function either subversively or as escapism' (Elsaesser 1987: 47). Elsaesser's and later theorists' point is that, by displacing social and ideological conflicts onto the private sphere of individual or family relationships, melodrama can in fact either diffuse those conflicts or call attention to them.[15]

In the case of *Calle Mayor*, it is clear that Isabel's story has a subversive function in the sense that it serves to reveal the effects that social forces have on individual psychology. Isabel may be the victim of the *gamberros*' cruel joke but she is also shown, in a more crucial sense, to be the victim of the pressures placed upon her by

[14] For a history of melodrama criticism, see Gledhill 1987: 5–39.
[15] See, for example, Schatz 1981: 225. Kinder follows a similar line in her study of Bardem's use of melodrama in *Muerte de un ciclista*; see Kinder 1993: 55.

her society.[16] Such pressures are clearly outlined in a key scene in which Isabel tells Juan the story of her life, a story organized around the chorus 'Isabel, ¿no tienes novio?' First it had been her girlfriends who had asked the question out of malice, then her aunts through a desire to compare Isabel with their own daughters, then her mother who was worried by the financial consequences of Isabel's spinsterhood, and finally it was Isabel herself who, shortly before meeting Juan, had come to the conclusion that she was a failure. This scene helps to reveal how Isabel has internalized the demands of her society, a society which, as the film graphically shows, has confined her to certain roles and certain spaces: the Cathedral, where she imbues the contradictory values of Catholic womanhood, the Calle Mayor, where she is exposed to that most effective form of social control, gossip, and, above all, the kitchen, corridors, and bedroom of her home, that is, the traditional spaces par excellence both of women and of melodrama.[17] But the film shows that there is another space available for women in this society: the brothel. By introducing the character of Tonia, the local prostitute whom we only ever see enclosed between the brothel's four walls, Bardem is able to give the full measure of the plight of women in contemporary society when he has her say of Isabel, towards the climax of the film: 'Ella también espera. . . Aquí las mujeres no podemos hacer otra cosa. . . Sólo esperar. . . En las esquinas, en los soportales de la Plaza, paseando por la Calle Mayor, detrás de las ventanas. . . Siempre esperando al hombre.'

Yet Isabel's melodrama has another function, one which is crucial to our understanding of the central aim of the film, which is to identify and denounce a particular moment in Spain's history (the 'aquí y ahora'). Isabel, like so many novelistic heroines before her, is a dreamer whose illusions are fired, as in the case of Arniches's Flora, by Hollywood films. In her first meeting with Juan, she had enthused over the gleaming new kitchens which feature so prominently in American films, and later, in the key scene at the building site, she plans out her future home in ways obviously borrowed from the movies she loves to watch. Hollywood films, therefore, have provided her with a way of imagining another space which

---

[16]   At the end of the film, Federico informs Isabel that the responsibility for her predicament lies with 'la ciudad, toda la ciudad'.

[17]   On the role of the home in melodrama, see Elsaesser 1987: 61–2.

Betsy Blair's character in *Marty* had also dreamed about: a home of her own. But Isabel's dream also has another, far wider, significance for Bardem. Over the years before the film was made, Franco's regime had gradually shed its fascistic rhetoric in an attempt to cement the rapprochement with the Western powers which had started with the onset of the Cold War, and also modernized the economy, which became less state-controlled and more market-oriented.[18] In a word, Spain was striving at this time to become a capitalist country and in so doing, as *Calle Mayor* shows, was attempting to seduce the population with consumerist dreams like that of Isabel, fostered by the foreign comedies and melodramas which were the main cinematic diet of the Spanish people.[19] Bardem, who has often attacked what he calls the 'cine falso [que] adormece al individuo',[20] literally punctures such dreams in the film by showing how Isabel almost falls down the deep hole which will become the stairwell leading to her future flat.

Our full understanding of the true nature of this change taking place in Franco's Spain, however, is secured by the presence in the film of Federico, a character who has often been seen as Bardem's mouthpiece.[21] Federico is a writer from Madrid who works on the philosophical and literary journal *Ideas*. He comes to the town in order to see his friend Juan, shortly after the latter's transfer there, but also to encourage Don Tomás, a local intellectual who, as Bardem's original screenplay makes clear, had once had a huge influence on Spain's youth,[22] to collaborate on the next issue of the journal. Don Tomás, however, who feels safe and comfortable slumbering away in the provincial town's casino, ultimately refuses to write anything for *Ideas*. In response, Federico upbraids him in one of the climactic scenes for what he calls his fear of the truth and his cowardice. Don Tomás is no better than the *gamberros* themselves,

[18] For a brief overview of these changes, see Carr and Fusi 1979: 49–78. Bardem himself once said that, in the 1950s, he was making films in a capitalist, rather than a fascist, society. Evans 1987: 34.

[19] Bardem and Berlanga's *¡Bienvenido Mr Marshall!* (1952), as Hopewell (1986: 48–50) has shown, had already made a similar point.

[20] Conde 1962: 11. The film itself openly attacks this 'cine falso' when Juan tells Isabel that Federico would consider the films she loves to be 'una mentira'.

[21] See, for example, Heredero 1993: 341.

[22] Bardem 1993: 8. Not surprisingly, this reference and the reference to the fact that the latest issue of Federico's magazine, which contained articles on Picasso and neorealism, had just been censored (ibid. 32) were suppressed by the censors in the final version of the film.

says Federico, for he too is unable or unwilling to see the reality that surrounds him.

These meetings between Federico and Don Tomás very much help to locate *Calle Mayor* in its precise historical context. The film portrays the present moment of change and uncertainty in terms of a relationship between generations. Franco's plan to modernize Spain's economy and thereby retain his grip on the country and the Spanish people is shown to be bearing fruit through the attitudes and activities of the *gamberros*. They represent the vanguard of Franco's capitalist experiment, that is, the new professional class which is gradually replacing the Falangist old guard in the running of the country. In the original screenplay, Bardem underlined this fact by including a scene in the bank where Juan works. As Federico watches how two clerks convince a family of peasants to take out a loan, Juan boasts that business has been going so well over the past years that the bank is becoming the true owner of the whole town (Bardem 1993: 104–6). This scene, through reasons of censorship, was reduced to a casual remark at the beginning of the final version of the film, but the point is still clearly made: the *gamberros*, like Isabel with her longing for a new home, are fully participating in the new capitalist dream offered them by the regime.

But these new Francoists do not represent the whole of the upcoming generation in Spain. As Bardem was making his film, the country experienced the first wave of serious unrest since the Civil War. The student rebellion on the streets of Madrid in February 1956 led to the declaration of Franco's first state of emergency and also, as we have seen, to Bardem's own brief arrest.[23] Bardem himself has underlined the generational significance of these events by saying that Spain was suddenly faced with 'un nuevo frente de lucha antifranquista, frente al tradicional de la clase obrera organizada. Son los estudiantes e intelectuales hijos de los fundadores ideológicos del regimen' (de Abajo de Pablos 1996: 47). In *Calle Mayor*, it is without doubt Federico who acts as a representative of this new 'frente de lucha'. And, from this point of view, his visit to Don Tomás could well be seen as an attempt by the disaffected young to make contact with, and gain support from, an older generation of intellectuals. In a sense, therefore, what Federico is

[23]   On the students' rebellion, see Carr and Fusi 1979: 146–7.

hoping to find in Don Tomás is a vestige of the pre-Civil War spirit of critical regenerationism, that is, the spirit which had led Unamuno in *En torno al casticismo* (1895) to denounce the moral and intellectual bankruptcy of the youth of his day,[24] and Antonio Machado in *Campos de Castilla* (1917) to sing a hymn of praise to the young Spain which was being born amidst the corruption and ruins of the old.[25] But the Don Tomás that Federico encounters is inert and resigned and is unable to provide any support for the new generation. He therefore bears witness to the tragic fact that the Civil War served to destroy a whole generation of intellectuals, either through execution, exile, or, in his own case, enforced silence.[26] The result of this has been a radical break in cultural continuity which has left the youth of Spain alone and having to find their own way forward in the world, their own path to truth.

In many ways, Federico's quest in *Calle Mayor* can be seen to represent the film's search for its own style. *Calle Mayor*, like Federico, searches for a connection with Spain's past, reaching back across the Civil War and making contact with the work of the regenerationists and, beyond, with the realist tradition of the nineteenth century. But, just as Federico finds Don Tomás wanting, so the film discovers that such literary traditions are not enough to capture fully the reality of the present moment. They may provide leads but they belong firmly to their own epochs, and film-makers in the 1950s need to find their own ways of portraying reality.[27] This is a fact which Bardem, once again, explores through the character of Federico.

The essential fact about Federico is that he is an outsider who stands apart from the social forces and pressures at work in the

[24] See above all the work's final chapter, entitled 'Sobre el marasmo actual de España'; in Unamuno 1969: i. 856–69. In this context, it is perhaps no coincidence that, in the original screenplay, Bardem had given his intellectual the name of Don Miguel.

[25] In the original screenplay, Federico's impassioned defence of the young Spain which is trying desperately to come to life, the 'otra ciudad que vive, que pugna por salir, que—saldrá' (Bardem 1993: 126), is directly and deliberately reminiscent of Machado's poem 'El mañana efímero'; see Machado 1990: 232–3.

[26] In this, he is very much a forerunner of the Fernando figure in Erice's *El espíritu de la colmena* (1973).

[27] In his Salamanca talk, Bardem claimed that contemporary Spanish film-makers were alone owing to the fact that the intellectuals had never shown any interest in, or support for, their country's cinema (Egido 1983: 51). Federico's attack on Don Tomás's 'cowardice' should also perhaps be read in this context.

town. But his role in the film is to help the other characters—especially Juan and Isabel—become outsiders too. This he does by taking a firm moral stance and encouraging the others to do the same. As a result of his demand that the truth be told, whatever the consequences, he forces Juan into a situation in which he has no choice but to separate himself physically and morally from the *gamberros*, and examine his conscience. Similarly, he forces the truth upon Isabel at the end of the film and leaves her in a position in which she is obliged to leave her illusions behind. Of course, the film provides no happy ending and we are left with the image of a Juan who has banished himself from the town and an Isabel entrapped behind her rain-spattered window, but it at least implies that the final social alienation of the characters is preferable to the moral alienation which they had previously suffered.

Federico's rigid moral stance is also the stance of the film as a whole.[28] Due to the threat of censorship, *Calle Mayor* could not openly enunciate its truths, so it aims instead to distance the spectators from what they are watching, to turn them too into critical outsiders. This it does in several ways. First, it offers them a film based on a fundamentally comic situation and then proceeds to disorient them as much as Arniches's work had done by showing that the *gamberros'* prank is anything but funny. Secondly, taking advantage of the popular appeal of American films, it draws the spectator in with the promise of a melodrama and then goes on to show that the premiss on which many contemporary Hollywood films are constructed, a comfortable bourgeois life, is, at least in the Spanish context, nothing more than a lie. Thirdly, it provides what seems to be a recognizably realistic portrayal of provincial life but gradually defamiliarizes what is presented on screen. It does this through grotesque exaggeration, through the use of foreign actors in some of the principal roles, especially Betsy Blair whose facial expressions and bodily gestures are clearly foreign to a Spanish audience, and, most importantly, through its unrelenting unmasking of the profound moral and social degradation of the town. In short, *Calle Mayor* decides that it is not enough or (given the existence of censorship) even possible simply to portray reality as classical realism had done; it also needs to confront and upset the

---

[28] Bardem once claimed that 'ese intelectual que meto en mis películas . . . lo hago para no engañar, para que las entiendan' (Bardem 1978: 10).

spectators' expectations and force them to take up a critical position in relation to what they see. Only in this way, only by creating a *crise de conscience* in his audience, could he hope to distance them from the conformism of his *gamberros* and, as he once put it, 'dirigir la mirada del espectador en otra dirección, hacia "lo mejor"' (Bardem 1962: 6).

This is the essence of Bardem's new realism which could perhaps be called (if any label is necessary) political or committed realism. Both Hopewell and Kinder, while praising *Calle Mayor*, seem to suggest that Bardem was something of a peripheral figure in the creation of the New Spanish Cinema of the late 1950s and early 1960s which, they claim, grew more out of Berlanga's, Ferreri's, and Fernán-Gómez's reworking of the Spanish *esperpento* tradition and Saura's contacts with the cinema of Buñuel and the French *Nouvelle Vague* (Hopewell 1986: 58–63, 71–6, 134–6; Kinder 1993: 87–126). There may be some truth in this. After completing the trilogy of *Muerte de un ciclista*, *Calle Mayor*, and *Los segadores* (1957)—which dealt with the social and moral problems of the haute bourgeoisie, middle classes, and peasants respectively—Bardem tended to make more occasional pieces until the death of Franco, when his ideological bias came powerfully to the fore in openly communist works such as *El puente* (1976). And yet it must never be forgotten that, with *Calle Mayor*, he produced a film which not only directly addresses the question of the direction in which Spanish cinema should go but also provides perhaps the most vivid testimony to the complex historical and cultural moment of its making.

REFERENCES

Alonso Dobz, Ángel (1988), 'Bardem: puedo considerarme propiamente un realista', *Cine cubano* (Havana), 121: 53–9.
Antolín, Matías (1978), 'Entrevista con Bardem', *Cinema 2002* (Madrid), 44 (Oct.): 40–4.
Aristarco, Guido (1956), '*Calle Mayor*', *Cinema nuovo* (Milan), 90–1 (1 Oct.): 145–8, 191.
Arniches, Carlos (1994), *El amigo Melquíades/La señorita de Trevélez*, ed. M. Seco. Madrid: Espasa Calpe.
Bardem, J. A. (1962), '¿Para qué sirve un film?', in *J. A. Bardem*, Madrid: Cuadernos de cine (UNAM) 4: 5–7 (1st pub. in *Cinema universitario*, 3 (May 1956)).

Bardem, J. A. (1978), 'Declaraciones', in *J. A. Bardem*, La Coruña: VI Certamen internacional de cine de humor: 10 (1st pub. *Nuestro cine*, 29 (1964)).

—— (1993), *Calle Mayor (guión original)*. Madrid: Alma-Plot Ediciones.

Bazin, André (1971), '*Cabiria*: The Voyage to the End of Neorealism', in André Bazin, *What is Cinema?*, ii, Berkeley and Los Angeles: University of California Press: 83–92.

Besas, Peter (1985), *Behind the Spanish Lens: Spanish Cinema under Fascism and Democracy*. Denver: Arden Press.

Bondanella, Peter (1996), *Italian Cinema: From Neorealism to the Present*. New York: Continuum.

Carr, Raymond, and Fusi, Juan Pablo (1979), *Spain: Dictatorship to Democracy*. London: George Allen & Unwin.

Clarín (1981), *La Regenta*. Madrid: Alianza.

Conde, Julián (1962), 'Entrevista con Bardem', in *J. A. Bardem*, Madrid: Cuadernos de cine (UNAM) 4: 9–14 (1st pub. *Excélsior* (Mexico City), 18 Jan. 1959).

de Abajo de Pablos, Juan Eugenio Julio (1996), *Mis charlas con J. A. Bardem*. Valladolid: Quirón Ediciones.

Edgar Neville en el cine (1977), Madrid: Filmoteca Nacional de España.

Egido, L. G. (1958), *Bardem*. Madrid: Editorial Visor.

—— (1983), *J. A. Bardem*. Huelva: Festival de Cine Iberoamericano.

Elsaesser, Thomas (1987), 'Tales of Sound and Fury', in Christine Gledhill (ed.), *Home is Where the Heart is: Studies in Melodrama and the Woman's Film*, London: BFI Books: 43–69 (1st pub. *Monogram*, 4 (1972)).

'Entrevista con J. A. Bardem' (1962), in *J. A. Bardem*, Madrid: Cuadernos de Cine (UNAM) 4: 17–29 (1st pub. *Tiempo de cine* (Buenos Aires), 1/5 (Feb.–Mar. 1961)).

Evans, P. W. (1987), 'A Bardem Retrospective', *Vida hispánica*, 36/3 (autumn): 33–4.

García Escudero, J. M. (1957), '*Calle Mayor*', *Film ideal* (Madrid), 5 (Feb.): 29.

Gledhill, Christine (1987), 'The Melodramatic Field: An Investigation', in Christine Gledhill (ed.), *Home is Where the Heart is: Studies in Melodrama and the Woman's Film*, London: BFI Books: 5–39.

Heredero, C. F. (1993), *Las huellas del tiempo: cine español 1951–1961*. Valencia: Ediciones Documentos 5 Filmoteca.

Hopewell, John (1986), *Out of the Past: Spanish Cinema after Franco*. London: BFI.

J. A. Bardem (1962), Madrid: Cuadernos de Cine (UNAM) 4.

J. A. Bardem (1978), La Coruña: VI Certamen Internacional de Cine de Humor.

'J. A. Bardem' (1957), *Film ideal* (Madrid), 5 (Feb.): 8–9.

Kinder, Marsha (1993), *Blood Cinema: The Reconstruction of National Identity in Spain*. Berkeley and Los Angeles: University of California Press.

Machado, Antonio (1990), *Poesías completas*. Madrid: Espasa Calpe.

McKay, Douglas R. (1972), *Carlos Arniches*. New York: Twayne Publishers Inc.

Monleón, José (1975), *El teatro del 98 frente a la sociedad española*. Madrid: Cátedra.

Oms, Marcel (1962), 'J. A. Bardem', *Premier Plan* (Lyon), 21 (Feb.): 3–64.

Pérez de Ayala, Ramón (1966), 'La señorita de Trevélez', in *Obras completas*, iii, Madrid: Aguilar: 321–6.

Schatz, Thomas (1981), *Hollywood Genres*. Philadelphia: Temple University Press.

'Tre domande a Bardem' (1957), *Cinema nuovo* (Milan), 108 (June): 328.

Unamuno, Miguel de (1969), *Obras completas*, i. Madrid: Escelicer.

4

Saura's *Los golfos* (1959; Released 1962): Heralding a New Cinema for the 1960s

MARIA DELGADO

CARLOS Saura (b. 1932) has produced one of the most varied and original bodies of work in the contemporary Spanish cinema. Over a period of forty years he has directed thirty-one full-length films, four short films, and a television adaptation of Jorge Luis Borges's story 'El sur'. Although he is perhaps best known in Britain for his more recent work, a series of flamenco musicals realized with a range of celebrated Spanish dancers including Antonio Gades and Cristina Hoyos, he was, during the 1960s and 1970s, Spain's most successful international director. His lengthy collaboration with producer Elías Querejeta gained both a series of international prizes, including Silver Bears at Berlin for *La caza* (1965) and *Peppermint frappé* (1967) and the Grand Jury Prize at Cannes for *Cría cuervos* (1975), and sufficient European distribution to ensure a conspicuous presence within the Spanish film community. In addition, his lengthy relationship with Geraldine Chaplin, a regular performer in his films from *Peppermint frappé* to *Mamá cumple cien años* (1979), provided him with a visibility which saved him from the crippling contingencies which befell his fellow directors.[1] Nevertheless Saura's career was forged within the restrictions of the tight censorship imposed by the Franco regime on its cultural practitioners. Although Saura's clashes with the censors in films such as *Llanto por un bandido* (1963), *La prima Angélica* (1973), and *El*

I am grateful to Dolores Devesa of the Filmoteca in Madrid for her assistance in locating material on *Los golfos*. I would also like to thank Paul Heritage, Jacqueline Roy, and Henry Little who offered valuable suggestions on earlier drafts of this chapter, Sandra Hebron for her incisive comments on the film and for providing such a focus for my interest in Spanish cinema over the past four years, and Roberto Romeo for discussing his film *Esperanza y sardinas* at length with me.

[1] A point made and elaborated by John Hopewell (1986: 134–5).

jardín de las delicias (1970) were considerable,[2] it is *Los golfos* (1959) his first full-length feature, that Saura considers the film which proved most difficult to make.[3] Initially conceived as a pseudo-documentary to be based on a series of articles written by journalist Daniel Sueiro on Madrid's Legazpi market, it evolved into a film which, as critic Marsha Kinder justly claims, 'helped to launch a new national film movement—the New Spanish Cinema' (1993: 99). Selected by a newly formed committee (which included such dissident figures as Juan Antonio Bardem as well as Franco's favoured film-maker José Luis Sáenz de Heredia) to represent Spain at the 1960 Cannes Film Festival, it launched the unknown Saura in an international arena. The film's selection proved contentious. Members of the committee who had initially upheld the film's selection were unhappy with Saura's decision not to provide a more upbeat ending. The film was still allowed to go to Cannes, but while it was there the dictatorship effectively distanced itself from *Los golfos*, awarding it only a 2b category, that accorded to films deemed of little national interest. This in effect paralysed effective distribution and the film was given only a limited release in the summer of 1962 with little possibility for the producers to recoup their costs. In addition, responses to the film were mixed, with a number of Spanish critics blasting it for an outright rejection of classical editorial methodology, a fragmented structure, the lack of psychological depth accorded to the characters, its supposed adherence to an outdated neorealist aesthetic, and, perhaps most importantly, in view of the reservations voiced by members of the selection committee, a bleak and pessimistic view of urban society which contradicted that expounded by the official regime.[4] Recognition of the film's importance came early from a number of conspicuous international sources including director Karel Reisz and critics Alan Dent (1961: 10) and Louis Marcorelles, writing in the *Observer*, who lauded it 'the one true revelation in the festival . . . the first great film of this director and perhaps the first of all Spanish films that

[2] See for example, Higgenbotham 1988: 12–15; Sánchez Vidal 1988: 36, 72–3, 86–7; Galán 1974.
[3] Carlos Saura, in a private, unpublished interview with the author, June 1990. See also Kinder 1993: 88.
[4] See, for example, the reviews published in *Cine mundo*, 428 (28 May 1960: 5) and *Revista internacional del cine*, 36–7 (Dec. 1960: 50).

deserves to be called great' (1960: 21). Recent reassessments of the film have similarly recognized the balanced use of non-exclusive cinematic strategies, a radical and complex narrative structure, and stylish cinematography in achieving a forceful ideological critique of post-Civil War Spain.[5]

Although the narrative is straightforward enough—centring on the adventures of a gang of boys as they engage in a range of illegal pursuits in the hope of raising enough money to enable one of their members, Juan, to debut as a bullfighter in the ring—Los golfos is not an easy film to digest. On one level, sequences often lack establishing shots, beginning abruptly with characters commenting on the action of a previous sequence, and they frequently cut in mid-action. In addition, incongruous jumps in time and space offer little expository material for the viewer. Shots are held beyond their theoretical cutting point, as in the final sequence where Juan's poor performance in the ring appears agonizingly prolonged. The insertion of non-causally motivated scenes, shots of the backs of characters' heads, an evasion of eye contact between character and camera, the camera's refusal to follow movement, and an excessive use of hand-held camerawork, all markedly present within the film, serve, on one level, to denaturalize classical cinematic methodologies, illustrating the text's materiality and its status as ideological construct. The film's oddly juxtaposed camera angles and a tendency to wander through locations while not necessarily centring on the boys themselves provide a brash discordant effect, more analogous to that achieved by the French New Wave directors than the more empathetic techniques of the neorealist cinema with which the film was often associated on its release. Past arguments regarding the neorealist influence on Los golfos have, however, hinged largely on three factors: Saura's use of unknown and untrained actors, the raw documentary feel to the cinematography, and a conspicuous use of recognizable impoverished outdoor locales—Legazpi market, the slums around the Manzanares river and Almudena cemetery, known at the time as 'La China'—in which the characters are positioned.[6] Saura has, however, repeatedly voiced his unease at seeing the film classified as neorealist, arguing that 'I've never felt Italian neorealism to be

---

[5] See, for example, Kinder 1993: 96–111 and D'Lugo 1991: 29–45.
[6] See, for example, views like that of Ibáñez (1960: 63–4).

mine. I've always thought it too sentimental. American gangster films of the 1930s and 1940s, on the other hand, I've always thought fantastic.'⁷ Marsha Kinder situates *Los golfos* in the 'dialectic between neorealism and Hollywood' (1993: 39), and whilst the film does display a debt to both, it is to the early work of Godard and Truffaut that the spirit of the film is most closely allied.

Thematically the film shares the motifs of delinquency and petty crime of Godard's *A bout de souffle* (1959) and Truffaut's *Les 400 coups* (1959). Like both films—also made in black and white and also evading the sentimentality and Catholic moralizing so characteristic of early neorealism—*Los golfos* was perceived as a statement on the predicament of its director. This was especially pertinent in Spain where a generation of film-makers were faced with a policy of non-cooperation by the Franco government. Both Saura and his co-scriptwriter Mario Camus, later to become a major film-maker himself, have spoken of the fact that for them the hooligans were a version of themselves; a way of dramatizing their story as aspiring directors struggling to create an alternative film culture within the limitations of the existing industry.⁸ The principal cast of *Los golfos*, like the director and his co-scriptwriters, were unknown figures. Only María Meyer, who plays Visi, the prostitute courted by Julián, and two of the gang, Manuel Zarzo (Julián) and Luis Marin (Ramón), were professional actors, albeit little-known ones. Juanjo Losada, who plays Chato, was discovered by Saura in El Rastro selling watches; Oscar Cruz was cast in the role of Juan, the aspiring torero, when Saura saw him training while searching for locations in Casa del Campo. The others were located through an advertisement. Not surprisingly the film was subjected to vindictive censorship scrutiny at every stage of its production. Four revisions of the script were undertaken which radically altered the initial draft Saura, Camus, and their co-scriptwriter Daniel Sueiro had conceived. Obliged by the censor to

⁷ Carlos Saura, in a unpublished, private interview with the author, June 1990.
⁸ See Braso 1974: 62. In a private, unpublished interview with the author, Mario Camus, in December 1991, stated: 'el papel de estos chicos, más o menos un poco fuera de la sociedad, un poco marginados era cerca de la sociedad española el mismo papel nuestro frente al cine español' (the role of these boys, more or less outside society, a little marginalized from society, was the same role we occupied in relation to Spanish cinema).

devise an altruistic purpose for their criminal activities, Saura turned to bullfighting, a motif which specifically locates the film, despite its associations with the American juvenile delinquent movie, within a Hispanic tradition of folkloric melodrama which is, as I will go on to indicate, systematically interrogated.

As with numerous features of the Nouvelle Vague Hollywood cinema is a powerful site of reference in the film, both deftly acknowledged and carefully deconstructed. The behaviour of the boys, like that of Belmondo's Michel Poiccard in *A bout de souffle*, is evidently modelled on American gangsters and teen rebels of the 1950s. Juan wears the baseball boots and straight-cut jeans associated with James Dean. Julián's quiff is similarly reminiscent of Dean. He is seen combing it with care in front of a large mirror in his otherwise austere flat, framed against postcards of young and beautiful screen idols. In a film bereft of father figures where the young male body is constantly positioned to be admired, these worshipped icons provide an ego ideal. Taboo desire for the father is projected onto these figures whom Julián especially attempts to impersonate. Interestingly rival images of the masculine ideal, like that of the avaricious impresario, representative of the heavily commercialized world of the fight, are presented as equally inadequate. His exploitative patriarch, as Kinder has also noted, is a sharp ideological departure from 'the Fascist glorification of the patriarchal family and its idealization of the bond between father and sons and also speaks to the historical reality of so many Spanish fathers having been killed in the Civil War' (1993: 99).

Paternal love is conspicuously absent from *Los golfos*. Here the gang functions as an alternative to the nuclear family with brotherly love presented as the definitive ideal. The boys' interest in each other's lives clearly exceeds that of their family members. The film is structured around a collective protagonist and the challenge of not concentrating on any one of the featured characters for any prolonged period of the narrative. Previous critics have concentrated on Juan's quest to become a bullfighter as the pivotal focus of the film but the text itself defies such a simplistic reading.[9] *Los golfos* dwells at length on the other gang members who do not function merely as secondary plot components. It is worth stressing

[9]   See, for example, Dent 1961: 1; the Cannes Film Festival programme for the film (1960), and Vas 1961: 139.

that the film opens not with Juan but with Ramón executing one of
the assaults needed to fund Juan's training at Don Esteban's.
Subsequently shots of Juan practising in the ring with the *novillo*
are juxtaposed with those of Chato, Julián, Manolo, Ramón, and
Paco. Their reactions to his moves in the ring—varying from Paco's
obvious enthusiasm to Ramón's distracted reading of a newspaper—are as important as the moves themselves for they situate
the various characters' responses to Juan's progress as a bullfighter.
For Ramón and Julián it is simply a commercial enterprise. For
Paco and Chato—significantly younger than Juan—Juan's body is
the centre of attention. His domination of the bull offers an expression of disciplined masculinity which is endorsed by the father
figure of Don Esteban who, as the session comes to an end, tells the
boys that 'Puede llegar a mucho' ('he could go far'), feeding their
collective dream of capitalist wealth. Money, as the boys are all
aware, buys everything. Even Chato, the youngest member of the
gang, knows the reality of an existence without financial security.
'Everything is a question of money,' he states, 'otherwise there's
nothing to be done.'

The overriding power of the capitalist imperative is established
from the very opening of the film when Ramón is shown robbing a
lottery seller hawking dreams of instant wealth to a gullible public.
The fact that she is asked if she has Chesterfields by a nameless and
practically faceless customer immediately locates the prominence
of American consumer items.[10] Throughout the film the boys are
located against products which sell the American dream. Julián,
Ramón, and Paco all actively promote the American model. The
1950s is, of course, the decade responsible for placing the adolescent male in front of the camera, thus offering an idealized image
of youth—as product, consumer, and object of desire—which could
be reflected throughout the mirror cinemas of the Western world.
The treatment of the young male body in films such as *The Wild
One* (1953), *Rebel without a Cause* (1955), and *East of Eden*
(1955) offered a reference point for disconnected teenagers everywhere. The dominant iconography of such films—blue jeans,
leather jackets, white T-shirts—is also visible in *Los golfos*. The
young men's attire clearly locates them as products of the
consumerism furiously promoted by the 1950s ethos. Julián's

[10]   A point also made by Kinder (1993: 100).

posture and gait, like his hair, is reminiscent of screen rebels of the 1950s. Like Dean's key characters, Julián is an outsider even within his own marginalized group; less willing to go along with Ramón's plans than the others, he is clearly his main rival for leadership of the gang. He challenges Ramón's authority by often arriving late for pre-arranged meetings; his allegiances we sense are mutable and based entirely on individual gain and status. 'Yo trabajo para mí' ('I work for myself'), he tells the group at the dance hall as they plot to assist Juan. In a film which celebrates the male bond, he lacks the communal ethos shared by the other boys, fracturing the gang's allegiances through his promotion of feminine glamour in his courting of Visi, the vulnerable local prostitute he offers to 'lend' to the gang and shows off on his arm in an attempt to 'be someone'. When he is first seen at home with his sister, a middle-aged woman calls in to see if he knows where her son Miguel is. 'Tonight he hasn't slept at home,' she tells him. Julián is curt and dismissive in his reply but his sister reminds him, 'Didn't you hang around with him for ages?' He lacks the unquestioning buddy loyalty displayed by the other gang members. Miguel's disappearance is almost a premonition of the fate to befall Paco, another disappearance to which Julián fails to allocate adequate importance.

In a later sequence, as Julián stands casually against the door of a bar watching a prostitute enter, a cigarette protrudes provocatively from his mouth in a manner reminiscent of the gangsterish Bogart or Cagney. He is posing as he would expect a screen outlaw to, playing his part in the surveillance exercise that precedes the theft of the tools from the lorry about to park outside the bar. There is a cruel irony in the fact that the hooligans—a derogatory term that lacks the more glamorous associations of 'gangster'—fail to realize that they are closer to the brash, adolescent, streetwise, dead-end kids of such Cagney vehicles as *Angels with Dirty Faces* (1938) and *The Public Enemy* (1931), duly punished for recognizing in crime an escape from a dire social predicament, than to the sophisticated gangsters themselves. This becomes clear in the garage break-in when they are abruptly put in their place by a large American. Julián wants to compete with the Americans. He wants their material goods, and the myth of their affluent lifestyle. 'Buena vida llevas,' he tells Visi as we see them having a drink together at an outdoor café. This he equates with the Americans who form her clients as a prostitute. 'How are the Americans?', he asks her and is obviously flattered when, having described them as 'regular', she tells him, 'you look very dandy'. 'Today you're coming with me,' he replies assertively, thrusting a number of notes into her hand, despite her protests to wait until later when they cannot be seen. In the male world where Julián exists, Visi is another commodity, but one which is doubly valuable because her presence on his arm verifies his heterosexuality. Women are significantly silent in the film, and kept largely to the margins. Visi is an object of exchange between the men, a function again doubly reinforced by her prostitution. Julián's reproduction of the patterns of behaviour witnessed in movie idols and pin-ups, his boasts of material affluence, and his spending on the visible luxury of having his shoes shined in the hope of impressing Visi clearly locate him as striving for an idealized masculinity which is a commodity he believes money can buy.

Ramón's behaviour is equally determined by American models—note how he, Paco, and Manolo are placed under a circular Coca-Cola sign outside the bar as they look out for a truck to arrive.[11] His plan for the garage break-in is full of intrigue and suspense, and he mentions that it should be executed 'a lo americano' (American style). Unlike his cinematic role models, however, he is unable to provide a flawless rendition of the heist and the operation is thwarted by the unexpected arrival of the loud American who gives Julián a single sharp punch to the stomach which leaves him breathless. All the boys are forced to hold the American down while Julián delays things further by screaming 'I'll kill him,' in an attempt to redefine his status, irrevocably wounded by a witnessed failure to match up to the American competition. 'America's a breeze,' Paco's earlier statement seeking to persuade Juan to emigrate to the States, rings particularly hollow as the boys pool all their physical might to contain the single American. Saura's hooligans are constructed by an ideology which promotes an idealized image from which they are pathetically distant. Their modest abilities as fighters, toreros, hoodlums, lovers, and pickpockets is brought into constant conflict with a myth which posits that they can indeed stand out from the crowd, a crowd in which the film constantly places them.

Their distance is doubly reinforced by the particularly Spanish

---

[11] A point also made by Kinder (1993: 107).

nature of the sport that Juan has chosen to excel in. The *corrida*, like the boxing ring, has proved a popular political metaphor for directors as diverse as Rouben Mamoulian, Luchino Visconti, Robert Rossen, Mario Camus, Martin Scorsese, and Roberto Romeo as an immediate means of dramatizing images of struggle and confrontation, of presenting through an individual, or in this case individuals, representing a particular social underclass the notion of ability—something which ironically Juan lacks—as a means of fighting one's way out of the ghetto. Mark Simpson locates struggle and simplicity as essential ingredients of the American dream of masculinity (1994: 155). *Los golfos* resituates these elements within a specific historical and geographic context and frames them within a recognizably Spanish motif. Bullfighting, Saura has commented, makes good theatre; an echo of a statement made by Nigel Collins in relation to boxing.[12] Ortega y Gasset wrote at the turn of the century of the circus and bullfight as the essence of theatre, the only surviving remnants of the popular religious theatre festivals of Dionysiac Greece, the Middle Ages, and the Renaissance (1966: 41, 90). There exists in such spectacles an unwritten consensus between performers and audience that this is theatre, and the responses of the audience—laughter, heckling, ridicule—are seen as an intrinsic part of the proceedings. The ring proves a daunting stage, its circular enclosure focusing all audience attention on the matador, enacting a ritualized performance of domination and submission. Interestingly, the first film directed by Camus, *Young Sánchez* (1963), initially developed with Saura as a script in 1960 in the immediate aftermath of *Los golfos*, concerns the aspirations of a struggling boxer to make it in a combative and corrupt professional environment. Analogies with the film-makers' predicament are once more suggested. In the boxing and bullrings, as in film, defeat is perceived in a particularly public manner, greeted, as in the final sequence of *Los golfos*, by the critical diatribes of antagonistic audiences.

Additionally, bullfighting functions, as in Roberto Romeo's *Esperanza y sardinas* (1996), as a means of showing the social pressures of a particular period—in Romeo's case depression-wrecked

---

[12]   Carlos Saura, in a private, unpublished interview with the author, June 1990; Nigel Collins quoted in 'Art in the Ring', *Omnibus* documentary, broadcast BBC1, 1990.

contemporary rural Alicante, in Saura's work the shanty towns springing up on the outskirts of Madrid in the aftermath of the Civil War, as Andalusian labourers flocked to the city in search of work. One of the latter film's early sequences shows the boys' descent from the bridge which marks the boundary between civilization and the shacks on the peripheries of the city where they live—a clear analogy for their marginalized status. Brief successive sequences then show the boys leaving their homes. Poverty and squalor prevail. Chato's home lacks running water, newspapers cover cracks in the wall, and the decor is sparse. Julián's flat is similarly austere, situated in a cramped building where the sound of crying children echoes around and inhabitants jostle for space on the stairs. Manolo lives in a derelict single-room shack with no proper windows or doors. There is no need to show the interior of Paco's home. There is enough of a visual identification with the sequences that have preceded it. As Paco slouches off, his elderly mother feeds the cackling chickens, the telephone poles in the distance providing a stark reminder amongst the feudal conditions that this is modern Spain. In a society where pigs scavenge alongside human beings—these 'golfos' form part of the anonymous mass. Mastering of the bull offers a chance to demonstrate themselves as being in control, scoring a victory against a society which would render them invisible. As Ramón tells the gang in the dance hall, 'a bullfighter isn't just anyone'.

Bullfighting, catering in Marvin D'Lugo's words 'to the basest values and instincts of the Spanish lower classes' (1991: 34), provides a socially acceptable (indeed institutionally endorsed) face for pent-up violence. In the release of violence which takes place in the ring, the crowd shares in a hysterical, sub-Dionysian ecstasy of histrionics. In the closing sequence of the film, the crowd's prolonged and agitated heckling proves a bitter humiliation for the inexperienced torero. Violence in the film functions ambiguously— both as a means of resisting a particularly bleak social system where corruption is rife, and as a destructive discourse (implicitly bound up with the fascist ideology which promotes it) which has the capacity to annihilate the torero, the gang's victims, and the gang members themselves, as witnessed by Paco's death—his hounding a premonition of the fate that is to befall Juan in the ring. The gang's attacks and assaults are used to fuel the stylized violence of the *corrida*. Violence engenders violence, providing an intricate pattern of associations in which, as Marsha Kinder notes, 'the modern random brutality of the American-style robberies is made analogous to the ritualized violence of the Spanish bullfight' (1993: 155). All the characters are embroiled in and tainted by an aura of violence which serves to illustrate the contradictions inherent in attempting to define themselves in opposition to an ideology whose language they are necessarily obliged to employ.

It is the feminized ceremonial aspects of the sport which Juan and Chato find particularly alluring. Juan is shown meticulously trying on his suit of lights and then modelling it assisted and observed by his adoring brother Chato. 'You look somebody,' Chato tells him as Juan stares admiringly into the full-length mirror. The reflected image provides a representation of what Lacan terms *l'objet petit a*, that which offers a temporary solution to the sense of lack (*le manque à être*) with which we are all born (1977: 1–7). The reflection in the mirror provides an image of unity which is a misrecognition of self. The image presented is of an unattainable perfection verified by an external source, his brother Chato. Juan therefore takes on the identity which is the desire of his brother and, by association, that of the other members of the gang. Like Narcissus, Juan loses himself in the illusory image of the mirrored reflection. This reflection can be linked to the other idealized mirrors—posters, calenders, and postcards—which offer Juan and the gang frozen glorified images of legendary toreros. One large German-language poster promoting the *corrida* in the impresario's office indicates its potency in exporting a limited image of Spain. Juan stares enraptured just as the younger boys who watch him practise stare in awe. In Juan and Chato's home, a worn calendar showing a matador captured in action is hung alongside a poor print of the Last Supper and a dedicated photo of an elegantly dressed couple. The repressive forces of Church and family are conspicuously absent from the lives of the boys, yet through their proximity to the calendar all are presented as mirrors through which the boys' behaviour is read. As with the postcards of film stars that adorn Julián's bare walls, these images are part of a complex web of references which, to use Althusser's phrase, 'interpellate' the characters through the social practices in which they engage into an ideology which they actively if unwittingly promote (1971: 153–6).

The perfect mirror image of the imagined ideal, a contrived and performed masquerade, provides an image of plenitude to a fragile male ego. The glitzy dazzling costume, the deliberate concentration on pose and deft, gracious movement, destabilize the voyeuristic gaze by presenting the male body as much as that of the female as a vehicle of display, an object of erotic contemplation. This femininity within the male has to be contained (or expelled) so that the myth of masculine prowess can continue to self-perpetuate. Consequently Paco, the gentlest and probably most likeable of the boys, is sacrificed. He becomes the victim of an ideology which celebrates sacrifice—both that of the bull and through Catholicism—that which Antony Easthope terms 'the son's feminine love for the father and complete obedience to him' (1990: 25). Paco's subservience to the father—as represented by both his celebration of the American model and his submission to the patriarchs of the gang Julián and Ramón—is never contested. There is no mother or girlfriend to desire who may challenge the male bond. Paco's status as the baby of the group is reinforced by his inability at the dance hall to secure a partner. 'Get off, baby boy, go and find your mummy,' he is told by the first woman he approaches. Even at the riverside picnic, as he goes off with a smiling teenage girl, Julián jokily goads him as 'chiquitazo' (little boy). His sordid death in a Madrid sewer, as he attempts to escape from an aggressive crowd of citizens bearing makeshift weapons, is not unlike that of Harry Lime in Carol Reed's 1949 film *The Third Man*. Lime, however, is clearly located as a father figure, a sophisticated black marketeer wishing to keep control of his territory. The young Paco remains, in psychoanalytic terms, infantile throughout; unable to face the threat of castration which the crowd pose, he retreats underground where he meets his death. Significantly his body is discovered draped in a discarded newspaper advertising *Gigi*. The baroque aestheticism and overt melodrama of Minnelli's 1958 film is here sceptically challenged by the stark image of a corpse framed against the poverty of an environment which cannot be escaped through *machista* fantasies of triumphing in the ring.

In this 'los golfos' are unlike the protagonists of the glossy *españoladas* or folkloric musicals of the 1940s and 1950s which nurtured a vision of the country as a haven of happy-go-lucky bullfighters and dark tempestuous bewitching *señoritas* who were punished for errant behaviour (as in the case of femme fatale Sara Montiel) or celebrated for their virtuous rectitude and selfless courage (as in the folk musicals of Peret or Marisol). The ideological currents of such films were deeply conservative, presenting a polarized view of gender roles and the exaltation of a nation whose moral, cultural, and socio-political superiority was so great as to make it the envy of the Western world. Spontaneous bursts into song by the celebrated *folklóricas* who starred in such propagandist vehicles served to draw attention to the exquisite instinctive performing abilities of the Spanish with socio-political problems erased from the screen as the worthy protagonists were shown capable of surmounting the economic hardships with which they were temporarily faced. Saura's *Los golfos* resituates the folkloric elements which formed the backbone of such features against a bleak and recognizable, as opposed to mythical or techni-colour, setting. The illusion of the spontaneous performer is undermined through the film's emphasis on the mechanics of production both in the self-conscious camerawork and editing and through allusions to the performed nature of the boys' roles—as both gangsters and, in Juan's case, torero. The positioning of 'los golfos' against inhibiting masculine myths of sexual prowess and flawless ability and control clearly locates the boys as both victims and perpetuators of patriarchal expectations. The only time prior to Juan's debut that the gang are seen anywhere near a professional bullring (Ventas) involves the theft of petrol caps, mirrors, and lamps by Manolo, Julián, and Chato from motorbikes parked outside the ring. They are in love with a narcissistic dream cruelly shattered in the film's long final sequence—the fight itself—where shots of Juan struggling clumsily in the ring are juxtaposed with close-ups of his suffering friends and an antagonistic public. As Juan's failure becomes all too apparent, the friends are drowned by and lost in the shouts of a hostile crowd. The crowds are filmed in small groups, their angry faces presented in oppressive close-up; a marked contrast to Juan's pathetic and vulnerable figure framed in the large arena in long shot. Through the crowd's presence, our own act of looking is articulated and replicated on the screen. Our position is made conscious through the reciprocal gaze that disconcertingly implicates us within an ideology of commercialized repression and prostitution. Juan is an object of spectacle exposed to the critical eyes of diegetic and non-diegetic spectators who are as dependent on images of the ego ideal as he is.

It is not solely the image of the *corrida* which has proved attractive to Saura. In the discipline of the bullfight there is a reflexive analogy with his own craft as a film-maker. The *corrida* has its own narrative, its own movements, stanzas, or acts. The fight is divided into structured cause and effect sections, each to be successfully realized before action can progress. In *Los golfos* Juan's failure to make progress during the course of the film—he is always framed attempting the same set of moves—acts as a premonition of his professional debut. Additionally, it is contrasted with the escalating violence which accompanies the boys' crimes, a violence unmatched by Juan's tame sessions in the ring. The performance Juan presents is mediated by the social stage in which it takes place. Saura's film is desperately aware of the socio-political relationships of those who gaze and those who are gazed at, and while the negotiation of conflict is ongoing, the austere physical environment in which the characters are situated clearly posits them politically as products of a specific social system which encourages prostitution in its widest forms whilst officially discouraging certain manifestations of it. Both Visi and Juan sell themselves and their affair at the end of the film solidifies a metaphoric analogy between bullfighting and prostitution. Nevertheless, as Kinder persuasively argues, 'while prostitution is an international institution, bullfighting (with its historical connections to "plebeianism" and melodrama) is far more culturally specific' (1993: 100).

Cultural specificity is inscribed in the film not merely through the deployment of the bullfight but also through the popular bastardized flamenco which underscores much of the action, marking its pace, commenting on its developments, and providing a point of reference for the characters' actions and attitudes. The guitar score by J. Pagan and Antonio Ramírez Ángel is one of a series of signifiers which situate the characters as Andalusian migrants. The lyric of one of the numbers, 'al pie de un árbol sin fruta' (at the foot of a tree without fruit), offers a blistering comment on the boys' relationship to the society they inhabit. Kinder also draws attention to the use of music in delineating specificity when she analyses the failed pickpocketing at the cosmopolitan bar Whisky a Gogo. Here the American-style diegetic jazz band score serves to stress Juan and Ramón's awkwardness in a setting where their difference is accentuated and all too apparent (1993: 108).[13] Their inability to perform in this environment demonstrates the way in which the iconographies which inform

---

[13] Kinder also examines the association of the flamenco guitar with Manolo, 'the Andalusian loner' (1993: 107), and the role of the flamenco score (1993: 101).

their behavioural practices are diluted and thus weakened by the mere act of translation.[14] They become pale imitators of the heroes they attempt to emulate.

The *copla* (ballad) sung by the two women in a corner of the flea market, El Rastro, as Chato and Paco are attempting to sell tools stolen in the previous sequence is a further example of the manner in which popular indigenous art forms can be used as a means of providing alternative realities in a society where 'truth' is officially and authoritatively written. The balled 'Cuatro asesinatos en Madrid' tells the story of José María Jarabo's assassination of four citizens in a bloody night of violence. The cautionary tale acts both as a premonition of the fate that is to befall Paco, who dies attempting to escape the wrath of a revenge-driven crowd, and as a moralistic warning of the dangers of crime as a means of funding vices. Elisabeth Bronfen's observation of how, 'set against mortality and oblivion, narrators . . . consume death' is relevant here, for it indicates how these storytellers fulfil their prophecy, 'positioned in an intermediary site between life and death. Their power of imagination is like a vampire, feeding off this exchange, for they rely on a preservation and production of "dead" figures—the teller's and the listener's temporary social death and the uncanny presence as absence that fictions embody' (1992: 349). The specificity of the singers' location (in the Rastro), and of the ballad (telling of a Spanish criminal) firmly locates the narrative (and its moral) within a local setting which sets up clear associations with the boys and their predicament. The sequence begins with a two-shot of the duo singing, cutting to a high-angle shot of Paco and Chato wandering through the flea market as the criminal's name is mentioned by the singers. The insertion at this particular point in the narrative of this musical interlude comments on the action already seen by the viewer—the attack on the blind lottery ticket seller, the theft of the tool box. The disruptive editing employed by Saura—the sequence appears initially to have no association with the previous episode—works to displace the viewer temporally and spatially as he or she struggles first to place the two women with regard to 'los golfos' and then to place Paco and Chato with regard to the women. As with the theft sequence where, after a dynamic build-up, Saura cuts to the two women just as Paco and Manolo

---

[14]   The theoretical framework of this point is provided by Phelan (1993: 97).

are attempting to dislodge the tool box, Saura again provides a jump cut, here as the ballad prepares to tell of Jarabo's fate and Paco and Chato simultaneously enter the shop to try and sell their loot.

These editing strategies, as both Kinder (1993: 105) and D'Lugo (1991: 40–1) have noted, are characteristic neither of Hollywood's classical cinema nor neorealism, rather they point to a rupture with established methodologies and the messages they implicitly carry; that which D'Lugo terms 'an interrogative practice of seeing' which questions 'the discursive practices that had naturalized the various myths of Spanishness that had formed and deformed the contemporary Spaniard' (1991: 7). It is not surprising, therefore, that despite the fact it was used to promote Spain abroad as an example of the regime's 'new' *apertura* (liberalism), *Los golfos* should have suffered crippling censorship at home, enduring an excessive number of cuts—ten minutes in a film running at ninety minutes. Direct heterosexual scenes like that of Visi and Juan lying in the bed of a shabby hotel room offended the regime's puritanical attitudes to sexual desire. Nevertheless, the casual male homoeroticism which provides an acceptable setting for the boys to nurture and express feelings which are habitually constrained by society remained untouched by the censor. Undoubtedly, the film's audacity in tackling taboo subjects—disappearances, prostitution, juvenile crime, the nation's social ills, the exploitation of a proletarian workforce—did not endear it to the regime, but a number of the cuts made seem to indicate a deliberate policy of sabotage on the part of Gabriel Arias Salgado, whose office was then responsible for film licensing.[15] Although most of the surviving prints of the film do not include the censored sequences, cuts aside *Los golfos* remains a key film within the Spanish film industry, breaking with the studio-shot films of the 1940s and 1950s, taking cinema firmly into the streets, offering a decisive response to the country's political, social, and ideological environment, celebrating the sublimated erotics of male cameraderie, interrogating the very medium and conventions of film, and, as with *A bout de souffle*, through a self-conscious collage of allusions to other texts, heralding a new cinema which was to challenge the very assumptions which had governed Spanish film-making to that point and which continue, as

[15] For a comprehensive list of the cuts made to the film see Brasó 1974: 69.

demonstrated by Roberto Romeo's *Esperanza y sardinas*, to exert a powerful influence on directors working today.[16]

REFERENCES

Althusser, Louis (1971), *Lenin and Philosophy*, trans. Ben Brewster. London: New Left Books.

Brasó, Enrique (1974), *Carlos Saura*. Madrid: Taller de Ediciones Josefina Betancor.

Bronfen, Elisabeth (1992), *Over Her Dead Body: Death, Femininity and the Aesthetic*. Manchester: Manchester University Press.

Dent, Alan (1961), '*Los golfos*', *Sunday Telegraph* (29 Oct.): 10.

D'Lugo, Marvin (1991), *The Films of Carlos Saura: The Practice of Seeing*. Princeton: Princeton University Press.

Easthope, Antony (1990), *What a Man's Gotta Do: The Masculine Myth in Popular Culture*. Boston: Unwin Hyman.

Galán, Diego (1974), *Adventuras y desadventuras de la prima Angélica*. Valencia: Fernando Torres.

Higgenbotham, Virginia (1988), *Spanish Film under Franco*. Austin: University of Texas Press.

Hopewell, John (1986), *Out of the Past: Spanish Cinema after Franco*. London: BFI.

Ibáñez, Enrique (1960), '*Los golfos*', *Documentos cinematográficos*, 2 (5 June): 63–4.

Kinder, Marsha (1993), *Blood Cinema: The Reconstruction of National Identity in Spain*. Berkeley and Los Angeles: University of California Press.

Lacan, Jacques (1977), *Écrits: A Selection*, trans. Alan Sheridan. London: Tavistock.

Marcorelles, Louis (1960), 'No Holds Barred at Cannes Festival', *Observer* (15 May): 21.

Ortega y Gasset, José (1966), *Idea del teatro*. Madrid: El Arquero.

Phelan, Peggy (1993), *Unmarked: The Politics of Performance*. New York: Routledge.

Sánchez Vidal, Agustín (1988), *El cine de Carlos Saura*. Zaragoza: Caja de Ahorros de la Inmaculada.

Simpson, Mark (1994), *Male Impersonators*. London: Cassell.

Vas, Robert (1961), '*Los golfos*', *Monthly Film Bulletin*, 28/332 (Oct.): 139.

[16] Roberto Romeo in a letter to the author states that 'The connection with Saura's film . . . does exist: in the characters who emerged from the streets, in the social (and a lot could be said here as the social landscape is almost the same in certain strands of people and that's forty years later) in black and white. . . . I can firmly say that I really liked *Los golfos* . . . and it did influence me but not knowingly.'

5

Culture and Acculturation in Manuel Summers's *Del rosa . . . al amarillo* (1963)

SUSAN MARTIN-MÁRQUEZ

THE last few years in Spain have witnessed a flurry of renewed interest in the socialization of children during Francoism. Luis Otero's deliciously ironic recreation of his own experience of ideological inculcation, *Al paso alegre de la paz* (1996), became a surprise best seller, leading to the rerelease of his 1987 novel *Gris marengo*, focused on the education of a Nationalist war martyr's son. Andrés Sopeña Monsalve's book of memoirs, *El florido pensil: memoria de la escuela nacionalcatólica* (1994), which has also enjoyed several reprintings, was quickly adapted for the theatre by the Basque company Tanttaka Teatroa; when this stage version moved on to Barcelona in the summer of 1997, tickets were sold out for nearly every performance. Continuing along the path established by Carmen Martín Gaite in her groundbreaking study *Usos amorosos de la posguerra* (1987) as well as in her earlier novel *El cuarto de atrás* (1978), Otero and Sopeña quote and reproduce graphic material from official textbooks, radio programmes, songs, comics, games, and films of the era, detailing the multiplicity of channels through which ideology was transmitted during the dictatorship. Yet these works do not necessarily claim that Francoist discourses were monolithically effective. While Martín Gaite reveals that during the post-war period certain forms of popular culture could be consumed in counter-hegemonic ways,[1] Otero

---

[1] For more on this aspect of Martín Gaite's work, see Sieburth 1994: ch. 5. Beginning the year of Franco's death, several compilation documentaries which also sought to highlight the ideological impact of popular culture during the dictatorship were released; they, too, seem to suggest that individual citizens could produce counter-hegemonic readings of propagandistic texts. Marsha Kinder argues, for example, that the complex juxtapositions of words, songs, and images in Basilio Martín Patino's *Canciones para después de una guerra* (produced in 1971, but not

highlights the occasionally ridiculous inefficacy of Francoist propaganda. Significantly, he dedicates *Al paso alegre de la paz* to the 'educadores, maestros y otros adultos del período denominado franquista que tanto me enseñaron a no escribir libros como éste. O sea: ¡todos hemos fracasado!'

It is one thing, of course, to enumerate the tragic successes and comic failures of Francoist acculturation several or many years after the dictator's death, and quite another to have done so during the dictatorship itself. The 1963 film *Del rosa . . . al amarillo*— cartoonist and Official Film School graduate Manuel Summers's debut feature—managed to achieve precisely that. Like Otero's and Sopeña's recent books, this film explicitly references a wide range of cultural texts circulating throughout Spain during the 1940s, 1950s, and early 1960s, and explores the complex ways in which they were received by children as well as by adults. Furthermore, Summers's work, a forerunner of Otero's and Martín Gaite's, suggests that on a micro-political level individual Spaniards could in fact stage localized rebellions against hegemonic norms by engaging in strategic 'readings' of these texts.

As a cultural product in its own right, *Del rosa . . . al amarillo* was widely consumed by domestic audiences. The most successful Spanish film ever entered in the San Sebastián Festival to that date, it received several awards: the Concha de Plata for direction (the public protested loudly when the Concha de Oro was given to another film), the Premio Revelación for the four main actors, the Perla del Cantábrico for the best Spanish-language film, and a Special Mention from the Federación Nacional de Cine-Clubs (García de Dueñas 1963: 33; Cotán Rodríguez 1993: 32). When the film opened nationwide it did extremely well at the box office, and remained in the Coliseum theatre on Madrid's Gran Vía for thirteen weeks. *Del rosa . . . al amarillo* also reached sixth place in a series of popular opinion polls conducted throughout the 1960s concerning the year's best films (Castro 1974: 430; Torres 1973:

released until 1976 owing to Francoist censorship) 'generate a plethora of subversive meanings' and that '[t]he film implies this subversive form of mental editing was accessible to those so-called inner exiles living within Francoist Spain, who could use their own popular memories of quotidian life to challenge the official meanings imposed by the state' (1997: 71). Other such works mentioned by Kinder include Martín Patino's *Caudillo* (1975), Jaime Camino's *La vieja memoria* (1975), and Gonzalo Herralde's *Raza, el espíritu de Franco* (1977).

115). Although production of Summers's work did coincide with the first codification of censorship laws (the Norms for Film Censorship went into effect in February 1963), the film pre-dated the National Film Development Measure of 1964 and was entirely self-financed. Curiously, however, *Del rosa . . . al amarillo* seemed to anticipate the goals of the latter legislation, which sought to guarantee the survival of the movies as a mass cultural form (albeit subject to tight restrictions), while simultaneously promoting a more 'open' art cinema—soon to be designated the New Spanish Cinema—whose success at international film festivals would impact favourably on the nation's image abroad.[2]

Del rosa . . . al amarillo is in essence a compilation of two short films depicting the experience of love in childhood ('Del rosa') and in old age ('al amarillo'). The first episode focuses on Guillermo (Pedro D. del Corral), an upper middle-class pre-adolescent boy captivated by Margarita (Cristina Galbó), a slightly older girl among his circle of friends. As their relationship develops over the course of several months, Margarita's friend 'Ratona' serves as go-between for the

[2] Although previously governmental subventions for films had been tied to a classificatory system promoting propaganda cinema—films that failed to champion the party line did not receive funding—the new law provided for an across-the-board subsidy of 15% of box-office take for all Spanish movies, thus encouraging the production of works with a wider popular appeal. At the same time, the measure elicited the support of recent graduates from the Official Film School in the creation of a cinema 'de destacada ambición artística', ostensibly modelled after the New Cinemas emerging throughout Europe, by offering them one million peseta advances for films designated of 'Special Interest'. According to Román Gubern and Domènec Font, New Spanish Cinema directors were in effect manipulated by the regime into producing a strictly regulated 'oppositional' cinema (1975: 124–5).

Summers's films immediately subsequent to *Del rosa . . . al amarillo* were produced under this new system, and they were indeed subject to much greater administrative control than was his debut feature (Santos Fontenla 1966). *La niña de luto* (1964), depicting the plight of a woman whose marriage to her fiancé is continually postponed owing to rigid Spanish mourning traditions, had to be modified to satisfy the censors. *El juego de la oca* (1964) tackled adultery, but the director was forced to change the ending so that the film's straying husband would dutifully return to his wife and children. When *Juguetes rotos* (1966), a trenchant documentary on Spain's abandoned cultural idols of the past, considered by many to be Summers's finest work, was also censored, the director abandoned all further efforts to create a critical 'art cinema'. His next film, *No somos de piedra* (1968), established the infamous *landismo* genre (which typically featured Alfredo Landa as a sex-starved male Spaniard in pursuit of curvaceous foreign bombshells), and from that point on Summers would cultivate exploitation fare of one sort or another almost exclusively. Looking back on his career, the director later admitted that 'yo tengo la fama de ser la "puta" del cine español', but insisted that 'si soy "puta" es porque yo quiero, y me permito el lujo de ser la más cara' (Castro 1974: 432).

young couple. When summer arrives, Guillermo attends a military-style camp while Margarita heads for the beach in Alicante, and the two exchange love letters. Back in Madrid, however, Margarita snubs Guillermo, and 'Ratona' informs him that Margarita now has a new 18-year-old boyfriend, whom she met at the beach. The second episode, considerably shorter and less developed than the first, focuses on Valentín (José Cerrudo) and Josefa (Lina Onesti), enamoured residents in a retirement home located in a convent and strictly run by an order of nuns; their relationship intensifies through the exchange of meaningful glances, gestures, and surreptitiously passed notes. Valentín attempts to convince Josefa to flee with him, but she refuses, and on the night he has designated for their escape, he waits fruitlessly beside the convent wall as Josefa sobs in bed. The next morning, Josefa is overjoyed to discover that Valentín has not left after all.

Shot in black and white with non-professional actors and in natural settings—somewhat paradoxically, in the interest of economy Summers set the first episode in and around his parents' apartment in Madrid's affluent Barrio de Salamanca—*Del rosa . . . al amarillo*, like so many Spanish films of the time, owes a clear debt to neorealist strategies. The film's critical edge, achieved through gentle humour and brief incursions into black comedy, also recalls Luis García Berlanga's early work. This comparison was in fact drawn in the press, as when the *Gaceta ilustrada* claimed of Summers that '[d]esde *Bienvenido Mr. Marshall* no había surgido en España otra personalidad más importante que la suya' (quoted in Press Book 1963). Summers also experiments with some of the aesthetic strategies characteristic of the European New Cinema movement, particularly the cinematographic creation of collage through the montage of textual fragments from other media such as ads and comics or the juxtaposition of objective and subjective sounds. Indeed, *Del rosa . . . al amarillo* is frequently cited—though rarely analysed—as a founding film of the New Spanish Cinema. Manuel Villegas López, one of the few critics to have considered Summers's work from a formal perspective,[3] emphasizes that the

---

[3] In their review published in *Nuestro cine*, Jesús García de Dueñas and Claudio Guerín Hill argue, rather inexplicably, that *Del rosa . . . al amarillo* is characterized by 'la no utilización de un buen número de recursos específicamente cinematográficos', and that the director is 'interesado sólo en lo que cuenta y jamás en cómo lo cuenta' (1964: 54).

director participates in the modern cinema's new conceptualization of time and space, noting of *Del rosa . . . al amarillo* that 'aquí ya maneja ese intercalado de escenas o simples imágenes, con las que pasa al otro lado de la realidad, al mundo de la imaginación, el ensueño, el deseo' (1967: 88–9).

By providing access to this 'other side of reality', experimentation with image and sound in this film serves to represent the marginalized subjectivities of children and the elderly. The soundtrack, for example, often reveals the characters' mental states. Typically, 'external' noises such as traffic or background conversation will fade out as the sound of 'inner reality' fades in. A voice-over frequently represents the thoughts of the protagonists; sometimes we hear their own voices (for example, when they are envisioning future conversations), while other times we hear them conjuring up those of different characters (if they are reading letters, for instance). Humorous moments abound, as when Valentín's voice, heard when Josefa reads his notes to her, pauses if Josefa must turn over a page, and whispers or falls silent whenever the vigilant nuns approach. Equally common is the use of non-diegetic music to reflect mood, although it is not always clear if we are meant to assume that this music is actually passing through the characters' heads, or if it is simply designed metaphorically to represent particular states of mind. As with the voice-over, this device is also used to comic effect: the jaunty piano music audible as Valentín begins to sneak a ladder from the kitchen out into the garden late at night stops abruptly as soon as a blind man enters the kitchen for some sausages—only to continue to 'play' once the man is out of earshot. Sometimes the music indicates otherwise invisible bodily reactions, as when a progressively more rapidly alternating series of notes suggests that Guillermo's heart races as soon as he catches sight of Margarita at the beginning of the film.

The image track too is exploited to represent the characters' interiority. Point-of-view shots often portray the world from their physical perspective, and may also reveal details concerning their perceptual capacities, as when a shaky patch of sky represents Guillermo's observations while marching through the countryside, or a blurry shot of Margarita's face simulates his vision while semi-conscious. This latter scene takes place in one of two dream sequences in the first episode; the other, in which Guillermo imagines meeting Margarita on the beach, is completely rose-tinted, symbolizing the boy's romantic mood. The film also includes several flashbacks. However, unlike the traditional flashback of classical film narrative, in which a highly coded transition, typically a close-up of the remembering character followed by a lap dissolve, introduces a linear, more or less realistic presentation of past events, the retrospective moments here are more akin to the modernist 'memory flashes' of the European New Cinema (Turim 1989: 206, 210). Thus, shots of Guillermo eating or attempting to sleep are intercut with brief close-ups of Margarita's face, or of her hand in Guillermo's, filmic fragments borrowed from a scene included earlier in the film.

Even though some of these techniques may have been novel for Spanish film-goers of the time, they would not have been particularly difficult for them to process. Summers was mindful of the need to communicate with his audience, and of the impossibility of achieving that goal if viewers did not understand his film's code: 'Si el receptor no está educado para la clave que utilizas', he observed in an interview, 'tendrás que pasarte a la clave del público, o no hacer nada, o decidirte a montar un departamento de películas educativas en el Ministerio de Educación Nacional, para que dentro de treinta o cuarenta años, puedas hacer las películas que tú quieras' (Castro 1974: 430).[4] Perhaps for this reason the memory flashes in Del rosa . . . al amarillo reference scenes already shown within the filmic narrative; unlike the brief images of an otherwise as-yet unseen soldier's arm in Alain Resnais's Hiroshima, mon amour (1959), for instance, the shot of Margarita's hand in Guillermo's is still fresh in the viewer's mind when it is recalled by the boy. Thus although it may employ somewhat similar formal strategies, Summers's film studiously avoids the creation of enigma or the emphasis on dense philosophical musings characteristic of much of the European art cinema of the time.

It is in fact significant that Del rosa . . . al amarillo's representation of interiority does not reveal any involved intellectual ruminations on the part of the protagonists. Rather, this film could be said to engage in a form of stimulus/response analysis: it reveals the

---

[4] Here Summers's declarations recall Pierre Bourdieu's on the same subject: 'Original experimentation entering the field of large-scale production almost always comes up against the breakdown in communication liable to arise from the use of codes inaccessible to the "mass public"' (1993: 129).

more immediate reactions of the characters to shifts in the external environment, and to discrete forms of cultural 'input'. In this way, *Del rosa . . . al amarillo* at times serves to ratify Louis Althusser's delineation of different 'state apparatuses' and their effect on a particular nation's citizens. According to Althusser, while Repressive State Apparatuses such as the police, the courts, the prisons, and the military exercise control over the individual through violence, the Ideological State Apparatuses, from the educational system to the Church, the family, and the media, bring about the formation of a compliant subject (1971: 142–5). Althusser qualifies somewhat the neat opposition between these two apparatuses, noting for example that although the ISAs work principally through ideology, they may also function secondarily through repression, as when they are shaped by censorship laws (1971: 145). In his well-known analogy, Althusser likens interpellation, the process by which ideology is simultaneously instilled in and practised by subjects, to hailing: it is as if the apparatus called out 'Hey, you there!' and the individual responded by turning around (1971: 174).

Del rosa . . . al amarillo exposes the ways in which myriad cultural discourses work to interpellate subjects under Francoism. The film provides a veritable catalogue of the different institutions and texts that serve as forces of acculturation during the dictatorship. First and foremost is the Catholic Church, which on occasion appears practically emptied of ideological content and converted into a pure agent of control. In Guillermo's school, for example, the teachers half-heartedly work to dominate their charges, preaching (sometimes hypocritically) the virtues of silence and good manners. It is the priest, however, who is shown to be the ultimate authority: when he enters the classroom students and teacher alike leap to attention, and the latter, adopting a servile pose, nods in respectful agreement as the priest inspects aloud the report card of each pupil and publicly humiliates those with low marks (most particularly, in this case, Guillermo, who has failed all subjects but drawing). In another scene, the priest becomes enraged when Guillermo attempts to defend himself against an inaccurate charge of cheating; '¡esto es intolerable!' he fumes, less interested in discovering the truth of the matter than in punishing Guillermo's insubordination. Achieving panoptic control—indeed, Michel Foucault's description of the modern society of surveillance is particularly applicable to Spain's Francoist period[5]—the ubiquitous gaze of the Church penetrates the domestic sphere as well: both the large painting and the imposing statue of the Virgin that preside over the hallway of Guillermo's home seem to bear witness to the small acts of transgression the boy commits without his parents' knowledge. Similarly, in the second episode, the residents of the retirement home must endure not only daily reminders of human mortality as the radio broadcasts a litany of news of death and destruction around the world, but also frightening sermons on the torments of hell. Looking to safeguard their eternal salvation, the nuns exercise strict vigilance over the residents, particularly Valentín, whom Sister Amparo begins relentlessly to pursue in the hope of catching him engaging in forbidden communication with his sweetheart. Just as the priest had confiscated the paper which he assumed Guillermo had copied, the nun will seize a letter to Josefa that Valentín, for his part, has indeed copied from a book of love letters.

In both episodes, it is evident that the Church plays a funda-mental role in the delimitation and control of gender and sexuality. Strict segregation of sexes is the rule: in accordance with the Francoist prohibition of coeducation, Guillermo is taught exclu-sively by men in his all-boys institution, while Margarita is educated by nuns in her convent school. In the second episode, male and female residents of the retirement home are not allowed contact with one another: they must eat in separate areas of the refectory, pray on opposite sides of the chapel, and spend their free time in different rooms. Significantly, the women 'dwell on high' in the more restricted space of the upper gallery while the men wander aimlessly about the patio below. Much of the residents' time is spend singing the praises of the Virgin. At times Josefa herself appears trapped within such modes of representation, as when she strikes poses reminiscent of those adopted by female

---

[5] For more on the panopticon, see Foucault 1979. Under Franco, a prison modelled on the panopticon was in fact constructed in Badajoz; political prisoners as well as common criminals were incarcerated there. In the 1990s the structure was transformed into a contemporary art museum, designed to serve as a reminder of past oppression even as it opens up a new 'space of freedom' (Holo 1997: 311–18).

Recent critical work has begun to show how the panoptic society of Francoism is figured in post-war novels. See Spires 1996, particularly ch. 1, and his analysis of Luis Martín Santos's *Tiempo de silencio* (a novel contemporaneous with *Del rosa . . . al amarillo*) in chapter 2, and Martin-Márquez 1995.

saints and by Mary in paintings or statues, with hands clasped together and eyes cast upward in devotion or downward in modesty or contemplation; in particular the final shot of the film, in which her uplifted gaze is framed within a round mirror, evokes medallion-shaped religious portraits. Josefa's ultimate refusal to flee with Valentín perhaps reveals her inability to escape a discourse that, for women especially, prescribes passivity and purity.

Under Francoism, Catholic teachings concerning gender and sexuality permeated a plethora of cultural texts, several of which circulate within *Del rosa . . . al amarillo*'s fictional universe. Guillermo's younger sister loans him a small card with a drawing of St Teresa reproduced in negative and with three small white dots over the nose. She bets Guillermo that after staring at the dots while counting to eighty, he will see a floating image of the saint; the camera registers a patch of empty ceiling as female voices singing religious choral music fade in on the soundtrack, and Guillermo avers that he has indeed seen the image. Helen Graham has remarked that the Franco regime's encouragement of public expressions of devotion was accompanied by an increase in miracles and visions among the masses (1995: 242), and the film slyly underlines the concomitant commercialization of religious sentiment through the St Teresa cards, as Guillermo's bubble-gum popping sister demands a *duro* from her brother after winning the bet. Although the card seems to have little effect on the children's avarice—the ironizing on this front continues when Guillermo, in need of a gift for Margarita, steals a bracelet from his sister immediately afterwards[6]—it does appear to influence gender socialization. During summer camp, for example, the St Teresa card inspires Guillermo to make a similar drawing in negative of Margarita, which he uses to conjure up her image as he marches in formation alongside his fellow campers, singing 'a ti sólo a ti yo quiero | nunca yo te olvido | con el corazón rendido | sólo a ti yo quiero'. By converting Margarita into a 'miraculous' apparition, Guillermo engages in a form of *marianismo*, placing his beloved on a pedestal

---

[6] The ascendancy of selfishness despite the Catholic context is also highlighted in another moment in the second episode characterized by black humour and reminiscent of Marco Ferreri's 1960 film *El cochecito*: when a retirement home resident expires, one of his disabled colleagues rushes over to stake a claim on the dead man's hand-cranked wheelchair.

that elevates her to sainthood and beyond the expression or pursuit of her own desire.

The popular film and kiosk literature referenced in *Del rosa . . . al amarillo* also conveys a dogmatic Catholic perspective on gender and sexuality. Margarita informs Guillermo that in her convent school the nuns show them movies such as *La señora de Fátima* (Rafael Gil, 1951), which depicts the famous appearance of the Virgin before three children in Portugal. This type of religious film, narrating miracles and charitable acts and featuring innocent children touched by God, heroic priests, maternal monks, and cheerfully selfless nuns, saturated the Spanish market throughout the late 1940s and 1950s. According to Diego Galán, these works sought to teach viewers that love must be sanctioned by marriage, that married couples must engage in sexual relations exclusively for the purpose of procreation, and that '[l]a mujer no monja no tiene otro fin en la vida que el de la maternidad o, como mínimo, el del sacrificio con respecto al esposo' (1975: 97–9). Similarly, the comic book that Guillermo surreptitiously reads at home during study time—the 'Guerrero del Antifaz'—is also designed to reinforce notions of gender-appropriate modes of existence, as well as to channel sexual desire safely into the confines of marriage. Terenci Moix has observed that although the heroes featured in comic books for boys popular during the Franco years, including the 'Guerrero del Antifaz', frequently exhibited a spectacular physique, the story-lines always emphasized their chastity. Despite the temptations presented by diabolically exotic women during his endless adventures in North Africa, the Guerrero remained absolutely pure; nor would he caress his virginal Spanish girlfriend Ana María until their union was sanctified by marriage, an event that was, of course, indefinitely postponed (Moix 1968: 123–5). Thus it is not surprising that when in *Del rosa . . . al amarillo* we are made privy to Guillermo's thoughts during mass, we learn that he prays to the Virgin that he might marry Margarita, as well as acquire the underarm hair and muscles that would bring him in line with notions of masculinity highlighted in comic books, and circulating, as the film makes clear, throughout Francoist society.

According to the cultural texts and institutions depicted in *Del rosa . . . al amarillo*, however, masculine desire and virility should be directed first and foremost towards the defence of the nation. Francoist historiography asserted that the divinely inspired

'Crusade' of the Civil War had returned Spain to its essential, pre-Enlightenment identity, characterized by religious, racial, and linguistic unity, as well as imperialistic values. The 'Guerrero del Antifaz' contributes to this discourse by intimating that the Civil War and the Reconquest are historical equivalents: both restore the nation's true destiny. Moix has noted that the 'Guerrero' idealizes this 'lucha con justificaciones de reivindicación histórica', portraying it as accomplished through a 'vida en comunidad masculina propia de los campamentos de *boy-scouts*' (1968: 125, 123). In fact, Guillermo is provided with the opportunity to experience this 'utopian' form of nationalistic communion in his boys-only summer camp: the campers spend much of their time marching in formation through the countryside, singing hymns that vow eternal loyalty to the Spanish flag, or to the girlfriend who waits at home, shedding tears for her heroic soldier. On the last day, their camp leader, carried away by patriotic fervour, bids the boys farewell with the following words, so characteristic of Francoist rhetoric:

Quisiera que estos días, en que hemos convivido como hermanos, compartiendo los mismos ideales, bajo el mismo sol y bajo el mismo cielo, quedasen engrabados en vuestro espíritu, para que en todo momento, a lo largo de vuestra vida, estéis preparados para la lucha sin tregua, en la guerra o en la paz, y sin descanso hasta vencer o morir, porque la vida es lucha.

Only within this military-like context does a representative of the Church assume a subordinate position. In a reversal of the situation in Guillermo's school, it is the priest who stands by meekly and is showered with spittle as the camp leader pronounces his impassioned speech.

The overblown nationalistic discourse of the regime has a notable impact on the children of the first episode. When Guillermo learns that Margarita's parents believe he is too young to have a girlfriend, he asks 'Ratona' to tell them that he intends to leave school early and become a commercial pilot or join the merchant navy. But Margarita informs Guillermo on two separate occasions that she would prefer him to join the navy, because 'así si mueres, que Dios no lo quiera, tendría el consuelo de saber que habías muerto por la patria'. The full intensity of Francoism's championing of ultimate sacrifice for the nation surfaces in a daydream in which Guillermo imagines himself as a critically wounded soldier.[7] While his earlier fantasy of a romantic walk on the beach with Margarita was rose-tinted, this one has a yellowish cast to it, which lends a documentary-like effect as it foreshadows the more sombre connotations of the second episode's theme colour (death and decay). In this complex montage sequence, which I will examine in greater detail later, little Guillermo is shot down while advancing alongside adult soldiers over a snowy battlefield. As he falls to the ground, his helmet tumbles off, revealing a photograph of Margarita tucked away inside; Guillermo extends a bloodied hand towards the photo, but collapses before reaching it. In the final shots of the sequence, Guillermo is carried into a hospital, and when he drifts into consciousness he finds nurse Margarita caring for him. By taking the nationalistic discourse concerning the glories of martyrdom literally—precisely as a child would—this dream sequence underlines the true perversity of Francoist socialization strategies.

Of the plethora of propagandistic texts circulating during the Franco years, Helen Graham insists that '[a]rticulating the regime's intent regarding such cultural forms is not, however, the same thing as ascertaining their impact on the constituencies of Spaniards consuming them' (1995: 238). As we have seen, *Del rosa . . . al amarillo* suggests that sometimes Francoist discourse did indeed achieve its desired effect, producing ideological conformity among the nation's citizens. Yet the film also explores the ways in which individual Spaniards could, in the terminology of Michel de Certeau, 'poach' on culture, co-opting 'high' and 'low' forms alike in the expression of their own, possibly counter-hegemonic, subjectivities (1984: 174). Graham suggests that during the Franco years this was most likely to occur whenever cultural institutions and texts propagated values in clear discord with the popular audience's own experiences (1995: 238). It is in fact this disjunction between prescribed modes of being and personal knowledge and desire that occasionally prompts the characters of *Del rosa . . . al amarillo* to consume cultural texts in more or less 'deviant' ways.

---

   7 In the video version of *Del rosa . . . al amarillo* (in Mundografic's series 'Antología del Cine Español') this daydream is misplaced: it is cut into a sequence in which Guillermo, now back in Madrid, puts on long pants, practises smoking, and heads off to find Margarita. In the film copy deposited in the Filmoteca Nacional, the daydream appears, as it does in the original script, immediately after Guillermo hears the camp leader's nationalistic speech.

Certeau insists that this type of consumption is in reality a form of production, and he likens the process to enunciation, since there is a 'resemblance between the ("enunciative") *procedures* which articulate actions in both the field of language and the network of social practices' (1984: 31, 19). For Certeau, the literal or metaphorical speech act 'is at the same time a use *of* language and an operation performed *on* it', characterized by a realization of some of the potential of the linguistic system and (perhaps most crucially) an appropriation of language by the speaker, and by an establishment of relationships with others and with time (1984: 33). In *Del rosa . . . al amarillo*, this process is presented quite explicitly with respect to Guillermo. The boy's reception of the 'Guerrero del Antifaz', for example, is portrayed in some detail. He first reads a passage from the comic book:

Guerrero: Dios os guarde, Ana María. Necesito hablaros de algunos asuntos de capital importancia para mí. No puedo ocultarlo por más
  tiempo. Os amo. No sé vivir sin vos.
Ana María: Pero. . .
Guerrero: No me interrumpáis, amor mío. Os adoro.

After reading this brief dialogue, Guillermo places his arm over the comic book and pulls up his sleeve to reveal a heart with his name and Margarita's that he has drawn on his skin, in effect literalizing the superimposition of one 'text'—his as-yet only imagined relationship with Margarita, inscribed on his own flesh—over another—that of the comic book. Guillermo then begins transcribing this superimposition onto a notepad: 'Hola Margarita. Hola Guillermo.' Changing his mind, however, he tiptoes to the bathroom to practise his half of the exchange orally before the mirror. In this performance, Guillermo seeks to update the language, although much of the stilted expression remains ('tengo que hablarte de ciertos asuntos de capital importancia para mí'). Then, on his way to play with his friends, Guillermo repeats the conversation in his head, inserting Margarita's responses; interestingly, although Guillermo's version involves the same silencing of the female interlocutor as the original ('no me interrumpas, vida mía'), it also includes a new line that calls for Margarita to express a certain complicity with this state of affairs ('Habla. Te escucho.'). Guillermo then plays 'rescatao', in which two opposing teams try to capture enemies while rescuing captives from their own side; the game replays the wartime scenarios portrayed in the 'Guerrero' comics, and this parallel does not escape the boy's attention. When Margarita is captured by the opposing team, Guillermo rushes across the street to save her—only to be caught himself. While the two prisoners contentedly hold hands, Guillermo plays his half of the dialogue over in his head again, but never recites it aloud; as he enjoys the delights of physical contact with Margarita, Guillermo discovers that failing to live up to the standards set by the Guerrero del Antifaz may in fact entail greater benefits.

Guillermo's tactics of consumption gain in complexity as the episode progresses. While at summer camp, the boy writes a letter to Margarita, and the camera reveals a volume of Rubén Darío's works on a nearby rock. A voice-over represents Guillermo's composition of a poem and a brief rhymed story:

> Margarita.
> Está linda la mar
> y el viento lleva esencia sutil de azahar
> tu aliento.
> Yo siento en mi alma una alondra cantar
> tu acento.
> Margarita. Margarita.
>
> Este era un rey que tenía un palacio de diamantes,
> una tienda hecha del día y un rebaño de . . . un rebaño de . . . de
>   elefantes,
> un kiosko de malaquita y un gran manto de tisú
> y una gentil princesita tan bonita, Margarita, tan bonita como tú.

Here Guillermo engages in a form of pastiche, imitating the *modernista* style of Darío's book *Azul*, characterized in linguistic terms by sonorous signifiers and exotic and/or sumptuous signifieds. Guillermo appropriates this high cultural text in order to articulate his own desire; his hesitations, for example over the 'rebaño de elefantes', humorously reveal, not simply his struggles with Spanish versification, but also his attempt to inject difference into the original schema. Furthermore, by inscribing Margarita into this 'foreign' context and transforming her into a charming princess, Guillermo apparently counters the xenophobic Orientalism of the 'Guerrero del Antifaz', which juxtaposed the ideally pure Spanish woman with the corrupt Semitic temptress. Yet as was the case with his earlier reception of the comic book, here Guillermo's personalized reading ultimately fails to subvert the gender politics of the source text: like any number of Darío's female characters, in the boy's renditions Margarita also becomes a precious object, yet another luxury good ripe for consumption.

Considerably more sophisticated in ideological terms is Guillermo's war martyr fantasy, represented through a rapid montage sequence of thirty-three shots; these include a number of odd, almost surreal images that betray the boy's angst and confusion concerning nationalistic and other cultural discourses. Much of the material appears to be archival footage from the Second World War, of Axis soldiers in heavy coats loading and firing cannons and charging across snowy battlefields, all orchestrated to music from Guillermo's summer camp: 'A ti sólo a ti yo quiero'. Guillermo sutures himself into this scenario via several shots in which, woefully outfitted in his camp shorts and armed with only a dagger, he scurries across the snow alongside several other adult soldiers, before collapsing in a bloody heap. Other curious fragments contribute to the disquieting effect: one soldier carries a rifle in his right hand and, inexplicably, an open umbrella—gaily striped—in his left; another, befuddled, wobbles ahead with a cane even as his companions have initiated a retreat. The entire series begins abruptly with an image that will also appear again later on: the camera moves in for a disorienting low-angle close-up of a soldier with his mouth wide open, as if screaming (the sound track registers only an explosion), with his eyes narrowed to slits behind oversized glasses, and with his fingers in his ears. It is tempting to associate this image with an earlier scene, in which Guillermo's language teacher chides a student who had put a finger in his ear for his lack of manners—only to repeat the gesture himself moments later.[8] Manners and civilization, Guillermo's fantasy/nightmare seems to suggest, are incompatible with war, which, contrary to what Francoist rhetoric and popular texts would indicate, is chaotic rather than ordered, bewildering rather than illuminating, pathetic rather than heroic.

Although the process is less meticulously developed, other characters in *Del rosa . . . al amarillo* also engage in cultural 'poaching'. Valentín, much like Guillermo, seeks inspiration for his notes to

---

[8] The hypocrisy of this teacher's insistence on 'buena educación' with respect to bodily comportment is further underscored in hilarious if somewhat understated fashion when he rises from his seat, revealing that the chalk marks that cover his dark suit are particularly concentrated around the area of his trousers' zip.

Josefa in other texts, specifically in Marcelo Peyret's *Cartas de amor*. Not until this book is confiscated, however, will Valentín learn to produce openly defiant letters that decry the injustice of his situation, as when, for example, he writes that he has been forced to compose his letter hurriedly in the bathroom, the only space beyond the nuns' surveillance.[9] For her part, although Josefa seems the most circumscribed by hegemonic forms, it is significant that the saintly poses she strikes are always linked to her feelings for Valentín; that is, she is most likely to mimic religious representations when she has received confirmation of Valentín's devotion. Valentín—quite unlike the other male residents, who stare either at the altar or vacantly off into space as they sing the Virgin's praises—directs broad smiles and provocative glances at Josefa as he warbles, 'santa, santa María, madre de Dios', several beats off the chorus of voices. Thus, while Josefa models her mannerisms after icons of the Virgin, Valentín converts Josefa into his own preferred object of veneration, injecting a generous dose of eroticism into the traditional *marianismo*. Both, in effect, work subversively to reinscribe themselves within the Catholic devotional context—without, it must be noted, ever quite escaping the restrictive sanctification of Woman characteristic of traditional religious expression.

By contrast, Margarita's consumption of cultural texts is often characterized by enthusiastic acceptance or uncategorical repudiation; she 'votes with her feet', in Graham's terminology (1995: 238). For example, Margarita rejects the moralistic religious films shown in her school, which she condemns as 'un rollo', voicing a marked preference for movies starring Burt Lancaster, whose height and good looks she admires. Despite her articulation of nationalistic clichés concerning martyrdom, Margarita appears particularly susceptible to the influence of foreign culture; this tendency is perhaps symbolized by her fascination with the Jorge Sepúlveda song 'Mirando al mar'. At first Margarita appreciates

---

[9] The confiscation of the book also takes place on a day in which the grim radio news programme is interrupted by the lively Cola-Cao jingle, whose words ('lo toma el futbolista para entrar goles | también lo toman los buenos nadadores | si lo toma el ciclista se hace el amo de la pista | y si es el boxeador—[pum, pum]— golpea que es un primor') seem to animate all of the usually passive male residents to small acts of rebellion: instead of playing a sedate game of dominoes, one group of men sets the blocks up to fall in a riffle; another man who habitually blows up a balloon decides to begin an impromptu game of volleyball with it.

this song mainly as a sentimental expression of nostalgia for an absent love, and Guillermo always chooses to read it this way too; indeed, it will serve as background music for his own rose-tinted summer fantasy of reuniting with Margarita on the beach, and will be heard again at the end of the episode as the jilted boy laments the loss of his sweetheart. But Margarita may also be drawn to the song's references to the act of gazing off into the sea — figuratively, gazing away from Spain. Along these lines, it is instructive to compare Guillermo's summer vacation, spent in a patriotic all-boys camp set somewhere in the Spanish interior, to Margarita's sojourn on the beaches of Alicante, which by the early 1960s would have been crowded with European tourists. It is not surprising that when Margarita returns to Madrid she appears markedly trans-formed; she has traded in her schoolgirl braids for a sophisticated new hairdo, and she wears heels and an expression of disdain for Guillermo, whom she evidently perceives as a provincial little boy, despite the fact that he now sports long pants and a cigarette.

Although Alicante, which is never actually portrayed on-screen, might be said to serve as an 'absent signifier' of cultural change in this film, there is another locus associated with shifting values that is indeed represented in *Del rosa . . . al amarillo*: Madrid. Unlike the oppressively restrictive domestic and institutional realms, the city streets signify freedom and ideological ambiguity in both episodes. Valentín enjoys a brief taste of this when he heads out with several other men to seek alms for a fellow resident's burial. One of the men takes the opportunity to flee, and the depiction of his escape is followed by a montage sequence set to festive *verbena* music (Estrellita de Palma's performance of 'Manolo de mis amores') that presents shots of carnival rides and automobiles traversing rainy thoroughfares; the infinite range of greys here contrasts dramatically with the Manichaean black and white of the nuns' habits, of the convent's chequerboard floors, and of the resi-dents' sombre mourning attire shot against stark white walls, otherwise omnipresent throughout this episode. Pedestrians — singles, couples, mothers with children, a soldier, a dog — pass by shop windows and cinemas advertising foreign films. The movie billboards in particular, promoting enticing titles such as *Más allá del amor*, with illustrations of lovers locked in passionate embrace or of intriguing climactic scenes (a woman in a maid's uniform brandishes a gun as a desperate man pleads with her), suggest that

some cultural texts circulating in the urban environment might
facilitate the conceptualization of alternative perspectives concerning gender, sexuality, and class.[10] Valentín enthusiastically writes to
Josefa afterwards: 'No exagero, Josefa mía. Todo era maravilloso:
la calle, los coches, la verbena. No sabes lo que me hubiera gustado
tenerte conmigo . . . nos hemos divertido mucho'.

For their part, the boys and girls of the first episode openly rebel
against rigorous sex segregation by reuniting after school in the
streets of Madrid's Salamanca neighbourhood, singing and dancing
the 'twist'—deemed to have a pernicious effect on youth according
to another film released in the same year[11]—and playing games
associated with captivity and freedom, or predicated upon transgression (the 'juego de las prendas', similar to 'truth or dare').
Perhaps most curious is the way in which the street is depicted as
liberated from the panoptic control so prevalent elsewhere in the
film. Various authority figures—priests, parents—are shown passing
by in the distance, but they make no effort to exercise surveillance
or discipline over the children; rather, within this realm, their
authority is questioned or dismissed. In one scene, for example,
Guillermo's friends, uninhibited by the presence of Margarita's
mother, address puerile but suggestive comments to the girl as she
plays with her dog on a nearby corner; in another, one of the boys
challenges a passing priest to return a stray football, addressing him
(ironically?) as 'macho'. Significantly, in the Plaza del Marqués de
Salamanca, the policeman on duty—who would normally serve as a
symbol of panoptic control—stands with his back to the children.
The policeman's supremacy over this space is further challenged
when the littlest boy in Guillermo's circle of friends, who has a cast
on his leg, kicks the officer's ample derrière to fulfil a dare in a game

[10] The first film (Más allá del amor) is Rome Adventure, directed by the
American Delmar Daves in 1962, in which Angie Dickinson's rich girl and Suzanne
Pleshette's librarian vie for the same man in Rome. The second film, directed by the
Hungarian Géza Radvány, is also from 1962 and features the actress Eva Bartok; it
was released in Spain under the title Operación caviar.
It must be noted, however, that Del rosa . . . al amarillo also implies that not all
citizens will be receptive to such potentially subversive cultural texts. Most eloquent
is the utterly impassive expression on the face of the woman who stares directly into
the camera as she walks by the dramatic poster for Operación caviar.
[11] In Juan Antonio Bardem's 1963 film Nunca pasa nada, a liberated
Frenchwoman and aficionada of the twist makes fun of a poster, typical of the era,
prominently displayed in a provincial Spanish bar: 'BAILES MODERNOS: Joven,
diviértete de otra manera'.

of *prendas*. The conditions of this game, established by another male member of the group, require gender-specific forms of rebellion: while a boy must symbolically usurp the power of the state by kicking the policeman, a girl must break with prescribed sexual passivity by kissing a boy of her choice. In effect, *Del rosa . . . al amarillo*'s treatment of Madrid anticipates later representations of the urban terrain in films by directors such as Pedro Almodóvar that, according to Marvin D'Lugo, highlight the 'power of the city as the agency of the individual's release from the constraints of the social suppression of the body and the mind' (1995: 138).

At the time of *Del rosa . . . al amarillo*'s release, however, critics did not characterize the film as unequivocally oppositional. Jesús García de Dueñas and Claudio Guerín Hill's reviews in *Nuestro cine*, for instance, are riddled with contradictory statements concerning the film's critical stance. Several apparently categorical assertions, including '[n]o hay en el autor ninguna pretensión crítica o moral' (García de Dueñas 1963: 34), or '[n]o existe aquí ninguna intención crítica' (García de Dueñas and Guerín Hill 1964: 54), are counterbalanced by observations such as '[l]a fuerza crítica de este episodio radica en lo implicado por cuanto vemos en la pantalla' (1964: 54). García and Guerín imply that Summers's film acquires an oppositional force only through the reception process: by meditating upon Guillermo's situation and attempting to imagine his future fate, for example, the viewer comes to recognize 'la invalidez de unas normas de educación y ambiente' (1964: 54). In a sense, their analysis confirms Manuel Villegas López's argument that the New Spanish Cinema requires an active viewer/co-creator: 'En el nuevo cine no se trata de ir al público para servirle la película, sino traer al público al film, hacerle intervenir en él' (Villegas López 1967: 65). Even more significantly, however, García and Guerín in effect advocate precisely the kind of negotiated reading of cultural texts depicted throughout *Del rosa . . . al amarillo* itself—a reading whose subversive force serves to weaken considerably the regime's efforts to construct a nation of citizens in complete conformity with Francoist ideology.

REFERENCES

Althusser, Louis (1971), 'Ideology and Ideological State Apparatuses (Notes towards an Investigation)', in Louis Althusser, *Lenin and Philosophy and Other Essays*, trans. Ben Brewster, New York: Monthly Review Press: 127–86.

Bourdieu, Pierre (1993), *The Field of Cultural Production*, ed. and introd. Randal Johnson. New York: Columbia University Press.

Castro, Antonio (1974), *El cine español en el banquillo*. Valencia: Fernando Torres.

Certeau, Michel de (1984), *The Practice of Everyday Life*, trans. Steven Rendall. Berkeley and Los Angeles: University of California Press.

Cotán Rodríguez, Zacarías (1993), *Manuel Summers, cineasta del humor*. Huelva: XIX Festival de Cine Iberoamericano.

D'Lugo, Marvin (1995), 'Almodóvar's City of Desire', in Kathleen M. Vernon and Barbara Morris (eds.), *Post-Franco, Postmodern: The Films of Pedro Almodóvar*, Westport, Conn.: Greenwood: 125–44 (1st pub. 1991).

Foucault, Michel (1979), *Discipline and Punish: The Birth of the Prison*, trans. Allan Sheridan. New York: Vintage.

Galán, Diego (1975), 'El cine "político" español', in Enrique Brasó et al. (eds.), *7 trabajos de base sobre el cine español*, Valencia: Fernando Torres: 88–107.

García de Dueñas, Jesús (1963), 'El festival agoniza', *Nuestro cine*, 21: 31–41.

—— and Guerín Hill, Claudio (1964), 'Estrenos por naciones: España', *Nuestro cine*, 24: 52–9.

Graham, Helen (1995), 'Popular Culture in the "Years of Hunger"', in Helen Graham and Jo Labanyi (eds.), *Spanish Cultural Studies: An Introduction: The Struggle for Modernity*, Oxford: Oxford University Press: 237–45.

Gubern, Román, and Font, Domènec (1975), *Un cine para el cadalso: 40 años de censura cinematográfica en España*. Barcelona: Euros.

Holo, Selma Reuben (1997), 'The Art Museum as a Means of Refiguring Regional Identity in Democratic Spain', in Marsha Kinder (ed.), *Refiguring Spain: Cinema/Media/Representation*, Durham, NC: Duke University Press: 301–26.

Kinder, Marsha (1997), 'Documenting the National and its Subversion in a Democratic Spain', in Marsha Kinder (ed.), *Refiguring Spain: Cinema/Media/Representation*, Durham, NC: Duke University Press: 65–98.

Martín Gaite, Carmen (1978), *El cuarto de atrás*. Barcelona: Destino.

—— (1994), *Usos amorosos de la posguerra española*. Barcelona: Anagrama (1st pub. 1987).

Martin-Márquez, Susan (1995), 'Vision, Power and Narrative in *Luna de lobos*: Julio Llamazares' Spanish Panopticon', *Revista canadiense de estudios hispánicos*, 19/2: 379–87.

Moix, Ramón-Terenci (1968), *Los 'comics': arte para el consumo y formas 'pop'*. Barcelona: Llibres de Sinera.

Otero, Luis (1996), *Al paso alegre de la paz: enredo tragicómico sobre la escuela franquista y pedagogías afines*. Barcelona: Plaza y Janés.

—— (1997), *Gris marengo*. Barcelona: Plaza & Janés (1st pub. 1987).

Press Book (1963), *Del rosa . . . al amarillo*. Eco Films/Impala/CB Films. (Available in clippings file for this film, Filmoteca Nacional, Madrid.)

Santos Fontenla, César (1966), 'Summers: el juego de la verdad', *Triunfo* (19 Nov.).

Sieburth, Stephanie (1994), *Inventing High and Low: Literature, Mass Culture and Uneven Modernity in Spain*. Durham, NC: Duke University Press.

Sopeña Monsalve, Andrés (1994), *El florido pensil: memoria de la escuela nacionalcatólica*. Barcelona: Crítica.

Spires, Robert C. (1996), *Post-totalitarian Spanish Fiction*. Columbia, Mo.: University of Missouri Press.

Torres, Augusto M. (1973), *Cine español, años sesenta*. Barcelona: Anagrama.

Turim, Maureen (1989), *Flashbacks in Film: Memory & History*. New York: Routledge.

Villegas López, Manuel (1967), *El nuevo cine español*. San Sebastián: XV Festival Internacional del Cine.

6

Fetishism and the Problem of Sexual Difference in Buñuel's *Tristana* (1970)

JO LABANYI

> Every perversion is an attempt to unsettle the boundaries
> between the real and the not-real
>
> (Kaplan 1991: 119)

BUÑUEL chose to film Galdós's 1892 novel *Tristana* because its
heroine has her leg amputated (Sánchez Vidal 1984: 330; 1994:
272). While acknowledging the recurrence of foot fetishism in
Buñuel's work, critics have largely seen his insistence on Tristana's
mutilated stump and artificial leg as a critique of a 'castrating'
traditional society: a reading encouraged by Buñuel's surrealist
iconoclasm and political exile, plus the scandal over the only other
film he made in Franco's Spain, *Viridiana*, which was stripped of its
Spanish nationality and banned in Spain after winning the Palme
d'Or as Spain's official entry to the 1961 Cannes Film Festival.
Tristana too had problems with the Francoist censors, who withdrew permission for Buñuel to shoot it in Spain in 1964 and several
times more in 1969, until they finally relented (Buñuel 1971: 8–9;
Sánchez Vidal 1994: 272). Buñuel changed the location from 1890s
Madrid to Toledo (seat of the Catholic Church in Spain and site of
the Military Academy famously defended by the Nationalists
during the Civil War) in 1929–35 (the Primo de Rivera dictatorship and the Republic): a period marked, in Buñuel's words, by
'overt social unrest' (Buñuel 1982: 239). Numerous sequences
open with shots of passing Civil Guards or priests or nuns.
However, as Linda Williams (1981) has argued in relation to other
films by Buñuel, *Tristana* is not a clear-cut denunciation of authority but an exploration of the collusion between desire and repression. Buñuel (1982: 238–9) liked Galdós's ambiguous depiction of
the film's protagonist Don Lope as patriarchal tyrant and anarchic

subversive. In film and novel, Tristana learns her desire for independence from him. And in the film, unlike the novel, Tristana succeeds in escaping Don Lope's home but chooses to return to it.

More importantly, Buñuel departs from Galdós's narrative by showing how the amputation of Tristana's leg, while physically 'castrating' her, gives her a newfound power over men. Peter Evans (n.d.) rightly notes that the film is less concerned with Don Lope's curtailing of Tristana's freedom than with his anxieties about his masculinity. The images of Tristana's 'castration' have to be taken together with those of Don Lope's severed head. The sequence where Tristana on the balcony exposes her 'castrated' body to a terrorstruck Saturno on the ground directly enacts the scenario which Freud posited as the origin of fetishism (foot fetishism in particular): that of the little boy looking up at his mother's genitals from below, seized by the 'horror' of sexual difference (the mother's lack of a penis, interpreted as a castration). As Freud ingenuously put it in his 1927 essay 'Fetishism': 'Probably no male human being is spared the fright of castration at the sight of a female genital' (1981: 354). The fetish, he suggested, functioned as a reassuring substitute for the woman's 'missing penis', allowing the man to disavow (deny/affirm) the woman's 'castration'. Tristana's artificial leg, sometimes attached to her body, sometimes not, plays this double function. The complementary images of Don Lope's severed head enact Freud's 1922 essay 'The Medusa's Head', where he argued that the Medusa's decapitated head functioned as a fetishistic disavowal of male castration anxiety provoked by the 'horrific' sight of the 'castrated' female genitals, since the snakes round her head functioned both as a sign of her missing penis and as a compensatory replacement, 'petrifying' the male spectator in the double sense of terrifying him and giving him a 'hard-on' (1940: 273–4). As Laura Mulvey comments in her essay on fetishism: 'fundamentally most male fantasy is a closed-loop dialogue with itself, as Freud conveys so well in the quotation about the Medusa's head. Far from being woman, even a monstrous woman, the Medusa is the sign of a male castration anxiety' (1989: 11). Buñuel's Medusa's head is male, making it clear that this is a fantasy of male castration. Tesson (1995: 170) notes that Don Lope's decapitated head first appears after Tristana pushes the penis-shaped bell-clapper; significantly, the bell-clapper looks like a limp penis and Tristana has to push it to make it 'perform'. Freud's theory of fetishism has so provoked feminist critics because it supposes that women are 'castrated' not by patriarchal authority but by their own biology: the theory itself mimics the fetishistic disavowal process by affirming women's disempowerment while exonerating men from blame and making women the cause of masculine insecurity. In this essay I shall read *Tristana* through successive feminist rereadings of Freud's theory of fetishism, for, like Freud, Buñuel posits the castrated woman as a castrator of men. I am not concerned here with the wider notion (Metz 1982; Williams 1981) that film, providing gratification through looking, is by definition a fetishistic medium: what interests me is Freud's suggestion that fetishism is a response to the 'horror' of sexual difference.

Laura Mulvey stresses that fetishism, supposing possession of a penis as the norm, specularizes women's bodies by turning them into 'fantasy male anatomies' (1989: 13). Buñuel's film shows how the 'castrated' Tristana, with her 'substitute penis' (artificial leg), functions as a fantasy image for males beset by castration anxiety (the ageing Don Lope, the adolescent Saturno constantly scolded for masturbating). But it also asks disturbing questions about who is in whose fantasy. Tristana steps out of the role that Don Lope has fantasized for her, using it to assert her independence; and she, as his fantasy object, fantasizes his castration (her visions of his severed head). Tristana wakes up twice from her repeated nightmare of Don Lope's severed head; the continuity editing makes it impossible to know at what point the dream sequence began, and on the final occasion at least, as Don Lope lies dying, her nightmare seems to be a projection of his terrors. Conversely, we cut from Tristana kissing Horacio to Don Lope waking, unsure whether any or all of the previous sequence was or was not dreamt by him. All of these surrealist breakdowns of the boundary between dream and reality erode male ontological security, as women refuse to remain fantasy objects dreamed by men, and male anxieties become nightmares dreamed by women.

Mulvey notes that the goal of male fetishism is to create stiff, phallic images of women that immobilize them, reassuring men that women are not so frighteningly different while denying the latter agency (1989: 6–13). Woman is given a substitute penis to castrate her symbolically: the phallic woman and the woman in bondage are identical. Mulvey also notes that the fetish functions as a detachable body part, signifying that the woman does and does not have a penis. Tristana's detachable artificial leg both counters and signals her disablement. In an unfilmed scene in the screenplay, the artificial leg is described lying on her bed, seen by her lover Horacio as he carries her to it, excited and repelled by her 'lack'. Its calf is ultra-feminine, its thigh ultra-phallic while also signifying Tristana's bondage: 'Amongst the silk and lace underwear we see an artificial leg, the lower part of which is perfectly shaped and clad in a fine silk stocking and a charming little patent leather shoe. The part corresponding to the thigh, however, is a mass of aluminium, straps and padding' (Buñuel 1971: 124). The straps remind one of the snakes round the Medusa's head. Tristana's fetishistic function is reinforced by the stiffness of Catherine Deneuve's acting. Almost from the start, Don Lope dresses her in smart clothes that require a rigid posture. He is not responsible for the amputation of her leg but his exclamation on first hearing she has a tumour is telling: 'This time she won't escape' (Buñuel 1971: 113).

Horacio, too, fetishizes Tristana by turning her into a specularized fantasy image, in his case by painting her portrait. Early in the film, Tristana polishes the portrait frame of one of Don Lope's former conquests, presaging her own reduction to possessed object. We are not allowed to see Horacio's portrait of her. On her visit to his studio he talks of wanting to finish her portrait, but when we glimpse the canvas on his easel it is a view of Toledo—appropriately, for in painting her he turns her into a 'view': his view.

However, the film is not about Tristana's disablement but about her progressive empowerment through 'castration' and fetishization. E. Ann Kaplan observes that Freud's notion of the fetish as a substitute penis creates a masculinized female image with which female spectators can identify as an expression of their own desires for empowerment (1983: 5). Tristana's fetishization both confirms that she is a 'castrated' woman and denies her sexual difference by masculinizing her. The first sign of her newfound authority is the stick she bangs on the ground from her wheelchair, echoing the stick which is an essential part of Don Lope's public masculine 'equipment'. The screenplay stresses the hardening of Tristana's features after her operation. Antonio Monegal has suggested that the amputation of her leg deprives her of her femininity (1993: 174). In fact, her 'castration' confirms her sexual difference from men, while her acquisition of an artificial leg plus stick masculinizes her. Like Don Lope, she now has three legs. Indoors, Don Lope loses his stick as he does in his confrontation with Horacio. But if in public Tristana has one real leg, an artificial leg, and a stick, indoors she retains three legs: one leg and two crutches. It is the sound of her crutches stomping up and down the corridor that most memorably conveys her power over the ageing Don Lope. She is also on her crutches when she exposes herself to Saturno. One is reminded of the Sphinx's riddle, 'What walks on four legs in the morning, two at noon, and three in the evening?' Oedipus solved the riddle by answering, 'Man,' like Freud leaving woman out of the picture. The Sphinx's riddle is, of course, about the ageing process. The passing of power from Don Lope to Tristana via his fetishization of her can be seen as the counter-productive result of his attempt to compensate for the phallic decline that comes with ageing.

Tristana's three legs are echoed by her three-legged grand piano which, as in Freud's notion that the fetish substitutes for the woman's 'lost' penis, replaces one she had lost previously. The first time we see Tristana after her operation, Buñuel indulges his love of visual puns, shooting Tristana's stump and one leg from under the piano so that the latter forms a triad framed by two piano legs, matched by the three-legged piano stool. The proliferation of wooden legs functions, like the snakes round the Medusa's head, as a fetishistic reminder/denial of the woman's 'castration'. The symbolic link between the piano and Tristana's 'castration' is clear: it is wheeled in as the doctor writes his 'sentence', and the film cuts from the doctor touching her leg to the maid Saturna polishing the piano. Here Buñuel is giving visual form to the verbal puns in Galdós's novel, where the piano is explicitly referred to as an 'organ': a 'little organ' ('organito'), and a 'superior organ' ('órgano expresivo de superior calidad') (Pérez Galdós 1987: 153, 168), for it signifies Tristana's 'lack' while providing a phallic compensation for it. The film clearly relates to the 1640 'miracle of Calanda' (Buñuel's birthplace in Aragón), when the Virgin restored the amputated leg of a male peasant who each day had rubbed his stump with holy oil, as Buñuel never tired of telling (Buñuel 1982: 21).[1] In addition to polishing the

1   Sánchez Vidal (1994: 274) notes that, according to legend, the peasant's wooden crutch was turned into two pairs of drumsticks, used in the Calanda Good Friday procession whose sound figures in several Buñuel films; these drumsticks were bought by an ancestor of Buñuel.

piano which functions as a fetishistic displaced image of Tristana's 'castration', Saturna later offers to 'rub' her mutilated body.

The fetishization of Tristana's wooden leg is paralleled by the camera's fetishization of male feet. When Don Lope visits Horacio after Tristana's operation, the camera closes on Horacio's boot being polished by a bootblack. Don Lope tells Horacio that Tristana 'is missing something': his boot represents the penis Tristana 'lacks' because he has the phallus denied her; however, the chain of associations between rubbing and amputated legs makes the bootblack's polishing an ironic reminder of castration. The camera also insists on Don Lope's tatty, floppy slippers, undermining the stiff, 'upright' posture he maintains in public. Tristana puts his slippers on his feet as he reads a newspaper article about the need to 'cure' Spain's 'gangrene', echoing the demands for an 'iron surgeon' to 'amputate' the nation's 'diseased limbs' that plagued left- and right-wing Spanish political rhetoric from 1900 till Franco took the metaphor literally. The newspaper Don Lope is reading is *El Socialismo Español*: the power he derives from Tristana putting on his slippers is subverted by their association with political demands for the 'castration' of the patriarchal order he represents. Tristana later rebels by throwing the slippers in the rubbish bin. The shots of the spaces left on the walls by the absent fencing rapiers and portraits of Don Lope's earlier female conquests, as these have to be sold off, also suggest that, beneath the virile public façade, Don Lope is—like Tristana—characterized by 'lack'. His fetishization of her is a defence as much against the very real possibility of his own 'castration'—the workers' rioting signals the end of his gentlemanly order and he cannot escape the ageing process— as against the imaginary threat of castration represented by women's bodies.

Barbara Creed (1993) has suggested that Freud's theory of fetishism posited the notion that men fear women because they see them as castrated, in order to mask a deeper fear of woman as castrator. Noting that in many horror movies the monster is female, she argues that, if men react to the female genitals with horror, it is not because these are perceived as lacking a penis but because they are imagined as a dismembering and engulfing *vagina dentata*. The problem is still the horror of sexual difference but Creed's explanation restores agency to women. She suggests that Freud's own difficulties in accepting women's agency made him posit the father as the source of the castration feared by the son, demonstrating that Freud overlooked the evidence in his case studies that it was the mother who threatened to castrate the child for masturbating (1993: 121). Creed notes that Freud's archetype of the phallic woman and that of the castrating woman 'are quite different and should not be confused; the former ultimately represents a comforting phantasy of sexual sameness, and the latter a terrifying phantasy of sexual difference' (1993: 157–8).

Creed's inversion of Freud's explanation of the male horror of sexual difference fits with the emphasis in *Tristana* on male castration. The creaking sounds as Don Lope's decapitated head swings from the rafters are almost a parody of the horror genre. It is possible to read *Tristana* as a horror film in which Tristana's increasing domination of Don Lope is caused, not by his fetishization of her, endowing her with a substitute penis, but by her 'monstrous' female power. The film does, after all, end with her hastening his death. In this reading the amputation of her leg, and its replacement by an artificial one plus stick and crutches, would signify not her castration but her 'monstrousness': witches have sticks. Tristana becomes increasingly vampire-like towards the film's end, her pallor emphasized by her garish make-up (indicated in the screenplay) and her black shawl echoing Dracula's cape, particularly in the final scene where she leans over the dying Don Lope like a vampire over its prey. This scene visually reverses the earlier shot of her leaning over Cardinal Tavera's tomb, suggesting the vampire's habit of drawing its strength from the dead. As he bends over the dying Don Lope, as when exposing herself to Saturno on the balcony, her over-painted red lips part in a monstrous smile, revealing her white teeth in an image of the *vagina dentata*. In the balcony scene, this image functions as a direct substitute for the sight of her genitals, granted to Saturno but denied the spectator. It is logical that Saturno should see the female genitals as castrating rather than castrated, since throughout he is violently reprimanded for masturbating by his mother Saturna. The film's two female characters, Tristana and Saturna, are both constructed as castrators of men.[2] The film is also about a man's fear of ageing: the

---

[2] Evans (n.d.: 98) notes that Saturna, as devouring mother, is a female version of Goya's painting *Saturn Devouring his Children*. In fact, Buñuel inherited her name from Galdós's novel where she has no such role.

monstrous-feminine and the (usually male) fear of ageing are both stock themes of the horror genre. In *The Hunger* (Tony Scott, 1983), Catherine Deneuve later acted the role of vampire in a classic horror film playing on these two terrors.

Louise Kaplan has similarly suggested that Freud's theory of fetishism is a cover for a male fear of women's agency, but rather than reject his theory she rewrites it. Defining perversion as 'a mental strategy that uses one or another social stereotype of masculinity and femininity in a way that deceives the onlooker about the unconscious meanings of the behaviors she or he is observing', she argues that Freud's essay on fetishism 'makes use unconsciously of the perverse strategy and is itself a fetishistic document' (1991: 9, 55). Kaplan's notion that perversion is a strategy of deception designed to distract attention from a deeper anxiety is particularly useful when dealing with a director like Buñuel who so perversely delights in misleading the spectator. As Kaplan notes, perversions are fictitious enactments or performances. The fetishist directs his or her own scenario, designed to 'screen out' what is really going on. Fetishism is a visual activity not because the fetishist is disavowing his horror on seeing the female genitals, but because he (or she, for Kaplan insists that women are also fetishists) is directing everyone's gaze at the 'screen' of surface appearance.

Kaplan's main thesis is that perversions are not so much sexual problems as 'pathologies of gender stereotyping' (1991: 196). Freud's 'Fetishism' is, for her, a fetishistic text because it sets up norms of masculinity and femininity to 'screen out' the troublesome evidence, recognized by him elsewhere, that 'gender normality' is an unattainable imaginary construct. Kaplan argues that standard notions of masculinity and femininity are themselves perverse enactments, and that fetishism, while apparently deviant, is in fact acting out a reassuring fiction of 'gender normality'. Thus male fetishism enacts a fantasy of phallic performance, while female fetishism acts out a masquerade of stereotypical femininity. But since fetishism, as a form of disavowal, is about having it both ways, there are further levels to the pretence. The man who subordinates himself to a phallic woman is allowing himself to satisfy the feminine (passive) side of himself which society makes him feel ashamed of, while pretending that he is being forced into it and anyway it is 'only an act'. This enactment enables him to perform sexually as a phallic man, reassuring him that he is in control because he is paying the woman to act his script. If the performance takes place with a fetish object, the sense of being in control is even greater. This complex transaction allows the man to have it both ways by simultaneously living out his feminine and masculine drives, while appearing on the surface to conform to the stereotype of the phallic man.

Kaplan suggests that, if perversion is regarded as an overwhelmingly male practice, this is because it has been seen as a sexual problem rather than one of gender stereotyping. If male perversion consists in impersonating masculinity so as secretly to indulge one's femininity, female perversion consists in impersonating a socially acceptable femininity so as secretly to indulge unacceptable masculine desires. The female fetishist turns herself into a fetish for men in order to exert power over them while appearing to be stereotypically feminine. Male and female fetishists are in collusion. As Kaplan notes, the feminine stereotype offers women many ways of disabling themselves as a mask for being in control: by dressing up as an object of desire, by being frigid, by obsessively cleaning (to take three examples relevant to *Tristana*).

Kaplan's argument is enormously suggestive as a way of reading Buñuel's film. All the film's main characters are male 'male impersonators' or female 'female impersonators', enacting a socially acceptable pretence of masculinity or femininity. This is evident even with Saturna and Saturno. The former, described in the screenplay as 'rather masculine in appearance' (Buñuel 1971: 15), rules the household by playing the role, with some telling lapses, of dutiful servant. Saturno's obsessive locking himself in the lavatory allows him to assert his phallic prowess (everyone, including the spectator, assumes he is masturbating interminably) while getting out of the masculine obligation to work. In an unfilmed scene in the screenplay, his bricklayer uncle says, 'he's not cut out for working on a site' because he is 'soft' (Buñuel 1971: 88).

This same-sex impersonation is particularly clear in the case of Don Lope, whom we repeatedly see 'making himself up' (literally and figuratively) in the bathroom. He is as specularized by his image in the mirror as Tristana in the scene where she makes up before exposing herself to Saturno. The gap between Don Lope's public image as a paragon of upstanding virility and his private reality when laid low with a cold or surprised in his long johns 'can only be described as lamentable', to quote the screenplay (Buñuel 1971: 84). What Don Lope seems to be ashamed of is not so much unacknowledged feminine desires as loss of virility with old age. With a typically perverse logic, he will justify standing down from his former role as duelling second by arguing that other men have become effeminate, freeing himself from the demands of masculinity while presenting himself as the only 'real man' left. It could be argued that Tristana's increasing domination of him is the counterproductive result of his fetishization of her, not because his 'sadistic' reduction of her to 'bondage' masculinizes her by endowing her with a substitute penis, but because—in a brilliantly perverse strategy designed to make his decline into 'feminine' vulnerability less humiliating—he creates a masochistic scenario that allows him to delude himself that she is 'forcing' him into submission, while continuing to believe that he is 'really' in control because he has written the script and is paying for the costumes. In which case, he is indeed deluding himself because the fantasy of submission is real.

On Horacio's first appearance, the screenplay indicates that he is 'dressed as an artist, the stereotyped image of the painter' (Buñuel 1971: 63–4). He and Don Lope, despite their apparent scorn for convention, impersonate two contrasting masculine stereotypes: those of gentleman and bohemian. As a painter, Horacio's concern is to turn human beings into 'models' of standard masculinity and femininity. When we first see him, he is 'fixing' his male model in a ludicrously 'typical' pose of 'erect' peasant virility, with *gorro catalán*, wineskin, and donkey. His first reaction on meeting Tristana is to ask if she will be his model.

Tristana complies with her fetishization because the elegant clothes Don Lope buys her make her not only hyper-feminine but also classy and superior, fixing her in a frigid pose just as she 'poses' for Horacio. She is also shown cleaning and ironing (in the novel, her mother was an obsessive cleaner); this allows her to play the feminine subordinate role while subverting it, as when she throws Don Lope's slippers out in the name of hygiene. Ginette Vincendeau has observed that Catherine Deneuve's star image embodies the stereotype of the French woman as sexy but impeccably dressed. Deneuve's first collaboration with Buñuel in *Belle de jour* (1967), which made her an international star, initiated a longstanding partnership with Yves Saint-Laurent; she has also modelled for Chanel (Vincendeau 1994: 43–4). *Tristana* draws on

Deneuve's star image to show how stereotypical femininity can be used as a perverse cover for masculine agency.[3] Vincendeau notes that Deneuve would, in the 1980s and 1990s, exploit her elegant image to play overtly strong female parts, and quotes her co-star Gérard Depardieu as saying: 'Catherine Deneuve is the man I would have liked to be' (1994: 47).

Tristana does not choose to have her leg amputated but, in turning this imposed restraint to her advantage by making increased feminine dependence a cover for increased masculine control, she perfectly illustrates Kaplan's definition of female perversion. Kaplan notes that fetishism replaces living human beings by dehumanized objects, and that the fetish 'holds together a body that is experienced as a container for leaking, fragmented parts' (1991: 33, 37). Tristana's artificial leg, with its straps to be fixed round the thigh, fulfils both functions. Much the same could be said of Don Lope's stiff suits which function as masculine 'straitjackets'.

Kaplan notes that the nineteenth century's increased emphasis on conformity to gender stereotypes created the category of the perverse: the 'abnormal' requires the concept of the 'normal'. She also observes that the late twentieth century's 'commercialization and standardization of so-called deviant sexuality' is 'a last-ditch effort to contain and regulate the gender ambiguities that are the lot of human beings' (1991: 6). One has to ask whether Buñuel's film contributes to this particularly devious form of gender normalization. There are two interesting things in Galdós's novel that Buñuel suppresses. The first (its main theme, for it belongs to the 1890s European cycle of 'New Woman' novels) is that of Tristana's desire for emancipation, not in the sense of power over men, but in that of earning her own living like a man. Her long discussions on the subject, particularly with Horacio, are reduced in the film to one brief comment: 'I want to be free, I want to work' (Buñuel 1971: 88). The second omitted aspect occurs in the novel's epistolary section which Buñuel found weak (Buñuel 1982: 238–9). In terms of gender, it is the most interesting part because in it an extraordinary homoerotic relationship develops between Don Lope and Horacio. Don Lope starts by helping the invalid Tristana write her

---

3 Kaplan's analysis suggests that the sexual perversions indulged in by Deneuve in *Belle de jour* should not be seen as the repressed 'other' to her role as bourgeois wife, but as an indicator that her conventional femininity is itself a perverse enactment. See Evans 1995: 151–72.

love letters to the absent Horacio, and ends up taking over the writing entirely. When Horacio comes to visit Tristana after her operation, he finds himself increasingly curtailing his meetings with her
to chat with Don Lope. The two men's mutual attraction is made
clear. Freud suggested that one of the functions of fetishism was to
disavow homosexual inclinations by masculinizing the woman's
body (1981: 353). Buñuel's *Tristana* can, like Freud's 'Fetishism',
be called a fetishistic text because its exposure of the perverse
enactment of stereotypical gender roles masks full acknowledgement of the gender ambiguity which the novel shows to be present
in both women and men.

Kaplan notes that the pervert has often been seen as a 'culture
hero' whose transgressions subvert conventional morality.
Perversion is, she argues, about 'unsettling reality' but 'the rebellion and the bravery are deceptions. For the pervert is rigid and
conservative' (1991: 41–2). Her analysis explains how Don Lope
can, to his friends' surprise, uphold traditional values while being
a sexual nonconformist: his refusal of marriage and monogamy
may shock society but it confirms his stereotypical masculinity by
freeing it from the taint of feminine domesticity (in public, at
least, for he still has his slippers). Kaplan's insistence that perversion is a product, rather than subversion, of the rigid gender
stereotypes developed during the nineteenth century echoes
Foucault's argument (1987) that Victorian morality did not so
much repress sexuality as create it, by talking obsessively about
it. Foucault turns on its head the idea that repression is in opposition to desire and that, to free the latter, one has only to abol-
ish the former, suggesting more uncomfortably that desire is
dependent on repression.

Thus Don Lope, as Tristana's guardian (legal but not natural
father) and seducer (natural but not legal husband), is having it
both ways by enjoying patriarchal power while indulging in scandalous sexual relations which proclaim publicly that he is a 'real
man'. His notion of freedom is a perverse strategy which uses
gender stereotypes to feign deviance while maintaining male
authority. When he claims that he and Tristana are happy because
they respect each other's freedom, he means that he does not want
to curtail his freedom by marrying her, and that he is confident
enough of her feminine compliance not to need to resort to coercion, though he will if necessary. As his authority wanes with age,

he turns to the institutional props he had previously despised, marrying Tristana and frequenting the company of priests. This loss of authority is presented as an emasculation. Unable to perform as a 'real man', he abandons the public, masculine space of the café and retreats into 'feminine' domesticity, surrounded by men in skirts (they sit sipping chocolate like old ladies). The abandonment of deviance involves abandonment of the pretence of conforming to the phallic stereotype.

The fact that Buñuel, unlike Galdós, allows Tristana to leave with Horacio, only to decide freely to return to her patriarchal tyrant when she is ill, implies that the freedom she was seeking was illusory and that desire depends on restraints. This suggests that desire is either perverse or is not at all, since it must simultaneously acknowledge and deny repression. Buñuel's conventional framing of characters while they are staring at something off-screen encapsulates the perverse logic that makes desire dependent on its negation. The film opens with Tristana and Saturna walking outside the city walls to meet Saturno; the final reprise ends with them walking back to where they came from: this open space, like the space to which Tristana escapes with Horacio, must be outside the film because it is unrepresentable. Tristana meets Horacio in a walled courtyard in the process of being rebuilt, another perverse combination of openness with closure. The same effect is produced by the emphasis throughout on exterior locations such as walled streets and colonnaded squares or courtyards that have the effect of interiors; and by the converse use of interiors that have a doorway, window, or corridor opening up onto a space beyond. The scene where Don Lope shuts the door in our face as he takes Tristana into the bedroom makes the point, while also teasing us, that desire can be realized only in a closed space.

Any political reading of the images of police, Church, and patriarchal repression in *Tristana* must take into account the film's demonstration, through its treatment of fetishism, that deviance and restraint go together. Fetishism is also, of course, a Marxist concept. Marx's definition of commodity fetishism as a concern with the surface appearance of 'things' that masks the underlying social relations between them is close to Kaplan's notion of perversion as a deception designed to distract the viewer's gaze from what is really going on. In a kind of disavowal, things are worshipped as commodities while their commodity status is denied.[4] It could be argued that Don Lope's acquisition and fetishization of Tristana is linked to his denial of the socio-economic relations governing his household (left to Saturna) and his society (work is a 'curse', and making money a 'dirty business' best left to 'Jews' like the dealer to whom he sells the family silver). In the film, unlike the novel, he inherits money from his sister ('Men make the laws,' she protests) just before Tristana returns: Tristana is another piece of property reverting to its 'rightful owner', like the silver which he buys back. (His phallic trophies—the fencing rapiers and portraits of his conquests—are never recovered.) Don Lope has originally 'inherited' Tristana from her mother, regarding it as 'natural' that she pass to a male owner. The Marxist theory of fetishism can be used to supplement Freud's analysis of the fetishistic disavowal of sexual difference, for it allows us to see how Don Lope takes advantage of the gender relations involved in commodity exchange while wilfully ignoring their gendered basis.

Fetishism is so appealing to a director who, like Buñuel, had his origins in surrealism because its use of objects as decoys, designed to distract attention from the real source of anxiety, invests 'things' with a perverse symbolic significance. As Mulvey (1996: p. xiv) notes, fetishism 'is the most semiotic of perversions'. The symbolic meaning of a fetish is always likely to be the opposite of what one thinks; indeed, it may have no 'deep' symbolic significance but function as a 'screen' diverting attention from what is really going on. Buñuel always resisted critics' attempts to explain the symbolism of his images. They, like fetishes, are perverse because they are 'screen images' analogous to the 'screen memories' analysed by Freud: diversionary tactics designed to frustrate the search for meaning. Such seems to be the function of the shell which Horacio clutches, or the various dogs in the film: the rabid dog shot by a Civil Guard as Tristana meets Horacio; Tristana's fox terrier, a perfect image of displacement, always being picked up and put down somewhere else.[5] Other elusive

---

[4] For Marx's theory of commodity fetishism, see McClellan 1977: 435–43. Mulvey (1996) links her earlier Freudian account of fetishism to that of Marx, arguing that cinema's fetishization of the female body functions as a disavowal of the industry's economic conditions of production.

[5] Sánchez Vidal (1984: 336) notes that, when he visited Buñuel in Mexico, he had a fox terrier named Tristana.

images function as enactments of the mechanism of disavowal, simultaneously affirming and denying difference: the visual rhymes between disparate objects that look alike (the cut from Don Lope's brasier to the similarly round, metallic *barquillero*'s wheel); Tristana's game of distinguishing between identical objects (columns, chickpeas, streets); the final reprise which ends by playing backwards the film's opening shot, except that Tristana and Saturna are facing the other way (the same yet different). Resistance to intelligibility is created by the use of deceptive continuity editing, and by the converse strategy of cutting the opening establishment shot and closing frames of almost every sequence (Buñuel 1971: 10). Saturno's lack of speech and hearing (Buñuel's invention; in the novel, where Saturno barely figures, some deaf mutes walk by as Tristana and Saturna meet him) foregrounds the resistance to meaning, as does Tristana's recourse to piano playing both to express and distract attention from her frustrated feelings. The sound of bells ringing is heard over the opening credits: the bellringer later tells Tristana that people no longer understand the language of bells.

The soundtrack over the final reprise consists of the opening bell-ringing played backwards, reinforcing the effect of a film rewinding and reminding us that what we have been watching is simply a 'screen image'. *Tristana* is a 'fetishistic' film because its use of deceptive 'screen images' exposes the characters' perverse masquerade of masculinity and femininity which simultaneously allows and denies gender ambiguity, while itself delighting in the perversity. It is also a fetishistic text because, like Freud's essay, it reinforces gender stereotypes in the process of deconstructing them. Whether we interpret Tristana's increasing domination of Don Lope as the triumph of the monstrous-feminine or as the counter-productive result of his fetishization of her, we have the story, not of a woman but of a man's fantasies of Woman. In either reading, the man's belief that he is in control is a delusion because he is finally destroyed by a woman. For all its sensitivity to the perverse games men and women play to reconcile their contradictory desires for domination and submission with acceptable norms of masculinity and femininity, *Tristana* in the end sends us back to Freud's notion that the basis of fetishism is man's 'inevitable' terror of woman.

REFERENCES

Amorós, Andrés (1977), '*Tristana*, de Galdós a Buñuel', in *Actas del Primer Congreso Internacional de Estudios Galdosianos*, Las Palmas de Gran Canaria: Cabildo Insular de Gran Canaria: 319–29.

Buñuel, Luis (1971), *Tristana*, ed. J. Francisco Aranda, trans. Nicholas Fry. Modern Film Scripts. London: Lorrimer Publishing.

—— (1982), *Mi último suspiro (Memorias)*. Barcelona: Plaza y Janés.

Caesarman, Fernando (1976), *El ojo de Buñuel: psicoanálisis desde una butaca*. Barcelona: Anagrama.

Creed, Barbara (1993), *The Monstrous-Feminine: Film, Feminism, Psychoanalysis*. London: Routledge.

Edwards, Gwynne (1982), *The Discreet Art of Luis Buñuel*. London: Marion Boyars.

—— (1994), *Indecent Exposures: Buñuel to Almodóvar*. London: Marion Boyars.

Evans, Peter W. (n.d.), 'Buñuel and *Tristana*: Who is doing What to Whom', in Pamela Bacarisse (ed.), *Carnal Knowledge: Essays on the Flesh, Sex and Sexuality in Hispanic Letters and Film*, Pittsburgh: Ediciones Tres Ríos: 91–8.

—— (1995), *The Films of Luis Buñuel: Subjectivity and Desire*. Oxford: Oxford University Press.

Foucault, Michel (1987), *The History of Sexuality: An Introduction*. Harmondsworth: Penguin.

Freud, Sigmund (1940), 'The Medusa's Head', in Sigmund Freud, *The Standard Edition of the Complete Psychological Works*, xviii, London: Hogarth Press: 273–4.

—— (1981), 'Fetishism', in Sigmund Freud, *On Sexuality*, Pelican Freud Library, vii, Harmondsworth: Penguin: 345–58.

Galeota, Vito (1988), *Galdós e Buñuel: romanzo, film, narratività in 'Nazarín' e in 'Tristana'*. Naples: Instituto Universitario Orientale.

Harvard, Robert (1982), 'The Seventh Art of Luis Buñuel: *Tristana* and the Rites of Freedom', *Quinquereme*, 5: 56–74.

Kaplan, E. Ann (1983), *Women and Film: Both Sides of the Camera*. New York: Methuen.

Kaplan, Louise J. (1991), *Female Perversions*. London: Penguin.

Lara, Antonio (1981), 'Lectura de *Tristana*, de Luis Buñuel, según la novela de Galdós', in Antonio Lara (ed.), *La imaginación en libertad: homenaje a Luis Buñuel,* Madrid: Universidad Complutense: 97–246.

McClellan, David (ed.) (1977), *Karl Marx: Selected Writings*. Oxford: Oxford University Press.

Mellen, Joan (1973), 'Buñuel's *Tristana*', in *Women and their Sexuality in the New Film*, New York: Horizon Press: 191–202.

Mellen, Joan (ed.) (1978), *The World of Luis Buñuel: Essays in Criticism*. New York: Oxford University Press.

Metz, Christian (1982), *The Imaginary Signifier: Psychoanalysis and Cinema*. London: Macmillan (1st pub. 1977).

Monegal, Antonio (1993), *Luis Buñuel, de la literatura al cine: una poética del objeto*. Barcelona: Anthropos.

Mulvey, Laura (1989), *Visual and Other Pleasures*. London: Macmillan.

—— (1996), *Fetishism and Curiosity*. London: BFI.

Partridge, Colin (1995), *'Tristana': Buñuel's Film and Galdós's Novel: A Case Study in the Relation between Literature and Film*. Lewiston, NY: Edwin Mellen.

Pérez Galdós, Benito (1987), *Tristana*. Madrid: Alianza.

Sackett, Theodore (1976), 'Creation and Destruction of Personality in *Tristana*: Galdós and Buñuel', *Anales Galdosianos* (suppl.): 71–90.

Sánchez Vidal, Agustín (1984), *Luis Buñuel: obra cinematográfica*. Madrid: Ediciones JC.

—— (1994), *Luis Buñuel*, 2nd edn. Madrid: Cátedra.

Tesson, Charles (1995), *Luis Buñuel*. Paris: Cahiers du cinéma.

Vincendeau, Ginette (1994), 'Catherine Deneuve and French Womanhood', in Pam Cook and Philip Dodd (eds.), *Women and Film: A Sight and Sound Reader*, London: Scarlet Press: 41–9.

Williams, Linda (1981), *Figures of Desire: A Theory and Analysis of Surrealist Film*. Urbana: University of Illinois Press.

—— (1987), 'The Critical Grasp: Buñuelian Cinema and its Critics', in Rudolf E. Kuenzli (ed.), *Dada and Surrealist Film*, New York: Willis, Locker & Owens: 199–206.

7

Between Metaphysics and Scientism: Rehistoricizing Víctor Erice's *El espíritu de la colmena* (1973)

PAUL JULIAN SMITH

THERE seems little doubt that Víctor Erice is the consummate Spanish art director. A recent reading of his first feature, *El espíritu de la colmena* (1973), by Santos Zunzunegui begins by stating that there is a 'fundamental agreement' amongst critics that Erice's work constitutes not only the high point of Spanish cinema of all time, but also one of the most notable examples of contemporary Spanish art in general (1994: 42). It is characteristic of Erice's reception abroad that in Britain *El espíritu de la colmena* is distributed in a video collection which bears the name 'Art House'. The most cursory examination of Spanish press coverage of Erice's career reveals the preconceptions implicit in such a term: his films are favourably contrasted with more commercially successful Spanish cinema; praised for their austerity, purity, and poetic lyricism; and held to be destined for an elite, minority audience.[1] Moreover, central to this question of art cinema is a questioning of the very possibility of cinema itself: Vicente Molina Foix cites Erice's second feature *El sur* (1983) as an example of an 'unrealized', utopian cinema, hampered by financial limitations;[2] Erice himself claims with reference to his third feature *El sol del membrillo* (1992) that, compared to that of painting, the language of cinema is 'wholly decadent', even 'dangerous' (García 1993).

I would like to acknowledge the help of the staff of the Filmoteca Nacional and Biblioteca Nacional (Madrid) and the British Film Institute (London); and to thank Andrés F. Rubio, for kindly sending me material from the archives of *El país*, Madrid.

[1] See e.g. Elsa Fernández Santos 1992; Ángel Fernández Santos 1992.
[2] Molina Foix 1983; see also Fernández Santos 1985.

In this piece I hope to examine the role of the unrealized or unrepresentable in *El espíritu de la colmena*, most particularly in relation to cinematic techniques, such as off-screen space and sound; but I also hope to historicize the question of art cinema, auteurism, and their relation to cinematic language by examining the emergence of a press persona for Erice in representative writings by and interviews of the director over twenty years and the complex Spanish responses to this very self-conscious project over the same period. Here I attempt a revised version of Erice's own critique of the supposed opposition between history and poetry. Finally I look at three specific contributions to the production of *El espíritu de la colmena* which both supplement and qualify the myth of the auteur as unique and solitary artistic creator: cinematography (Luis Cuadrado); performance (Ana Torrent); and scriptwriting (Ángel Fernández Santos). My aim is not to minimize Erice's achievement but rather to historicize its reception and to call attention to the contributions of others without whom *El espíritu de la colmena* would not exist. The original synopsis of the film states that 'El viejo caserón donde viven las niñas se va llenando de la presencia de algo impalpable que sólo Ana parece fundamentalmente decidida a descubrir' ('El espíritu de la colmena' n.d.). If *El espíritu de la colmena* is reliant on the positing of an unrepresentable (or untouchable) which is to be uncovered or drawn into visibility, then Erice's career has also benefited from just such a resonant absence, an unexamined appeal to the category of 'art' which can now be submitted to analysis.

A sense of wilful isolation or abstraction is stressed by Erice in a very early interview with José María Palá in *Film ideal* on the release in 1969 of *Los desafíos*, the portmanteau movie in which Erice had directed one of the three segments (Palá 1969). Erice calls attention to the particular circumstances of the shoot. Filmed far from Madrid in a remote country location (a village abandoned by its inhabitants when a new reservoir was created), the film required a sense of 'convivencia' (of co-operation or communality) amongst cast and crew. Indeed, on returning from the location to their hotel Erice claims that some of his colleagues chose to swim across the reservoir, rather than take the boat (Palá 1969: 218), a detail which he says is important in that it helped to create an 'atmosphere' of 'mystery' around the film, a mystery to which even he as director

did not fully have access (Palá 1969: 219). Unaware of his characters' motivations, Erice trusts to the actors who add a contribution
which they have learned themselves during the collective enterprise
of film-making. Such privileged knowledge, claims Erice, is not
learned in film school. Attacking not just Francoist censorship but
also 'anachronistic' Spanish production practices, Erice states that
he is interested only in auteurist cinema and that at the moment of
self-expression one cannot give up 'what one is' (Palá 1969: 220).

Erice's artistic isolation and presence-to-self are here qualified
in a somewhat unexpected manner by his sense of cinema as
'convivencia', a paradox I will explore later. But on the opening of
El espíritu de la colmena some four years later Erice insisted once
more in interviews on the purity of his artistic vision (Comas
1974). Condemned to publicity work in the long interval between
his first projects because of an inability to procure funding for
features, Erice claims modestly that he must remain faithful to
himself, as his 'limitations' make him unable to take on any project
in which he does not believe. The only concern of an auteur is to
maintain a rigorously moral posture, an absolute commitment to
oneself, and a complete fidelity to one's beliefs (Comas 1974: 35).
Inversely, however, Erice stresses that 'cinema is an industrial
entity' and claims that the poor reception of some films comes not
from their auteur's lack of vision but rather from a mundane,
commercial limitation: the distributors' frequent ignorance of the
films for which they are responsible means that Spanish publicity
campaigns are often inappropriate for the films they are promoting
and fail to match product and audience (Comas 1974: 36).

For Erice, then, the auteur is defined both by his artistic integrity
and by his antagonistic relation to the commercial norms of the
industry. And this is true not only of Spain, but also of Hollywood.
It is no accident, then, that Erice should edit with Jos Oliver a
collection of critical essays on the apparently unlikely figure of
Nicholas Ray (1986). In their introduction to the volume the
editors stress the existential isolation of Ray, who experienced the
'decisive' alienation of modernity (1986: 13); his work constitutes
not so much a break ('ruptura') with cinematic norms but rather an
act of 'dissidence' within them, establishing a problematic link
between the past and the future of film, without giving up on
aesthetic innovation. Ray thus experienced exile as an 'internal
condition', one which he lived in his native land (1986: 14),

condemned to solitude (1986: 15) as the product of 'classical humanist training'. In his own, brief essay on Ray (1986: 17–21), Erice claims that the latter's life and work are inseparable: his films are not discursive, do not communicate a truth: rather they are 'pure exteriority . . . unfurled to the infinite' (1986: 19). But this sense of an impossible, unrealized cinema, itself based on a primary alienation (Erice cites the 'most beautiful and revealing' title *We Can't Go Home Again*), is coupled with a tragic destiny at the hands of the industry: Erice and Oliver state that some of Ray's films were 'mutilated' by his producers (1986: 13).

As geniuses frustrated not by artistic but by commercial constraints, the identification between Erice and Ray is clear. And when *El espíritu de la colmena* was revived on the tenth anniversary of its release the Spanish press agreed with this assessment. For example, a positive piece in the rightist *Ya* (written to coincide with a round table on the film at the prestigious Ateneo in Madrid) was in no doubt that Erice's first two features were amongst the best Spanish films of all time (Fernández 1983). However, although the writer stresses the universality of Erice, whose films are addressed to 'any human being capable of thought and feeling', he also claims that Spanish spectators are the only ones able to understand their 'complex network of references and feelings' and to intuit that the central theme of Erice is the 'continuity of tradition and life' in Spain. *El espíritu de la colmena* is thus inserted into a narrative of national identity which becomes increasingly problematic: rejecting the claim frequently voiced in an earlier era that the 'Spanish genius' was less suited for film than it was for other media such as painting, the journalist goes on to state that Francoist censorship was never an obstacle to great film-makers: proof of this (he claims) is that both *El espíritu de la colmena* and *El sur* could have been shown under the dictatorship without any problem. Although freedom of expression is, of course, necessary and welcome, it must always be adapted ('adecuarse') to the customs of each people ('pueblo').

It is clear, then, that Erice's poetic abstraction and metaphysical absorption were easily co-opted by the right even under the Socialist government of the 1980s and even as consensus as to the nature of Erice's achievement became ubiquitous. But what was the response of the national press and the specialist film journals to the release of *El espíritu de la colmena* in the last days of the dictatorship? Was there the same degree of unanimity?

Although *El espíritu de la colmena* won the main prize (Concha de Oro) at the San Sebastián Film Festival of 1973, its reception was mixed. The interview already cited above claims that the cheers from critics in the stalls of the main screening theatre were matched by the jeers and stamps of the public in the balcony. The journalist also proposes another significant division: while the Madrid press was positive towards the film, the Barcelona papers were hostile. Examination of press clippings held at the Filmoteca Nacional (many of which lack full attributions) reveals that even the established and mainly Madrid-based critics of late Francoism had mixed feelings about the film. One supporter of Erice states that one of the film's great merits is its 'universality', a universality which does not, however, prevent it from being purely auteurist: personal and subjective (B. A.). Another supporter claims that for once Spanish cinema, normally 'impoverished, shaky, and colour-less', has produced a 'miracle' worthy of French masters such as Godard or Truffaut or of the 'essential form' of silent pioneer D. W. Griffith (Rubio 1973). Even those who doubt the value of the film as a whole praise it for transcending the particularities of the time and place in which it is set: Erice has 'raised himself' ('se ha elevado') up to the level of the internal world of child psychology; here he finds poetic inspiration, classical simplicity of narration, and purity of expression (Cebollada 1974). When one critic, uniquely, praises Erice's 'social commitment' it is only in the context of celebrating the emergence of a 'sensitive, profound, and lyrical auteur' (Crespo 1973). More typical is the reviewer who cites Erice's lack of concern for the social conditions of the time in which *El espíritu de la colmena* is set (1940): scorning the tempta-tion to call attention to this 'dramatic date in our history', Erice, we are told, 'gains universality' and shows his 'independence of any kind of ideology' (9 Oct. 1973).

Universality is thus an alibi for the refusal to consider any social or political considerations to which the film might give rise. It is thus inevitable that the most right-wing critics of the film (those who show most hostility towards it) are also those who distinguish most sharply between the 'success' of the scenes centring on the children and the 'failure' of those concerning the adults. Thus the reviewer in *El alcázar* wrote that the world of the girls was 'a true creation', while that of the adults exhibits 'vacuous meandering' (Martialay 1973). *El pueblo* praises the intelligence of bees, who, unlike Erice's characters, work together towards a clear aim: in *El espíritu de la colmena*, on the contrary, all is 'Baroque' and 'confusion', with the married couple lacking 'human vitality' (17 Oct. 1973).

The enigmas and ellipses of Erice's plot are thus both celebrated by some critics for their poetic lyricism and decried by others for their dangerous obscurity: *El pueblo* claims the film is a 'crossword puzzle without answers'. In the face of such wilfully fragmented narration, the critic's breast cannot swell with the 'patriotic pride' that would normally be felt at a Spanish film's international recognition. The debates on universality and obscurity are thus inseparable from competing discourses of nationalism: opponents (such as *El alcázar*) attack Erice's genuflection to 'modern' (read: 'foreign') experimentalism and supporters (such as *Nuevo diario*) qualify their comparisons with French or US masters by claiming that *El espíritu de la colmena* is Spanish 'through and through'.

The short review in trade journal *Cineinforme* (A.F. 1973) coincides with the rightist view in attacking the 'weakness' of *El espíritu de la colmena*'s plot and the 'falseness' of the roles of the parents, while celebrating the 'lyricism' and 'humanity' of the psychological study of childhood. Such timeless qualities, however, are somewhat qualified by the context of the review, which is fortuitously placed according to alphabetical order between two features more characteristic of films released commercially in the Spanish market that month: a French *policier* and an execrable Italian *peplum* (classical epic).[3] And if we turn from the daily national press to the specialist monthly film journals we find, perhaps unexpectedly, a much greater attention to the historical specificity of Erice's film, in relation to both the period in which *El espíritu de la colmena* is set and the moment in which it was released and was battling for an audience with more commercial productions, often from foreign sources.

Dirigido por named *El espíritu de la colmena* 'film of the month'. Jaume Genover's sensitive review (1974) begins by stressing once more the 'puzzle'-like structure of Erice's plot, which requires an active participation from the audience which some spectators will be unwilling to give. Citing the isolation of each

---

[3]   *Il était une fois un flic* (Georges Lautner, 1971); *Maciste, il gladiatore più forte del mondo* (Michele Lupo, 1970).

character from the others (as previous critics had also done), Genover moves beyond the stylistic vindication of Erice's poetic dislocation of narrative to draw a crucial connection between film form and history: the separation of each member of the family, confined to their own 'cell' of the eponymous hive, directs the spectator to the 'historical moment in which the action is situated' and to its unvoiced correlatives: the presence of the 'intellectual' father in an impoverished and uncultured village and his 'unusual' profession of beekeeping are transparent signs of his political unorthodoxy; the mother's letters to an unknown recipient reveal 'all the anguish of the War'. Moreover, the necessary failure of the young girls' fantastic aspirations is a transparent 'symbol' of the unavoidable repressions of the period. The film is thus not confined to the time and place in which it is set; but those circumstances and that location are 'specific' and 'concrete'.

Alvaro Feito's argument in *Cinestudio* is rather similar (1973). Feito argues that *El espíritu de la colmena* is the first Spanish film of its time to be wholly 'modern' (controversial, open to differing interpretations, requiring the active participation of an adult spectator); and that the characters are by no means as 'symbolic or universally abstract' as 'triumphalist' (i.e. Francoist) critics would have us believe (1973: 47). On the contrary, the spirit of the beehive is, quite simply, 'the spirit of Spanish society in 1940': hierarchical, functional, and wholly closed in on itself. The repressions and fears of the children are thus as much socio-political as psychological, the 'creation of a historical period . . . which does not eliminate, but rather amalgamates the diverse influences to which any human life is subject, situated as it is in a specific historical context' (1973: 48).

Writing in the broadly Marxist tradition of progressive opponents of the regime, Genover and Feito are thus impatient with what they see as the idealizing abstractions of the daily press, and take for granted a necessary relation between artistic form and historical moment, but one which is inevitably complex and mediated. One of those mediations is the contemporary Spanish film industry. Thus Genover stresses the role of producer Elías Querejeta (unmentioned in the national press), who brought to the project his customary 'team' of technicians including cinematographer Luis Cuadrado; and Feito mentions the class component in Erice's reception: *El espíritu de la colmena* has received extravagant praise from the progressive bourgeoisie ('progres') and perhaps coincides too cosily with the expectations of a certain intellectually elite metropolitan audience, amongst whom are to be found members of the national press and of festival juries (Feito 1973: 48). The institutionalization of Erice's art cinema by an ascendant liberal establishment is thus already clear even to those critics who vindicate *El espíritu de la colmena*'s political and social challenge to the Francoism which still clung to power on its release.

Ironically, as democracy became definitively established in the Spanish state so readings of the film became increasingly abstracted, thus justifying the warnings of leftist intellectual critics on *El espíritu de la colmena*'s release. A crucial moment in this process is Vicente Molina Foix's typically subtle essay of 1985 in a special number of the prestigious *Revista de occidente* on war, Francoism, and film (Molina Foix 1985). Reading the film as 'the war behind the window' (that is, the domestic replaying of a national scenario), Molina claims that *El espíritu de la colmena*'s theme is the 'obligation to absent themselves from reality produced in the characters by the Civil War and its political effects' (1985: 113). For Molina, all of the characters (not just the children) are defined by their relation to fiction: the mother by her letters and the father by his diary, both of which are directed to an unknown addressee (1985: 113). The film, then, is not (as previous art critics had suggested) a 'symbolic film on the War', since it lacks both a contrast between 'the two Spains' and a dialectic between the worlds of winning and losing parties (1985: 115). All possible elements of historicity are thus 'erased' from *El espíritu de la colmena*, rendering it not so much a metaphorical reflection on the war as a study of the simulations of the real enacted by fiction on the world (1985: 116). Transcending the barrier between *énonciation* and *énoncé* (Spanish *decir* and *lo dicho*), Erice expands the boundaries of filmic verisimilitude, lending his images the quality of phenomenological reality itself (Molina Foix 1985: 118).

With his customary subtlety, then, Molina suggests that the resonant absences and silences of the film (its appeal to the unrepresentable) are themselves an imaging of the effects of history, of a political repression which rendered its victims speechless and diverted their energies from the public, social arena into the private realm of fantasy. But in his contention that *El espíritu de la colmena* represses the dialectic of power, neglects metaphor in favour of simulation, and thus blurs the binary between fact and fiction, Molina not only problematizes previous Marxian readings made on the film's release, a time of more urgent political commitment; he also prepares the way for later, increasingly abstract readings which will expand his own reference to the structuralist poetics of, say, Christian Metz and wholly neglect any sociopolitical implications of the film, just as the Francoist critics of *El alcázar* and *El pueblo* had done before them.

The most developed and theorized of such readings is Santos Zunzunegui's essay, which, the author tells us, won a prize as best unpublished essay at a conference on Cinema and History held in Orihuela in 1992 (1994: 42). Zunzunegui claims to base his study on Erice's own challenge to the Aristotelian binary of history and poetry: Erice has shown that there is 'no real division' between the two (1994: 43). Zunzunegui argues convincingly that Erice's critical writings must be taken in conjunction with his filmic works as part of a single project; but his chronological narration of that project (which seeks quite properly to avoid any facile linearity) remains wholly intracinematic: it is a succession of encounters with the work of filmic masters on the screen (Visconti, Pasolini, Mizoguchi) (1994: 44–8). Tellingly, Zunzunegui cites with approval what Erice claims to have learned from von Sternberg's Dietrich films: a 'path towards abstraction' (1994: 48).

For Zunzunegui, then, *El espíritu de la colmena* follows a road of abstraction or 'dereferentialization', which lends the 'signifying practice' a 'particular density' (1994: 49). Abandoning anecdotal elements in the narrative, Erice also lends objects a resonant (yet non-specific) opacity by shooting them straight on: a frontal angle which lends locations such as the abandoned building in which the fugitive hides an anthropomorphic quality (1994: 53). With its multiple openings (credit sequence, unestablished first shots; 'primal scene' of the *Frankenstein* screening) the film is devoted to an 'internal referentialization' which renders 'external referentials' (reality effects) wholly secondary (1994: 55). In a rather similar way, the narrative as a whole can be abstracted into 'mythemes' (paradigmatic 'coagulations' of syntagmatic strands) (1994: 56) and a structural logic in which temporality is negated, giving way to a circular 'figurativization' which always refers back to itself (1994: 59) and a 'mythic operator' in which all movement is eliminated (1994: 65). Here Zunzunegui calls attention to one of Erice's (or perhaps more properly Luis Cuadrado's) most significant formal techniques: the lack of establishing shots, which means that 'all shots function as close ups', that is, are 'abstracted from their space-time coordinates' (1994: 66). Surpassing 'banal referential-ism', *El espíritu de la colmena* thus points to an impossible space beyond the image which Zunzunegui calls 'essentiality' or 'firstness' (1994: 69).

Zunzunegui is to be praised for his close attention to film form. But although he does not deny that Erice's 'disconnections' gesture towards a concrete referent (the 'double physical and moral void' of the post-war, 1994: 69), it is clear that the 'path towards abstraction' Zunzunegui discerns in Erice is also his own. This is not the place to ask why the structuralist and semi-otic poetics of Greimas, Lévi-Strauss, and the early Barthes (all cited reverently by Zunzunegui) should still be so influential in Spanish literary and cultural studies some twenty years after it fell out of favour in other countries. Zunzunegui himself offers a fragmentary genealogy of film studies in Spain when he refers to a piece on *El espíritu de la colmena* by Javier Maqua and Marta Hernández which, he claims, introduced the use of narratological terms to film study in Spain, thus clearing the way for a criticism which would no longer be reliant on gossip and impressionism: Zunzunegui cites film journals such as *La mirada* and *Contracampo* in the period 1978–87 as exemplary here (1994: 48 n.120). I would suggest, however, that specialist film journals of the Transition were often more politically engaged and less enam-oured of abstraction than Zunzunegui suggests;[4] and, ironically, Zunzunegui's universalism merely echoes that of the 'impression-istic' press he so despises. In spite of his title, then, Zunzunegui's 'logical model' neglects not only history, but also dream: the scientific rigour and technical lexicon of structuralist poetics is notably inappropriate for the study of a film such as *El espíritu de la colmena* in which desire and fantasy are so prominent. Zunzunegui can only point, beyond his graphs and diagrams, to an unrepresentable 'essentiality' which goes wholly unexamined. The cult of the text (of its circularity, self-reference, immanence) is thus complicit with the cult of the auteur who also aspires to

---

[4] See the references to *Contracampo* critics of the late 1970s and early 1980s in Smith 1992: 134–6, 142–3, 153, 158, 160, 163.

self-sufficiency and transcendental abstraction, who claims that history and poetry are one.

Yet we have seen that Erice himself acknowledges, intermittently at least, that cinema is an 'industrial entity' and the product of a community of co-workers. Having considered both popular and academic approaches to *El espíritu de la colmena*, we can now look more closely at how auteurism is qualified by collaboration in the film with reference to the three areas of cinematography, performance, and scriptwriting. My aim is both to historicize the act of film-making and to materialize elements often held to be transparent, innocent, or invisible: light, childhood, and off-screen space and sound. Rather than succumbing, then, to Erice's path towards abstraction, I follow a different route, one which attempts to acknowledge both technical virtuosity and psychic virtuality.

Luis Cuadrado's cinematography is invariably cited by critics as being an essential contribution to the success of *El espíritu de la colmena*. It is more difficult, however, to assess the exact nature of that contribution. In his volume on the history of Spanish cinemtography Francisco Llinás reproduces an extended interview with Cuadrado by Jaime Barroso which sheds light on both his working practices and his conceptualization of the relation between film and the real (Barroso 1989). Cuadrado begins modestly by stating that the cinematographer's role is simply to reproduce in the form of images the director's ideas (n.d.: 229). However, it is not quite as simple as it sounds: for the question of creating or, more properly, re-creating cannot be limited to 'capturing' or 'photocopying' the world. As film is incapable of reproducing the natural look of objects, the 'naturalness' sought by the director must be 'invented' by the cinematographer. Moreover, although 'creative discussion' with the director is important, no director has been able to advise Cuadrado on the technical means he uses to produce the final effects of the film; indeed, only Carlos Saura has any specialist knowledge of cinematography at all (Barroso 1989: 230, 231). Scouting for locations before the shoot is also a collaborative process, but one in which Cuadrado's contribution is definitive: while it is important, once more, that the director should explain how he intends to shoot each scene, exteriors are determined by the cinematographer's priorities: the direction of light and position of the sun at each point in the working day; the adaptation of his own preferred lighting design to the kind of lighting required by the film. Cuadrado's preference in interiors is for indirect lighting, reflected off a sometimes complex combination of white cards, sheets, or translucent papers. This is particularly appropriate for a frequent and tricky shot (prominent in *El espíritu de la colmena*): filming an actor by a window (1989: 246).

It is clear, then, that according to Cuadrado's account of his working practice, the 'magical' or 'mysterious' effects praised by critics and often attributed to Erice are the result of strictly technical means. But, moreover, that technique (to which the director has no access) is inextricable from a certain theory of representation elaborated by the cinematographer from his practice: Cuadrado claims to favour 'realist photography'; but by this he means an 'expressionism' which reproduces the 'sensation' of the real, the emotion it provokes in the spectator, not its exact appearance ('realidad minuciosa', Barroso 1989: 233). That relation between history and poetry (between the particular and the general), that tension between referentiality and abstraction that we have seen in both the writings of Erice and the responses of critics to *El espíritu de la colmena* (generally considered to be 'Erice's film'), are thus also present in the theory and practice of *El espíritu de la colmena*'s cinematographer, who also and uniquely controls the technical means without which there would be no film.

One of those means is colour. Jesús González Requena has given an original account of the 'consciousness of colour' in Spanish cinematography which pays particular attention to Cuadrado and *El espíritu de la colmena* (1989). Like Zunzunegui, González Requena's theoretical touchstone is semiotic or formalist: citing Shklovski he claims that the role of art is to transform the object, defamiliarizing the everyday, and substituting revelation for mere recognition (1989: 121). But González Requena also offers a historical account of colour. Thus, in general, the second half of the twentieth century has seen three major changes: the massive expansion of audiovisual technologies, which have 'invaded' perceptive experience with intense, even 'violent' colours; the inversion of the historical relation between matter and colour, whereby the latter is no longer dependent on the former, and indeed often flaunts its status as an arbitrary choice, independent of the object to which it is attached; finally, the rise of plastic, which has 'sacralized' this arbitrary relation, creating ever more pure and dense colours, and sacrificing texture to wholly homogeneous surfaces (1989:

119–20). More particularly in Spain, these developments had
quite specific effects on cinematography: the expansionist 1960s
were a time of increasing consumerism in which the middle class
saw itself reflected in the vivid colours of advertising and the
garish Kodak tones of the dominant genre of the period: the bourgeois, urban comedy: 'Flat and brilliant urban colours, reminiscent of plastic, of postcards, and of sunsets, irrepressibly modern
and commercial . . . these were the colours that dominated the
Spanish cinematographic landscape of the 1960s' (1989: 122).
González Requena traces next the 'clean break of the 1970s':
rejecting both the 'granitic greys' of Francoism and the Kodak
colourized consumerism a new tendency emerges, which replaces
plastic colours and TV kitsch with local landscapes in their diversity of texture and colour, with subtle, shaded, and warm tones,
and with intimate, atmospheric, and metaphorical photography
(1989: 123).

El espíritu de la colmena clearly belongs to this reactive
tendency. For González Requena the novelty of its look was, paradoxically, its direct link to the 'perceptive memory' of Spaniards
who could see beyond the 1960s: for them, its setting was at once
recognizable and dense with associations. The browns, creams, and
greys of the exteriors, the warm yellows and oranges of the interiors, both palettes suggest to González Requena 'dense, subtle . . .
atmospheres' (1989: 123). This chromatic density is confirmed by
contradictory forces in the composition. On the one hand, we find
the static symmetricality of the composition of exteriors (the two
windows of the abandoned building; the horizontal long shots of a
road or railway in a deserted landscape). But on the other we find
the unsettling liminal nature of interiors and the 'vertical
affirmation of the subject' (the mother writing by a window; the
child standing against the landscape). Most importantly, González
Requena stresses texture: the human face is presented as 'a rough
surface which . . . reveals that it shares its matter with other
surfaces' (1989: 123). Thus the face of the woman announcing the
film show in the opening sequence is similar in texture to the rough
walls of the buildings which surround her; the facial wounds of the
villagers are extended into the highly textured features of the
village itself (1989: 124).

Compared to the mythic immobilism of, say, Zunzunegui,
González Requena suggests a textured temporality: Cuadrado's

cinematography is not abstract, but reveals rather the trace left by time in bodies and buildings. Moreover, in place of Zunzunegui's 'essentiality', González Requena cites the Lacanian 'real': that impossible place outside representation, which is not, however, wholly separate from the trace of textual and psychic movement.[5] And if we look now at the question of performance we shall see that just as the magic of light may be historicized, drawn itself into visibility, so the supposed innocence and abstraction of childhood can also be read for its insistent historicity and inevitable temporality.

It is notoriously difficult to read performance in film, so specific are codes of facial and bodily movement to cultural context. The problem is multiplied when the actor is a child and the performance offers itself as purely 'natural'. Erice has suggested that the sequence in which Ana (the character) sees *Frankenstein* for the first time was the first time that Ana (the actor) had herself seen the film (Elsa Fernández Santos 1992). This 'firstness' or priority of the unrepeatable event, captured by Erice uniquely on a hand-held camera, points towards the 'magical' moment of 'primeridad' cited by Zunzunegui in *El espíritu de la colmena*. In an interview in women's magazine *Dunia*, run under the emblematic title 'The Power of the Look' (Pando 1989: 137), the adult Ana Torrent has confirmed this identification of presentation and representation in a unique moment of innocence: she was not aware of giving a performance but was simply 'playing' before the camera.

Torrent also acknowledges, however, that Spanish audiences have internalized their memory of her as a child (Pando 1989: 136). And if we look back to press cuttings of the 1970s a more complex story emerges. Posed against a varied range of backgrounds (an aquarium, a DC9 aeroplane, a cinema in which *El espíritu de la colmena* is playing) the child Ana is shown always with the same impassive face she presents in the film: the dark, blank stare which embodies 'the power of the look'. Journalists invariably comment on the 'special attraction' of her 'large, wide' eyes, the 'most expressive look of our cinema' (García Rayo 1975). But while in the late 1980s *Dunia* read the meaning of those eyes

---

[5]   González Requena does not however give a reference in Lacan's text for this term; nor does he acknowledge that its meaning is problematic and much debated. For one version of the real see Zizek 1992.

as being that 'there was still a place [in late Francoist Spain] for a forbidden ideal of freedom', earlier interpretations are quite different. An extended interview in *Ya* praises not only the 'naturalness of her performance' but also the 'simplicity of her Hispanic face', claiming that there are 'many Anas' in Spain, many young girls of her generation, facing so many difficulties with such a great capacity for endurance. The 'magical face' invoked in *Telva* magazine (15 Mar. 1976) is also quite specifically Spanish, held to embody both the spirit of the nation (there are frequent references to the dark eyes of Goya portraits) and the history of that nation at a particular moment.

The most sensitive and revealing interview is by novelist and contemporary chronicler Francisco Umbral on the release of Saura's *Cría cuervos* two years after *El espíritu de la colmena* (Umbral [1975]). Umbral also cites Torrent's 'dark tragic eyes, worthy of a sad child in a Goya portrait'; but he seems equally taken by her tiny hand covered in elastoplasts and her 'catastrophic' teeth. On the one hand Umbral claims that she is 'a little girl and nothing more' and that the impression she makes on film comes from a simple, even mechanical technique: she is forbidden to smile on camera, and her gaze thus takes on a 'veil' of adult seriousness. But on the other hand Umbral compliments Torrent on her beauty, asks her where babies come from, and compares the pleasure she takes in snacks and sweets to an 'ordered orgy'. He ends with an exclamation: 'Oh, those eyes, dear God, those terrible eyes.'

These hints of infantile sexuality (which could hardly be voiced by a women's magazine such as *Dunia*) are confirmed in a later piece in *El país*, in which Umbral, five years later, looks back on the earlier encounter and compares himself to the 'dirty old man' ('hombre del saco') seducing children with poisoned sweets as evening falls in the park (Umbral 1980). But if the journalist plays the part of the paedophile (even 'vampire') then the child herself is cast as 'Lolita', her innocence 'stolen' by the adult whose heart is swollen with 'blood and embarrassed love': in the figure of the child, in the doll-like, Goya eyes, Umbral saw the body of the adolescent she was to become coming towards him: 'nicely grown up ['crecidita'], reader. Nicely grown up.'

Just as the 'universality' of *El espíritu de la colmena* served critics as a screen protecting them from the film's political implications, so the 'naturalness' of Torrent's performance, the 'darkness' of her look, work as a veil, masking both the nationalist dimensions of her image (the mirror of Spanish womanhood) and the disturbingly sexual resonances of the plot (in which a child gives herself to a monstrous man in the dark). Playfully ironic and archly seductive, Umbral not only discloses the repressed eroticism of the spectator's response to child actors; he also reveals a less sublimated yet more complex process: the way in which audiences trace the chronology of their own lives in the shifting appearance of performers on screen. By anticipating the erotic evolution of Ana (the actor, and perhaps the character) Umbral illuminates the historicity of our own libidinal response to cinema, a historicity which at once responds to and recoils from the 'magical' suspension or abstraction of bodies imaged and unchanging on the screen. He points, then, to an off-screen space in which Torrent scratches her hand, eats sweets, grows up, but in which she and her audience will carry with us the material trace of the power of her look, a power that is at once poetic and historical, experienced in isolation and as part of a community of spectators, of citizens.

We have seen, then, that both cinematography and performance made specific contributions to that process of 'convivencia' described by Erice in the shoot for *Los desafíos*, contributions which are perhaps more self-conscious than has previously been supposed. Even the adult Torrent, who claims she had simply 'played' before the camera, is contradicted by the child actor Ana, who reveals differences in working practices: with Erice, unlike with Saura, she learned her lines before shooting began (Elsa Fernández Santos 1992). The question of the contribution of co-scriptwriter Ángel Fernández Santos is more complex as it raises the problem of artistic priority. For while the two share the credit for the screenplay, in the typewritten script held in the Biblioteca Nacional (Fernández Santos and Erice 1973) Fernández Santos's name comes first; while in the film itself it comes second. In a lengthy piece in *El país*, published to celebrate the tenth anniversary of *El espíritu de la colmena* (Fernández Santos [1983]), Fernández Santos (a faithful supporter of Erice's subsequent films, in which he himself played no part) gives his account of the origins of the script. According to Fernández Santos this was such an intimate process of collaboration that the childhood memories of each man alternated in the narrative: thus Erice provided the mushroom picking and monster games of the children; Fernández Santos the well, the fugitive, and the school anatomy lesson. Fernández Santos attributes to Erice a decisive stroke: the 'amputation' of the original frame narrative set in the present in which the adult Ana returns to the village in which she grew up to visit her dying father. This cut led to an internalization of the narrative: deprived of an on-screen storyteller, spectators are obliged to recreate the story inside their own consciousness, using the 'secret look, indebted to a secret identity and poetic time, which exists behind the eyes of every human being'.

Fernández Santos thus takes the internalization of the narrative to be also a universalization of it: the two men's private memories become, immediately, those of the audience. What he reveals, however, is that that abstraction is the effect of a specific and conscious decision on the writers' part and one which arose from a familiar problem in scriptwriting, the attempt to retain a unified point of view. And if we go on to contrast the Biblioteca Nacional script with the final film version we note a continuing erasure of the historical frame of the narrative which extends into analogous changes in shooting style and the relation between sound and image. To start at the very beginning: the opening shots of the film (after the title pictures drawn by the child actors) are long shots of the truck carrying the movie apparatus and of the building in which the film will be shown, followed by medium shots of the projectionist unloading his equipment surrounded by boisterous children and the town crier announcing the show. The script opens on a black screen in silence on which the title appears, fading out onto a shot of a 'hermetically closed' beehive, without a single bee in sight. A dissolve links this to the following montage, also shown in silence:

Master shot of a village. Most of the houses are grouped together around a hollow, by a small river.
Inside the village, but mainly on the outskirts, we can see ruined houses, and others that are empty and uninhabited.
Ruined walls.
Blackened walls.
Windows with their panes broken.
A house on the outskirts, in the middle of the plain, a farm labourer's house, abandoned. Next to it, a well.
An artillery gun, overgrown with moss, destroyed by a blast, turned into scrap iron.

An abandoned trench.
A pair of soldier's boots, in the bottom of a ditch, their soles in tatters.
A common grave. A cross. By the tomb, a lot of wild flowers.[6]

Here there is a very explicit reference to the trace of history in the landscape (guns, boots, and graves), not to mention an emphatic parallel between the emptiness of the hive and the mortal decrepitude of the village. The next shot in the script (of a bee feeding at a flower) hints, like the blossoms by the grave, at the possibility of a rebirth also absent from the opening of the film as it finally appeared. If the loss of this historical frame renders the opening sequence of *El espíritu de la colmena* abstracted, non-specific, what remains nonetheless is the texturality of the images cited by González Requena: the traces of time in the faces and buildings we are shown.

Elsewhere Erice (or Cuadrado) eliminates spectacular camera effects or movements specified in the script. Thus the sequence in which the children watch *Frankenstein* begins in the script (but not the film) with a 'blinding white light directed straight to the camera lens' (Fernández Santos and Erice 1973: 8), a reverse angle from the screen's point of view. Or again, the sequence in which Ana looks down the well on her second visit to the abandoned building ends in the script with the camera, hitherto held motionless in extreme long shot, 'violently penetrating the interior of the well, focusing on the opening from the darkness surrounded by walls on all sides: this opening against which we see [Ana's] head leaning over, standing out against the sky' (1973: 43). In the film, we simply cut to closer shots of Ana and the well, followed by a shot from her point of view looking down into the well. Once more the showy subjective shot from the point of view of the 'thing' (screen or well) is cut.

Eliminating both historical reference and virtuoso camera movement, the film also intensifies the use of off-screen space and sound already hinted at in the script by rendering what we see and hear more abstracted and less grounded within the frame. For example, the script is divided throughout into two columns on each folio, with visual instructions on the left and sound and dialogue on the

  [6]   Fernández Santos and Erice 1973: 1. Zunzunegui (1994: 52) also cites this passage from the published version of the script (Fernández Santos and Erice 1976: 1).

right. Sound effects off-screen are precisely orchestrated as they are in the film itself: Teresa (known as 'the woman' in much of the script) thus pauses as she writes her letter and looks to the window as the distant whistle of a train is heard (1973: 10); or again, the script specifies that in the scene in which Fernando joins his estranged wife in bed and she pretends to sleep, he does not appear in frame as we hear him approach and remove his clothes and shoes (1973: 33). Indeed he is wholly impersonalized in the direction, which reads: 'Someone opens the door off-screen.' The script also refuses to specify the motivation or sometimes, indeed, the actions of the characters: when the two girls first visit the abandoned building we are told that Ana 'seems' to follow her sister faithfully, 'as if' obeying an agreement they had previously made (1973: 41). In the same sequence we are told that Ana 'may' be cold and that it is 'impossible' to know if the two girls speak to one another (1973: 42).

Historical abstraction, technical discretion, and undecidable motivation thus seem to go hand in hand. What is important to note, however, is that the consistent use of sound bridges (the staggering of sound and vision from one sequence to another) is always in the form of sound off, not sound over: that is, unlike the voice-over of, say, *El sur*, in which the main character offers an authoritative commentary on the action from a disembodied position outside it, the effects or dialogue which play over a sequence in *El espíritu de la colmena* always derive from another location within the diegetic space: thus we know, for example, that the ominous clumping noises heard as the girls discuss *Frankenstein* late at night derive not from the monster but from the father we have seen pacing in his studio in a previous shot. Strictly speaking, then, *El espíritu de la colmena* is a film not so much of the unrepresentable but of the unrepresented. The dislocation of image- and soundtracks points not to an 'essentiality' to which actors and spectators have no access, but rather to an atomization of filmic space in which no subject accedes to an intersubjective realm beyond their immediate, sensual experience. This atomization and dislocation can be read (as Molina Foix does) not as metaphysical, but rather as historical in origin.

In the last sequence of *El espíritu de la colmena* Ana invokes the monster, addressing the night sky with the words 'Soy Ana' (It's me,

Ana). A female voice is heard, singing eerily and wordlessly on the soundtrack. This is another example of the path towards abstraction followed by Erice (by Cuadrado, Torrent, and Fernández Santos): in the script she sings a song about a woman waiting at night for her lover, taken from a sixteenth-century *Cancionero* (1973: 128). But the sequence also reveals the role of the Other in the constitution of a sense of self: it is by giving herself to the monster (to the unknowable lover whom she awaits) that Ana finds her own (sexual?) identity. There is no denying the magical, mysterious effect of this scene on many audiences, like its predecessor in which, eyes closed once more, the child offers herself to the monster by the river. What I have suggested in this piece, however, is that such effects are the result of quite specific technical means (of cinematography, performance, and scriptwriting); and that those means are themselves subject to the commercial constraints of the film industry and the discursive limitations of those critics, whether journalistic or academic, who are paid to comment on its products. Like Ana, then, the director has no unique and solitary identity, no sense of self without the Other (crew, industry, audience) with whom and to whom he offers his vision.

But if we, like the Nicholas Ray whom Erice admires so much, 'cannot go home again' to the old myth of auteurism or, still less, the unquestioning reverence of the 'Art House', nor should we take refuge in metaphysics or scientism, which remain the dominant critical approaches to *El espíritu de la colmena* in Spain.[7] For, as we have seen, the first is complicit with a rightist politics of nationalism (of the 'Spanish genius' or 'spirit of the nation'); while the second can address neither the historical nor the psychic dimensions of film (neither the 'war behind the window' nor the 'look behind the eyes'). The connection between film form and social practice will always be complex; and any study of reception risks impressionism and triviality. The challenge, then, is not to suspend too soon the conflict between history and poetry, between reference and abstraction; to elaborate a reading of *El espíritu de la colmena* which does justice to its extraordinary resonance and complexity without either reducing it to empirical evidence or abandoning it to the ecstasy of abstraction.

----

7 I have attempted to offer just such a reading (both historical and theoretical) for another contemporary Spanish film-maker in Smith 1994.

REFERENCES

B., A. (n.d.), '*El espíritu de la colmena*', no source given.

Barroso, Jaime (1989), 'Entrevista con Luis Cuadrado', in Francisco Llinás (ed.), *Directores de fotografía del cine español*, Madrid: Filmoteca Española: 228–47.

Cebollada, Pascual (1974), review in *Ya* (10 Oct.).

Comas, Juan (1974), 'Víctor Erice nos dice: entrevista', *Imagen y sonido* (Jan.): 35–6.

Crespo, Pedro (1973), '*El espíritu de la colmena* de Víctor Erice', *Arriba* (10 Oct.).

'El espíritu de la colmena' (n.d.), unpub. typescript, Filmoteca Nacional, Madrid.

Erice, Víctor, and Oliver, Jos (1986), *Nicholas Ray y su tiempo*. Madrid: Filmoteca Española.

F., A. (1973), review in *Cineinforme*, 186 (Nov.): 23–4.

Feito, Álvaro (1973), review in *Cinestudio*, 127 (Dec.): 47–8.

Fernández, Manuel (1983), 'Diez años de "El espíritu de la colmena"', *Ya* (23 Nov.).

Fernández Santos, Ángel ([1983]), 'Mirar desde detrás de los ojos', *El país*.

—— (1985), 'Una hermosa elegía inacabada', *El país* (25 May).

—— (1992), ' "El sol del membrillo" de Víctor Erice y Antonio López, provoca una fuerte división de opiniones', *El país* (12 May).

—— and Erice, Víctor (1973), 'El espíritu de la colmena'. Unpublished.

—— —— (1976), *El espíritu de la colmena*. Madrid: Elías Querejeta.

Fernández Santos, Elsa (1992), 'Los buscadores de luz', *El país* (3 May).

García, Angeles (1993), 'Víctor Erice dice que "El sol del membrillo" es para minorías que "están en todas partes" ', *El país* (20 Jan.).

García Rayo, Antonio (1975), 'Ana María Torrent: con nueve años, dos películas', *Ya* (23 Nov.).

Genover, Jaume (1974), review in *Dirigido por*, 9 (Jan.): 25.

González Requena, Jesús (1989), 'La conciencia del color en la fotografía cinematográfica española', in Francisco Llinás (ed.), *Directores de fotografía del cine español*, Madrid: Filmoteca Española: 118–65.

Martialay, Félix (1973), review in *El alcázar* (12 Oct.).

Molina Foix, Vicente (1983), 'El año en que triunfamos peligrosamente', *El país* (25 June).

—— (1985), 'La guerra detrás de la ventana', *Revista de occidente* (Oct.): 112–18.

Palá, José María (1969), 'Conversación con Víctor Erice y Julia Peña', *Film ideal*: 217–22.

Pando, Juan (1989), 'Ana Torrent: el poder de la mirada', *Dunia*, 18: 136–7.

Rubio, Miguel (1973), '*El espíritu de la colmena*', *Nuevo diario* (14 Oct.).

Smith, Paul Julian (1992), *Laws of Desire: Questions of Homosexuality in Spanish Writing and Film 1960–1990*. Oxford: Oxford University Press.

—— (1994), *Desire Unlimited: The Cinema of Pedro Almodóvar*. London: Verso.

Umbral, Francisco ([1975]), 'Idolos sin pedestal: Ana Torrent', unidentified press clipping.

—— (1980), 'Spleen de Madrid: Ana Torrent', *El país* (5 Sept.).

Zizek, Slavoj (1992), 'Pornography, Nostalgia, Montage', in *Looking Awry: An Introduction to Jacques Lacan through Popular Culture*, Cambridge, Mass.: MIT Press: 107–22.

Zunzunegui, Santos (1994), 'Entre la historia y el sueño: eficacia simbólica y estructura mítica en *El espíritu de la colmena*', in *Paisajes de la forma: ejercicios de análisis de la imagen*, Madrid: Cátedra: 42–70.

8

Furtivos (Borau, 1975): My Mother, my Lover

PETER WILLIAM EVANS

La muerte es esencial porque sin ella no hay auténtica cacería.
(Ortega)

Furtivos (1975), with its dark narrative about matricide following a son's discovery of his wife's murder by his own mother, is a major landmark of Spanish film history.[1] Its nightmarish odyssey into the furtive desires of inwardly damaged slaves of a culture in crisis follows an almost Dantesque pattern of personal and public torment. In its desire to shock the audience into awareness of its own complicity in barbarism the film recalls the Buñuel of *Un chien andalou* (1928) and the Hitchcock of *Psycho* (1960). One of a cluster of hard-hitting films (including *Cría cuervos*, 1975, and *Camada negra*, 1977) that appeared around the time of Francoism's timely farewell, it met with both critical and commercial success. For many years it broke box-office records (Heredero 1990: 353), earning critical approval from, among others, Vargas Llosa, Francisco Umbral, and Julián Marías (Sáez 1989). Inevitably outraging apologists for the *ancien régime* (see the review in a *Fuerza nueva* supporting journal (Sánchez Vidal 1990: 122)), it also offended animal rights sympathizers in Spain for its apparently brutal treatment of the dog substituting for the wolf in the horrific scene where Martina clubs it to death with a shovel (Heredero

I am greatly indebted to José Luis Borau who, in conversation, clarified many points and provided me with key information related to the making of the film. Naturally, I take responsibility for all questions of interpretation and any unintentional inaccuracies of fact.

[1] The film is very loosely based on the life of a real 'alimañero' who lived and hunted wolves in the Bosque del Saja (Heredero 1990: 345).

1990: 352; Sánchez Vidal 1990: 120).[2] As Agustín Sánchez Vidal points out in a chapter of exemplary scholarship, *Furtivos*—appearing at a time when censorship had not yet disappeared in Spain—reflects the enormous energy and courage of Borau not only in getting the film made at all, but also in resisting the demands of the censor and in eventually arranging its effective distribution and exhibition, at the San Sebastián Film Festival (Sánchez Vidal 1990: 115–20). Borau's refusal to capitulate to the censors' demands ensured that some of the film's most crucial elements (e.g. the character of the *Gobernador*, scenes at the girls' reformatory, and Milagros's woodland striptease) were relatively untouched in order to maintain its hard-hitting, *tremendista* qualities.

Less allusive and abstract than Borau's previous film *Hay que matar a B* (1973), *Furtivos* brought together the disparate but complementary talents of José Luis Borau (as director but also here actor and producer), Manuel Gutiérrez Aragón (as scriptwriter, and director of some scenes, specifically those featuring Borau in the part of the *Gobernador*, Santiago), and Luis Cuadrado, whose photography in this and other films often recalls—as Marsha Kinder and others have noted—the chiaroscuro effects of Spain's great painters, especially El Greco and Ribera (Kinder 1993: 226–9). Aesthetically, the film reflects the recognized tastes of these individuals in a film that for all its thematic innovations—though even here comparisons have been made with Valle-Inclán, Cela, and other writers—refuses to succumb to unnecessary formal experimentation. Borau, whose fondness for Hollywood has been noted by John Hopewell (1986), has defended the shot/countershot style of the film, distancing himself from, say, the rapid cutting trademark of a Jancsó, or the more languid pace of an Antonioni. However alien to Hollywood the uncompromising treatment of its difficult thematics, there remains in the narrative pace and visual style of the film the memory traces of the work of the great directors like Ford, Lang, and Hitchcock so admired by Borau. Cuadrado's photography of a deceptively calm and lush autumnal forest landscape—where the greater part of the action takes place—combines with the elliptical style of the Borau/Gutiérrez

---

[2] Though, curiously, *Pascual Duarte* (Ricardo Franco, 1975), with its far more brutal scenes in which a dog is shot and a horse repeatedly stabbed to death, seems to have escaped censure.

Aragón narrative to conjure up the shadowy atmosphere of uncertainty and despair so characteristic of Francoism's last hurrah.[3] Franco's view of Spain as 'un bosque en paz' is refocused as a secret hellish prison teeming with creatures intent on mutual destruction.[4]

The key narrative elements of this dystopian pastoral, related to the ultimately disastrous consequences of the love triangle between the mother, Martina (Lola Gaos), son, Ángel (Ovidi Montllor), and daughter-in-law, Milagros (Alicia Sánchez), have been read in predominantly allegorical and psychological terms. The allegorical resonances, using the rudiments of the melodramatic plot as an image for the ills of a country straitjacketed by Francoism, derive from the key metaphor of the hunt. Owing nothing here to Ortega's definition of the hunt as the over-civilized individual's reason-abandoning attempts to recover Dionysian energy in the Bacchic *mise-en-scène* of nature, the woodland setting seems more like a sculpted figurative landscape for Spain's pre-1975 history. The film's literary inspiration is rather Azorín's 'Un pueblecito: río frío de Ávila' with its more cynical view of the countryside as a place—far from exemplifying a rural idyll—raging with nature's furious battles for survival. From this point of view the countryside has been seen as an image of Spain, the *Gobernador* (Borau himself) as the embodiment of contemporary political realities, Martina the destructive forces of tradition, and Ángel and Milagros, representative of the

---

[3] As Borau remarks, to create this effect several locations were used: 'Cuando fuimos a localizar el Bosque del Saja nos dimos cuenta de que los bosques reales, donde están los lobos, no son precisamente muy cinematográficos, ya que son de maleza, no muy altos de árboles ni despejados de ramas, llenos de vegetación, intricados y espesos. Un lobo se mueve entre las zarzas y los arbustos y no se le puede ver, pero eso no es fotografiable: es decir, que los bosques de alimañas no son wagnerianos. Necesitábamos, por tanto, un bosque menos enmarañado, donde los actores pudieran desenvolverse y la luz entrar por algún lado para que la cámara de Luis Cuadrado lograra el efecto plástico que buscábamos. Lo encontramos al norte de la provincia de Madrid, en el hayedo de Montejo el más meridional de Europa.' However, as Heredero points out, the setting was not appropriate for all the shots Borau had in mind, so other locations in north Navarre, around Segovia and in the Pyrenees, were also used (Heredero 1990: 346–7).

[4] Borau himself points out that *Furtivos* is about secrecy and persecution, as the film's title makes clear: 'Durante el desarrollo del guión se produjo un cambio fundamental, de forma accidental, descubrí en el diccionario el significado de la palabra "furtivo". Entonces ni siquiera sabíamos que ése sería el título de la película . . . "Furtivo" es todo aquel que hace algo a escondidas. Cosa que yo, si he de ser sincero, no sabía. Pensaba que furtivo y perseguido venían a ser sinónimos' (Heredero 1990: 346).

population, the victims of that dark history. Spanish audiences of the time could hardly have missed these obvious connections, especially as Franco himself was known to be a keen huntsman. The portrayal of the *Gobernador* as a narcissistic, slightly effeminate big baby, an impression heightened by the prissy, high-pitched voice of the dubbing actor (Rafael Penagos), preferred to Borau's gruffer tones, would have done little to undermine these associations.[5] His fussy, strutting intrusion into the lives of the *pueblo* may be further viewed as the pitiful attempts of the social order— specifically, the conservative forces of Francoism—to repress the turbulent desires of a nation preparing for their monstrous return.

The film's project—the exposure of these raging desires and the overthrow of repressive measures—raises several problematic issues, chief among them being the representation of motherhood in such negative terms, a pattern repeated in the equally brilliant subsequent Borau/Gutiérrez Aragón collaboration *Camada negra* (1977) where, as in *Furtivos*, the mother feeds her offspring the deadly pap of a venomous ideology. Martina's portrayal of the incestuous tormentor of her son and daughter-in-law, so vividly and terrifyingly depicted in the famous poster designed by Iván Zulueta, invites accusations of misogyny, its images of motherhood collapsing unconscious and real or socially authentic versions of motherhood in a nightmarish projection of the 'phallic mother'.[6] The poster represents the mother as an embodiment of the abject, of the monstrous-feminine, in a way that distorts and simplifies the carefully ambivalent treatment of motherhood in the film itself. Here, significantly, the mother's spiky vulpine face is featureless except for a cruel predatory mouth, agape to reveal sharpened fangs. The hair, like strands of barbed wire, is brushed back from a forehead of diabolically purple, red, and orange hues. There are no eyes to humanize the face which, beneath its ghostly, haggish brow, becomes a mask of horror fitted onto a skeleton of a torso from which emerge spindly arms that culminate in claw-like fingers

---

[5] Until the early 1970s Spanish films were usually post-synched, with the actors recording their lines in the studio. In this film the voice of Ángel, as well as the *Gobernador*'s, is dubbed. In the case of the former this was due to Ovidi Montllor's thick Valencian accent, highly unsuitable for a character supposedly born and bred in the north of Spain.

[6] For a fuller discussion of Kleinian reformulations of Freudian discussions of motherhood, see Kaplan 1990: 107–23.

digging into the shoulders of her traumatized son. The drawing of the torso curiously recalls to some extent the disturbing cover of one of the most provocative of popularizing feminist books on the cultural history of women, Germaine Greer's *The Female Eunuch* (1971). The cover of the first edition draws attention in somewhat grisly fashion to what would now perhaps be termed, after Judith Butler and others, the 'performativity of gender' (Butler 1990), through its representation of the female torso as a kind of theatrical costume made of human skin, a sort of sleeveless uniform worn by women in conformity with the demands of socially defined roles, in the drama of sexual difference. The breast-dominated singlet-vest costume of female flesh finds its even more gruesome parallel in the *Furtivos* poster where, again, the upper part of Martina's body seems like a skeleton, lit up, like the forehead, by infernal colours, over which hangs Martina's grotesque female-eunuch uniform of parched Oedipally textured skin.

The image of the predator, witch, or castrating mother, to which in discussions of the film many have referred (e.g. Fiddian 1989), comes to life here in its most terrifying form. Borau has himself referred to his conception of the narrative in terms of the Hansel and Gretel fairy tale, drawing attention to the script's formulaic references, for instance, to Martina as a 'witch' and to the *Gobernador* as a 'king':

Por debajo de su apariencia realista y rural, *Furtivos* es a la vez una tragedia y un cuento infantil, incluso hay personajes que se caracterizan a sí mismos como tales: en un momento determinado a Lola Gaos la llaman *bruja*; ellos son los niños perdidos en el bosque, que vuelven de la mano a casita; la madre llama al gobernador rey mío . . . como en los cuentos de reyes, princesas y bosques. (Borau in Sánchez Vidal 1990: 123–4)

Here, though, as elsewhere, the text refuses to be compromised by narrow readings, and Borau refocuses his own remarks on the fairy-tale inspiration of the film by also claiming that the film is a sort of intertextual narrative, playing with the idea of Lola Gaos as a female Saturn, the offspring-devouring, Galdós- and Buñuel-inspired terrible mother, Saturna, from *Tristana* (1970).[7] His further comment, too, to Gutiérrez Aragón about his desire to make a film about Lola Gaos in a forest (Sánchez Vidal 1990: 110)

[7] Lola Gaos had also, of course, appeared as the lewd photographer at the beggars' Last Supper in an earlier Buñuel film, *Viridiana* (1961).

draws attention, beyond myth and intertextuality, to other more contemporary interests. The film clearly raises questions about subjectivity, especially in relation both to the desire of individuals (adults as well as children) to resist control, and to the construction of motherhood, through the idiosyncratic semiotic and kinetic attributes of a major actress of the Spanish cinema, an aim that inevitably mediates the changing attitudes to gender roles in what was about to become a period of political and social transition.

In a sense, of course, all these levels of meaning are interrelated. And even though ultimately each is in itself too limited if alone considered the key to the film's intelligibility, perhaps the fairy-tale associations initially allow one more easily to approach the complex nature of their involved structure and attendant issues. In a discussion of the Hansel and Gretel story Bruno Bettelheim remarks that the children's departure from home, followed by their ordeals in the witch's gingerbread house, symbolize the individual's learning curve of experience, in which a lesson is taught about the importance of curbing id-driven desires, of submission to the demands of the ego, and the recognition of the destructiveness of orality, a theme highlighted through the food imagery associated above all with the gingerbread house. In this account, the witch is also the mother:

Having overcome his Oedipal difficulties, mastered his oral anxieties, sublimated those of his cravings which cannot be satisfied realistically, and learned that wishful thinking has to be replaced by intelligent action, the child is ready to live happily again with his parents. This is symbolised by the treasures Hansel and Gretel bring home to share with their father. Rather than expecting everything good to come from their parents, the older child needs to be able to make some contribution to the emotional well-being of himself and his family. (Bettelheim 1988: 165).

As Fiddian has remarked (1989: 300), the parallels between the fairy tale and the film break down most obviously in their closures. In the fairy tale, the children learn their lesson and enter the social order; in *Furtivos*, this ending is denied because the film questions the legitimacy of that order, given its predominantly Francoist premises. Yet even though fairy tale and film conclude in radically different ways—in the former, a safe return home, in the latter, Milagros's murder by Martina, Martina's killing by Ángel, and, we suspect, Ángel's suicide—the Oedipal parallels offer useful ways of pursuing the film's interest in contemporary issues related to the construction of identity.

Although never explicitly stated—in line with what many have recognized as the film's aesthetics of allusion and understatement—it seems clear that prior to involvement with Milagros, Ángel has been having an incestuous relationship with his mother. Not a common theme in Spanish cinema even after Franco (other examples include *Pascual Duarte*, Ricardo Franco, 1975; *Vacas*, Julio Medem, 1991; and *Contra el viento*, Francisco Periñán, 1990)[8], the treatment of incest has nothing here of the somewhat romanticized aura of a film like *La luna* (Bertolucci, 1979), where the mother–son relationship is largely deprived of the ideological determinants so crucial to *Furtivos*. The expression of mixed delight and contempt on Martina's face as she comforts the grieving Ángel once he learns of Milagros's apparent decision to abandon him for her first lover, *El Cuqui*, the gangster, speaks volumes about a history of sexual intimacy. For all the tenderness of his feelings towards Milagros, Ángel's aim in pursuing her has really been motivated primarily by a desire for liberation from the nightmarish control of his mother. The revealing testimony of facial kinetics mapping out a history of abuse is compounded by her teasing remarks about his penis. Ovidi Montllor's baleful expression poignantly captures the complexity of feeling that bears witness to his own family romance of sexual shame.

As the dominant partner of this unlikely couple, Martina—her reptilian eyes peering out from the jaundiced skin to observe in secret the unwelcome affairs of her son and daughter-in-law—embodies the social order's darkest image of abjection. In *The Monstrous-Feminine*, Barbara Creed draws on Julia Kristeva's notion of the abject to theorize representations of monstrous motherhood in the cinema. Described by Kristeva as that which refuses to respect positions and rules (Creed 1993: 9), the abject is also, as Creed remarks, something that highlights the 'attraction as well as the horror of the undifferentiated' (1993: 9). On this reading, part of the attraction of the horror film genre—to which *Furtivos* is only distantly related—would seem to lie precisely in its treatment of taboo subjects arousing in audiences perverse pleasures as well as revulsion. In her discussion of the aesthetics and mechanisms of the horror film Creed goes on to argue that this ambiguous fascination with abjection often involves the monstrous representation of

---

8 All these films deal with brother–sister relationships.

mothers. Again drawing on Kristeva, she argues that 'all individuals experience abjection at the time of their earliest attempts to break away from the mother' (Creed 1993: 11).

In its representation of motherhood, through the Saturnine presence of Martina, *Furtivos* clearly relies heavily on the ambiguous dynamics of abjection. From one point of view, Martina is systematically portrayed as a figure of horror; her predatory features and rasping voice, seemingly emanating from the depths of an undead corpse rather than from the throat of a live human being, confirm her as the dreaded witch/mother archetype of every control-fleeing male's worst nightmares. But if Martina were no more than that the film might well stand condemned as an unproblematic endorsement of misogynistic stereotype, another text serving up a *mujer devoradora/bruja* for rejection by all castration-fearing *ingénus*. In its very careful sidestepping of such crudity the film succeeds instead in signposting reasons why a mother's incestuous control of her son—for control is the film's key concept—becomes the dominant impulse behind her desire to validate what Creed refers to as her 'problematic relation to the symbolic realm' (Creed 1993: 12). In *Furtivos* control is given its most extreme form in Martina's incestuous victimization of her son Ángel.

In an illuminating analysis of a difficult subject, Estela Welldon begin by attempting to expose the taboos on discussion of mother–son sexual involvements, drawing attention to social attitudes too compromised by idealization to admit the true extent of this problem, before formulating her far-reaching conclusions about the circumstances that lead to such perverse behaviour in mothers. A constant feature of the patients who come to her for treatment with perverse histories of this kind is, in the case of mothers, a legacy of self-doubt and abuse, both leading to acts of abuse committed against a son who becomes, as perhaps is customary in all perverse behaviour, the target of displaced anger. In such instances, too, in what is clearly a pattern, as Welldon argues, of arrested emotional and sexual development (Welldon 1992: 93), the victimizer regards the victim as an extension of her own body, a de-individuated, dehumanized adjunct of the self, a process which clearly reflects on the social as well as the psycho-biological power structures in which women are caught up:

The aetiology of perversion, I believe, is intertwined with the politics of power; one aspect is psychobiological and the other social. It is possible that this difference of response is caused by society's inability to see woman as a complete human being. The difficulties in acknowledging that mothers can abuse their power could be the result of total denial, as a way of dealing with unpalatable truth. Woman is seen as a part-object, a mere receptacle for man's perverse designs. The apparent idealization with which society hides female perverse attitudes ('Women don't do those awful things') actually contains a denigrating counterpart. Until recently a lack of legislation on female perversion reflected society's total denial of it.

The study of power politics might throw new light on the understanding of motherhood functions. Perhaps if women had a longer tradition of belonging to the power structure their attitudes to men and children would not be governed, as they are now, by a weakness which they strive to turn into possessiveness and control. (Welldon 1988: 104–5)

Furtivos brilliantly explores the areas of power and disempowerment covered by Welldon's analysis, casting Martina as its monster of power-crazed abjection, but also insisting on the circumstances and origins of her monstrousness. Although motherhood here to some extent fulfils ideological expectations, with its portrayal of Martina often stressing the apparent ease with which she adapts herself to the demands of her role, the film also highlights the frustrations and ultimately the perversions to which acquiescence in the socialization process often leads. This film corresponds to the pattern noted by Marsha Kinder (1993) *vis-à-vis* Spanish cinema during this period, of films marked by the absence of the father. That absence often results, as Nancy Chodorow also argues in a more general discussion of parent–child dynamics, in the mother's seductive attention of the child:

Just as the father is often not enough present to prevent or break up the mother–daughter boundary confusion, he is also not available to prevent either his wife's seductiveness or his son's growing reciprocated incestuous impulses. (Chodorow 1984: 105)

The real father here is not only absent but also unknown, although it is not too fanciful to speculate that he might be the *Gobernador*. The ideological father, of course, is the great patriarch of Spain, whose public omnipresence and private absence plays no small part in the tortured construction of his wider family, the country at large.

In a specific discussion of *Furtivos*, Robin Fiddian remarks that Martina accepts her ideological place—however disgruntled—

acting as cook and provider for son, community (while not providing gingerbread the house offers more adult fare in its capacity as
inn or bar), and, symbolically, a nation (Fiddian 1989: 297). She is
a figure 'integrated . . . in the fixed order of patriarchy' (Fiddian
1989: 296), but the film also shows the resentment and anger of a
woman constrained by the social and economic injustices of a
conservative order. Martina's contemptuous refusal of the gratuity
offered by one of the *Gobernador*'s entourage, and her resentment
of the *Gobernador*'s attitude towards her and his 'hermano de
leche', who may even turn out to be his incestuous son/brother,
Ángel (has Santiago, too, been sleeping with Martina on his peri-
odic visits to the country?), may be read as clues of a repressed
deeper rage against, specifically, her own situation and, more
generally, the condition of most women in Spain at that time. The
brunt of that fury is perhaps most acutely felt by her recognized
son, Ángel, whom she treats ambivalently, at times berating him for
failing to live up to ideal standards of stereotyped macho masculinity (as when she complains about having to shoulder responsibility
for what she considers are his physical duties), at others retarding
him, continually infantilizing him, and, through abuse, guaranteeing his failure to develop fully as a man. As Adrienne Rich remarks,
the matriarch's possessiveness and control, an unproblematical
desire for the exercise of power, is perhaps better interpreted as
'survival—strength, guts, the determination that her children's lives
shall come to something even if it means driving them, or
sacrificing her own pride in order to feed and clothe them' (Rich
1984: 203). To some extent—in line with Adrienne Rich's general
argument—Ángel is Martina's agent in the system, the confused
child-man, simultaneously her challenge to the system, since he is
after all, as game poacher, a law-breaker—patriarchy's transgres-
sor—and her compensation for that system's victimization, above
all, of women. The monstrous-femininity of Martina might more
reasonably be viewed as an angry revolt against the kind of attitudes exemplified by figures like Juan Ametller Portella in
Pedagogía familiar:

A las hembras hay que cuidarlas con el mismo esmero y cuidado que a los
varones, no empantalonarlas, no permitir que jueguen al estilo varón, ni
juegos propios de varones, reprimir todo gesto, todo ademán, toda actitud
propia del hombre, no tolerarle malas crianzas, como responder varonil-
mente o con altivez a una reprimenda o advertencia dada. Darle a conocer

que esa actitud desdice de toda hembra o niña auténticamente femenina. Eso es muy formativo y convence a la hija. Y así como al varón se le debe impedir el que barra, el que juegue con muñecas, el que friegue, el que corte o cosa, el que gesticule o actúe como mujer; de la misma manera, hay que impedir que la niña o señorita transporte potes, haga mudanzas, mueva pesos en el interior o fuera de la casa, e incluso impedir con todo el rigor posible que se imponga o pretenda dominar al niño varón, así sea él inferior en edad. (Juan Ametller Portella in Aguado et al. 1994: 387)

The aggression of the mother does not only find expression in her savage butchering of the captive wolf, and the murder of Milagros, but also in the ambivalent treatment of her son. The assault on the wolf seems like a displaced attack on what in the eighth circle of hell Dante calls the 'Sins of the Wolf'. Here the wolf suffers the fury of Martina's rage against the female usurper, Milagros, and of her incoherent, wayward feelings against the fraud and malice of Francoism. Human physical aggression is directed exclusively towards animals, thus avoiding the romanticization of violence so characteristic of the Hollywood cinema (e.g. in films like *Bonnie and Clyde*, Arthur Penn, 1967). Violence against helpless animals merely shocks and, by analogy, exposes the horror of violence perpetrated by humans against one another. The psychological violence to which Martina subjects her son to some extent derives from inchoate feelings of rage against the system of which she is both an emblem and a victim. As José, the oldest brother of the black brood in *Camada negra*, puts it, while the mother (María Luisa Ponte) may seem to hold the reins of power in the family, the patriarch really does so.

In obedience to the confused desires of a woman whose maternal role within the social order is both centralized and marginalized, both revered and trivialized, Ángel is encouraged to accept his place in the patriarchal world, to become proficient in the use of guns as a hunter and poacher—where the hunting terrain clearly becomes the symbolic ambience of sexual potency—while at the same time, paradoxically, remaining tied to his mother's apron-strings in an incestuous bond that prevents him from gaining true independence and full integration into patriarchy. This paradox of ill-matched ambitions for her son reflects Martina's contradictory situation as a woman, someone attempting to use her offspring—whom she regards as an extension of herself—both as the screen for her own displaced desire and as the potential source of transgression against the power of the very system which, at another level, she respects and endorses.

Martina both fears and welcomes the price of her son's entry into the social order, in her ideologically warped psyche displacing onto him her contradictory feelings of hostility and gratification aroused by a system of which she has become twice a victim, first by the introjected ideals of a phallocentric order and, secondly, by the revenge meted out by her tormented and equally victimized son.

Borau's *Furtivos* is remarkable not only because of its uncompromising treatment of controversial material, but also because it is one of a handful of films marking the first stage of more direct challenges to the prejudices of a regime on the verge of final breakdown. In its representation, above all, of women, especially mothers, it provides an opportunity for the release of muffled voices. Martina's voice is the sound of the repressed returning in monstrous form. Later films, especially those made in the late 1980s and 1990s by women directors like Pilar Miró or Icíar Bollaín (the former a pupil of Borau's, the latter appearing as an actress in his latest film, *Niño nadie*, 1997) living in times marked, as Anny Brooksbank-Jones points out (1997), by enormous progress in the lives of Spanish women, indirectly acknowledge a debt to films like *Furtivos*. *El pájaro de la felicidad* (1993), for instance, and *Hola ¿estás sola?* (1995) represent female experience beyond the limits of monstrous-feminine images constructed in a climate of institutionalized prejudice. But they are the heirs to a legacy partially handed down by a film like *Furtivos*.

In its representation of the male, the film seems deliberately intent, above all through its uncompromising portrayal of the traumatized Ángel, on instilling that necessary anxiety in men both on- and off-screen defined by the transitory delusions and securities of Francoist constructions of masculinity.

In some ways the film is the Spanish *Psycho* (made by one of Borau's great heroes). The mother–son relationship is the key element in the overall pattern of abuse, of victims and victimizers, and of whole-sale exploitation, whose determinants, to a large extent intelligible through acknowledgement of the destructive power of ideology, are ultimately made to seem as dark and mysterious as the perverse desires by which the film's characters are ceaselessly tormented. Given the historical realities of the time, the lasting impressions of the film are the cries for freedom associated with the figure of *El Cuqui*, disturbing the silence of the countryside with the rasping noise of his motorcycle, the flight of Milagros from the ideological cloisters of the reformatory, and Ángel's final release from the prison of maternal abuse in the snow-covered landscape where he sentences Martina to the fatal consequences of a seemingly inevitable act of matricide.

REFERENCES

Aguado, A. M., et al. (1994), *Textos para la historia de las mujeres en España*. Madrid: Cátedra.
Bettelheim, Bruno (1988), *The Uses of Enchantment: The Meaning and Importance of Fairy Tales*. Harmondsworth: Penguin Books (1st pub. 1976).
Brooksbank-Jones, Anny (1997), *Women in Contemporary Spain*. Manchester: Manchester University Press.
Butler, Judith (1990), *Gender Trouble: Feminism and the Subversion of Identity*. New York: Routledge.
Chodorow, Nancy (1984), *The Reproduction of Mothering: Psychoanalysis and the Sociology of Gender*. Berkeley and Los Angeles: University of California Press (1st pub. 1978).
Creed, Barbara (1993), *The Monstrous-Feminine: Film, Feminism, Psychoanalysis*. London: Routledge.
Fiddian, Robin W. (1989), 'The Roles and Representation of Women in Two Films by José Luis Borau', in Jennifer Lowe and Philip Swanson (eds.), *Essays on Hispanic Themes in Honour of Edward C. Riley*, Edinburgh: Edinburgh University Press: 289–314.
Greer, Germaine (1972), *The Female Eunuch*. New York: Bantam Books.
Heredero, Carlos F. (1990), *José Luis Borau: teoría y práctica de un cineasta*. Madrid: Instituto de la Cinematografía y las Artes Audiovisuales.
Hopewell, John (1986), *Out of the Past: Spanish Cinema after Franco*. London: BFI.
Kaplan, E. Ann (1990), 'Motherhood and Representation: From Postwar Freudian Figurations to Postmodernism', in E. Ann Kaplan (ed.), *Psychoanalysis and Cinema*, New York: Routledge: 128–42.
Kinder, Marsha (1993), *Blood Cinema: The Reconstruction of National Identity in Spain*. Berkeley and Los Angeles: University of California Press.
Rich, Adrienne (1984), *Of Woman Born: Motherhood as Experience and Institution*. London: Virago (1st pub. 1976).
Sáez, Elena (1989), *José Luis Borau*. Málaga: XVII Semana Internacional de Cine de Autor de Málaga, Publicaciones Semanautor.
Sánchez Vidal, Agustín (1990), *Borau*. Zaragoza: Caja de Ahorros de la Inmaculada.
Welldon, Estela V. (1992), *Mother, Madonna, Whore: The Idealization and Denigration of Motherhood*. London: Guilford Press (1st pub. 1988).

9

Sex Change and Cultural Transformation in Aranda and Abril's *Cambio de sexo* (1977)

MARSHA KINDER

IN March 1997 I attended a sold-out screening of *Cambio de sexo* (1977) in Los Angeles that was part of a 'Vicente Aranda Tribute' within the American Cinematheque's annual series on 'Recent Spanish Cinema'—a screening which enabled me to see this film with new eyes. Recognizing many persons in the audience and overhearing conversations about the film, I realized this was not the typical crowd for the annual Spanish series, which usually has a particular interest in Hispanic culture. Rather, these enthused spectators were primarily gay males or fans of Victoria Abril, whom most of them probably came to know in Pedro Almodóvar's outrageous melodramas, such as *¡Atame!* (1989), *Tacones lejanos* (1991), and *Kika* (1993); or in the French nominee for the 1995 foreign-language Oscar, *French Twist*; or in Aranda's *noir* thriller *Amantes* (1991), his only box-office success thus far in the United States.

Seeing *Cambio de sexo* with this reception community made me want to address three issues: the relationship of this film to an international genre of subversive melodrama that takes sex seriously as a political issue; the casting of Victoria Abril as a transsexual, which helped launch a star discourse of eroticized sexual mobility that other film-makers like Almodóvar would later build on; and the use of sex change as an effective trope for cultural transformation, particularly within the specific context of Spain during the mid-1970s. While the American Cinematheque audience seemed attuned to the first two issues (which provided easy access into the text), they seemed less aware of the third. This essay will address these three issues as they are manifest in two different readings of the film—one set specifically within Spain's period of political transition between the death of Franco in 1975 and the election of the Socialists in 1982, and the other a transcultural and transhistorical reading that helps explain why *Cambio* can still be a cutting edge text for an international gay audience in the 1990s.

Produced in 1976 and first released in 1977, *Cambio* tells the story of José María, an effeminate 17-year-old boy living with his bourgeois family in the provinces outside Barcelona. Tormented at school by fellow students who call him a 'maricón', he is unjustly expelled by the principal because his 'abnormality' is too threatening to the other boys. Although supported by a loving mother and sister, he is treated harshly by his father, who takes him to a Barcelona night club for his sexual initiation as a man. The plan backfires, for not only does the boy fail to perform with the whore hired by his father, but he also discovers a stunningly beautiful female impersonator (played by real-life transsexual Bibi Andersen in her screen debut) who provides a new imaginary of sexual transformation. Running away from home, he goes to Barcelona where he can experiment more freely with cross-dressing. Although inexperienced, he successfully rents a room from a sympathetic landlady (played by comic actress Rafaela Aparicio) and gets a job as a hairdresser in a salon. In these two feminine spaces his effeminacy is not only tolerated but appreciated. His sexual transformation from José María to María José is accelerated by a visit from his sister Lolita and a chance meeting in the salon with Bibi Andersen, who becomes his customer and mentor. After a violent incident with his first date, he tries to castrate himself. Once recovered, he returns to his family but is again rejected by his father. Back in Barcelona, he is recruited by Bibi to become a female impersonator in the night club where she performs. In an impromptu audition staged by Bibi for her boss Durán (played by Fassbinder veteran Lou Castel), these two gorgeous creatures do a tango that evokes the one performed by Dominique Sanda and Stefania Sandrelli in Bertolucci's *Il conformista* (1969). As María José undergoes rigorous training to become a convincing woman, she begins to rival Bibi both on stage and with Durán, with whom she falls in love. After overcoming several romantic difficulties, the couple flies to Morocco for the surgery that completes José María's sex change and enables them to fulfil their goal of heterosexual marriage.

Historicizing the Trope of Sexual Mobility

The year of *Cambio*'s release, 1977, was also the year when Spain held its first free elections, legalized its Communist Party, and officially abolished censorship. Despite these liberalizing changes, there was still good reason for caution, for radical left-wing films were still the target of right-wing terrorist bombing (as in the case of Gutiérrez Aragón's *Camada negra*, 1977) or even of government delays and harassment (as in the case of Miró's *El crimen de cuenca*, 1979). Partly because of the 1973 assassination of Franco's hand-picked successor Admiral Luis Carrero Blanco by Basque terrorists, many Spaniards expected the post-Franco transition to be violent. Thus it still made sense to filter political critiques through a discourse of sexual transgression, as had been done during the Francoist period.

Cambio was based on a news story published in the French journal *Le Nouvel Observateur* which Aranda's Catalan collaborator Carlos Durán had read in 1972, about a Belgian transsexual who died after the surgery that transformed him into a woman. Working with Joaquín Jordá, Aranda wrote a script called *Una historia clínica* (A Clinical History), which was rejected by the censors and which had to wait until the death of Franco before being transformed into *Cambio de sexo*. According to Aranda: 'When we went to present the script to the Ministry in 1976, we had no problems. We didn't have to make any cuts because, although censorship was still in force, it was already less rigorous' (quoted Alvares and Frías 1991: 103).

The economic sphere also provided good reasons for using sexually explicit material. After the suspension of censorship, Spain was flooded with foreign films that included big-budget Hollywood movies as well as soft-core porn, which drew Spanish spectators away from the domestic product. Moreover, partly because of the growth of home video and the diversification of Spanish television, movie attendance drastically declined (from 331 million spectators in 1970 to 101 million in 1985), with the Spanish percentage of this shrinking market also decreasing from 30 per cent in 1970 to 17.5 per cent in 1985. The use of outrageous sexual material was one way for Spanish film-makers to compete for the liberated Spaniard's attention within this unstable market.

Cambio was not the only Spanish film of the mid-1970s to use sexual mobility as a trope for post-Franco cultural transformations or to feature a protagonist who 'comes out' both sexually and politically. But whereas other key works (such as Jaime Chávarri's *A un dios desconocido*, 1977, Eloy de la Iglesia's *El diputado*, 1978, and Jaime de Armiñán's *Al servicio de la mujer española*, 1978) tended to emphasize the past (shown in flashbacks or dramatic reconstructions) and to restage familiar Oedipal scenarios in this new arena of political instability, *Cambio* was the first to focus on the actual process of sexual transformation itself. Nor did these other films deal with transsexualism or even cross-dressing, except for *Al servicio*, where the protagonist only pretends to be homosexual to entrap a reactionary female radio star, on whom he displaces the rage he feels towards his dead mother (whom he impersonates with the aid of his nanny). Another notable exception, besides *Cambio*, is Ventura Pons's fascinating 1978 documentary about a well-known Catalan artist who was also a transvestite, *Ocaña: retrato intermitente*. I do not mean to suggest that *Cambio* was necessarily more 'progressive' than these other films from the 1970s, for it does not deal with the political realities of the gay movement (which were addressed by *Il diputado* and, to a lesser degree, by *Ocaña* and *A un dios desconocido*) and, more significantly, it does not even include any homosexual characters. According to Stephen Tropiano,

The unprecedented popularity of gay-themed films by a mass audience during Spain's democratic transitional period (1975–1978) was due to de la Iglesia's ability to link homosexuality as a marginalized form of sexuality to current sociopolitical issues . . . De la Iglesia, a committed Marxist, is equally concerned with other forms of 'difference'—economic, political, and social—which marginalize individuals in patriarchal Spain. Thus by politicizing homosexuality, the writer/director broadens the appeal of a subject matter that had been virtually absent from Spanish cinema until the early 1970s. (1997: 158)

The fact that heterosexual directors such as Aranda and Armiñán turned to transsexuality as a trope for political change demonstrates this process of 'broadening', even if it cannot be traced so directly to de la Iglesia as Tropiano claims, for these same dynamics were also used in Armiñán's earlier film *Mi querida señorita* (1971), which provides the most interesting comparison with *Cambio*. Perhaps one reason these straight directors turned to the gay world for the sexual trope was the 1970 passage of the Social Danger and Rehabilitation Law, which 'criminalized homosexual acts and empowered the police to arrest any man suspected of homosexuality because of the potential threat he posed to society' and which 'included a reeducation component . . . to "guarantee the reform and rehabilitation of the dangerous with more technical means of purification" ' (Tropiano 1997: 158). According to Tropiano, by 1972 this law, 'the most severe anti homosexual legislation in modern Spanish history', helped launch the Spanish homosexual rights movement. It was in this gap between the passage of the law and the birth of the gay movement that *Mi querida señorita* was produced.

Played by José Luis López Vázquez, the protagonist of *Mi querida señorita* is a bourgeois middle-aged woman from the provinces who, after being surgically transformed into a man, moves to Madrid where he is free to work and pursue his desire for his former young maid across traditional barriers of class and generation. Made during the Francoist era, this remarkable film was nominated for a foreign-language Oscar, partly because it was able to use sex change as an effective trope for political transformation, particularly within a nation that supposedly consists of 'the two Spains' (those dedicated to preserving the nation's cultural and moral purity versus those committed to the ongoing project of modernization). The 'free man' trapped within the ageing body of a repressed provincial spinster was analogous to those libertarians who were suffering an 'inner exile' under Franco, waiting to be reborn in a modern, urbanized, post-Franco Spain. The film implies it is simply a matter of an essentialist core being trapped in the wrong body or within the wrong government, waiting to be freed. Thus, when the doctor (played by Armiñán's producer and co-writer José Luis Borau) tells the protagonist, 'You are strong and courageous, but you are *not* a woman!', his diagnosis might be essentialist and highly problematic on the register of gender, but within the political subtext it was, indeed, strong and courageous. Instead of witnessing the surgery, we see the long train ride to Madrid and through the new eyes of the transsexual the streets of this bustling urban centre where the process of cultural transformation is already well in progress. Ironically, although the film celebrates the liberation that the transsexual finds in the city and although it grants a desiring gaze to both genders, neither the male nor female body is eroticized. The representation of sexuality remains very discreet, not only because of the censorship norms of the times but also because the political subtext is the primary source of the film's subversive power.

In contrast to *Mi querida señorita*, *Cambio* shows a wariness about Spain's new libertarian identity, implying it might someday prove to be the oppressive double of the fascist regime it had replaced, a wariness that was partially justified by the series of moral scandals (including a secret campaign to eradicate Basque terrorists) that led to the 1996 defeat of the Socialist government after thirteen years of uninterrupted left-wing rule. Thus, more than these other films from the 1970s, *Cambio* anticipated later works produced in the early Socialist era, such as Antonio Giménez Rico's documentary *Vestida de azul* (1983), Imanol Uribe's *La muerte de Mikel* (1983), and Almodóvar's *La ley del deseo* (1986), which all show how the legacy of Francoist repression is still internalized within a supposedly hyperliberated Spain.

Cambio de sexo *as Subversive Melodrama*

From a 1990s perspective, *Cambio* seems firmly positioned within the genre of melodrama, which highlights sexual and generational conflicts within the family and features stylistic excess and lurching ruptures of tone. This form was used subversively by Fassbinder and Bertolucci (whose work is invoked within *Cambio*) as well as by other well-known European auteurs such as Visconti, Pasolini, Bardem, and Buñuel. Yet in November 1994 at a panel at New York University on 'Spanish Cinema in the 1990s: Sexuality, Melodrama, and Global Desire', Aranda denied that any of his work was melodrama, for he claimed the term was pejorative and that this genre was incompatible with the kind of realism he cultivates in his films.

Cambio can be read as a realistic 'clinical history' of a transsexual, particularly since the story was based on a real-life event discovered by documentary film-maker Carlos Durán (who is credited with the story idea and after whom one of the main characters is named). From this perspective, the film documents the case of a female subject trapped in a male body who must undergo a long process of transformation that culminates in a surgical procedure, which is described in graphic detail. Yet since her driving ambition is to become a 'real woman' who can find love and happiness in a heterosexual marriage, her saga could also be read as a transsexual woman's film, a subgenre to which both *Cambio* and *Mi querida señorita* belong. While the realism of the 'case study' helped disavow the political implications of the subtext (particularly for the censors), Armiñán and Borau deliberately positioned that subtext within the familiar genre of domestic melodrama—a practice, as I have argued elsewhere, that was common in Spanish cinema during the Francoist era and that also seems operative within *Cambio* (Kinder 1993: esp. ch. 2).

Nevertheless, at the NYU conference, Aranda identified the term 'melodrama' with theatre and seemed unaware that this genre had been redefined as a subversive rather than a regressive form, particularly in Peter Brooks's seminal book *The Melodramatic Imagination* (1976), which was published the same year that Aranda's film was made. Defining the melodramatic imagination as 'an abiding mode in the modern imagination' that is characterized by excess and that cuts across many periods, cultures, and art forms, Brooks claims the extravagant representations and moral intensity of melodrama simultaneously place it in opposition to the realistic mode and yet require a realistic context to rupture: 'Within an apparent context of "realism" and the ordinary, they seemed in fact to be staging a heightened and hyperbolic drama, making reference to pure and polar concepts of darkness and light, salvation and damnation' (1976: p. ix).

This is precisely how melodrama functions in *Cambio*, where an elaborately structured series of extravagant theatrical performances rupture the ordinary realism of the case study, which leads not to polar concepts of morality and class (as in *Mi querida señorita*) but more specifically to conflicts between male and female sexuality, patriarchal law and transgressive desire, mainstream norms and subversive marginality, romance and travesty, loss and recuperation. Unlike other recent popular drag movies from other nations like *To Wong Foo, Priscilla, Queen of the Desert*, and *Paris is Burning*, none of *Cambio*'s performances is played for laughs; instead, they raise a complex set of subversive ironies. This particular form of melodrama enables the film to be read productively across different cultures and periods and in relationship to recent queer theory. For it invites an alternative reading that problematizes not only the optimism over

Spain's political changes but also the essentialism of the unified gender identification achieved by José María through surgery and the heterosexual dream that drives it. It is this kind of reading that distinguishes *Cambio* from its predecessor, *Mi querida señorita*.

In this alternative reading the iterative nature of *Cambio*'s theatrical performances is crucial because it implies that gender and sexuality are not freely chosen by an individual through any singular act but are materialized through a series of repeated actions that are regulated by social and historical forces—a process that has been theorized most powerfully by Judith Butler.

Performativity cannot be understood outside of a process of iterability, a regularized and constrained repetition of norms. And this repetition is not performed *by* a subject; this repetition is what enables a subject and constitutes the temporal condition for the subject. This iterability implies that 'performance' is not a singular 'act' or event, but a ritualized production, a ritual reiterated under and through constraint, under and through the force of prohibition and taboo, with the threat of ostracism and even death controlling and compelling the shape of the production, but not, I will insist, determining it fully in advance (1993: 95).

In *Cambio*, José María's decision to 'become a real woman' is not only repeatedly prohibited by his father and commanded by his heterosexual lover Durán but also repeatedly urged by his sympathetic female mentors (his sister Lolita, his landlady Doña Pilar, and his transsexual friend Bibi) who have absorbed the culture's gender norms through education, mass media, and the family.

The first pair of transformative performances is witnessed by José María in the company and at the command of his censorious father, whose own sexual stability is compromised by his presence in this drag club and by his exaggerated womanizing machismo, which is presented as a form of drag. Like the potential male lovers whom José María will later encounter in Barcelona, the father displaces any sign of his own sexual instability onto his son by harshly condemning and threatening to physically punish the boy's so-called 'abnormality'. Yet these repeated prohibitions help shape and eroticize the boy's transgressive fantasies—a dynamic that is mirrored in the first rupturing performance.

Unfolding like a surrealistic dream, the first performance begins with a man in white walking onto the stage and being attacked by four topless female dancers, who appear to be raping him, which suggests the sexual instability of the heterosexual male. This sexual transgression is interrupted by a prim lady who is discreetly dressed in a long, high-necked red dress from a past era and whose spectacles emphasize her role as voyeur. As the lady picks up a dead chicken (a Buñuelian icon), the four topless women assemble a mirror before her, as if to reveal what lies beyond (or behind) her dignified persona. Her mirror image (who is played by a different woman) begins to strip. As if to prevent this female split subject from exposing herself and her erotic desires or perhaps to express his own aggressive sexuality, another man in white enters the scene and shoots the naked imaginary signifier, splattering her body with blood. This performance evokes Butler's retheorization of Lacan's mirror phase.

The body in the mirror does not represent a body that is, as it were, before the mirror: the mirror, even as it is instigated by that unrepresentable body 'before' the mirror, produces that body as its delirious effect—a delirium, by the way, which we are compelled to live. (Butler 1993: 91)

   This description aptly applies to the performers on stage—not only to the 'split' female who, like José María, experiences a gap between the inner and outer self but also to the killer with his phallic weapon, who mirrors the hypermasculinity of José María's father with his phallic cigar. It applies equally well to father and son who are watching this spectacle that mirrors their own relationship. The mirror scene has a delirious effect on the boy which compels him to adopt this performance as a prophetic scenario that he will re-enact in a series of castrating performances—on stage, in bedrooms and bathrooms, and ultimately in the surgical theatre of the hospital. This process is facilitated by the fact that two of the performers will figure prominently in his sex life: the mirror image is played by Fanny, his father's whore who is hired to initiate him sexually and who later will humiliate him as he performs on stage; and the first man in white turns out to be María José's love interest Durán, whom her love will save from his demeaning life with strippers. The second, murderous man in the white coat prefigures the doctor who will perform the surgery that eliminates the gap between the female subject and her imaginary. Not yet understanding such symbolic meanings, José María, when asked whether he likes this number, responds, 'Yes, it's fun.'
   This act is immediately followed by the stunning transvestite headliner, Bibi Andersen, who is introduced as 'a mystery of

nature' and 'the biological enigma of the century'. As if offering an alternative condensed version of the previous act, she performs a provocative striptease, which ends with the display of her penis. As she says in a later scene, the penis is crucial to the act, for it proves the double nature of her performance (both as a dancer and as a woman) which must be read against two different sets of norms; without it, she has to rely merely on *her* own talent without the uncanny spectacle of the freaky hybridization of the sexes. Not surprisingly, the reactions of the spectators-in-the-text to this performance are more personally engaged. Obviously threatened by the display of the penis on a performer who has aroused his desire, the father asks Fanny, 'Is it stuck on?' Revealing the jealousy she feels toward this rival performer, Fanny responds: 'The tits are stuck on, the rest is his own.' Disavowing his earlier experience of pleasure, the father assures her: 'I like the old dancers better.' Meanwhile, José María remains silent, absorbed in his own delirium over this new set of thrilling possibilities.

The next pair of performances concern María José's first 'date' in Barcelona. The first is private: José María is home alone on a Sunday, luxuriating in a female masquerade for his own pleasure and a queer reception of popular culture. While listening to a women's programme on the radio (the kind that is central in *Al servicio de la mujer española*) and while watching a soap opera on television, he first dons a virginal white communion gown and vogues dramatically on the bed, then puts on a sexy red dress, as he freely adapts the dialogue and gestures transmitted over the airwaves. He wears this red dress to the public space of the night club where he meets a handsome, moustached Burt Reynolds lookalike who is wearing a white jacket (like the two men in the first prophetic performance).

The second performance occurs the next day when María José, dressed to look like a young innocent schoolgirl, waits for her date, who rides up on a motorcycle wearing a helmet and a racing driver's uniform. Since both are deceptively costumed, there is misrecognition on both sides: she mistakes him for a cop until he takes off his helmet, and he thinks that when she said, 'I'm not exactly a woman!' she meant that she was a virgin, not a transvestite. Yet, as in the injustice at school with which the film opened, the only consideration is the discomfort of the empowered heterosexual male (a category fetishized in the huge poster of Mark Spitz that dominates the room in which her deflowering was to be performed). When the Reynolds impersonator discovers María José's penis, he hits her; in response, José María tries to cut off his own balls, drawing blood as in the first prophetic performance.

The next pairings of performances are more complex, leading us to compare what happens at home with his father and in Barcelona with Durán. To help his son return to 'a decent life', the father assigns him an arduous regimen of work, which may allude to the re-education programme mandated for suspected homosexuals by the Social Danger and Rehabilitation Law. The performance of these repetitive tasks is presented in a montage sequence accompanied by classical melancholy music. When the father discovers women's lingerie in his son's bedroom, he forces him to dress as a woman. Intuitively realizing that this command is designed to test the sexual stability of the father more than that of the son, José María meets his challenge. Discreetly drawing the curtains behind rather than in front of him, as if to shield his naked body from the gaze of us spectators in the movie theatre, he boldly confronts his father with frontal nudity and then with his convincing drag in a red dress. As if that were not sufficient provocation, he then vogues with a sexy come-on gesture, which elicits a slap from his father. In demonstrating that his own sexual mobility is as threatening to his father as it was to the Reynolds simulacrum, José María is liberated from his patriarchal dominance and is free to return to Barcelona.

In Barcelona, the sequential order of the contrasting double performances is reversed. First, there is another dress-up sequence where he is directed not by his censorious father but by a sympathetic surrogate mother, his landlady Doña Pilar. Not only does she advise José María about make-up and wigs, but she loans him a wonderful outfit from 1944, which he wears when he goes to the club and first meets Durán. Evoking the vintage costume of the dignified lady in the first prophetic performance (as well as the gowns worn by Sanda and Sandrelli in Il conformista), this dress is worn by María José in the transgressive tango with Bibi (who replaces Fanny as mirror reflection), which brings the two sides of the divided woman (lady and stripper) closer together in a collaborative number now performed in synch. Telling María José that she 'could become a spectacular woman . . . even better than Bibi' (a promise motivated by Bibi's altered status as a transsexual) and assigning her a new theatrical name alliterative with his own

(Diana Darcy), Durán becomes a Pygmalion who commands her to undergo rigorous training that is designed 'to wipe out all masculine mentality'. In case one misses the analogy between these labours and those assigned by José María's father to make him a 'man', this sequence is also presented as a montage accompanied by melancholy classical music, but this time the imagery consists of huge stylized facial close-ups (evocative of Bergman's *Persona* and of similar transformative sequences in Nicolas Roeg and Donald Cammel's *Performance*) rather than realistic medium and long shots as in the earlier work montage. Bibi helps supervise the training, which couples her with Durán as surrogate parents and Oedipalizes the rivalry between the two female impersonators. Although María José performs both sets of labour, she continues to offer resistance—both to Durán's domination and to the repetitive tasks of steaming, plucking, creaming, piercing, and exercising that are required of any *body* that wants to be made over into a so-called 'desirable woman'. Insisting she is a 'natural' woman who had no masculine mentality to begin with, she tries to fetishize the breast and womb in place of the phallus. For her, it is a matter of body parts—of getting rid of the penis, which she fears Durán wants her to expose on stage (the way Bibi did in the original pair of performances), which will evoke the same castrating behaviour from him that it did from the Reynolds lookalike and her father. As María José puts it, 'I don't want to show it . . . I want to forget it . . . I don't want to be an enigma like Bibi, just a real woman.'

The next two pairs of performances are presented as an extension of this training and as the development of the problematic relationship between María José and Durán; like the original pair, they both have a prelude involving an angry encounter with another woman. The first pair is introduced by a rehearsal (with an older female coach and Durán looking on), which is followed by the actual debut performance of the same number. Preceded by a disturbing primal scene (like the one in the first prophetic performance) where Bibi arrives with champagne and finds María José kissing Durán, the next performance is similarly interrupted, this time by Fanny and a male customer who hits María José with a champagne cork while she is dancing on stage. When María José asks Durán to fire Fanny, he refuses. These performances reveal María José's growing sense of frustration with Durán, which erupts in the transgressive performance that follows.

Set within a flamenco bar where transvestites freely mingle with straight gypsies who are equally marginalized within Spanish culture, this public performance is the only one in the film where there is no barrier between performers and spectators. For the first time, we see María José dancing for her *own* pleasure. She performs with a wild, drunken abandon that is sexier than the carefully choreographed moves of her previous numbers. The dance becomes most transgressive when she clutches an empty wine bottle between her legs, mocking the phallus that has oppressed her because of its position not on her own body, from which it is easily detachable, but within the symbolic order. As if reversing the situation from the opening prophetic performance, this scene of transgressive pleasure is interrupted by Durán, who makes her retreat in fear and aggressively pursues her with a castrating verbal attack: 'You're nothing but a shitty transvestite . . . I'll never think of you as a woman!' Accusing her of travestying herself, he is actually threatened by her mocking of the phallus, on which his own powers as a heterosexual male are propped. In Butler's terms, she challenges its originary position by showing it is not a given and therefore can be replaced.

In expiation for this transgressive performance at the gypsy bar, María José performs the number that Durán wants her to sing, 'Mi cosita'. After coyly performing as an innocent Little Bo Peep who claims she will keep her 'pretty little thing' a secret, she lifts her skirt and reveals (in a flat cut to an inserted genital close-up) María José's (but not Abril's) tiny penis. Redirecting the mockery from the symbolic phallus to her own body part, she submits to Durán's castrating domination, which inserts rather than removes the penis. This time it *is* stuck on! She suffers a humiliation greater than Bibi's, for it is overdetermined by three subordinate identifications: as child, as female, and as physically inadequate male. It is this submissive performance that makes Durán ask for her forgiveness and declare his love: 'I wondered why I did it . . . I don't know.' To answer his question, we must recall the original prophetic performance where he is almost raped by four women. By castrating and infantilizing his boyfriend, Durán maintains the illusion of his own 'pure' masculinity and disavows his own homoerotic desire. From this perspective, the ending is as closeted as the opening.

This is where Aranda and his co-writer Jordá claim they wanted the film to end. Instead, they added an epilogue that provided a 'happy' ending that was more appealing to audiences and that humanized Durán, who, according to Aranda, could be seen as merely 'an exploiter of circus freaks' (Alvares and Frías 1991: 110). It also provided further ironies. From these declarations of love there is a flat cut to an aeroplane (an image parodied in the ending of Almodóvar's *Laberinto de pasiones* where the nymphomaniac heroine flies off with her bisexual Iranian royal), which shows them on their way to Morocco for the surgery (the same trajectory later pursued by the transsexual played by Carmen Maura in *La ley del deseo*, whose sex change is literally designed to please her incestuous father who rejects her). On the political register, Morocco is also the site from which Franco launched his coup that would convert Spain to fascism—an ironic connection that helps question whether the sex change really is so transformative.

José María's surgery is also presented as a series of interlinked performances. First, she is subjected to a battery of tests administered by patriarchal authorities, which, like the two earlier work montages, are designed to regulate her true gender and which earn their stamp of approval, 'You are *not* a homosexual!' After being warned that there is 'no going back', the happy couple is shown a medical slide show, with graphic drawings that (like the reversal of José María 's given names) demonstrate this sex change is basically a simple inversion: 'The skin of the penis, still with its tube-like shape, is turned inside out . . . and inserted into the new cavity . . . [which] is a functioning vagina.' The second performance, the actual operation, is performed in the hospital's surgical theatre. Only briefly suggested, it is quickly displaced by José María's dream, which hearkens back to the original prophetic performance. Costumed as bride and groom, María José and Durán dance in slow motion to melancholy music that evokes the transformative work regimes. As if repeating the moves of the transgressive tango earlier performed by Bibi and María José, they spin in circles and then he gently lays her down, in a deathlike posture. As he retreats, a bloody stain materializes on her white gown, suggesting the death of the phallus and its power. She awakens with him by her side, asking, 'Am I a woman now?' Though he tells her not to talk, she observes, 'I dreamed I died, now that I'm a woman.' Kissing her, he declares: 'You're alive and you're a woman . . . you've always been a woman.' She closes her eyes again, evoking the fate of the Belgian transsexual who died of a haemorrhage, the ending that Jordá actually preferred (Alvares and Frías 1991: 109). The image dissolves to a large close up of María José staring directly into the camera as a male voice-over declares, 'Six months later, María José experienced her first feminine orgasm.' These declarations about her sexuality and pleasure are hardly reassuring for they are voiced by the patriarchy which still controls the enunciation of the body and the text, while she is left with dangling questions and with silence.

Ironically, the only thing gained through all this arduous labour and suffering is the restoration of the heterosexual norm and the replacement of one tyrannical patriarch by another—a replacement of her father by her husband and, one might add, by Abril's director, Vicente Aranda.

Victoria Abril's Star Discourse of Sexual Mobility

The misinterpretation of José María's line, 'I am not exactly a woman!' acquires new resonance when applied to the dynamics between Aranda and Abril, who was only 16 when *Cambio* was shot and only 15 when he first spotted her in a film on TV. As Alvares and Frías astutely observe, 'The adolescent image of Victoria Abril permitted her character to be situated on an ambiguous plane between the two sexes' (1991: 106)—an observation which is consistent with Butler's claim that there is no pre-existing material body onto which sex or gender are imposed but rather the body and its sex are materialized through regularizing, reiterated norms. In the case of Abril, these norms would be inflected by the roles she played in Aranda's movies.

Aranda originally signed Angela Molina for the part of María José and was planning to use one of her brothers for the earlier scenes as José María, but she withdrew. This choice would not have required the sexual transformation to be performed on screen, as it is with Abril. As in *Mi querida señorita*, where the sexual transformation moves in the opposite direction (from female to male instead of from male to female), the transsexual is played by an actor of the gender to which the character aspires. This choice enables spectators of both genders to identify with the process of sex change—seeing a man playing a woman who aspires to be a man, and a woman playing a man who desires to be a woman—for both films involve a sex change in both directions.

Not only did Aranda give Abril her first demanding role in *Cambio* that established her as a sexual shifter, but he also cast her as Juan Marsé's protagonist Mariana in his film adaptation of *La muchacha de las bragas de oro* (1980). At first he did not believe that Abril was capable of playing a role that demanded female sensuality: 'I was accustomed to seeing Victoria as a kind of cabin boy in *Cambio de sexo* and thus I could not bring myself to see her as the luscious Mariana' (quoted Alvares and Frías 1991: 117). But after a long search for the right actress, he finally decided to give her the role:

After much thought, one night we said, 'Why not Victoria?', and we called her . . . When we were looking for her, she was then on tour singing. She was being taken around by her husband, Gustavo Laube, who was also her 'manager' and who almost ruined her. We saved her from the songs. (Quoted Alvares and Frías 1991: 118)

It is ironic that Aranda should make this comment when he himself cast Abril as a musical performer in *Cambio* and (like Durán) required her to sing 'Mi cosita'. Like Laube and Durán, Aranda could be seen as another patriarchal Pygmalion who shaped her image and sexuality through a series of regulating performances. Although Abril may be identified more strongly with Almodóvar by American spectators, in Spain she is closely associated with Aranda,[1] for he first gave her the roles that proved no matter how extreme or explicit the sexuality with which she was identified, she still retained credibility, sympathy, and dignity with audiences worldwide, an achievement to which a hyperliberated Socialist Spain also aspired.

According to Alvares and Frías, it was *La muchacha* rather than *Cambio* that consolidated the relationship between Aranda and Abril, whom, despite her petite stature and slender body, he would cast as a highly sensual figure in many films to come, including: *Asesinato en el comité central* (1982), *El crimen del Capitán Sánchez* (1985), *Tiempo de silencio* (1986), *El Lute, camina o revienta* (1987), *Se te dicen que caí* (1989), *Los jinetes del alba* (1990), *Amantes* (1991), and *Libertarias* (1996). Although she is not a great beauty, Abril's sexual intensity and the expressiveness of her body and face would lead other directors to cast her to play

---

[1] See Alvares and Frías 1991.

an impressive array of equally extreme sexualities, all of which she could make convincing regardless of how excessive the melodrama or how parodic the tone: whether it was the single mother who abandons her career as a scientist to enter the fantasy world of her autistic son in Salgot's *Mater amatísima* (1979); or the Mexican prostitute who murders the sadistic border guard and former client who has been terrorizing her in Borau's *Río abajo* (1984); or the incestuous daughter of a cardinal in Regueiro's *Padre Nuestro* (1985); or the porn queen who falls in love with her kidnapper in Almodóvar's *¡Átame!* (1989); or the parricidal daughter in Almodóvar's *Tacones lejanos* (1991) who is so obsessed with her famous mother that she first marries and then murders her mother's ex-lover and becomes impregnated by her mother's transvestite impersonator; or the monstrous 'video vamp' cyborg (to poach Paul Julian Smith's apt description) who 'takes pleasure in the confusion of boundaries' and who is 'masculinized as quest hero' in Almodóvar's *Kika* (1993);[2] or the victimized Spanish housewife in Josiane Balasko's *French Twist* (1994) who manipulates her adulterous French husband and lesbian lover into letting her move from one bed to the other; or the alcoholic prostitute who fights her way back to independence and self-respect in Llanes's *Nadie hablará de nosotras cuando hayamos muerto* (1995).[3] Even when playing in a non-Spanish film such as *French Twist*, Abril's mobile sexuality evokes the radical cultural and political change that Spain has undergone.

When we see major stars such as Abril or Maura performing such complex sexualities, particularly alongside a real-life transsexual like Bibi Andersen,[4] the iterative power of their sexual mobility is subversive, regardless of the specifics of the narrative. The frequent reiteration of such performances in Spanish films helped construct a new stereotype for a hyperliberated Spain—one that was popularized most successfully worldwide by Almodóvar

[2]   Smith 1996: 47–50. An image of Victoria Abril as Andrea, the video vamp, enlivens the cover of this book.

[3]   For an extended reading of Abril's performance in *Nadie hablará de nosotras cuando hayamos muerto*, see Kinder 1997: 1–32. Kinder 1993 also contains detailed readings of her performances in *Río abajo*, *Amantes*, and *Tacones lejanos*.

[4]   This juxtaposition would be repeated by Gutiérrez Aragón in *La noche más hermosa* (1984) and in several films by Almodóvar, including *La ley del deseo*, in which Abril has a brief, uncredited appearance, *Tacones lejanos*, and *Kika*.

but that was also extended through the star discourses of Antonio Banderas and Abril, who both crossed lines of nationality and gender. As if to reaffirm the Spanishness of his own mobile sexuality, at the height of the media hype around Banderas's crossover to Hollywood and his scandalous affair with Melanie Griffith, when asked by an American journalist which of his leading ladies was the sexiest, Banderas replied, 'Victoria Abril is the best kisser.'[5]

Abril represents not merely the cliché of the whore with a heart (or panties) of gold, but a woman whose spirit is so intense that, no matter whether expressed through sexuality, madness, motherlove, or violence, the fire of her passion purifies her soul. It is this intensity that enables her to embody the proverbial two Spains with their opposing extremes of uncompromising orthodoxy and unrestrained anarchy. This is the quality that makes her such an effective icon for the dramatic and unpredictable cultural transformations that were taking place in Spain in the wake of Franco's death in the mid-1970s and what helps keep *Cambio* alive in the 1990s for an international gay audience that increasingly believes (along with Butler, Smith, Tropiano, and other theorists) in the performativity of both gender and sexuality.

REFERENCES

Alvares Hernández, Rosa, and Frías, Belén (1991), *Vicente Aranda and Victoria Abril: el cine como pasión*. Valladolid: Semana Internacional de Cine de Valladolid.

Brooks, Peter (1976), *The Melodramatic Imagination: Balzac, Henry James, Melodrama, and the Mode of Excess*. New Haven: Yale University Press.

Butler, Judith (1993), *Bodies that Matter: On the Discursive Limits of 'Sex'*. New York: Routledge.

Kinder, Marsha (1993), *Blood Cinema: The Reconstruction of National Identity in Spain*. Berkeley and Los Angeles: University of California Press.

—— (1997), 'Refiguring Socialist Spain: An Introduction', in Marsha Kinder (ed.), *Refiguring Spain: Cinema/Media/ Representation*, Durham, NC: Duke University Press: 1–32.

[5] Rebello 1995: 37. For an extended discussion of the star discourse around Banderas, see Kinder 1997.

Rebello, Stephen (1995), 'Interview with Banderas', *Movieline*, 6/11: 37.

Smith, Paul Julian (1996), *Vision Machines: Cinema, Literature and Sexuality in Spain and Cuba, 1983–1993*. London: Verso.

Tropiano, Stephen (1997), 'Out of the Cinematic Closet: Homosexuality in the Films of Eloy de la Iglesia', in Marsha Kinder (ed.), *Refiguring Spain: Cinema/Media/Representation*, Durham, NC: Duke University Press: 157–77.

10

Feminism, Politics, and Psychosis in Fernán Gómez's *Mi hija Hildegart* (1977)

DOMINIC KEOWN

THERE can be little doubt, even in a cinematographic context as anomalous as post-war Spain, that there can have been few careers as peculiarly incongruous as that of Fernando Fernán Gómez's. His performance as actor, author, and director has ranged consistently from the highly acclaimed to the most rigorously censured: a creative trajectory which, perhaps not unsurprisingly, has been exactly paralleled in the perception of his endeavour in the sphere of political resistance to the regime.[1] As a result, it is not unusual that a similar disequilibrium should characterize his disturbingly provocative essay of 1977, *Mi hija Hildegart*.

The screenplay—an adaption by Rafael Azcona and the director himself of Eduardo Guzmán's unsettling biography of 1973, *Aurora de sangre*—recounts the cause célèbre four decades earlier of the notorious filicide Aurora Rodríguez Carbelleira (Amparo Soler Leal). Born into a middle-class Galician family at the end of the last century and appalled by the nymphomaniacal inability of her sisters to escape the limitations of the female condition, this would-be emancipator, educated at home by her father in a menacing amalgam of utopian socialism and the dubious but widespread scientific messianism of the epoch, embraces unquestioningly the possibilities offered by eugenics as a means to achieve the liberation of her sex. On the death of her mentor, this singular individual resolves to use her inheritance to realize a scheme to produce a daughter who, in the guise of some type of epic revolutionary heroine, will deliver woman from her state of oppression. To this effect, she 'selects' a

---

[1] The professional and personal trajectory of Fernán Gómez has been well documented and a reliable global vision is offered Galán and Llorens 1984.

suitable father for the master plan—a priest in the Spanish navy (Carles Velat)—whom she erroneously considers to possess those qualities of unsullied spirituality and reformatory zeal necessary for the realization of her genetically inspired ideological enterprise.

Shortly after a dispassionate fecundation she moves to the capital in 1914 where her daughter Hildegart (Carmen Roldán) is born. From her earliest years, the young girl is subjected to the most rigorous of educational discipline in line with the great project of her mother. By the age of 14 she has already passed her *bachillerato* and, after playing a prominent role in the Juventudes Socialistas, joins the ranks of the UGT. In 1932 she gains a degree in law at Madrid University and, already fluent in German, English, and Russian, enrols thereafter to read medicine. After a series of ideological disputes she is expelled from the Socialist Party and enlists in the Partido Republicano Federal, continuing her numerous publications in the left-wing press.

As is not unusual in these superhuman schemes of transcendence, however, disaster is soon to make an appearance. After a chance meeting with Hildegart's father, Aurora discovers she has been tragically duped: her co-genitor is revealed as no utopian reformer but a wanton libertine. Given her recalcitrant faith in eugenics, the protagonist develops a neurosis which comes to envisage the same dissolute fate for her daughter. In what is evidently a fit of paranoid-schizophrenia, she convinces herself that her offspring's decision to leave home and go to England is not due to the reality of her overbearing parental control and a desire to mature intellectually but is, in effect, both a manifestation of latent promiscuity and its inevitable ideological corollary: the hijacking of her progeny's revolutionary ideals by the forces of international reaction. As a result, she murders her daughter, shooting her four times as she lies asleep in her bed on the morning of 9 June 1933. In the subsequent trial, an event which the film describes in some detail, Aurora is found guilty of murder and sentenced to twenty-five years' imprisonment only to be transferred to a mental institution where she spends the rest of her life.

Historical Parallels

Although this case study is fascinating for its own intrinsic interest, it is abundantly apparent why it should be even more immediately relevant to a contemporary Spanish audience experiencing the day-to-day socio-political trauma of the Transition. The relevance of the parallel examination of the female condition at three crucial points of contemporary history is patent and requires little elucidation.[2] In the first instance, we receive a lyrical account of the harshness of existence of women during Aurora's formative years wherein, towards the end of the last century, patriarchal control over the family was total and uncompromising. Through the innocent eyes of the daughter we perceive the mother's dilemma as she desperately attempts to achieve a separation from her spouse but is coerced into accepting the inevitability of her intolerable attachment given that any estrangement would mean the certain loss of her children.

In due course we move to the era of the Second Republic—where the main body of the film is set—and are privileged with a further example which crystallizes the crude exploitation of women in this epoch. In the location of a fairground, esperpentically grotesque in its montage—exemplary of the much-commented theatricality of Fernán Gómez's cinematic expression—a *pim pam pum* stall has four women unceremoniously flung from their beds each time a target is hit by one of the male punters.[3] Finally, we are shown the present-day reality of the female condition as Eduardo Guzmán (Manuel Galiana), Aurora's biographer—who was actually acquainted with Hildegart and her mother—recounts the story in detail to the attendant waitresses of a red-light bar who, in their position of subordinate dependence, are shown to be as enslaved as their earlier counterparts. Indeed, the identity of the common situation is emphasized at the end of the final scene by how Eduardo rolls up his newspaper and, in a gesture of abject futility, throws it at the hookers in a manner which necessarily recalls the action of the earlier episode at the fairground.

The austerity of the repeated monochrome with its isolated splashes of red employed with great subtlety in these related scenes, the euphony of their various melodies and cacophony of busy street

---

[2] Further information on the female condition in Spain in the 20th century is available in the seminal survey Graham and Labanyi 1995. Of particular relevance are Graham 1995; Montero 1995; Brooksbank-Jones 1995.

[3] Marsha Kinder offers a complete explanation of the *esperpento* and its relevance to the Spanish theatrical and cinematographic tradition in her excellent survey *Blood Cinema* (Kinder 1993: 115–20). A more ideologically oriented study of this phenomenon is offered by Keown 1996.

noises, fairground bustle, shots, etc., together with the impression of a synchronic temporal scale effected by the repeated flashback in the narrative all serve to underline the homogeneity of the female condition in each of the three cases. The net result, of course, is an implicit statement of the lack of real progress in the area of emancipation in the Spain of this century despite the various periods of attempted reform. More disturbing for the spectators of 1977 is the realization that on two previous occasions in recent history—at the end of the last century and in the years of the Second Republic—the initiatives to achieve socio-political advance proved spectacularly abortive. The movie posits correspondingly the discomfiting question as to when real progress will be achieved in this respect: a topic of some poignancy for an audience aware of the severity of the reaction of the recalcitrant Right to the reformist programme of the Súarez administration and, more alarmingly, the continued plotting against the inchoate democracy among reactionary circles in the military which would shortly reach its culmination in the *Tejerazo* of 1981.

It is not merely the obvious historical parallels as regards female emancipation, however, which would disconcert the audience of the Transition. The film is, in essence, a character study of the protagonist, some of whose traits would be particularly familiar to viewers of the period. Despite her enlightened and progressive instincts, Aurora is an authoritarian tyrant. We are shown this inclination from the very start as, in the lyrical reminiscences of her childhood, she exerts a menacing control over her doll and looks forward eagerly to exercising a similar constraint over her future offspring. As is revealed in due course, her presentiment proves entirely accurate when, in later life, we see her violently force her daughter to live in accordance with the questionable morality of her own messianic purpose whilst she, sitting censoriously in the wings, vicariously delights in the development of the child's personality inasmuch as it coincides with her predetermined programme. The slightest deviation perceived from the ardour of the maternal strictures is brutally repressed, as is evinced graphically in the bathroom scene by the strong-arm removal of make-up from the 18-year-old's face and, finally, by the horrendously callous filicide.

There is not the slightest human warmth emanating from her person, an impression enhanced by Amparo Soler Leal's aggressively aloof representation of the character. Apart from the fleeting

moments of intimacy seen initially with her mother, Aurora struggles chronically to establish any type of cordiality in her relationship with those around her. In the first instance it is apparent that
from her own puritanical high moral ground she cannot relate to
her sisters in the slightest, reducing their relationship to a simple
detestation of the wantonness of their sexuality. The condition of
detached superiority recurs when she adopts the same lofty position with her fellow inmates in the remand prison in Madrid and is
accordingly beaten and reviled. Ironically, the severity of her ideological discourse is totally removed from their life experience and
she is cast out and disowned by the very class and gender whose
situation she is so keen to improve. Cold, implacable, and distant,
she exerts a tyrannical control over all those who fall into her
sphere; and there is little need to mention that such detached
intransigence and Pharisaic paternalism are features alarmingly
reminiscent of the late dictator, as would be immediately appreciated by the audience of the time.[4]

There are certain other items which emphasize the connection.
Aurora, like the Generalísimo, is a Galician sharing the same home
town of El Ferrol. More intriguing is the peculiar coincidence in the
hysterical amalgam of sexual and macro-political considerations
posited by the movie. Aurora sees her daughter as a victim not only
of the exterior forces of reaction but also of incipient promiscuity
against which she must be protected. The Dictator, in a similarly
paranoid fashion, sought to preserve Spain from the international
subversive influence of liberalism and progress; and this political
xenophobia was accompanied by the identical fixation with
protecting the moral innocence of the country—the 'reserva espiri-
tual del occidente'—through the sexual repression of women, a
phenomenon Hopewell summarizes so efficaciously in the single
phrase: 'Female sexuality was a contradiction in terms under
Franco' (1987: 78). Indeed, the conviction that the ideological and
sexual fall from grace are inextricably intertwined is dwelt upon
with some insistence as the camera returns on two occasions to a
graphic view of the corpse for us to notice that Hildegart is shot,
significantly, twice in the brain and once in each breast.

As a consequence, it becomes readily apparent how certain

---

[4] These facets of the Dictator's personality and his obsession with power are
well documented in Juan Pablo Fusi's revealing biography (1985).

unsavoury yet recognizable characteristics of the Dictator become transposed onto the avowedly progressive sentiments of the protagonist. Needless to say, the implication of such a juxtaposition is of particular interest. At a crucial moment in Spanish history the director seems intent on alerting us to the dangers of authoritarianism not only on the right but also on the left of the political spectrum, an unusual stance at a time when the communist agenda enjoyed hegemony amongst the creative elite. However, this procrastination and absence of affiliation to any 'committed' position is characteristic of Fernán Gómez's career. Though an anti-Francoist of conviction, his acratic instincts—like those of his illustrious contemporary Luis García Berlanga—could not allow him to embrace with any fervour the totalitarian programme offered during the dictatorship by the Soviet-inspired left, taken by many at the time to be the sole alternative to Francoism. In addition, his propensity to collaborate in films which epitomized the official ideology of the regime left him a marginalized figure, severely compromising his political credibility. As a result, he was frequently criticized for his apparent ideological indefinition and doubtful commitment to the communist-inspired mainstream of creative resistance.[5]

Mothers and Daughters

Despite the immediacy of this political speculation and its acute relevance to the period of the Transition in Spain there is an additional, evocative dimension which imbues the film with a subtler, more haunting element. We refer, of course, to the psychological drama which unfolds disturbingly along Oedipal lines as the movie develops. Marsha Kinder has isolated pertinently the fixation in

---

[5] The director deals with these facts plainly in his autobiography. First he refers to the commonly held assumption that the PCE offered the only alternative to the regime: 'No eran pocos los ciudadanos sin definir políticamente que creían a pies juntillas que cuando Franco desapareciese . . . lo que tendríamos aquí sería un comunismo; o sea un socialismo del estado al estilo de la URSS.' He is also quick to distance himself from such totalitarianism: 'Eso era lo que a mí me parecía mal de lo que predicaban—me predicaban—mis amigos comunistas. Era necesario un Estado fuerte . . . No había conseguido apartar de mí—no lo he conseguido todavía—la idea de que el Estado es enemigo de los individuos' (Fernán Gómez 1990: ii. 167–8).

Spanish literature and cinema with this particular archetype; and there is every reason why this should be the case. The primal scene of family romance deals with only the personal rivalry but is also redolent with the struggle for power and control. Given the sensitivity of the Spanish creative psyche to the question of parental authoritarianism as expressed institutionally through the political machinery of repression, it is hardly surprising that the topic becomes something of a commonplace in art as the critic reveals— most pertinently in our case—with reference to the figure of the domineering mother.

In the Spanish Oedipal narrative, mothers frequently stand in for the missing father as the embodiment of patriarchal law and thereby become an obstacle both to the erotic desire of the daughter and to the mimetic desire of the son . . . This pattern is fairly commonplace in Spanish literature, where the 'material' is frequently represented as a force that obsesses both mother and child—as a woman's passionate desire to have a child or to dominate the one she possesses and as a child's passionate yearning to be united with the lost mother or to defy the one who is present. (Kinder 1993: 199)

The reference to the mother as an 'obstacle to the erotic desire of the daughter' could not be more pertinent to the present study; yet although the relation of this struggle to contemporary Spain is readily apparent, there can be no question that this archetypal dimension imbues the essay with a more universal quality, as becomes evident if we consider our case within the parameters of Laura Mulvey's perceptive meditations on the nature of the female condition:

Woman's desire is subjected to her image as bearer of the bleeding wound, she can exist only in relation to castration and cannot transcend it. She turns her child into her own desire to possess a penis (the condition, she imagines, of her entry into the Symbolic). Either she must gracefully give way to the word, the Name of the Father and the Law, or else struggle to keep her own child down with her in the half-light of the Imaginary. Woman then stands in patriarchal culture as signifier for the male other . . . still tied to her place as bearer of meaning not maker of meaning. (Mulvey 1992)

It is difficult to imagine a more revealing analysis of the female psychosis particularly in the context of our film, as Aurora condemns her daughter to inhabit the nether regions of her own

imaginary world. By way of contrast, Bernarda Alba would constitute an example of the alternative, obsessive subscription to
parental authority; although both cases are exemplary of women
embracing the role of the male other. Jacques Lacan has elucidated
further the destructive dimension of the mother–daughter relationship, particularly germane to the two filicides in question and their
fixation with the phallic lack.

El papel de la madre es el deseo de la madre. Esto es capital. El deseo de
la madre no es algo que pueda reportarse tal cual, que pueda resultarles
indiferente. Siempre produce estragos. Es estar dentro la boca de un coco-
drilo, eso es la madre. No se sabe qué mosca puede llegar a picarle de
repente y va y cierra la boca. Eso es el deseo de la madre . . . Entonces traté
de explicar que había algo tranquilizador . . . Hay un palo, de piedra por
supuesto, que está allí, en potencia, en la boca, y eso la contiene, la traba.
Es lo que se llama el falo. Es el palo que protege si, de repente, eso se
cierra.[6]

In both these cases the 'crocodiles', in what might be described as
a classic psychotic state, devour their daughters in the manner
imagined by the analyst. It is not insignificant that they have
recourse to the phallic substitute of the rifle (Bernarda Alba) and
the pistol (Aurora) in order to exert compensatory control. The
crucial scene in the bathroom—perhaps the most memorable of the
entire film—is fundamental to our study in this respect. As the
mature Hildegart prepares to go out on a date her mother drags her
furiously from the door into the bathroom where she wipes all the
make-up from her face. She then strips her daughter and writes
'Aurora' with an eye pencil over all her erotogenous zones. The
primal scene of the family romance sees the children as the possession of the parents, as Freud was to elucidate pertinently with reference to the Hegelian Master/Slave paradigm, and the mother's
name written upon her daughter's body is clearly analogous to this
possession.[7] Moreover, the sexual autonomy implicit in Hildegart's
romantic sortie and the independence evident in her decision to
separate from her mother is not only a threat to the mother's role
as substitute for the symbolic father, as was the case with Adela and

[6] Lacan 1992: 118. A fascinating study of the conflictive relationship between
mothers and daughters is provided by Nancy Friday's psychological survey (1994).
Particularly relevant is the chapter entitled 'Competition' (160–200).
[7] The nature of this struggle for control with possession as the fundamental
stimulus is elucidated most pertinently in Lacan 1966.

Bernarda Alba, but also confronts Aurora with the reality of her lack of phallus which will in due course prove intolerable.

In this respect it is interesting to consider Mulvey's comments on Julia Kristeva's meditation on the problematic relation of woman to the poetics of the patriarchal order.

Woman, in these terms, only stands for what has been repressed, and it is the male poet's relation to femininity that erupts in his use of poetic language. The next step would, from a feminist point of view, have to move beyond woman unspeaking, a signifier of the 'other' of patriarchy, to a point where women can speak themselves, beyond a definition of 'femininity' assigned by patriarchy, to a poetic language made also by women and their understanding. (Mulvey 1989a)

It is intriguing to note that, after a certain fashion, Aurora's struggle for female emancipation is conceived verbally along similar lines. It is not irrelevant, for example, that Hildegart is given the name of a visionary, reformist saint: a celebrated critic of the ecclesiastic status quo as evinced by her caustic censure of emperors, kings, and popes alike.[8] More significant, as regards Kristeva's speculation, is the reason the protagonist discloses for this choice. Aurora explains to the prison inmates that she made this selection since, in German, the name is a compound of the words 'garden' and 'knowledge'. The archetypal relevance here is patent and ties in well with our context as Aurora attempts to reinvent or rewrite the history of the human condition from its very origin. The creative aspect of this desire for female liberation, however, is inevitably usurped as the protagonist falls prey to the psychosis which impels her to act in accordance with the familiar scheme as described by Lacan.

It is in this psychological context that we can appreciate further the aptness of the *mise-en-scène*. The repeated flashbacks imbue the narrative with a synchronism which is most appropriate for the examination of the archetypal conflict suffered by the mind of the main character. The prolonged, explanatory discourse of both Aurora and the biographical narrator is also highly reminiscent of the confession and explanation enacted between patient and analyst. Also relevant in this respect is the manner in which the narrative imitates the genre of a peculiar detective story wherein the individual who unearths the clues to the crime is, paradoxically,

[8] More information is offered in Farmer 1992: 231.

also the assassin. Laura Mulvey has explained how this dimension is entirely in keeping with an investigation of the nether world of the psyche with reference to the dramatic representation of Oedipus.

Not only does the old mystery of Oedipus' own parentage remain unsolved . . . but a murder has been committed and the criminal must be revealed . . . In this process Oedipus takes on the role of investigator. But it only gradually emerges that he is telling his own story, revealing, as detective hero the hidden meaning behind his actions . . . It is here that the Oedipus story, once again, both works within a given narrative code and represents a twist, a deviation from a particular composition's scheme (Propp's term). In this case the detective himself is the criminal . . . The detective story is a narrative that carries the hero to another space, a nether world. Exploration of this space depends on a re-telling of events, the investigation of an immediate past that lies within the experience of the characters involved in the drama.[9]

There are certain related elements in our film which complement the Oedipal narrative of telling and retelling. A series of genealogical motifs—the question of parentage and kinship is, as Mulvey confirms, fundamental to this myth—also underline the psychological nature of the confrontation with the patriarchal order. Aurora insistently displays her photo album giving the life history of the members of her family. Equally intense are the recurrent splurges of red which accompany the narrative and, evocative of prostitution and (spilt) blood, refer us inevitably—and in all their Lorquian intensity—to the themes of sexuality, procreation, life, death, and, more pertinently in this case, heredity and legitimacy. In similar terms, it is entirely fitting that the final third of the film should develop into a courtroom drama. Not only do we witness in this respect the trial of the filicide and her extraordinary justification of the crime—the telling of her own story—but also,

---

⁹ Mulvey 1989b. Also of interest in this respect are Mulvey's comments on the modern urban detective genre which relate pertinently, albeit tangentially, to our study of Aurora's psychosis. 'The nether world of the city, seething with bars, prostitutes and criminals, also the uncontrollable working class, could provide a mythic terrain for scenarios of adventure and constitute a modern space of liminality similar to the no-man's land through which the heroes of antiquity travelled. But whereas the ancient or the folk tale heroes embarked on a linear journey outside the city space, the journey of the urban detective is a *descent into a hidden world of what is repressed by bourgeois morality and respectability to decode and decipher signs and restore order through the process of reason*' (1989b: 187, my emphasis).

on a more allusive plain, we see the ultimate subjugation of a woman who has dared to transcend the limitations of the female condition in defiance of the symbolic law of the father and is now being called to account.[10]

Una película fallida

As is not unusual in the unpredictable career of Fernando Fernán Gómez, the general response to this film was particularly ambiguous. On the one hand, the cinema critics were quite scathing in their dismissal of the production, a censure which extended to all areas of the piece, as evinced by Carlos Balagué's brutal review in *Dirigido por*. For this commentator, the director's attempt to imbue a Brechtian style of historical distancing is deprecated as 'un deseo de prolongar al cine el aséptico academicismo de sus trabajos teatrales . . . llevando su labor hacia un terreno escasamente imaginativo'. In similar vein, the division of the film into various temporal blocks leading to the long endpiece of the courtroom drama affords the narrative 'un ritmo terriblemente moroso y cansino'. The reviewer likewise prefers not to appreciate the evocative value of the monochrome flashbacks which, far from effecting a lyrical synchronism conducive to the exploration of psychic atemporality, are dismissed as 'totalmente gratuitos'. The historical parallelism—another central pillar of the piece—is in turn considered laboured, as is exemplified by the *atrezzo* of Aurora's flat which, it is argued, emphasizes the theatricality of the production in its attention to detail which 'confiere un rigor pintoresco al trabajo del ambientador'. Finally, the commentator ends with the cutting remark that Fernando Fernán Gómez 'no era el director apropiado para el proyecto', suggesting that the enterprise would have been better served by the likes of Víctor Erice (Balagué 1977).

Ramón Freixas echoes these sentiments when he complains in much the same way about the academic tone of the film which

---

[10] I am indebted to members of the Lacanian circle in Valencia, particularly Pilar Dasí, Isabel Robles, and Jaume Pérez Montaner, for their assistance on the psychoanalytical dimension of this study. Unlike the psychiatrists who were engaged by the defence during the trial to establish Aurora's insanity and merely confused the court with pedantry, Pilar Dasí has produced an exemplary case study of the protagonist giving a clear analysis of the violence of the psychosis (Dasí 1997).

gives rise to a 'mullido conformismo'. What is worse is the extension of this censure to the areas of screenplay, direction, and
production, wherein 'una escritura impersonal, un ritmo premioso,
una realización plana, contaminada de atonía narrativa determinan
su categoría de celuloide rancio'. As a result, it is 'un film errado .
. . cuyo tono es inadecuado y desafinado' (Freixas 1993). Ángel
Pérez Gómez showed himself to be equally blunt about the pack-
age overall. His words seems to sum up the critical response as a
whole as he laments how 'un tema apasionante resulta al final
machacado por una realización torpe, ambigua y carente de imaginación creadora. La historia ni siquiera llega a estar correctament
"ilustrada", ya que su narrativa, tanto a nivel material como
ideológico, se resiente de fallos lamentables y clamorosos' (Pérez
Gómez 1978: 9–36).

Harsh words indeed. Nonetheless, such caustic reaction is in
no way unfamiliar to Fernán Gómez. In his autobiography, the
long-suffering director refers not without some disgruntled irony
to the *homenaje* he was afforded in Huelva in 1981 wherein, far
from receiving any great eulogy of his *œuvre*, he was constantly
reminded of the shortcomings of his labour. The charges levelled
against this particular film are exemplary of the general tone of
disparagement.

Me enteré también de que . . . mis trabajos teatrales tienen un aséptico
academicismo. Que en *Mi hija Hildegart* llevé mi labor hacia un terreno
escasamente imaginativo. El ritmo era terriblemente moroso y cansino.
Había planos totalmente gratuitos. Una secuencia grotesca. Una
planificación tan vetusta como forzada. Inútiles movimientos de cámara.
    Al cabo de los años, con casi todas estas censuras estoy de acuerdo,
pero todavía no comprendo cómo no encontraron otro profesional más
merecedor del homenaje. (Fernán Gómez 1990: ii. 199)

Given the severity of the critical response, it is hardly surprising
that the movie has all but disappeared as an item of interest from
the Spanish cinematic panorama. Indeed, the condemnation was so
damning that, not unlike Aurora, the chastened director seems to
have all but disinherited his offspring, hardly referring to it in an
autobiography which, by way of contrast, deals in great detail with
all his other endeavours. In fact, on the rare occasions it crops up
in this work it is usually qualified by the epithet 'mi fallida
película', which is, curiously, how it is also described by Augusto

Torres in his *Diccionario del cine español* (1994: 209). In effect, the tendency to ignore this essay as some type of unfortunate mistake has been so universal that in his seminal examination of the cinema as social and historical document during the Transition a critic as apparently well prepared as Carlos Heredero makes no mention of it in the body of his synopsis nor, more alarmingly, in his appended and would-be complete filmography of this theme in the period concerned (Heredero 1989).

Fortunately, as is not infrequently the case, the wisdom of the cinema-going public tends to eclipse that of the professional critics and, by way of contrast, there can be no doubt as to the positive response that this essay elicited amongst Spaniards in general; a fact which tends to attest the real quality of the piece. A first indication of this phenomenon was the rapturous warmth of the applause when the film was premièred at the San Sebastián Festival in 1977.[11] More convincing in this respect, however, was its success at the box office. The movie enjoyed an appreciable run of 4,064 days, attracting an audience of over a million and grossing just under 122 million pesetas, being outshone only by such block-busters of the same year as Garci's *Asignatura pendiente* or Berlanga's *Escopeta nacional*, and emulating with ease other notable essays on socio-historical questions such as Camino's nostalgic *Largas vacaciones del '36* or Lazaga's flippantly evasive *Vota a Gundisalvo* (Pérez Gómez 1978: 165–73).

This unqualified success is perhaps not surprising at a crucially important historical juncture when the Spanish population was, in general, particularly sensitive to studies of an in-depth socio-political nature. The curious question remains, however, as to the reason for the inability of *Mi hija Hildegart* to convince critical opinion of its real cinematic value despite its evident quality. As might be expected, much of the censure gravitates around what is perceived as the excessive theatricality of the production. Much mention is made of the excessively 'academic' dimension to the film and its reliance on 'timeworn' Brechtian dehumanization which, it is argued, further problematizes the static dimension considered a deficiency in the scripting.

However, it is difficult to find any of these criticisms entirely

---

[11] This is one of the few references the director makes to the film in his autobiography (Fernán Gómez 1990: ii. 260).

convincing. In the first place they could equally be levelled, say, at much of the contemporary work of Saura, for whom empathy in characterization and dynamism at the level of narrative were hardly prerequisites. Indeed, it would not be excessive to sustain that employment of these 'theatrical' techniques is, in fact, extremely well considered. One of the most intensely moving moments of the film, for example, is the catharsis produced during Aurora's serenely determined walk to murder her daughter in her bedroom. In the placid tranquillity of the early morning Aute's evocative arrangement of a haunting lullaby intones; a tender motif which, recurring at times of family affection, stands in stark contrast at this moment to the cold presence of the phallic pistol with which the murderous act will be perpetrated.

Fernán Gómez, moreover, is no novice to the director's profession and has written copious theoretical tracts precisely on the subject of the relationship between theatre, literature, and the cinema. Indeed, he has commented pertinently on the dramatic dimension of psychopathology itself, particularly in the sphere of delusion evident, in our case, in Aurora's obsessive protestations of sanity.

Las teorías de Freud fueron en seguida pasto alimenticio de los dramaturgos. Se habló de que ya Eurípides las había intuido, y esto les dio carta de naturaleza. Buena parte del teatro mundial estuvo impregnada del pensamiento freudiano durante nuestro siglo. El pensamiento de Freud era en sí teatral, se prestaba a sorpresas, demostraba que los cuerdos eran locos, y los locos cuerdos: los buenos malos. Muchas de sus historias daban ya hechas las estructuras de las obras, los argumentos de un drama.[12]

It might not be inappropriate, however—and this is purely an intuitive observation—to look beyond the actual details of the reviewers' censure to posit a different explanation for their general unease when confronted with this film. It is tempting, for example, to attribute the overall critical dissatisfaction not to any gratuitous 'theatricality' or 'academicismo' but rather to a sense of discomfiture relating to the generic indeterminacy of the piece wherein an uneasy hybridity is seen to surround the question of categorization. In the

---

[12] Fernán Gómez 1995: 165–6. In this theoretical study on literature and the cinema there is an entire section devoted to the relationship between theatre and cinema (pp. 139–67).

case of an Almodóvarian comedy this indeterminacy might prove spectacularly successful; but this essay, with its weighty subject matter, might well have failed to impress a critical body of the pre-Movida period precisely because of its indefinition. It is difficult, for example, to specify exactly what class of film we are being presented with. Is it a social-historical document, a psychological study, a detective story, a courtroom drama, or even a horror movie, a variation on the Frankenstein theme wherein a monster creates and murders a human?

In truth, a case may be made for all of these options and none of them; and the proposition that the reviewers may well have become disaffected by the confusion in this area remains intriguing. There can be little doubt, however, that our assimilation is problematized least if—despite the appreciable box-office success—we release ourselves from the restrictions of genre and approach the piece less exclusively as an art film. When considered from this perspective, free from the generic limitations listed above—and again the comparison with Saura is valid in terms of narrative technique and eclecticism—the quality of the film may be appreciated for its speculation on all these levels—from the socio-historical to the psychological and even the detective mystery—which allows a much more positive and rewarding reading of what has for long been unjustly considered a problematic 'película fallida' and consigned spectacularly to the annals of oblivion.

REFERENCES

Angulo, J., and Llinás, F. (1993), *Fernando Fernán Gómez: el hombre que quiso ser Jackie Coogan*. Guipúzcoa: Patronato Municipal de Guipúzcoa.

Balagué, Carlos (1977), 'Crítica', *Dirigido por*, 47 (Aug.) (unpaginated).

Brooksbank-Jones, Anny (1995), 'Work, Women and the Family: A Critical Perspective', in Helen Graham and Jo Labanyi (eds.) (1995), *Spanish Cultural Studies: An Introduction*, Oxford: Oxford University Press: 386–92.

Dasí, Pilar (1997), 'Los estragos de la interpretación materna: Hildegart o el Jardín de la sabiduría', *Finisterre Freudiano*, 7 (Jan.): 99–102.

Farmer, David Hugh (1992), *The Oxford Dictionary of Saints*, Oxford: Oxford University Press.

Fernán Gómez, Fernando (1990), *El tiempo amarillo*, 2 vols. Madrid: Debate.

—— (1995), *Desde la última fila*. Madrid: Espasa Calpe.

Freixas, Ramón (1993), 'Entre la convención y la sumición', in J. Angulo and F. Llinás (1993), *Fernando Fernán Gómez: el hombre que quiso ser Jackie Coogan*, Guipúzcoa: Patronato Municipal de Guipúzcoa: 59–76.

Friday, Nancy (1994), *My Mother My Self*. London: HarperCollins.

Fusi, Juan Pablo (1985), *Franco: autoritarismo y poder personal*. Madrid: Ediciones El País.

Galán, Diego, and Llorens, Antonio (1984), *Fernando Fernán Gómez: apasionadas andanzas de un señor muy pelirrojo*. Valencia: Fundación Municipal de Cine, Fernando Torres.

Graham, Helen (1995), 'Women and Social Change', in Helen Graham and Jo Labanyi (eds.) (1995), *Spanish Cultural Studies: An Introduction*, Oxford: Oxford University Press: 99–115.

—— and Labanyi, Jo (1995), *Spanish Cultural Studies: An Introduction*. Oxford: Oxford University Press.

Heredero, Carlos (1989), 'El reflejo de la evolución social y política en el cine español de la Transición y de la Democracia: historia de un desencuentro', in *Escritos sobre el cine español 1973–87*, Valencia: Filmoteca de la Generalitat Valenciana: 17–32.

Hopewell, John (1987), *Out of the Past: Spanish Cinema after Franco*. London: BFI (1st pub. 1986).

Keown, D. (1996), 'The Critique of Reification: A Subversive Current in the Cinema of Contemporary Spain', in W. Everett (ed.), *European Identity in Cinema*, Exeter: Intellect: 61–73.

Kinder, Marsha (1993), *Blood Cinema: The Reconstruction of National Identity in Spain*. Berkeley and Los Angeles: University of California Press.

Lacan, Jacques (1966), 'L'Agrésivité en psychanalyse', in *Écrits*, Paris: Seuil: 101–24.

—— (1992), 'Seminario 17', in *El reverso de la psicoanálisis*, Barcelona: Paidós: 101–24.

Montero, Rosa (1995), 'The Silent Revolution: The Social and Democratic Advances of Women in Democratic Spain', in Helen Graham and Jo Labanyi (eds.) (1995), *Spanish Cultural Studies: An Introduction*, Oxford: Oxford University Press: 381–5.

Mulvey, Laura (1989*a*), 'Film, Feminism and the Avant-garde', in *Visual and Other Pleasures*, London: Macmillan: 111–36.

—— (1989*b*), 'The Oedipus Myth', in *Visual and Other Pleasures*. London: Macmillan: 177–201.

—— (1992), 'Visual Pleasure and Narrative Cinema', in *Screen* (ed.), *The*

Sexual Subject: A Screen Reader in Sexuality, London: Routledge: 22–34.

Pérez Gómez, Ángel (1978), *Cine para leer 1977: historia crítica de un año de cine*. Bilbao: Mensajero.

Torres, Augusto (1994), *Diccionario del cine español*. Madrid: Espasa Calpe.

11

El corazón del bosque (Gutiérrez Aragón, 1979): Mist, Myth, and History

JOHN HOPEWELL

EL *corazón del bosque* (1979) was the film that made Manuel Gutiérrez Aragón, plumping him on the always slippery plinth reserved for Spain's most acclaimed cineaste, lionized by the left, the darling of its hard-core intelligentsia, fodder for Sunday supplement features. These were unlikely laurels for a wayward, discreetly savage, and ironic critic of an increasingly sanitized society. But he was to maintain a Spanish directors' pole position for nearly a decade until Pedro Almodóvar's *Mujeres al borde de un ataque de nervios* (1988) consecrated a mainstream Spanish cinema and replaced a meta-text of political debate by a postmodernist discourse whose extra-filmic referentiality was popular culture and Hollywood cinema.[1]

Yet *El corazón del bosque* also spawned the Legend of Gutiérrez Aragón, an *idée reçue*, returned by few, of a film-maker whose work, rather like the film's high beech wood, is dazzling but near impenetrable. 'Anyone can approach the world which his characters live in, but nobody can decipher it,' avowed Miguel Juan Payán and José Luis López in 1985.[2]

Gutiérrez Aragón certainly fires on very heavy artillery: Sigmund Freud, and the structural anthropologist Claude Lévi-Strauss. His films merely depart from such writers' ideas rather than illustrating their accuracy. But anyone who does not know, at least superficially, their Sartre from their Barthes could well get left behind. More than anything else, however, Gutiérrez Aragón remains, in the best sense

---

[1] And whose radicality turned on its sexual politics. See Evans 1996 for a definitive introduction.

[2] They went on to write a whole book to try to underwrite this: Payán and López 1985.

of the word, a oddity. As a chubby 20-year-old (he was born in Santander in northern Spain in 1942) he began studying in 1962 at Madrid's Escuela Oficial de Cine (EOC). A hotbed of dissidence, it furnished most of the leading young liberal cineastes of the 1970s. Yet Gutiérrez Aragón's films at first poked rather than broke through. *Habla, mudita* (1973), a discreet parable about 'the irony of language',[3] was overshadowed by Victor Erice's stunning debut of the same year, *El espíritu de la colmena*. Gutiérrez Aragón got sparse public credit for co-scripting José Luis Borau's epoch-making *Furtivos* (1975). *Camada negra* (1977) became famed for driving neo-fascists to firebomb a cinema; critics celebrated *Sonámbulos* (1977)—for its unintelligibility.

Spain's transition from dictatorship to democracy from 1975 to 1977 flamed a national cinema whose breadth and intellectual vitality mark it as a fleeting golden age.[4] But by the time *El corazón del bosque* was released, Spain's radical cinema and radical political pretensions had faded. 'When we finished it, I said to Luis [Megino, the producer of the film], we might as well eat the film with chips. A few months before we could have placed the film, but now there's no market for it.' *El corazón del bosque* finally opened at Madrid's top Alphaville art house in late 1979, played for some six months, and took a nationwide 42.7 million pesetas ($288,000), becoming a *succès d'estime*. Part of the picture's allure proved to be, ironically, its now rare radicality.

The Transition saw a rich debate about Spain's past and what should be its future. Made by an always questioning member of the Spanish Communist Party (PCE),[5] *El corazón del bosque* drives far deeper. Its concern is not so much what has—or should—happen, as how people come to believe in what has happened or should happen, the creation of personal, popular, and political myths, and the need, however fictitious they may be, for their existence. The theme vertebrates some of the greatest modern Spanish films,[6] echoing throughout the whole of Gutiérrez Aragón's work, but never to such moving effect as in *El corazón del bosque*.

---

[3] Gutiérrez Aragón's own words in what still remains a central interview: Llinás, Pérez Perucha, and Santamaría 1979.

[4] For details see a seminal essay, Pérez Perucha and Ponce 1986.

[5] Gutiérrez Aragón resigned from the PCE the day after it was legalized in 1977. For his reasons, see *Sonámbulos*, *El corazón del bosque*, or Torres 1985.

[6] See González Requena's key essay (1989).

Since 1980, Spanish film directors have haltingly sought to appeal more broadly to a new generation of audiences for whom the Spanish Civil War is as distant as the Siege of Troy. Gutiérrez Aragón has tried to ride this change. Up to *Sonámbulos*, he declared later, he had thought that cinema 'necessarily explored its own language as poetry and painting had done'. Now he saw the danger of films becoming 'art for cinephiles' when they should be mass art. From the rites-of-passage drama *Maravillas*, Gutiérrez Aragón has usually worked within genres, used stars, and adopted the pictorial plushness favoured by the PSOE film authorities from 1982.

Spain can now boast three artistic generations of film-makers — those who performed political guard duty under Franco, the post-Franco hedonists (Almodóvar, Trueba), and a new New Spanish Cinema, dating broadly from the first films of Julio Medem and Juanma Bajo Ulloa.[7] Gutiérrez Aragón sits to the left of the first of these cadres. But he has never abandoned his interest in the structures and limitations of belief, or in making films which are more than the sum of their narratives. He remains now one of the last of the Mohicans, a figure whose deep sense and sensuality still add weight and richness to contemporary Spanish film-making.

Gutiérrez Aragón swears that in his films nothing happens by chance. A first step into the labyrinth of *El corazón del bosque* may well be, far more than with most films, to confirm what happens at all. Set in September 1942, its prologue introduces El Andarín, a *maquís* leader entrenched in the drizzly forests on the border between Asturias and Cantabria in northern Spain. Having attacked an electricity supply depot, he waves in triumph from in front of a lighthouse; at the local dance, he struts a gallant paso doble with local womenfolk. A young girl, Amparo, looks admiringly on.

Ten years later, Amparo's brother, Juan P., ostensibly an exiled member of the PCE, arrives in the region to persuade El Andarín to lay down his arms. While they dance at the local fair (*romería*), Amparo tells Juan P. that the band's saxophonist is her fiancé Suso, a shoemaker. At home, she adds that the *maquís* will meet him at a winter stable for cattle (*invernal*). On his way, Juan P. is shot at

---

[7] The thesis from an overview of recent Spanish film-making, Holland and Hopewell 1997.

by the Civil Guards,[8] but rescued by El Andarín. He awakes at the *invernal*, just as El Andarín leaves. El Andarín does not want to meet him, the cottager says. His daughter confides that El Andarín is pockmarked by a terrible skin disease. When Juan P. asks how to find him, she sings a song.[9] Climbing the slopes above the cottage, Juan P. spies some old crones laden with wood: they turn out to be Civil Guards, who run at him shooting. The Civil Guards later execute the cottager. In the forest, Juan P. finds a milk-jar left for El Andarín. He drinks from a Guard's flask while the Guard frolics on top of his horse. At night, other horsed Civil Guards clop by pulling a ox-cart; on it are the corpses of *maquís* killed in an ambush. A body tumbles to the ground. The man, Atilano, is still alive.[10] Like Juan P. he was born in the region. Following the clues in the song, the two find powdered milk by a fig-tree and red sausages beside a stream. Sunning himself with Juan P. in a tree, Atilano says that El Andarín is now on his own and recounts memories from his childhood. Reaching a road down the mountain, Atilano tells Juan P. that if he wants to find El Andarín, he should ask Amparo.

Juan P. returns to a maizefield by Suso's house. Amparo and Suso hold an open-air wedding lunch. That night in the barn Amparo tells Juan P. that El Andarín is in the maizefield. Amparo goes to talk to him. El Andarín hides his sore-marked face and, when the Civil Guards approach, flees.

Defeated, Juan P. boards a bus to leave the village but suddenly decides to search out El Andarín. Following the clues in the peasant child's song, he reaches El Andarín and hands him a face cream.

---

[8] However bizarre, each and every event in the forest can be given a practical explanation. Here the Civil Guards appear to have got wind that the PCE has sent a member to the region. One Guard sings an ancient local song to see if Juan P. can join in or is from outside the area. Juan P. does so—temporarily fooling the Guards into not shooting at him.

[9] 'Si la zorra va a higos . . .', a real-life song popular in northern Spain. Its second-line refrain suggests where food left for El Andarín—hence the *maquís* himself—may be found. The song goes something like this: 'If the vixen goes looking for figs, there will be song on its way | it will find a fig-tree | . . . wet its coattails | the stairway will flood | it will see its black shadow | the friend will shake its hand.'

[10] Atilano's 'resurrection' obeys both mythic logic—Juan P. performs symbolic rites associated in ancient myth with reanimation, closing and opening his eyes, and giving Atilano food—and a practical reason. As was not unknown in the Civil War, Atilano appears to have survived an execution squad.

As the Civil Guards close in, Juan P. and El Andarín flee higher up the mountain into the forest, Juan imploring El Andarín to lay down his arms. When Juan is shot in the foot by the pursuing Civil Guards, El Andarín tends him in a cave. The next day Juan shoots El Andarín. Returning to the village, Juan is nursed by Amparo. The Civil Guards burst into Amparo's house, tipped off by Suso. An epilogue explains that Amparo and Suso had several children. When Juan P. returns—very possibly from prison—to live with Amparo, Suso leaves to set up a shoemaker's shop in Llanes, the nearby town. All three meet once a year, the day of the local fair.

El corazón del bosque, an upper-case, intertitle explanation stridently insists, is 'based on various events and people who existed in the same hills and woods where the film was shot'. 'When you tell a story with a historical background, you have to get the epoch, the details right: the concomitant style, and all those things which buffs discover in the film, can come afterwards,' Gutiérrez Aragón has said (Llinás, Pérez Perucha, and Santamaría 1979: 33–4). *El corazón del bosque* is carefully documented in its dates and historical background. By September 1942, when the film begins, the Second World War was beginning to turn against the Axis powers of Germany and Italy. Marshalled by the Partido Comunista Española (PCE) in exile, the resistance movement in Spain entertained not-unreasonable hopes that, once the Axis was beaten, the Allies would remove the neo-fascist General Franco from power.

Ten years later, cold-shouldered by the USA and UK, devastated by hunger, imprisonment, and executions, many of Spain's former Republicans were hard put to find their next square meal, let alone lead another war against Franco. In 1948, the Spanish PCE ordered the *maquís* to end their armed resistance to Franco. Those who stayed were less freedom fighters than fugitives.

One immediate way into *El corazón del bosque* is to see it, like so much social or elliptically political cinema made in Spain from the 1960s, as an act of demystification, presenting a revisionist reading of a subject which was obfuscated in cinema under Franco, such as Arturo Ruíz Castillo's daring *Dos caminos* (1953), whose finale naturally had to urge *maquís* to recognize the errors of their ways, or further films in the 1950s which went on to exalt the virtues of Franco's police or Civil Guards.

On both these points of armed resistance or the Civil Guards, *El corazón del bosque* begs to differ. If Juan P. asks El Andarín to lay down his arms, it is not because armed resistance is morally misguided but because it is outmoded. The Civil Guards come off worse: brutally murdering the cottager, who has abandoned armed resistance. The Civil Guards are a force for repression, their shadowy figures, ill focused in the 1952 dance scene, forcing Juan P. and Amparo to hide their feelings when they see each other, despite the fact that they have probably been separated for years.

While knowledge of its historical background is vital to understanding its pro-filmic action, a 'counter-Franco' reading of *El corazón del bosque* seems limited. Formal censorship was abolished in Spain in November 1977. By 1978 films—such as Mario Camus's tearjerker *Los días del pasado*—and books—such as a translation of Paul Preston's *Spain in Crisis*—were already appearing which treated the subject of the *maquís* at length. If the film demystified anything by this time, it was the *maquís* and PCE apparatus itself. By 1952 the first's resistance was neither glamorous nor useful; and the second kill their own comrades.[11] If anything, *El corazón del bosque* could be broadly read as a prescient paean to the ideological death of the left in the late 1970s and beyond. 'Today, in Western Europe, the known political left also has death in its soul: there are no alternatives, the idea of a revolution no longer figures on the horizon,' Gutiérrez Aragón commented in 1979. However carefully documented, though, *El corazón del bosque* eschews a savage naturalism. In contrast, its psychological and sexual relations, narrative structures, its framing and lighting style, and even forceful forefronting of storytelling insistently invoke myth.

Three key scenes—very unlike each other in style but all among the most memorable in the film—underpin its mythic dimensions.

1. Through an almost comic in-your-face use of phallic imagery, the film's highly Freudian prologue sets a psycho-social scene. Backed by the Llanes lighthouse El Andarín projects his temporarily elongated figure over the landscape, waving his machine gun in triumph. Framing in the next shot shows merely his legs as he

---

[11] El Andarín's assassination is not historical embellishment. As early as 1945, the PCE ordered the execution of two resistance leaders, Gabriel León Trilla and Jesús Monzón, for not toeing the party line. See Preston 1978.

walks along the beach. At the fair, echoing the use of *droit de seigneur* on festive days, he enjoys the privilege of dancing with the local womenfolk.

El Andarín is immediately established as a patriarch, the lord or 'king' of the region, a father figure for the villagers. The film returns forcibly to this father image at its climax. It can of course be argued that Amparo only views El Andarín as a 'Father-King' in a Freudian sense. But one point that anthropologists stress in considering kinship is that this should be considered from the point of view of social relations, not biological fact. Again, disfigured by illness, El Andarín is still only a monster in a metaphorical sense of the word. And Juan P. obviously does not literally marry Amparo at the end of the film.

Reinterpreting its symbolic relations between individuals, *El corazón del bosque* reveals startling similarities with both the Oedipal and Theban myths (the last involving Theseus' slaying of the minotaur, a monstrous symbol of its father Minos, with the aid of Minos' daughter Ariadne and her celebrated thread).

A mythic reading also provides productive access to some of the film's most abstruse detail. *El corazón del bosque* borrows heavily from Lévi-Strauss's myth analysis in its emphasis on cooking (where fresh raw food is transformed by cultural means) and the suppression of incest (for example, a man gives away his sister in marriage), both of which transform nature into culture.

As a narrative device, the culture/nature contrast marshals many of the film's images. Juan P. arrives at the village, for instance, when it is celebrating its annual fair—a place where food and drink is prepared and sold (the first human action we see as the camera cuts from the fairy-lights to the crowd is a young woman buying a bottle of wine), and where the swains of the region traditionally consolidate their relationships with future wives (when we first see the adult Amparo she is chatting with two other girls from the village; blurred in the foreground a group of young men amble by). Juan P.'s carefully graduated journey towards and back from the heart of the forest—a place where only nature exists—starts here. Amparo takes him to her house, hiding him in the stable whose floor is littered by apples (raw food to be transformed into cider). Juan P. listens to the sound of cows (animals, but domesticated ones). At the cottage he watches peasants scythe grass (raw food lightly prepared for animals). In the forest, he finds a milk-jar (raw

1. *Los golfos*: feckless youth in Franco's Spain

2. *Tristana*: the pleasures and horrors of sexual difference

3. *El espíritu de la colmena:* the power of the look

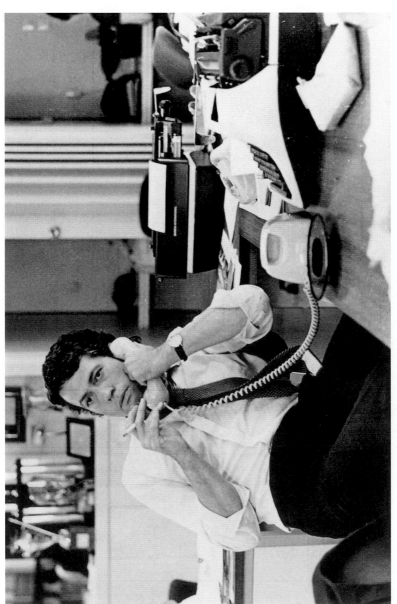

5. *Gary Cooper que estás en los cielos*: new man, old issues

6. *¿Qué he hecho yo para merecer esto?*: the Spanish 'Woman's Picture'

7. *Jamón jamón*: the specularised male

8. *Vacas*: experience and perception

sustenance drunk with little preparation by rural people of that time). But he ends up drinking only water. When he returns to Amparo's house, she, Suso, and friends are celebrating their wedding the next day. The table is chock-a-block with black pudding, red sausage, cider, bread, and sponge cake. After the lunch finishes, the camera tracks along the remnants of food on the table before the film cuts significantly to a photo of two sisters, perhaps distant aunts of Suso, then to that of an old couple, quite possibly his grandparents, while Amparo prepares her dress for her wedding night.

From the moment when Juan P. arrives at the village, the film loses touch with chronological time in the day-to-day sense. Traditions seem timeless, events blur in their chronology, we are in a primitive world (with, nevertheless, sophisticated cultural relations) where an individual's position within culture is more notable than any sense of future.

After Juan P. shoots El Andarín, the dying *maquís* raises his hand a few feet off the ground. 'I've known you since you were this small,' he tells Juan P. in an act of neo-paternal recognition.

2. When Juan P. appears at the local dance in 1952, Suso strikes up 'Solamente una vez' (Just Once). Yet the song's romance is usurped by an elegant interchange of glances between Juan P. and Amparo. Mostly filmed in medium shot, so that the two are continually separated by the crowd, their looks establish a covert complicity between them which goes beyond the fact that Juan P. is a member of an outlawed political party.

3. When Juan P. asks the cottager's daughter how he can find El Andarín, by way of answer she sings a popular song, which is also a riddle. When Juan P. initially tries to interpret the song, he fails, and gets lost in a seeming magical forest of fairy tale with its own laws and its own near anthropomorphic life. He only succeeds in interpreting the leafy labyrinth when aided by Amparo, who lends him her boots.

A father-king figure; insinuated incest; a labyrinth: perhaps the most productive way into the film is through myth analysis, such as that practised most famously by Claude Lévi-Strauss, for whom myths were not so much fallacious history as a sacred tale. Heavily influenced by Freud, Lévi-Strauss affirmed that studying primitive mythology or classical myths could reveal repeated events and figures which, when compared and contrasted through their binomial tensions (Nature/Culture or Man/Animal), reveal nothing less than universal collective wishes.[12] 'Megino and I elaborated our memories and materials in a mythical manner,' says Gutiérrez Aragón. 'A rural society of that time in the mountains of Santander functioned almost like a tribe. You could find structural traits of an astonishing primitivism,' he adds (Llinás, Pérez Perucha, and Santamaría 1979: 36).

Concentrating like Lévi-Strauss in his analysis of the Oedipal myth on the 'incidents' of the tale—characterized by the 'status' of individual characters and their symbolic relations—*El corazón del bosque* begins to seem far more familiar:

1. Juan P. and Amparo are the son and daughter of a King, El Andarín.
2. Amparo copulates with her King-Father.
3. Juan P. is ranged against the King and has to penetrate a labyrinth. He consults an oracle (the cottager's daughter) who sets him a riddle.
4. Amparo betrays her father and helps Juan P. to penetrate the labyrinth by means of her magical boots.
5. Juan P. solves the riddle and kills the King, who has become a monster.
6. Juan P. succeeds the King.
7. Suso, Amparo's husband, imprisons Juan P.
8. Juan P. returns and banishes Suso.
9. Juan P. 'marries' Amparo, but they have no heirs.

But this world is threatened, and dying. When starting to plan *El corazón del bosque* Gutiérrez Aragón observed that for the Greeks, the implacable was destiny, for the Spanish it was history. The central tension of *El corazón del bosque* is the contradiction between myth and history. Myth, which orders people's lives, adds weight, value to the chaos; history withers attachments, creates and destroys myth. As Jesús González Requena notes, in Gutiérrez Aragón's work, myths 'sprout' ('apuntan'), but their universes are not wholly mythical.

---

[12] 'The only thing which continues to interest me passionately is knowledge,' Gutiérrez Aragón said in 1979. For a brief, if sceptically Anglo-Saxon, introduction to Claude Lévi-Strauss, see Leach 1982.

For one thing, by 1952 history has begun to control and manipulate myth, its codes and derivatives. A decade before, El Andarín's attack struck, significantly, at the forces of the (notably urban) oppressor's communication lines: its electricity. His success is fleeting. When Juan P. travels back to the region in a lorry (carrying an icon of agrarian culture, milk), he senses lights outside. The Llanes lighthouse (which El Andarín 'takes' in 1942)? No. The hotel (a symbol of pacific urban incursion into rural areas? Neither. The lights are the motorbikes of Civil Guards, patrolling the roads to stop El Andarín attending the *romería*. By 1952, the Civil Guards have subverted other forms of communication in the region, its ancient songs ('Que me oscurece'), its dress (they disguise themselves as woodcutters), its birdsong (they imitate the owl-hoots used before by the *maquís*).[13]

The crux of the film turns on the reasons why Juan P. returns to kill El Andarín. González Requena groups Gutiérrez Aragón's *œuvre* with many recognized modern classics of Spanish cinema — including Víctor Erice's *El espíritu de la colmena* (1973) and *El sur* (1982) — as films where 'someone tells or listens to stories' or 'the film itself, evidencing its enunciatory gesture, emphasises the act of telling a story'. None of these films, he adds, 'can — or wants — to be taken as myth. And this is because what's debated in them . . . [is] the very difficulty of myth. And its necessity' (González Requena 1989: 92).

For the cottager's child, El Andarín becomes 'him', someone who does not need and should not, like a god, be given a name. The delicate tension between El Andarín's human condition, illness, unattractiveness on one hand, and his heroic status on the other, echoes throughout the film. When the main part of the film begins, El Andarín is nearing, but has not arrived, at the status of a demigod, the subject of legend. In the milk-van on the way to the *romería*, its other occupant tells Juan P., 'They're looking for him . . . El Andarín. Every year he comes down [from the mountains] to dance with his girlfriends, or so they say.' Atilano fears that El Andarín will die 'like a dog', but still swears his valour. 'He didn't denounce us, he's incapable of denouncing anybody,' he adds.

If myth had any hidden, collective sense, at least to Lévi-Strauss, this was that, if society is to go on, daughters must be disloyal to their parents and sons must destroy (replace) their fathers.[14] Juan P. recognizes that, in the struggle against Franco's regime, El Andarín has become an anachronism, his time has gone. But, exploring the forest with Atilano, he discovers his own rural roots, the way a goldfinch sings, the old chestnut about a cow which was given beer to increase its milk yield: Atilano's memories are his own. Juan P. recognizes that El Andarín belongs to the same world and seeks him out to kill him, releasing a myth of his own rural world from the ravages of history. As he retreats downhill, the body of El Andarín is already fading into the landscape.

The tension between history and myth permeates framing, editing, and light in *El corazón del bosque*. At the dance, the elegant shot/reverse field set-up progresses from medium shot to a two-shot of Amparo and Juan P. to their final intimate isolation: a classic romantic resolution. But this is modern romance of a curious kind, undercut by suggestions of past incest.

At the wedding lunch, a hand-held camera snazzily leads to a near fly-on-the-wall documentary style, as the characters celebrate, for Lévi-Strauss at least, the most ancient keystone to culture: a man giving away his sister to another. The 'giver' meanwhile lies off-camera in a maizefield, grovelling like a pig. And in the forest, the shafts of light—a symbol in divine painting of knowledge[15]— give some shots an almost sacred feel. In others, Juan P. is lost in the darkness of ignorance, ill framed, while the camera forefronts a miasma of shrubbery, mud, and natural chaos.

Myth and ideology lend sense to an otherwise chaotic and value-less world. But they are a product of history. Here lies the film's deepest political reading, one which, 'our left (both reformist and revolutionary) seems to ignore in an act of recalcitrance', writes Pérez Perucha (1979). But there are no victors in *El corazón del bosque*. Love—romantic narratives which give sense to an individual's life—proves equally time-laden. In an act of tempered

[14] And tragedy occurs when characters refuse to recognize their obligations: in *El corazón del bosque*, El Andarín's obligation to lay down his arms, and Juan P.'s to forget his incestuous interest in Amparo.

[15] As in Rembrandt's portraits, Juan P. sometimes suggests a loss of will, a receding into darkness in which light becomes an animating principle and a source of knowledge. *El corazón del bosque* was lensed by Teo Escamilla, a self-declared disciple of Luis Cuadrado, the director of photography on Erice's *El espíritu de la colmena*.

triumph, at the film's ending the camera pans from mountain and forest to the valley below. Hovering above is an eagle, the god of the skies, a suggestion perhaps of El Andarín's now mythical status. Below Suso mends a shoe, an seeming affirmation of his status in a rural world. But, undercutting this elegiac finale, the epilogue tells us that Suso now lives in the local town. The images show a lifestyle which in the future time of the text no longer exists. Amparo and Juan P. end up living with each other, so affirming an elementary bond to a rural life and each other, but their status seems diminished; no longer at the cusp of events, they simply tend cows. History has proved implacable: resistance to Franco has moved to the urban world, the big city. The film's credits roll to its theme music, the pointedly named 'Solamente una vez', once, a long time before, proclaimed by Suso to be 'the latest novelty from America'.

REFERENCES

Evans, Peter William (1996), *Women on the Verge of a Nervous Breakdown*. London: BFI.

González Requena, Jesús (1989), 'Escrituras que apuntan al mito', in *Escritos sobre el cine español 1973–1987*, Valencia: Ediciones Textos Filmoteca.

Holland, Jonathan, and Hopewell, John (1997), 'Spanish Cinema Now', in Peter Cowie (ed.), *Variety International Film Guide, 1998*, London: André Deutsch.

Leach, Edmund (1982), *Lévi-Strauss*. London: Fontana Modern Classics.

Llinás, Francesc, Pérez Perucha, Julio, and Santamaría, José Vicente (1979), 'Entrevista con Manuel Gutiérrez Aragón', *Contracampo*, 7 (Dec.).

Payán, Miguel Juan, and López, José Luis (1985), *Manuel Gutiérrez Aragón*. Madrid: Ediciones JC.

Pérez Perucha, Julio (1979), 'Dos observaciones sobre el cine de Manuel Gutiérrez Aragón', *Contracampo*, 7.

—— and Ponce, Vicente (1986), 'Algunas instrucciones para evitar naufragios metodológicos y rastrear la transición democrática en el cine español', in *El cine y la transición democrática español*, Valencia: Filmoteca Valenciana.

Preston, Paul (1978), 'La oposición antifranquista', in Paul Preston (ed.), *España en crisis*, Madrid: Fondo de Cultura Económica: 217–35.

Torres, Augusto M. (1985), *Conversaciones con Manuel Gutiérrez Aragón*. Madrid: Editorial Fundamentos.

12

Female Subjectivity in *Gary Cooper que estás en los cielos* (Miró, 1980)

RIKKI MORGAN

PILAR Miró already had a reputation as a controversial film-maker by the time she released her third feature film *Gary Cooper que estás en los cielos* (1980). *La petición* (1976) had subverted the norms of period drama with its exploration of power and sadism and female sexuality and *El crimen de Cuenca* (1979) had broached the inflammatory themes of institutional corruption and police torture in bold realist mode. Eager readings of this latter film as a metaphor for the present provoked the threat of a military court martial against which Miró was still battling as she filmed her next feature. Continuing a number of themes which had already emerged in her earlier work, *Gary Cooper* was another high-risk project, charting unknown territory in a number of ways. This was Miró's first venture into production (a co-operative company relying on the contribution and collaboration of friends and colleagues) and her first film with a contemporary setting (Pérez Millán 1992: 175–6; Martínez Láinez 1981: 22). It also rejected the easy appeal of a well-known star in favour of the relatively unknown Catalan actress Mercedes Sampietro. In terms of its commercial potential, the major risk factor attached to the film's thematics, register, and pace.

Miró's work demonstrates a recurrent preoccupation with questions of communication, alienation, and existential frustration across a now very broad range of generic forms, prompting many critics to see her as a contemporary auteur. As almost the only female film director with an established career during the transition period,[1] and given the frequent—though by no means exclusive—focus on

This study of *Gary Cooper* develops some initial thoughts about the film mentioned in my article on Miró's 1993 film *El pájaro de la felicidad* (Morgan 1994–5).

  1 Josefina Molina was the only other female director to produce a significant body of work in the transition period and the early years of democracy.

women protagonists and female thematics in her work, it was perhaps inevitable that she quickly became regarded as a feminist film-maker. Miró herself, however, repeatedly denied any suggestion of a consciously adopted feminist position and in interviews and articles around the time of the release of *Gary Cooper* her protests were particularly strong: 'No creo haber hecho una película feminista' (Botaya 1980: 33); 'El cine feminista me carga' (J.S. 1980: 66).

Ronald Schwartz's comments typify some of the assumptions which have prompted both celebrations and condemnations of Miró's work as 'feminist': 'The controversy surrounding the career of Pilar Miró stems from the motivations behind her films. Unlike her contemporary Josefina Molina, Miró is a very dynamic personality. Unmarried and independent, she is trying to re-educate the modern Spanish woman by posing and exposing their problems as the raw material of a new type of cinema that may be loosely referred to as "feminist cinema" ' (Schwartz 1986: 130). If Schwartz arguably overstates the relevance of authorial intentionality and takes a rather patronizing view of female spectators, many other critics were also quick to identify several parallels in *Gary Cooper* with Miró's own experiences, not least her life-threatening illness in the 1970s and the fact that her own career, like her protagonist's, was carved out within the hostile, male-dominated world of television. These external factors and Miró's very public image have undoubtedly influenced the way in which her films are read, and the presumption of what we might call an 'autobiographical discourse' may indeed lend authenticity and authority to the film's representation of the protagonist's subjective experience.

However, although several feminist film theorists have identified the importance of authorship to understanding the way in which female subjectivity is represented and how specifically gendered discourses may be privileged, particularly in work by female directors, recent feminist film theory has placed greater emphasis on the discursive activity within the text itself and the relationship between the spectator and the text (Kuhn 1982: 9–13; Silverman 1988: 193; Cook 1985: 189). Precisely what constitutes 'feminist film' is, of course, notoriously difficult to define. Indeed, whether it is possible to talk about a 'feminist text' at all is a moot point when the production of meaning is focused so emphatically on spectatorship and reception (Kuhn 1982: 7–15). Nevertheless the spectator's relationship with the text is clearly influenced by the operation of a complex set of identification processes whereby form and content can work together to privilege particular psychological or ideological subject positions. In a cinema largely dominated by male subjectivity, the introduction of a dominant female subject voice can in itself represent a challenging development. In its broadest sense, therefore, feminist film might be understood as that which privileges a specifically female voice and discourse, thereby seeking to challenge patriarchal constructions of femininity. This study will seek to identify the ways in which female subjectivity is privileged and problematized in *Gary Cooper que estás en los cielos* and the possibilities the film offers for a range of feminist readings, particularly in relation to female subjectivity as an existential and a cinematic issue.

Gary Cooper que estás en los cielos focuses on main protagonist Andrea Soriano, a successful director of television drama and documentary programmes in her thirties. A medical examination confronts her with the non-viability of her recently discovered pregnancy and the need for a life-threatening operation to remove a cancerous tumour. This physical and emotional crisis launches her into an urgent bid to reconsider and make sense of her now threatened life through the examination and review of her personal and professional aspirations and relationships. Both the subject matter and aesthetic approach of the film clearly reflect Miró's conscious position with regard to the film industry and film culture in Spain, as her comments on the release of *Gary Cooper* indicate: 'tenía necesidad de hacer una cosa de este tipo y ver qué pasaba. En España el cine no ha salido de la comedia o de la farsa. A excepción de Saura, no se consiguen plantear los problemas de un modo serio y haciendo una introspección profunda en nuestra propia manera de ser' (Rovira 1980). Eschewing the more conventional plot-driven, action-oriented style and structure of the Hollywood type of narrative which dominated Spanish cinema screens then as now, the film's hermeneutic drive rests on a personal psychological quest articulated in highly intimist mode. The film ultimately rejects the comfortable closure of a traditional narrative resolution, ending as Andrea is anaesthetized in the operating theatre for the critical surgical intervention which she may not survive.

Both narrative and formal aspects of the film work together to establish female subjectivity as dominant, not least in the constant presence of protagonist Andrea. The temporal structure is linear, alternating between sequences featuring Andrea at work in the television studios, alone in her apartment, seeking out or conversing with friends, family, and colleagues, and moving slowly but relentlessly towards the time of her operation. The intimist, reflective mood is created and maintained through an abundance of close-ups, point-of-view shots, and lingering detail shots which foreground the protagonist's psychological and existential dilemma and privilege her emotional and psychological viewpoint. These strategies combine with narrative and dialogue to produce a quite untypical female film 'heroine'.

Some have noted the proximity of the film's narrative structure to that of the western, a genre associated with a lone figure pushing back the frontiers of uncharted territory: 'Hay quien me ha dicho que hice un *western* tradicional con su peculiar estructura itinerante, y donde el/la protagonista tiene que enfrentarse a un problema vital que debe resolver en un espacio concreto de tiempo. Yo no me había dado cuenta, pero es así. Quizás por eso la invocación al héroe que da título a la película es comprensible después de vista' (Miró 1985: 10). In many respects Andrea's lone quest clearly echoes Cooper's (some would say futile) 'long and desolate night of the soul' in *High Noon* (Fred Zinnemann, 1952) as she faces her personal crisis alone (Johnston 1989: 261). However, if Gary Cooper was likeable even when he was the 'baddie', Miró's heroine apparently enjoys no such redeeming appeal (J.S. 1980: 66). Indeed many (predominantly male) commentators have found her quite objectionable, largely because of an introspection interpreted as self-obsession, and her apparently incomprehensible refusal to explain her predicament to those close to her. John Hopewell finds her behaviour 'bizzare' (Hopewell 1986: 184), and Vidal Estévez finds her frankly egotistical: 'se debe creer en su fuero interno poco menos que salida del muslo de Jupiter, o la diosa Minerva, con la que todo el mundo está en deuda sin que ella se sienta obligada en ningún momento a explicitar sus demandas' (Vidal Estévez 1981: 56). The film steadfastly refuses to recycle conventional stereotypical images of the female heroine to secure Andrea's dominance of the narrative and, as Carmen Rabalska points out, 'one does not find the usual erotic or fetishist image of the bruised or victimised females that become the deservers of our sympathy. In sharp contrast, Andrea chooses to toughen herself against her harsh experiences in an unfeminine way' (Rabalska 1996: 175). One might well argue, however, that Andrea's 'flawed' character and her antipathetic traits not only increase her verisimilitude, but also, as we shall see later, are open to quite radically subversive readings.

Andrea's behaviour must clearly be considered within the context of her critical physical and emotional *situación límite*: 'La película está basada en las reflexiones de una persona en un momento crítico de su vida. Este tipo de reflexiones que solemos hacernos ante la muerte de una persona joven' (Miró 1985: 10). Faced with the possibility of her own imminent death, she instinctively begins to question the meaning of her own life, recognizing that this is determined by the evidence of her past actions and confirmed through her relationships with other people. Her sharp recognition of this daunting reality is indicated as she silently mouths the poignant words of one of the characters in her television production of Jean-Paul Sartre's *Huis clos*: 'Se muere demasiado pronto o demasiado tarde y sin embargo la vida esta allí terminada. Pasada la raya hay que hacer la suma.' Her remaining forty-eight hours before the operation are dominated by her urgent need to put the record straight as her comments and gestures throughout the film constantly indicate. She tells Bernardo that 'me gustaría que después alguien encontrara todo ordenado, todo en su sitio' and is repeatedly shown adjusting the position of ornaments in her home, smoothing the counterpane on her bed, and so on. 'Hay que estar preparado,' she tells Julio, echoing the words of Hamlet.

Andrea's examination of her life and relationships is punctuated by intermittent scenes from the rehearsal and recording of *Huis clos* (1944), a dramatization of Sartre's theories concerning the nature of individual consciousness as argued in his *L'Être et le néant* (1943) (McCall 1967: 110–11). The significance of this drama-within-the-drama self-consciously points to the film's existential concerns and indicates a philosophical framework against which these might be considered.

Drawing on Hegel's notion of the duality of the conscious self—comprising both 'the transcendent self, or observing ego' and 'the immanent self, or the observed ego'—Sartre developed his understanding of human consciousness in terms of Being-in-Itself (the material existence which humans share with all other matter) and Being-for-Itself (the conscious self-awareness that separates humans from other living creatures). Since the conscious being is initially 'without essence or definition', individuals have both the freedom and the responsibility to make choices, define themselves by their actions, and thereby assert their Being-for-Itself (Tong 1989: 196–8). The three central characters from *Huis clos*, who are all dead, are a persistent reminder of the fact that humans are judged on what they leave behind and that the opportunity for self-definition is limited to the span of each individual's living lifetime. 'Somos lo que hemos elegido,' Inez reminds Garcin, who protests that 'He muerto demasiado pronto. No me dieron tiempo para actuar.' If Andrea is to affect what may stand as the final account of herself, time is short. This sense of urgency haunts the entire film.

The parallel themes of death and the brevity of life are ever present, not only in the shape of Andrea's impending operation, but also in secondary narrative events such as the death threats her journalist boyfriend Mario receives from anonymous right-wing extremists, or the terrorist attack where the camera focuses relentlessly on the removal of a young girl killed in the incident. These themes are constantly reiterated in the film's intertextual references and in its sound and visual images: Andrea's seemingly frivolous purchase of a Roman vase, a relic which has survived the passage of time, which she carries obsessively around the apartment with her on the eve of her operation; persistent detail shots of water disappearing down the plughole of her bathtub or raw egg washed down the sink; music from Massenet's *Werther* which she plays persistently on the gramophone. Time is at a premium at every level of the film: the short notice for the operation, recording and editing deadlines at work, and the time constraints imposed by both Andrea's and Mario's busy professional lives on their relationship. Her efforts to talk to him are always located at his workplace, whether at the press office of *El país*, at the Palacio de Moncloa where he awaits an interview with a minister, or at the site of a terrorist carbomb attack he has rushed to cover. When Mario says he needs time to see if their relationship can be salvaged, her response is poignantly misunderstood as intransigence: 'Tiempo es justo lo que no puedo darte.' Similarly her attempts to elicit some meaningful evidence of communication from her mother are characterized by a disturbing sense of finality: 'Si de verdad creyeras que te vas a morir mañana, ¿qué me dirías?'

According to Sartre, the process of self-definition and assertion of Being-for-Itself are dependent on the objectification of other conscious beings. An inevitable element of conflict is thus introduced into human relations as competing subjectivities vie for dominance, relegating rival consciousnesses to the position of 'Other' (Tong 1989: 196–7). The idea that the 'process of self-definition is one of seeking power over other beings' inevitably influenced the theorizing of gender relations within the patriarchy (Tong 1989: 192). Feminist appropriations of Sartre's theory of consciousness posited woman's designation as Other and her consequent historical marginalization as the direct result of the threat she posed to male subjectivity. Simone de Beauvoir, whose work was influential on Spanish feminism in the 1970s, argued that women had to claim their subjectivity, their Being-for-Itself, and transcend their 'Otherness' by claiming their rightful place in society, the workplace, and intellectual life.

In *Gary Cooper* Andrea's capacity for self-assertion initially seems unquestionable. From the opening sequence of the film she is established as a strong, independent, dynamic, even domineering personality. In the short sequence tracking her from her arrival at Televisión Española studios to the recording set, the extent of her professional success is clearly established in the congratulations she receives from colleagues on her recent international award for a documentary programme. The use of a travelling camera, relatively rapid editing, and a combination of long and cross-angle shots establish a pace and sense of movement which contribute formally to her construction as a positive, energetic, forward-moving, and determined character. The sequence culminates in an interview with her colleague Begoña in which she makes an emphatic statement of her professional ambitions and commitment, forcefully emphasized in direct-to-camera imaging with its attendant connotations of honesty and intimacy: 'Mis planes de futuro . . . hace diez años que tengo los mismos: dirigir una película—cuando me dejen. Una película, dos películas, veinte películas. . . . John Ford dirigió setenta películas, Howard Hawks cincuenta y ocho, Hitchcock cincuenta. Yo no quiero ser menos'.

Andrea's professional ambition and evident success and her general pursuit of independence appear to indicate the successful assertion of her Being-for-Herself both as an individual and as a woman within the hostility of the patriarchal context. These achievements, however, seem to have exacted their price: 'Es una mujer fuerte, decidida, brillante en su profesión, en la que ha conseguido el puesto que tiene planteando una lucha diaria en su campo profesional: Andrea quiere hacer una película, y ella está acostumbrada a pisar fuerte en la vida, aun a riesgo de arrastrar a menudo a su propia realización afectiva' (Miró 1985: 10). In terms of her affective relationships with others we discover early in the film that Andrea has determinedly shaped her own lifestyle and refused to compromise her independence and ambition. This has often made her relations with others stormy. The stagehands preparing the set for *Huis clos* comment on her forceful manner: '¡Qué corte, tío!', and the dialogue with her colleague Begoña is tense with thinly disguised rivalry which Begoña finally articulates in her resentful comment: '¿Te crees que me gusta hacer este programa imbécil mientras tú haces un función maravilla?' Subsequently her personal relationships with her mother and boyfriend reveal similar tensions. In her relationships both with Bernardo, her *primer amor*, and with her current partner, Mario, Andrea's independence and self-sufficiency became an inevitable point of conflict as is demonstrated by Mario's comment that 'Tú marcas el paso, siempre tú' and his resentful repetition of the accusatory 'tú decides' throughout the film. In the final sequence of the film Bernardo tells Andrea that the reason that he left to take up his scholarship abroad was because not only did she vehemently defend her own independence but 'también decidiste lo que yo tenía que hacer: aceptar aquella beca, marcharme y renunciar a casarme contigo'. His own indecision had been resolved by her intolerance of weakness: 'Era como diciéndome: si eres tan asquerosamente débil te despreciaré toda mi vida.'

The announcement by the doctor delivers a severe blow to Andrea's sense of authority, control, and independence. These feelings of disempowerment are reflected in the pace and formal construction of the shots and soundtrack for the sequence at the clinic which contrast starkly with the positive pace and style of the opening sequences. Following this critical moment, Andrea's reflections invite the spectator to reconsider the initial impressions of her self-sufficiency. It gradually becomes clear that her apparent insensitivity and coldness towards others is a protective armour concealing her essentially human vulnerability in both her personal relationships and the professional sphere, although it is not until near the end of the film that she finally admits this to Bernardo: ' "Quiero no necesitar a nadie para no quedarme decepcionada", dice. Es esta necesidad que tiene Andrea de ser fuerte en un mundo hostil' (Rovira 1980: 21).

Andrea's construction of a public and private persona of strength and independence also conceals an essential irony since she remains dependent on others for recognition and confirmation of that image. This irony is reflected in Sartre's argument that, as individuals simultaneously struggle to establish their own consciousness and self-image as dominant, they are also dependent for confirmation of their dominance on conscious recognition by others: 'I can know myself only through the mediation of the other' (Sartre 1969: 51). Sartre also warns of the dangers implicit in this dependence on the other, since the real self may be concealed or effaced by the self-image which is projected for the benefit of the other. Such behaviour constitutes an abdication of responsibility to the real self—what Sartre refers to as *mauvaise foi*—and thus poses an obstacle to Being-for-Itself. Furthermore, the reflection back to the subject of this inauthentic image may ultimately result in a self-deceptive acceptance of the self-image as self-knowledge (Catalano 1974: 78–91). As Catalano explains: 'In bad faith, we actually manage to convince ourselves that our lies are true. . . . The paradox is that we are conscious of lying to ourselves and yet believe [have faith] in our lies' (Catalano 1974: 86). In *Huis clos* this concept of bad faith is illustrated in the efforts of the main characters to convince each other of their preferred self-image: for example, Estelle's obsession with her appearance and concealment of her infanticidal past or Garcin's pretence of bravery to conceal his actual cowardice. Various secondary characters in Miró's film also demonstrate similar patterns of behaviour. Andrea's mother's thought and activity, for example, is exclusively focused on her obsession with her health, appearance, social agenda, and the petty banter, opinions, and impressions of her friends.

The location of the whole film within the context of television and theatre provides a particularly apposite context for its concern with authenticity, given the essential blurring of the boundaries between reality, representation, and artifice inscribed within these particular forms of cultural production. Significantly, the actor who plays the part of Garcin in Andrea's production draws attention to the way in which his own performance and role-playing extend beyond the confines of his professional dramatic roles into his own life: 'Tú ya conoces todos mis trucos de cómico,' he tells Andrea. Even his confession to Andrea is a simultaneous continuation of the artifice. When Andrea tells him about her forthcoming operation he tells her: 'Si sales de ésta y cascas después que yo, no olvides de decirles a todo el mundo lo maravilloso que estuve en la escena de la despedida.'

In the process of her self-examination, Andrea herself begins to recognize the deceptive power of the constructed self-image which is so central to Sartre's understanding of *mauvaise foi*, and she gradually comes to a realization that in both professional and private areas of her life her behaviour and image were in fact less self-determined than they initially seemed. Her success and the nature of her television work, for example, has clearly been controlled and determined institutionally. We might recall that Andrea's own forceful representation of her ambition was clearly signalled as performance by its location within the context of a television interview and the fact that her aims were expressed in terms of standards and benchmarks established by other directors (predictably all men, given the male domination of the film industry) such as Ford and Hitchcock. Significantly, when she is finally offered the opportunity to make the film she claimed was her life-long ambition, Andrea turns it down. Having told her producer that she is going on a trip, rather than share the truth with him, she says: '¿Te das cuenta? Si se estrella el avión, todo lo que habré hecho en mi puta vida serán las cuatro mierdas que vosotros me habéis encargado.' Whilst this outburst points to the limitations *imposed* on her creative work, it also implies a recognition of her own *complicit* acceptance of this situation. Her refusal of the film opportunity now indicates a desire to reassert herself and break out of this collusion in the limitation of her own creative potential.

Similarly in her affective relationships Andrea now recognizes that aspects of her apparently unassailable independence, strength, and assertiveness may paradoxically reveal an accommodation to her idea of what others expect or require of her. Her relationship with Mario is a case in point. In conversion with Julio, after a sexual encounter which seems less prompted by desire than by a need to reassert herself following her confirmation of Mario's affair with a photographer, Julio compares Andrea favourably with his own live-in partner who resents his continuing contact with his wife and is demanding he get a divorce, and argues that 'Tú no eres así. Tú tienes una identidad lo bastante sólida como para ignorar estas cosas.' Andrea, however, now acknowledges both some of her own weaknesses and aspects of the deceptive superficiality in this identity she has constructed for herself: 'Estás equivocado. Esto es lo que os queréis creer vosotros para sentiros más cómodos. Y algunas somos tan estúpidamente orgullosas como para representar ese tipo . . . ¡hasta el final! No se lo cuentes a nadie pero yo lo paso igual de mal que Pilar porque Mario no tramita su anulación, porque su mujer sigue lardeando el apellido, porque yo también soy la pequeña burguesa que me enseñaron a ser, y. . . bueno. . .' The authenticity of Andrea's apparent power, authority, and independence up to the point of her personal crisis now seems doubly compromised: in the professional sphere by her de facto acceptance of the conditions imposed by others, and in her relationships by deferment to the presumed wishes of others. The ironic implications of this strange conundrum relate very specifically to her position as a woman seeking to assert herself in the male-dominated professional world and in patriarchal society as a whole.

A number of contemporary feminist theorists have argued that, notwithstanding the self-evident gains of feminism, female access to power still often seems to be conditional upon women's operation within the social and symbolic order established by the patriarchy (Tong 1989: 213). Society has traditionally required men to display characteristics and behaviour associated with physical and emotional strength, aggression, power, and control. Andrea's behaviour in *Gary Cooper* has often been referred to as 'unfeminine' and certainly displays many of these 'masculine'-coded characteristics, as other characters' reactions and references to her qualities of assertion, independence, toughness, and so on attest. In the workplace, in particular, her behavioural strategies seem to indicate a successful appropriation of what Steve Neale refers to as the 'narcissistic male image—the image of authority and omnipotence' (Neale 1992: 281). On one occasion, when faced with Andrea's accusations of jealousy and desire, Begoña ignores her confrontational question and offers to help her finish an urgent editing job. However, her caustic comment—'o prefieres seguir sintiéndote omnipotente?'—also indicates her perception of the self-deceptive nature of the all-powerful image Andrea tries to project. Although this strategy may have enabled Andrea to carve out a career and compete on 'equal' terms with her male colleagues, her adoption of these values and behaviour patterns also suggests further implications of *mauvaise foi*. On the one hand she is conforming to a role predetermined and prescribed by the patriarchal order, and on the other it is an assumed role which denies aspects of her real self. In this sense, Andrea's situation seems to illustrate feminist arguments that in order to assume their due place in social economic and professional spheres of life, women have been required to sacrifice their difference since the celebration of the 'masculine' also constitutes a denial of the 'feminine' (Tong 1989: 213).

One essentially undeniable element of female identity, of course, is the concrete reality of the female body. It is therefore particularly significant that the crisis which precipitates Andrea's process of existential self-questioning is focused on her female body and the specificity of her womanhood. It is the invasion of her body by a gender-specific cancerous growth associated with the specifically female condition of pregnancy which initially poses the threat to Andrea's apparently successful life. Her body is thus posited as the source and signifier of her physical morality and both notionally and formally associated with diminished subjective control and objectification: the cold clinical terms in which the doctor informs her of the dangers of the operation in voice-over and the distancing images all contribute to the communication of the sense of loss of control and alienation summarized in Andrea's final comment to the doctor: 'Me parece que ni siquiera puedo opinar.'

The formal characteristics of the sequence also foreground a further aspect of representational objectification of the 'feminine' through the objectifying look of the cinematic gaze in a series of fetishistic detail shots focusing repeatedly on parts of Andrea's always prostrate body—her feet in stirrups, her raised knees as the doctor carries out an internal examination, her womb reduced to the dehumanizing scanned image on the screen of the monitor. These images—later (literally) mirrored in her contemplation of her own body in the looking glass—embody the conceptual link between the cinematic gaze and the controlling look of the dominant consciousness. For Sartre the look was the symbolic control mechanism by which the dominant consciousness fixes the other as object, once more reflecting Hegel's concept of the 'transcendent self' as the 'observing ego' and the 'immanent self' as the 'observed ego': 'Although *le regard* is neutral in its implications, most of Sartre's examples and terminology seem to justify interpreting it as the stare of judgement or of hostility.' We will recall Andrea's discomfort under the penetrating look of her mother examining her through her opera glasses. This look 'is that which comes to me unexpectedly and suddenly transforms me from subject to object, even though sometimes—as in pride—I feel that I am the object of admiration' (Barnes 1974: 64). Feminist film theory of the 1970s was particularly interested in the way in which cinematic practices might be seen to reproduce phallocentric designations of woman as Other through the complex structure of the look. Laura Mulvey, for example, applied aspects of Freudian psychoanalytical theory to the activity of spectatorship, noting the consistent objectification of the female figure through voyeuristic and fetishistic scopophilia (the sexually gratifying contemplation of objectified bodies on the screen). She argued that the controlling gaze in mainstream cinema was thus predominantly coded as male (Mulvey 1989: 14–29).

A critical moment in the film occurs when Andrea confronts the reflection of her *own* body in the mirror and directs her fear and anger at the image before her: '¿Te vas a morir? ¿Me vas a hacer esa cabronada?' The sequence is imaged in another series of fetishized shots recalling, but contrasting in tone with, the scopophilic imaging to which Mulvey referred. Andrea thus accuses her body of the ultimate betrayal of her female subjectivity and consciousness, signifying as it does her symbolic and representational objectification and the reality of her physical mortality.

However, although the body (particularly the observed body) seemingly denotes Otherness and object status, Sartre himself recognized the body as the outward evidence of our consciousness and subjectivity. 'It is through the body that the self is manifested to others' (Catalano 1974: 170–5). Notwithstanding the problematic aspects of biological essentialism, the *female* body is also central to the notion of *female* subjectivity and consciousness and thus becomes a critical site for the tension between self and Otherness. Sartre contended that this essential duality of the conscious being (the coexistence of self and otherness) could only be resolved in the impossible fusion of the self and the other. The fascination of Sartre's characters in *Huis clos* with the mirror (featured in the film's first extract from the play) thus becomes understandable as a function of their desire for the unattainable unity of the self and other. The 'mirror phase' in Lacanian psycho-analytical theory, of course, had posited the child's (mis)recognition of its own reflected image as a key moment in the formation of the consciousness and integration into the Symbolic Order of the adult world: 'The self comes to see itself as a real self only by first appearing to itself as a mirror image of the real self' (Tong 1989: 221). These ideas may help us to understand the critical importance of the 'mirror sequence' in *Gary Cooper* in terms of the development of Andrea's acceptance of the reality of her own (female) self and for the construction of the film's feminist narrative and aesthetic discourse. As she looks at her own image in the mirror, she becomes simultaneously the instigating subject (the observing ego) and the observed object (the immanent ego) of her own look, thus offering a symbolic representation of the fusion of the conflicting elements of consciousness. Her confrontation with the multiplicity of conflicting and contradictory meanings attaching to her body also marks a key point in her psychological development, emphasizing the gender specificity of her identity and subjectivity.

Within the narrative structure of the film, this sequence marks the beginning of a new phase in her behaviour in which she attempts to be more honest with herself and establish more meaningful relationships with those around her. The path of her existential quest is again foreshadowed in the film's extracts from *Huis clos*: Garcin observes that 'Ninguno de nosotros puede salvarse solo. O nos condenamos juntos o nos salvamos juntos.' If Andrea's tentative efforts to communicate affection or acknowledge fault or vulnerability seem largely to fail, the reason for this partly relates ironically back to the success of her earlier image of self-sufficiency and toughness. Her dilemma is again reflected in the dilemma of the *Huis clos* characters who demonstrate that 'L'enfer c'est les autres': 'Sartre has emphasized this point: "The only valid relationship is with other people. That can go even to hell. In order for it not to be hell, *praxis* must exist. The characters of *No Exit* are in a passive changeless situation in which each of them is inevitably fixed in his essence by the others." Hell, then, is other people when they brand us with an image we cannot accept as our own, and when we have no possibility to act so as to change that image' (McCall 1967: 124).

The failure of Andrea's attempts to establish satisfactory communication with those around her also prompts her to seek out alternative Others. If hell is others, heaven, it seems, can only be found in the Imagined Other, and a number of critics have identified what they interpret as Andrea's retreat into nostalgia and fantasy in her dialogues with the photograph of her adolescent film hero Gary Cooper, or her taped monologue to her first love Bernardo (Vidal Estévez 1981: 57; Rovira 1980: 21). It is with these two that she is able to express herself most authentically, whether in her admission of vulnerability and dependence on others—'Necesito que tú me respondas,' she tells Bernardo—or in her prayer that Gary Cooper will 'líbrame de todo mal'. Andrea is clear, nevertheless, about the mythical status she has bestowed on both men: in the case of Bernardo she recognizes that 'No podía vivir contigo, pero podría morir en paz a tu lado,' and Gary Cooper's place within the realms of myth is recognized in her echo of the Lord's Prayer which gives the title to the film.

The obstacle to communication seems largely attributable to her difficulty in finding an adequate means of expression for the needs and emotions she is trying to communicate. On the one hand this is clearly related to her long-standing denial of her own vulnerability and the fear of relinquishing her ostensibly dominant position: it is only with characters who share a power relationship with her in which she is clearly dominant that Andrea is able to talk about her impending operation—her neighbour at the flat, and one of the actors in the production of *Huis clos*. On the other hand Andrea's silence may well indicate a tacit denunciation of the inadequacy of the language of patriarchy to express her feelings.

Lacan argued that language (significantly acquired around the time of the 'mirror stage' and thus prompting parallels with Andrea's cathartic experience before the looking glass) is the essential instrument by which the Symbolic Order of patriarchy is internalized. It has been argued that in its refection, codification, and internalization of the gender binaries underpinning patriarchal social structures, language is an essentially male construct, incapable of articulating female subjective experience. Women are, nevertheless, forced to use it to gain access to the Symbolic Order. Hence 'Femininity is squelched, silenced and straightjacketed because the only words that women are given are masculine words' (Tong 1989: 221). This interpretation of the significance and operation of language is clearly consistent with our earlier conclusions about Andrea's adoption of 'masculine' behavioural strategies in order to operate within the context of patriarchy and it may also provide a key to understanding Andrea's steadfast refusal to tell anyone close to her about her problem and articulate her fears. Carmen Rabalska further argues that Andrea's stubborn silence might be read as 'politically strategic', articulating a radically alternative feminine discourse which distinguishes itself from the patriarchal associations of language, along the lines of the alternative (non-linguistic) communication codes developed by a number of feminist writers and artists (Rabalska 1996: 174–5). Andrea's apparent rejection of the language of patriarchy is also reflected in the *filmic* language of *Gary Cooper* which articulates its arguably feminist discourse. We have already noted many of the film's departures from the narrative and stylistic conventions of mainstream cinema and, as Rabalska again points out, it also rejects the common scopophilic practices of specularization and fetishization of the female protagonist and 'defies any possible eroticising intent in the male gaze' (Rabalska 1996: 174). It is the mirror sequence again which offers a formal articulation of the film's appropriation and redirection of the look. Sharing the optical and psychological point of view of Andrea (herself a director of television films) at the moment in which she contemplates the reflected image of her body in the mirror, the spectator also experiences her subjective reappropriation of the objectifying cinematic gaze.

Gary Cooper clearly addresses the question of female subjectivity at every level of the film's narrative, symbolic, and aesthetic discourse. Through Andrea's cathartic experience of the proximity of death and her examination of her life and relationships, the film calls for a radical questioning of the ways in which female identity and authenticity may have been compromised in the strategies women have been obliged to adopt in order to compete on 'equal' terms with men within the patriarchal status quo. It further suggests that female consciousness must be asserted on its own terms and through its own signifying practices if it is to be authentic and empowering. In the same way that the protagonist strives to reclaim her female identity and subjectivity, rescuing it from patriarchal distortion, Miró's formal strategies reappropriate the dominantly male practice of cinema by actively subverting the established practices of representation and looking in order to articulate a specifically female voice.

REFERENCES

Barnes, Hazel E. (1974), *Sartre*. London: Quartet Books.

Botaya, Guillermina (1980), 'Pilar Miró: "el cine feminista me carga muchísimo" ', *El correo* (18 Dec.): 33.

Catalano, Joseph S. (1974), *A Commentary on Jean-Paul Sartre's Being and Nothingness*. Chicago: University of Chicago Press.

Cook, Pam (1985), *The Cinema Book*. London: BFI.

Hopewell, John (1986), *Out of the Past: Spanish Cinema after Franco*. London: BFI.

Johnston, Sheila (1989), 'High Noon' (review), in *Time Out Film Guide*, London: Penguin: 261.

Kuhn, Annette (1982), *Women's Pictures: Feminism and Film*. London: Pandora Press.

McCall, Dorothy (1967), *The Theatre of Jean-Paul Sartre*. New York: Columbia University Press.

Martínez Láinez, F. (1981), ' "Gary Cooper . . ." gustó en Moscú', *Brun* (21 July): 22.

Miró, Pilar (1985), 'Silencios y soledades de "Gary Cooper" ', *El país* (8 Nov.): 10.

Morgan, Rikki (1994–5), 'Woman and Isolation in Pilar Miró's *El pájaro de la felicidad* (1993)', *Journal of Hispanic Research*, 3: 325–37.

Mulvey, Laura (1989), 'Visual Pleasure and Narrative Cinema', in *Visual and Other Pleasures*, London: Macmillan: 14–26 (1st pub. 1975).

Neale, Steve (1992), 'Masculinity as Spectacle', in *Screen* (ed.), *The Sexual Subject: A Screen Reader in Sexuality*, London: Routledge: 277–87.

Pérez Millán, Juan Antonio (1992), *Pilar Miró, directora de cine*. Valladolid: 37 Semana Internacional de Cine.

Rabalska, Carmen (1996), 'Women in Spanish Cinema in Transition', *International Journal of Iberian Studies*, 9/3: 166–79.

Rovira, Bru (1980), 'Pilar Miró, el miedo a la soledad y la lucha por la independencia', *Tele expres* (18 Dec.): 21.

S., J. (1980), 'La película intimista de Pilar Miró', *La vanguardia* (18 Dec.): 66.

Sartre, Jean-Paul (1969), *Being and Nothingness*. London: Methuen & Co. Ltd. (1st pub. 1943 under the title *L'Être et le néant*).

Schwartz, Ronald (1986), *Spanish Film Directors (1950–1985): 21 Profiles*. New Jersey: Scarecrow Press.

Silverman, Kaja (1988), 'The Female Authorial Voice', in Kaja Silverman, *The Acoustic Mirror: The Female Voice in Psychoanalysis and Cinema*, Bloomington: Indiana University Press: 187–234.

Tong, Rosemarie (1989), *Feminist Thought: A Comprehensive Introduction*. London: Routledge.

Vidal Estévez, M. (1981), 'Gary Cooper que estás en los cielos, de Pilar Miró (España, 1980)', *Contracampo*, 19 (Feb.): 56–7.

13

Re-imaging the Community: Imanol Uribe's *La muerte de Mikel* (1983) and the Cinema of Transition

MARVIN D'LUGO

El cine vasco es una pompa de jabón. Una pompa brillante que puede deshacerse en cualquier momento.

(Imanol Uribe)[1]

Antihegemonic Cinema in Transition

Imanol Uribe's *La muerte de Mikel* (1983) is one of the earliest demonstrations of the possibility of a popular and commercially viable Basque cinema. At the same time, however, the film poses an emotionally charged refutation of the intransigent identity politics at the root of regional cinemas. This apparent ambivalence reflects the underlying project of *Mikel*: to contest the Manichaean logic that shaped the cultural politics of cinema during the first decade after Franco's death, and, more generally, to bring audiences to rethink the chain of allegiances and affiliations that have formed and deformed the notion of community for Spaniards.

During the early post-Franco period, regional cinema (*cine de autonomías* or *cine de las nacionalidades*) was understood largely as an avenue of regionalist propaganda, that is, as the vehicle through which film-makers, principally Catalans and Basques, advanced some form of regional cultural pride and boosterism. These films often affirmed the regional culture in ways that challenged the very notion of the unified nation so fiercely defended by earlier Francoist ideology. In Catalan cinema, which had histori-

---

[1] 'Basque Cinema is a soap bubble. A shining bubble that can burst at any moment.' As quoted in Angulo et al. 1994: 156.

cally rivalled Castilianized Madrid-based film production, even before the Civil War, the tendency toward themes of historical vindication dominated works such as Antoni Ribas's *La ciutat cremada* (1975); Josep Maria Forn's *Companys: procés a Catalunya* (1979); Jaime Camino's *España, otra vez* (1968) and *Las largas vacaciones del '36* (1976); and Francesc Betriu's *La plaça del Diamant* (1982).

In the Basque Country, however, as John Hopewell notes, the emphasis was on films with more contemporary themes, stressing modern Basque culture rather than resurrecting folkloric clichés (Hopewell 1986: 233). Basque cinema lacked Catalan cinema's industrial and cultural advantages, for it had neither the infrastructure for developing a regional film industry nor the homogeneous linguistic community that had enabled Catalan cinema to develop so quickly and successfully after 1975 (Monterde 1993: 123). To overcome these obstacles, film-makers were compelled to underplay ethnic difference and, instead, to seek broader audiences beyond the Basque region. Though historians of Basque cinema could proudly point to the distinctive expression of traditional cultural images on screen in Néstor Basterrechea and Fernando Larruquert's 1969 lyrical documentary of Basque culture *Ama Lur*, that film, and others that similarly attempted to define Basque culture narrowly, failed to connect with wide audiences, or even with most critics. It was not until the formulation of the 1978 constitution, which recognized regional autonomous communities, that Basque film actually achieved wide attention within and beyond the Basque Country with Uribe's controversial first feature-length film, the documentary *El proceso de Burgos* (1979).

The success of this work, as well as Uribe's next film, the taut thriller *La fuga de Segovia* (1981), a dramatization of the escape of political prisoners from a jail in Segovia, was equalled and surpassed by the even stronger commercial appeal of Eloy de la Iglesia's *El pico* (1982). De la Iglesia's film further expanded the expressive register of Basque film through its new formulation of themes of identity. These included pairing regional political issues with gay characters in a plot that explores the relation of family structures to larger regional and national culture. As Paul Julian Smith argues, the originality of de la Iglesia's vision lay in the alignment of themes of political and sexual marginalization within Basque society (1992: 152–4). These early films, however, relied

Political Basque

heavily on the sympathies of audiences both within and beyond Euskadi who saw the cinematic assertion of Basque identity as part of the more general repudiation of Francoism.

Made less than a year after *El pico*, *La muerte de Mikel* effectively challenges that formula for Basque films by reworking aspects of de la Iglesia's material—the convergence of sexual and political identities—in order to interrogate the basis of that cultural community. Ironically, the result is a film that questions the legitimacy of patterns of affiliation, be they familial, social, cultural, or political. Though often erroneously categorized as a film of gay advocacy, *La muerte de Mikel* only mobilizes the theme of homosexuality, as one critic noted, as a metaphor to expose and transcend the very confines of regionalism, to demonstrate the 'difference' that provokes intolerance (Pérez Gómez 1984: 24).[2] The identity crisis provoked by the hero's recognition of his sexual identity, amidst an array of competing allegiances within a regional culture, becomes the conduit through which audiences are brought to see the implications of individual and collective identities beyond the confines of a narrowly defined regional agenda. Also, the pointed critique of major elements of the Basque community—traditional family structures, political parties of both the left and right, even the Church—suggested a polemical theme that had very few antecedents in the previous cinema of the Transition. In fact, with *La muerte de Mikel*, for the first time in the brief history of post-Franco cinema a Spanish film defiantly challenged both the cultural and political claims of the regional autonomies and the territorial ideology of a unified Spain. As such, Uribe's film demanded of its audience an uncommon willingness to scrutinize the traditional national fiction of unified Spain and, as well, to read against the grain of regionalism and regional cinema.

Mediating Regional Cinema

Perceived at the time of its release as an indictment of the intolerance of individuals and groups within contemporary Basque society,

---

[2] The distinction I want to make here is between films that use gay characters and themes as part of other projects, as opposed to the patterns of certain filmmakers to develop what is, in effect, a gay sensibility. For a discussion of this see particularly Bergmann and Smith 1995.

La muerte de Mikel goes well beyond a mere reflection of social conflicts by problematizing for its audience the very idea of the community. Its insistent focus is on that slip-zone of cultural indeterminacy within which the individual finds him or herself torn between competing conceptions of the community, and, consequently, of individual identity. Through the film's self-conscious strategies of enunciation, Uribe revisits two central questions that made possible the advent of Spanish regional cinema and have since shaped regional culture. The first is a solipsistic issue of what constitutes the cultural community. The second is the question of how that community might be sustained over time. In some respects the new constitution of 1978 that first legitimized the historical autonomies of the Basque Country and Catalonia, while also formulating fifteen other autonomous 'comunidades', avoided intellectual debate by privileging the territorial as opposed, for example, to the linguistic definition of regions. As a result, it fell to regional governments to define the inherent bonds of affiliation of their own communities. It was these entities, ironically, who, in aggressive ways, replicated many of the same institutional practices that had previously bolstered the territorial ideology of Francoism that opposed the regional autonomies. For instance, as Pilar Miró notes, the Catalan government invested heavily in the dubbing of Hollywood blockbuster films into the Catalan language in order to reinforce the primacy of Catalan (Miró 1988: 32).

With a more enlightened approach, the Basque government established its own regional television network, Telebista, in 1982, with the aim of promoting Basque culture and the Basque language. Though of considerably less demographic impact, cinema continued to be considered of critical importance. It was argued that film was a cultural commodity that could create and actualize the national fictions that defined the Basque Country as a cultural community with a distinctive heritage. What is more, motion pictures travel, thereby stabilizing regional cultural identity within a transnational arena (Lasagabaster 1995: 353–4). It is precisely this dialogical function of regional cinema, its mode of address to local as well as outside audiences, that seems to explain the continued investment in commercial film projects first by the Catalan and later by the Basque regional government, even at a time when all statistical indices showed that domestic cinema was continuing to lose its audiences to American film (Hopewell 1991: 114).

In 1982 the Basque Parliament established a film subsidy policy aimed at supporting the development of a regional film industry where previously there had been none.[3] Subscribing to the same logic that Benedict Anderson outlined regarding the importance of 'print capitalism' in the formation of nineteenth-century nation states, namely the positive effect of the mass media in bringing large populations to begin to think of themselves as nations (Anderson 1991: 37–46), there was an increasing interest in the mass visual media as a way of developing and maintaining the intricate network of ideological supports for identification, affiliation, and allegiance within the Basque community. It is in this context, therefore, that *La muerte de Mikel* came initially to be seen as one more demonstration of the regionalist impulse of Basque culture.

Yet the film also reflects the more problematic side of cultural politics of the transition period. For instance, some film-makers who were regional exponents began to sense their own ambivalent status as marginal within Spanish culture while somehow also linked to the dynamics of cultural production outside of Spain. Thus emerged what Marsha Kinder has identified as the tension of micro- and macro-regional cinema, which very often exploited this ambivalence through the deployment of themes that dramatized the refiguration of previously marginal identities (1993: 429–31). These tensions account for a more perplexing kind of regionalist cinema, one that seemed to play the margins against the centre. One of the most conspicuous exemplars of this tendency was Bigas Luna, whose films persistently emphasized the shifting lines of affiliation that situated the autonomous region culturally and economically between Madrid, where it was merely a marginal site in an Iberian society, and a European macro-region where, in fact, it was part of a broader and more diverse cultural community.

---

[3] In exchange for a subsidy of up to 25% of the film's production budget, film producers were asked to comply with a very liberal set of requirements: film production in 35mm; exterior location shooting within the Basque Country; technical crews that were comprised of about 75% individuals residing in the Basque Country; and, if the film were not shot in Euskara, the Basque language, a copy of the final film in that language provided to the Consejería de Cultura. These provisions, it was hoped, would help support the development of a technical infrastructure for the continued expansion of a Basque film industry. For more details see Monterde 1993: 122–5.

To a certain degree, we find this same insistent liminality shaping the development of Uribe's career as it comes into polemical focus around *La muerte de Mikel*. Through his early documentary *Ez* (1976), which dealt with local resistance to the building of nuclear reactors in the Basque Country, Uribe became publicly identified with regional issues. His reputation was enhanced by *El proceso de Burgos*, as it established his credentials as a marketable political film-maker as well. The commercial success of that film both within and beyond the borders of the Basque region, as well as Uribe's next work, *La fuga de Segovia*, derived, in part, from the general interest anti-Franco themes enjoyed in the early years of the Transition. Uribe was also one of the prominent supporters of the short-lived Asociación de Cineastas Vascos. Thus, by the time he made *La muerte de Mikel*, the third part of what critics called his Basque trilogy, his name was already closely linked in the popular press with the thematics of Basque cinema.

Yet, such an identification with Basque politics is only part of an intricate double-tiered development of Uribe's authorial style during the crucial years of the Transition. On one level we may consider his career as being constructed publicly around his identification with a regionalist discourse. Textually, however, there is a progression in Uribe's films that seems to run counter to this contextual identification with Basque themes. According to Santos Zunzunegui, we see this in tracing the treatment of historical events from *El proceso de Burgos* to *La muerte de Mikel* in which the focus of filmic action moves from the public to the private sphere, from the explicit format of documentary in the first film, to an intermediate stage of dramatized historical events in *La fuga de Segovia*, finally, to a fictional narrative only broadly situated in relation to historical events in *Mikel*. By the conclusion of the trilogy, the presence of ETA commandos, for example, is viewed not as the central focus of the film, but rather as historical background that momentarily halts the protagonist's personal drama. This trajectory, as Zunzunegui contends, reflects the film-maker's self-distanciation from the Basqueness of his earlier period of political advocacy toward a radically different accommodation as a regionalist within the larger cultural community of Spain. With *Adiós, pequeña* (1986), the next film he makes after *Mikel*, the Basque region serves simply as a convenient backdrop for a *noir* film (Zunzunegui 1994: 54–68).

What ultimately comes to be reflected in *La muerte de Mikel* is thus less a straightforward affirmation of regional culture than a destabilization of the previously defined borders of cultural production that shape cinematic regionalism as well as the film-maker's accommodation within those borders. Even more, the film goes beyond a mere reflection of a violent social reality as Uribe's subtle narrational structure seeks to mobilize the active and self-conscious engagement of his audience in the reassessment of these issues of identity politics.

Re-imagining the Community through Film

The facile classification of *La muerte de Mikel* as an example of regional cinema is usually based on the film's inclusion of topical details of Basque culture such as its focus on Basque political groups, its setting, as well as its funding, involving subsidies from the Basque government (López Echevarrieta 1984: 234–5). Such a taxonomical approach to *Mikel*, however, seldom takes into account fully the film's problematic pattern of enunciation. The story is told in a self-conscious manner that problematizes those elements of Basque culture specifically and Spanish regional culture generally that otherwise go unquestioned, namely, the individual's sense of identification, affiliation, and allegiance with clan and community.

From its title sequence, which announces the protagonist's death, the usual emphases of cinematic story have been rearranged so as to move spectators beyond mere engagement with plot and to focus on the essential evaluation of Mikel's life and death. The filmic 'story' is enunciated through a perpetual present tense (Zunzunegui 1994: 63), beginning with the funeral mass for the dead Mikel, that frames the series of flashback events that gradually situates within the narrative of Mikel's life those characters who have gathered to witness his funeral. At about the midpoint in the film, the frame shifts to the silent vigil conducted by members of the Basque Autonomy Party taking place just outside the church where the mass is going on. Besides underscoring traditional religion and modern political activity as the axes that shape contemporary Basque identity, this elaborate framing mechanism has other key functions: first, to engage the audience actively in the decipherment of the story in ways that approximate the detective genre or the whodunnit as viewers conjecture about the identity of the person or persons responsible for Mikel's death; secondly, to recast spectatorial sight around the paired rituals of the mass and the political protest so that the viewing process becomes aligned with the fictional characters' act of 'bearing witness' to the commemoration of Mikel's death. In this manner, the telling of Mikel's story, equated with the spectator's act of viewing, evinces a highly original form of cinematic reflexivity in which spectatorship simulates the ritual formation of a new community shaped by the moral bonds dramatized within the film.

By placing these rituals in the foreground of the film's narrational process, particular prominence is given to what Anderson has called in the context of nation-building the 'imagined community'. Explaining this term and concept, Anderson notes: 'It is *imagined* because the members of even the smallest nation will never know most of their fellow-members, meet them, or even hear of them, yet in the minds of each lives the image of their communion. . . . it is imagined as a *community*, because, regardless of the actual inequality and exploitation that may prevail in each, the nation is always conceived as a deep, horizontal comradeship' (1991: 6–7). This sense of the imagined community is frequently alluded to by the characters within the flashback sequences that comprise the principal narrative line of the film. Similarly, both the priest conducting the mass and the protesters grouped outside the church attempt to transpose Mikel's death from an isolated, individual event shrouded in some ambiguity into a martyrdom enacted on behalf of their own notions of the larger community.[4]

More than merely a strategy for telling Mikel's story to the audience, the framing device of the funeral mass and protest dramatizes the competing public spectacles that embody opposing ideas of

---

[4] In this regard, it is useful to recall the comments of Ernest Renan, upon whose essay Anderson built his *Imagined Communities*. In 1882 Renan noted the special condition that blood sacrifice and martyrdom held for the process of building national consciousness: 'A nation is therefore a large-scale solidarity, constituted by the feeling of the sacrifices that one has made in the past and of those that one is prepared to make in the future' (1990: 19).

that community. What will ultimately be recognized as the self-referentiality of *La muerte de Mikel* is rooted in the exploration of these and other social performances through which individuals—the spectators of such socially symbolic events—are interpellated as subjects into particular groups. In pointed ways, these social performances are made to mirror the community of off-screen witnesses comprised of the cinematic audience, viewing but also judging their own relation to the icons and myths that shape their identification with communal culture.

Though the flashbacks suggest a complex weave of characters, events, and time, the details of Mikel's life that emerge from these scenes are relatively simple. In a small Basque town not far from Bilbao, Mikel (Imanol Arias) and his wife Begoña (Amaia Lasa) are in the throes of a marital crisis. Mikel's friend Martín (Martín Adjemian) urges him to see a psychiatrist in Bilbao. There Mikel also meets a female impersonator, Fama (Fernando Telechea), in a night club. They spend the night together but the next morning Mikel repents his actions. When Fama shows up in the small town, Mikel is thrown into panic. At first angry at Fama's presence, he becomes motivated by the latter's words, and decides not to hide his gayness, even kissing Fama in public.

This openness about his homosexuality causes his colleagues in the Basque Autonomy Party to remove his name as a candidate from the local election lists. His mother (Monserrat Salvador) is less troubled by Mikel's sexual identity than by the gossip his candour about his sexual relations will provoke; she demands that he keep his behaviour discreet. In an action apparently unrelated to these matters, Mikel is arrested and tortured by the police in order to force him to betray others with prior involvement in the ETA terrorist movement. He discovers that his friend Martín had informed upon him to the police. Mikel is released and tells Begoña of his determination to leave the town and go to live in Bilbao. The next morning Mikel's dead body is found, presumably a suicide. At the funeral, the party members stage a protest outside the church, claiming that Mikel was killed by the authorities and that 'his death belongs to the people'. The funeral cortège is disrupted as the police and the demonstrators clash.

The final image of the film is that of Mikel's mother staring stoically out from the window of her house, suggesting that it was

ETA Political NARATIVE

she, not the police, who killed Mikel.⁵ The function of this final shot is not so much narrative as hermeneutic, responding to the question implicitly posed by the political demonstrators' claim that the police killed Mikel. The image thus moves the spectator once more to become actively involved in the narrative and thematic decipherment of Mikel's story.

The various flashback sequences each include brief vignettes that underscore the complexity of the varied relations that define Mikel's identity. The most central of these are the melodramatic details of the traditional family in crisis. At the outset, we see Mikel torn by a struggle between two strong female characters: his mother who embodies the narrowly defined and closed world of the small Basque community in which she lives, and Begoña, who is identified early on with geographic mobility and European culture. This duality may be read as a microcosm of the cultural and social tensions of Basque society itself, divided between closed traditionalism and a more expansive modernity. But, even more, the opposing mindsets reflected by the matriarch and her daughter-in-law suggest the conflict between an intransigent world view and one that is able to accommodate itself in new and changing environments. These are, in fact, the ways that the two women will respond to Mikel's sexual crisis.

A crucial bridge between the fate of individuals and that of larger collectives is presented in a brief but pivotal scene showing a car carrying a young couple who are shot down by the government police for having passed without stopping at a roadside checkpoint at night.⁶ This action precipitates the first political demonstration involving Mikel as a central figure of anti-government protest. More importantly, by positioning the innocent couple within the framework of larger communities, Uribe reminds his audience that

⁵ Santos Zunzunegui cogently argues that this final shot parallels a similar scene at the beginning of the film when Mikel peers out the window of his apartment and views his mother across the street dressed in black. Taken together, these two scenes serve as the conceptual framing device that synthesizes visually the underlying polarization of ways of seeing that will eventually lead to Mikel's murder by his mother. See Zunzunegui 1994: 63–4.

⁶ This brief scene, which seems to hark back to Uribe's roots in political documentary, was the basis of extensive press debate about the forced nature of the film's political themes. Manuel Vidal Estévez defends the inclusion of the scene as part of Uribe's larger plan of placing under scrutiny the full array of the political and social stereotypes of contemporary life. See Vidal Estévez 1994: 42–4.

the individual or, in this case, the couple, is never fully disengaged from the actions and activities of larger groups.

In piecing together the narrative fragments that comprise that story, the audience finds itself questioning the hierarchy of loyalties, of kinship, of social practices, ultimately of the place of personal desire within the context of those more public, social allegiances. What sets in motion the series of dramatic events leading to this hermeneutic task and the subsequent rethinking of the imagined community is Mikel's painful recognition of his own sexual desire among those conflicting social allegiances. That desire, however, is clearly situated within a narrative that insistently points to the blurring of the lines that differentiate personal from public identity. The rethinking of community through the process of the film thus becomes a rethinking of the status of the individual within society as well.

The Spectacle of the Community

One notable way in which this kind of spectator engagement is channelled into a productive interrogation of the patterns of contemporary society is through the textual insistence on the staging of moments of public performance that revolve around Mikel's body. These scenes detail the ways individual identity is appropriated into more general discourses of the community. As well, these are public spectacles; all are moments that engage a community by mobilizing sight, involving a register of gazes—looks of complicity, of 'bearing witness', of individuals acknowledging their connectedness to the larger group. Such dramatizations of looking establish the self-referential link between the audience and the film.

Though apparently unrelated to each other, these performances are, in fact, efforts to naturalize the meaning of the community, or, conversely, to contest certain naturalized communal meanings through which individual identity is negotiated. As the filmic narrative unfolds, it becomes clear that the dialectic transacted between presumed naturalness and the naturalization of affiliations in these scenes forms the underlying conflict which the audience is asked to ponder.

We have already noted that two of the most conspicuous of these performative moments are build into the frame of the film:

the ritual mass for Mikel and the silent vigil held by members of the Basque Autonomy Party as a protest against what they claim is the government's torture and murder of Mikel. The funeral mass and the protest vigil pointedly share the cultural specificity of contemporary Basqueness by involving the audience in bearing witness to the clashes between political and religious definitions of that community. The two discourses also acknowledge the power of ritual to shape and mobilize groups. Within the mass and the vigil, sight becomes the signifier of social meaning; individuals come to see, but also to be seen. Indeed, the motivation of the protesters outside the church parallels that of the mass as the priest formulates it: to bring others to bear witness to the death of a fellow member of the community. For the protesters, that act of bearing witness signifies registering resistance to the government as well as affirming affiliation with the Basque autonomy movement.

The actions of the rally organizers, however, are understood, at least by the audience, to be self-serving and manipulative. Having rejected Mikel's political candidacy precisely because of his sexual orientation, the party now hypocritically embraces him as a martyred victim of state violence. By contrast, the Church, in the person of the priest, seems clearly to embody a higher moral order of tolerance as voiced in the spectacle of the mass. With the first image, even before the credits appear, we see the interior of the chapel as the camera pulls away to situate the spectator's view within that moral community who have come to pay homage to Mikel's life. The representation of the enlightened religion posed within the film, is, as we come to understand, a rebuke of a narrow and intolerant Catholicism. Yet, ultimately, the priest's words aimed at convincing the assembled mourners of Mikel's martyrdom are recognized as textually equivalent to the actions of the political demonstrators outside the church. Each is guilty of having constructed Mikel's identity to suit its own institutional goals.

The truth of Mikel's death, as the film reveals in its final lingering freeze-frame, lies elsewhere, with Mikel's mother who, as a series of shots and images suggests, is her son's murderer. This resolution of the hermeneutic question—Who killed Mikel?—is posed in the closing image of the film so as to suggest that the interrogation of the nature of the community needs to be re-examined beyond the chain of familiar social icons or simple narrative closure. That reassessment process will eventually lead the contemplative spectator to move outside the isolated discourses of groups in order to note the pressures exerted by those groups on Mikel as he attempts to assert his own identity.

These pressures are pointedly dramatized in another series of public performances related to the nature of sexual identity as constructed by and within the social community. The first of these is a social affirmation of masculinity that takes place during the local celebration of the town's patron saint. The performance in question involves a group of men on the dock who hold on to a heavy rope suspended across the harbour to a nearby boat. Each contestant stands in a rowboat as it passes under the suspended rope; the contestant must grab a live cock tied to the rope as the men on the dock proceed to loosen or pull the rope, thereby dunking each contestant in the water until he gives way and falls in.

This atavistic ritual suggests something of a rite of passage, a test of each participant's manhood as measured against the power of the group. An equally important part of the ritual involves the community bearing witness to the individual's prowess, as emphasized by the reaction shot of the assembled townspeople to the efforts of the various young men, among them Mikel, to hold on to the rope. The scene underscores what Homi Bhabha has called the 'pedagogy' of cultural narratives, an activity that functions to teach and re-teach to members of the community their own historical origins (1990: 297), in effect, to 'fix' a socially constructed notion of masculine identity.

That invocation of primitive origins is underscored in the sequence in two ways: on the level of iconography, the centrepiece of each contestant's attention is the traditional symbolic representation of maleness, a cock or rooster. On a more formal level, the public staging of the event emphasizes sight and visibility as the cement of social unity, functioning as a self-conscious acknowledgement by the members of the community, performers and spectators alike, of their shared identity. Interestingly, the implications of sight as part of the foundational force of the community will later be echoed in the conversation between Mikel's mother and the priest when she argues that her son should keep his sexual activities discreet and *guardar las apariencias* (keep up appearances).

The same scopic structure of this ritual of masculinity is repeated when Mikel visits the boisterous Bilbao night club where Fama, the transvestite, performs. Transvestism here is not a mere incidental element of the characterization of the gay character. Rather, it functions implicitly to contest the larger community's adherence to the traditional belief in gendered identity as a natural, biological fact, by presenting femaleness now as the result of a social performance.

Unlike that earlier scene, within which masculinity was presented as a construction produced through ritual before an assembled community, Fama's performance unsettles those previously fixed identities. In later scenes, his very presence will be understood as threatening the fixed borders that neatly define all the other patterns of socially constructed identity, and, by implication, the variations of the imagined community, social as well as political. We see this with his visit to the rural town where he persuades Mikel not to hide his own sexual orientation any longer. What results is a brief moment that strikingly combines the elements of all the previous public performances we have noted: Mikel's public kiss of Fama on the street of the little town will set in motion the events that eventually lead to his own murder. That kiss precipitates the party's rejection of Mikel and his mother's admonition about his public behaviour.

Understood within the context of enquiry into the concept of community, the scene of the kiss becomes the most decisive public performance of the narrative, joining the private and public spheres of Mikel's identity, and similarly linking the two spatial and thematic polarities of Basque social life: the city and the town. The two participants of this performance, Mikel and Fama, are noteworthy not because they are gay, but rather because their open demonstration of gayness marks them as occupying a liminal space between the fixed identities that otherwise stabilize the traditional community. Set against the chain of social polarizations described elsewhere in the film, this liminality is perceived as dangerous because it reveals the impermanence of the presumed immutable marks of identity of various social groups.

While activating a series of repressions of visibility, Fama's presence as a liminar, situated between the borders defined by traditional regional culture—between urban and rural space, male and female genders, conservative and radical social behaviours—seems at the same time to open up a space of enquiry for the filmic audience as well. That space, however, is not one simply defined by issues of sexuality, as Mikel's life and death show. It is the entire logic of community affiliation that becomes unravelled in the audience's interrogation of the events that surround Mikel's real story: his insistence on his own, rather than the community's, definition of his identity.

Concluding Mikel's Story

La muerte de Mikel is distinctive even among regionalist films in that from the outset it relies heavily on the engagement of its audience in questioning essential cultural meanings through a process of 'deciphering' a cinematic text rather than merely absorbing a pre-constructed message. The underlying logic of the film, its seeming indeterminacy, derives not only from its insistence on the scopic register that shapes individuals into spectators and then engages them in cinematic stories, but also on Uribe's scrutiny of the ways individuals are interpellated into social discourses. Central to the form as well as the substance of Uribe's theme is the film's avoidance of simple thematic and narrative closure. Things do not simply end. Individuals continue to interrogate self-consciously the hermeneutical meaning of the filmic image as well as its import within the cultural fictions of Basque regional identity with which that image is associated. By problematizing narrative, character, and events, Uribe's film seeks a more demanding and sophisticated level of engagement, one in which cinema itself self-consciously becomes the agency through which Spaniards may ideally realize a new form of imagined community.

REFERENCES

Anderson, Benedict (1991), *Imagined Communities: Reflections on the Origin and Spread of Nationalism*, rev. edn. London: Verso.

Angulo, Jesús, and Heredero, Carlos F., and Rebordinos, José Luis (eds.) (1994), *Entre el documental y la ficción: el cine de Imanol Uribe*. San Sebastián: Filmoteca Vasca.

Bergmann, Emilie, and Smith, Paul Julian (eds.) (1995), *¿Entiendes? Queer Reading, Hispanic Writing*. Durham, NC: Duke University Press.

Bhabha, Homi K. (1990), 'DissemiNation: Time, Narrative, and the Margins of the Modern Nation', in Homi K. Bhabha (ed.), *Nation and Narration*, London: Routledge.

Hopewell, John (1986), *Out of the Past: Spanish Cinema after Franco*. London: BFI.

—— (1991), 'Art and a Lack of Money: The Crises of the Spanish Film Industry 1977–1990', *Quarterly Review of Film and Video*, 13/4: 113–22.

Kinder, Marsha (1993), *Blood Cinema: The Reconstruction of National Identity in Spain*. Berkeley and Los Angeles: University of California Press.

Lasagabaster, Jesús María (1995), 'The Promotion of Cultural Production in Basque', in Helen Graham and Jo Labanyi (eds.), *Spanish Cultural Studies: An Introduction*, Oxford: Oxford University Press: 351–5.

López Echevarrieta, Alberto (1984), '*Cine vasco: de ayer a hoy*' época sonora. Bilbao: Ediciones Mensajero.

Miró, Pilar (1988), 'Diez años de cine español', in Samuel Amell and Salvador García Castañeda (eds.), *La cultura española en el posfranquismo: diez años de cine, cultura y literatura (1975–1985)*, Madrid: Playor: 27–32.

Monterde, José Enrique (1993), *Veinte años de cine español (1973–1992): un cine bajo la paradoja*. Barcelona: Ediciones Paidós.

Pérez Gómez, Ángel A. (1984), 'Un año de cine en España', in *Cine para leer: 1984*, Bilbao: Ediciones Mensajero: 7–33.

Renan, Ernest (1990), 'What Is a Nation?', in Homi K. Bhabha (ed.), *Nation and Narration*, London: Routledge: 7–22.

Smith, Paul Julian (1992), *Laws of Desire: Questions of Homosexuality in Spanish Writing and Film 1960–1990*. Oxford: Clarendon Press.

Vidal Estévez, Manuel (1994), 'La trilogía vasca del cine español', in Jesús Angulo, Carlos Heredero, and José Luis Rebordinos (eds.), *Entre el documental y la ficción: el cine de Imanol Uribe*, San Sebastián: Filmoteca Vasca: 31–44.

Zunzunegui, Santos (1994), 'El largo viaje hacia la ficción', in Jesús Angulo, Carlos F. Heredero, and José Luis Rebordinos (eds.), *Entre el documental y la ficción: el cine de Imanol Uribe*, San Sebastián: Filmoteca Vasca: 53–68.

14

Epílogo (Suárez, 1984)

XON DE ROS

GONZALO Suárez's *Epílogo* stands as a marker in the cultural history of democratic Spain. The film registers the changing poetics of that period from the late 1960s to the early 1980s which saw the development of modern cinema: from the subversive cinema of the 1960s generation, whose aesthetics were absorbed and commodified in the films of the 1970s, until the 1980s where there was a drift back into genre revisited as parody or pastiche. From the vantage point implicit in its title *Epílogo* offers a reflection on the demise of the second wave of modernism against the background of the culture industry. The opposition between high art and mass culture, first formulated in the debate about commodification in art by the ideologues of the Frankfurt School, was called into question by the growth and prominence of broadcast television during the 1970s. This growth changed our perception of cinema which has, in the meantime, come to represent a locus of artistic respectability and authorial recognition in academic fields of study. At one level the film shares Max Horkheimer and Theodor Adorno's indiscriminate pessimism about the products and processes of mass culture, whose audiences were regarded as passive accomplices in the commodity fetishism of capitalism (Horkheimer and Adorno 1972), but the film is also a celebration of the protean heteroglossia of the mass media. From this perspective it concurs with the utopianism of those theorists, from Walter Benjamin to Hans Magnus Enzensberger and Frederic Jameson, who celebrate the progressive potential of the mass media's cultural products in their challenge to the auratic work of art (Benjamin 1992; Enzensberger 1974; Jameson 1979). Whereas high and mass culture are interrelated in *Epílogo*'s discursive level, the film's narrative expresses a dialectical opposition between the two spheres. It is precisely the 'waning' of this polarity, together with the dissolution of the sphere of the real into that of representation, suggested in the configuration of *Epílogo*'s concluding sequence, that has come to characterize postmodern aesthetics. *Epílogo*'s textual indeterminacy, its simultaneous resistance to and incorporation of competing discursive practices, articulate the social circumstances and historical conditions of its production and reception, offering a privileged site for cultural analysis. Adopting this approach, it is important first, therefore, to consider the medium of television and its underlying presence in the film, a presence which extends to its textuality, aesthetics, and thematic concerns. The phenomenon of hybridization resulting from the film's assimilation of television's language has to be understood in the context of the period's increasingly close interaction between cinema and television.

After Franco's death and before the passing of the new legislation on cinema early in 1984, the first financial agreement between Spanish television (RTVE) and the film industry was a decisive factor, together with the abolition of censorship in 1977, in modifying the trends of Spanish cinema. Among the provisions of the first co-production deal, orchestrated by the UCD government in 1979, was that television funding should be primarily directed to film adaptations of well-known literary works. The success of the first projects prompted a further agreement between RTVE and independent producers in 1983–4. The co-operation between the two media was intended to revitalize Spanish cinema, which was undergoing the worst crisis in its history. It was also meant to preserve the past tradition of Spanish cinema by means of enforcing a quota system on imported films. Following the lead of other nations in Europe, RTVE became not only an important source of funding but also a historical archive for cinema. However, despite the series of protectionist measures, the decline of the Spanish film industry was widely acknowledged by critics and film-makers alike. It was crushed by the monopoly of American distribution corporations and by the establishment in Spain of multinational production companies, and lacked the infrastructure to fight for an audience which had deserted cinema in favour of television and the domestic video.

But whereas Spanish cinema was lagging behind its European counterparts in their common struggle against the crisis, the growth of television during the 1980s was unprecedented.[1] The Spanish broadcasting system was to be set up as a model for multi-national states. The enormous expansion of television networks, with the launching of several new channels run by autonomous governments and later private corporations, alongside technological advances such as teletext, cable, and satellite systems, gave rise to a spectacular increase in television audiences and also to an overflow in commercial advertising, whose revenue turned the Spanish market into one of the most profitable and competitive in the world. At the same time, with the dramatic expansion of its networks, television required more and more the services of cinema as a source of material. From this point until the end of the decade the relationship between the two media developed into one of mutual dependence, forcing a redefinition of both their creative spaces and their respective audiences. *Epílogo* bears witness to this process.

During the crisis, television became a sanctuary for many film-makers who found more freedom to experiment and to develop their professional careers in this medium than in the ever more conventional and formulaic cinema officially fostered in Spain, particularly in the impasse of the first years of the Socialist govern-ment. Gonzalo Suárez was one of the film-makers who found in the mass medium a way not only to survive the crisis, but also to explore the semiotics of the film image through the new technology. From 1978 to 1983 and after ten long feature films, he retired from cinema and devoted himself to fiction writing and to advertising, making a number of television commercials. During this time, he established his own production company, Ditirambo Films, which, initially designed for publicity films, was also to be instrumental in his subsequent development as an independent film-maker. He returned to film-making with *Epílogo*, which was produced in collaboration with television. The film represents a turning point in Suárez's career and shows the extent of his involvement with the new medium, whose discourse and conventions are so embedded in the narrative that the dialogue between film and television becomes central to the concerns of the film. This fact is reinforced in the casting of the three leading actors, whose careers had found a new

[1]   A résumé of the period and a bibliography on the subject are given in Jordan 1995.

lease of life with the literary adaptations, either for cinema or for television serials, made under the first co-production deal between the two media. A commentary on the period's connection between literature and cinema can be read in the film's marked literary component.[2]

Epílogo's complex dramatic structure unfolds on three narrative levels, steered by a network of on-screen and off-screen internal narrators, and by the camera. The framing story is cast in the visual style of *film noir*[3] and its action, set in the present, centres on an interview in a hotel room between Laína and a literature student about the former's relationship with two writers: Rocabruno and Ditirambo.[4] The interview is cast in low-key lighting, and the portrayal of the two women closely recalls *noir* stock characters. Whilst the interviewer, who is at first taken for a journalist by Laína, adopts the role of a private eye, her questions becoming more and more personal, her interlocutor is presented with the traits of the femme fatale: a beautiful but jaded woman in *déshabillé*, cynical, foul-mouthed, and liberally indulging in alcohol and cigarettes. Laína's reminiscences materialize on the screen in a more conventional, realistic frame and *blanc* lighting. The narrative, a series of flashback sequences corresponding to two different periods in the past separated by a ten-year gap, spans various episodes in the relationship between the protagonists. The action begins in the countryside, then moves to an urban landscape some ten years earlier, and finally reverts to the more recent past in the chain of events which took place at the beginning of the section. This inset story in turn comprises three enactments of fictional pieces authored by the main characters. Displaying a mixture of styles, these self-contained units are often marked by returns to the inset

---

[2] The plot not only revolves around the story of two writers and their work, and is scattered with literary references (Shakespeare, Chesterton, Simenon), but it also contains stories which Suárez had published before in his collections *Gorila en Hollywood* (1980): 'Ombrages', 'El auténtico caso del joven Hamlet', and 'Combate'; and *Trece veces trece* (1972): 'Cómo ganar un combate inútil'. For an informed study of Suárez's literary career see Cercas 1993.

[3] I use the expression *film noir* to refer to a transgeneric visual style which informs the detective genre but may appear in other configurations. For an illustrative description of *noir* style, see Place and Peterson 1976.

[4] The characters of Rocabruno and Ditirambo had first appeared in Suárez's novel *Rocabruno bate a Ditirambo* (1965). Suárez himself played Ditirambo in both his short film *Ditirambo vela por nosotros* (1966) and his long feature *Ditirambo* (1967).

story, whose fragmented editing includes a brief interlude which takes us back to the framing story. The film's intricate narrative pattern is eventually resolved in the last sequence, which returns to the framing story, now accompanied by a voice-over device. The voice belongs to one of the writers, Rocabruno, who, therefore, is revealed as the ultimate narrator of the film.

In order to facilitate the identification of the sequences discussed in this analysis we can summarize the film's narrative layout as follows:

A. 1. Present (street, corridor, hotel room)
B. 2. Recent Past (countryside)
C. 3. Atemporal (story no. 1)
B. 4. Recent Past (countryside)
B. 5. Distant Past (city)
D. 6. Atemporal (story no. 2, part I)
B. 7. Distant Past (city)
D. 8. Atemporal (story no. 2, part II)
A. 9. Present (hotel room)
B. 10. Distant Past (city)
B. 11. Recent Past (countryside)
E. 12. Atemporal (story no. 3, part I)
B. 13. Recent Past (countryside)
E. 14. Atemporal (story no. 3, part II)
B. 15. Recent Past (countryside)
A. 16. Present (corridor)

In its sequence, the film's formal logic is reminiscent of the 'flow' of textual material that Raymond Williams (1990) describes as a distinctive feature of television. According to him, television experience, unlike film or theatre, depends on a 'flow series of differently related units', which are perceived as unified by the viewer. The unmarked transitions between units produce a flow of images where unconnected material becomes a continuous programming sequence. Several strategies are deployed to keep the viewer's attention fixed on the flow. Intervals between units are blurred by new items interspersed among them. They can be connected either explicitly, as in trailers devised to stir our expectations, or more subtly conveyed through situations or motifs which allude directly or indirectly to other units, or even by interspersing commercials that include characters or actors that appear elsewhere in the sequence. Even when the units are apparently unconnected the viewer tends to apprehend the sequence as a whole experience which, according to Williams, is determined by the medium itself. Williams's essentialism has been contested by Rick Altman (1986), who argues that the level of flow is proportional to the rate of commercialism and of spectator commodification determined, not by the technology, but by the specific cultural practice.

Competition for an audience was a relatively new phenomenon in Spain. Even though the debate over the introduction of private television channels had begun in 1978, the first licences were only granted in 1988 and implemented in 1990. However, both the two state-owned channels run by RTVE and the regional televisions depended to a very large extent on advertising revenue, and this fact determines the medium's unstable position between a public and a commercial system. Prominent among the strategies to increase audience rating is the pattern of flow which *Epílogo*'s segmented formal organization, with its diverse, internally coherent units and slow narrative progression, closely recalls. Its assimilation within the film highlights the theme of competition for an audience implicit in the practice.

The effect of flow in *Epílogo* is created by an alternate series of segments with different conventions and visual styles. As with television, the units are related to the preceding ones or to those larger units into which they are inserted. The proleptic style of the trailer is parodied in two scenes. The first of these is in the restaurant where the three protagonists improvise the dialogue which is subsequently re-enacted by other actors in the 'Young Hamlet' episode (D). The same situation will be repeated later in the film before the episode of the boxers (E). The homogeneity of flow is also conveyed by the presence of the same actors playing different parts in two or, in the case of Ana, more episodes. Motifs such as the punch-bag, the comic, and, most conspicuously, the television set — the film's leitmotif and an image of the ubiquity of mass culture — appear in several segments. There is also one sequence whose style closely corresponds to the staple of commercial television: the advertisement film. It is the horse race that the three main characters contemplate in the country fair (B.11), which is shot in the characteristic multiple camera technique of television. The visual qualities are intensified by slow-motion action, and rapid cutting to the protagonists' faces in close-up. In the soundtrack, synthesizer music emphasizes the atmosphere of a commercial. This essentially visual scene is echoed in the last interspersed story (E). This episode is cinematic, in both its mode of narration and its techniques. However, in the final sequence, synthesizer music similar to that used in the background of the horse race marks the televisual quality of the images of the fight between the two boxers. The voice-over commentary, detailed close-ups, variety of perspectives, and slow motion recall television's coverage of professional spectator sports, which Adorno (1991: 77) sees as an emblem of the schema of mass culture.

Moreover, different television formats are reproduced or parodied within the film, particularly in the interspersed stories which represent the writers' fictions. They highlight specific traits of television broadcasting which differentiate its practices from those of feature film. The characteristics of the first interspersed story (C) correspond to those of the situation comedy. This type of programme is a character comedy based on humour which reflects a conflict between two opposing forces left unresolved. The scene is constructed around an incident and consists of a verbal confrontation between two characters. Its theatrical quality is produced by the centrality of the dialogue and the merely illustrative function of the images. The static vision of the sitcom format is represented in the character of the eccentric confined to a wheelchair.

The connection of the 'Young Hamlet' episode (D) with television is stated in the opening sequence, where most of the television sets in the shop window display reproduce images from this story. It is shot in a style that parodies the conventions of North American soap operas. Specifically, it reproduces the format of the plutocratic family sagas whose original and most successful example is *Dallas*. As in the glossy American serial, the setting is a luxurious villa and the subject a wealthy family's internal feud. The villainous stepfather and his glamorous wife, always dressed in expensive outfits, are characters which could be easily accommodated within the milieu of the Ewing family. Their lives seem surrounded by an identical atmosphere of psychological violence, verbal confrontation, and melodrama. The only difference lies in the fact that the fictional aspect of the narrated reality in the film is caricatured by the actors' stilted performances. The worldwide popularity of *Dallas* at the beginning of the 1980s alarmed highbrow ideologues of mass culture. They regarded the phenomenon merely as an image of the colonization of popular culture by American consumer capitalism. However, as media reception studies have convincingly argued, the popularity of *Dallas* had more to do with the hefty manipulation of television's conventions than with the fascination produced by the style of life portrayed.[5] The use of Shakespeare's work in the plot-line, whilst representing mass culture's assimilation of the 'serious' art of the past, is not only an ironic commentary on a serial whose low standard with regard to content had been generally criticized, but also the inclusion of *Hamlet*'s play-within-a-play scene, in the context of *Dallas*, alludes to a defining factor of those dramatic modalities, series and serials, specific to television: the pattern of repetition, either of format, situation, or characters, which gives the audience an instant familiarity with the form and guarantees its continuity.

Finally, *Epílogo* also displays several features which are characteristic of broadcast television: wordiness, prevalence of close-ups and television's typical 'talking heads', instances of shallow focus as well as stripped-down *mise-en-scène*. These traits, however, are shared, with varying emphases, by the two media. It was precisely the realization that many cinematic codes (editing, camera movements, spatio-temporal configuration) were common to other artistic practices that made film semioticians in the late 1960s redirect the focus of their attention from the textual production to spectatorial dynamics.

This emphasis on the 'reader' is prominently inscribed in *Epílogo*. The fact that the two repositories of this role are female characters brings into play the traditional identification of women with mass culture: from the paradigmatically naive, emotional, and passive consumer embodied in the film by Ana, to the modern mass culture audience, described by Adorno (1991: 139) as 'supposedly disillusioned, alert and hard-boiled', represented in Laína. These two attitudes, in turn, relate to different media: literature and film, and television, respectively. The interrelated issues of spectatorship and gender have dominated a large part of the critical discussion in film theory for the last two decades. Theorists of cinematic specificity such as Jean-Louis Baudry and Christian Metz introduced the subject, exploring the issue of subject positioning effected

5 For a study of the phenomenon, see Ang 1985.

by what was termed the cinematographic apparatus (Metz 1982). In
Epílogo, Ana embodies the childish, regressive, and desexualized
subject, trapped in the 'Imaginary stage', which Metz, drawing on
Lacanian terminology, describes as a paradigm for his model of
cinema's spectatorial experience. At the same time, the submissive and
sexually ambiguous roles she adopts in the episodes seem to illustrate
Laura Mulvey's description of the masculinized and passive position
offered to the female spectator in traditional cinema, a position which
has since been questioned by feminist theorists of the gaze.[6] In
contrast, Laína's attitude is detached and dialectical. Her position,
which appears free from the scopophiliac drive that the male protagonists flaunt, is closer to the definition of the broadcast television
viewer.[7] The discursive relationship that television establishes with its
audience is illustrated in the sequence where Rocabruno tells Laína
the story 'Cómo ganar un combate inútil' (B.10). Rocabruno's
projected shadow gives the narration a cinematic tone. Whilst Laína's
attitude is diverted between the narration and extratextual concerns,
Rocabruno tries to elicit her concentration by creating a sense of
complicity through direct address, asking her to write down the story,
and placing himself in an investigative role within the story.

The preoccupation with the spectator in the film's narrative is
borne out by the ultimate frame of the film which shows the stylistic traces of those genres that 'actively acknowledge and inscribe
within their structures the practice of reading'.[8] *Epílogo* opens with
the scenario of a *film noir*. As we have seen, the visual style and the
dramatic structure of a large part of the film are associated with

[6] Laura Mulvey's seminal essays (1975; 1981) opened the ongoing debate
around the female gaze. Taking issue with Metz's essentialism she argued that the
spectator's position is not inherent to the medium of film but the result of textual
strategies which are culturally and historically determined. For critical commen-
taries on Mulvey's model see Stacey 1988.

[7] Rick Altman describes the competing regimes as follows: 'Hollywood narrative film is mainly non-discursive. It refuses to recognize the presence of the viewer,
making that viewer adopt instead the stance of the voyeur, a stance that depends on
a dependable and continuous level of attention. With TV the audience is not secure.
Television competes with surrounding objects of attention just as the products it
advertises do; it is thus far more discursive as a whole, addressing the audience and
involving spectators in dialogue, enjoining them to look, to see, to partake of that
which is offered up for vision' (Altman 1986: 50). Ellis (1992: 163–4) examines the
differences between the cinema's 'gaze' and the television's 'glance'.

[8] Stephen Neale discusses the notion of genre from a structuralist psychoanalytic perspective (1992: 42).

television. Except for a brief sequence in the middle, it is not until the last images, with the voice-over and flashback device, that the film reverts to full-blown *noir* style. However, this mode of cinema sets the tone for the whole film. *Epílogo*'s retrospective narrative structure, organized around a triangle of protagonists, is very similar to that of the private eye genre, where the plot hinges on the reconstruction of a crime and revolves around a triangle formed by the detective, the victim, and the murderer. The overall structure of the film conforms to the whodunnit, where the narrative contains not one but two stories: the story of the crime and the story of the investigation.[9] The re-enactment of the relationship between the two writers, the central narrative thread, is subject to the temporal discontinuities which characterize *film noir*. Moreover, motifs and themes belonging to the crime tradition pervade the film. The recurrent presence of the pistol and the reiteration of the jazz tune are reminders of this underlying genre.

The prevalence of *noir* cinematography not only gives a cohesion to the narrative but has a deeper thematic significance. Even though television cop series replicate some of its visual conventions, *film noir* is essentially cinematic. It first appeared in America during the 1940s and 1950s as a spin-off from gangster and thriller genres. *Panorama du film noir*, the first survey and critical study, was published in France in 1955, in the wake of the debate about the 'politique des auteurs', which had been triggered by the influential film magazine *Cahiers du cinéma*.[10] Auteurist critics reacted against the literariness and social realism of French art cinema and the sociological emphasis of its critics, valorizing instead a formalist approach in film criticism and popular American cinema. The auteurist's interest in *mise-en-scène* informed the movement of the Nouvelle Vague, which from 1959 to 1964 produced a series of experimental films whose iconoclastic style, loose plots, and aesthetics of dislocation were distinctive hallmarks. Most Nouvelle Vague film-makers belonged to the critical circle of *Cahiers* and championed from its pages Hollywood genres, films, and auteurs. Their films combined homages to American cinema with an innovative approach to film-making, acknowledging in their cinematography

---

[9] According to Tzvetan Todorov's classification of the genre (1977: 44).

[10] The favourable critical reception of the genre in France was prompted by the popularity of the 'Série Noire', a collection of detective novels published by Gallimard in 1945, from which the term *noir* derives.

the influence of television, particularly in its interview and reportage techniques. Godard, Truffaut, and Chabrol, particularly, employed the *film noir*, its structure, motifs, and conventions, as a referent in many of their films. In *Epílogo*, this style functions beyond the limits of self-referentiality or nostalgic homage. Relevant to the film's thematic concerns is the fact that the French New Wave film-makers had earlier been the critics who first formulated the principles of an auteurist approach for film criticism in which the visual discourse was valorized as the ultimate expression of a romanticized notion of an auteur's personality, understood as expressing an individual world view constructed through thematic or stylistic consistency. In their critical practice they would focus on the highly formalized American popular commercial cinema, and would greatly prize the visual suggestiveness of the *film noir* tradition in their ranking of auteurs. And this is precisely the issue that *Epílogo* highlights through its references to *film noir*. *Epílogo*'s circularity is in itself a statement in favour of style, even if this style has been exposed in the film as corrupt and manipulative. It is interesting to note that the name of the boxer who wins the fight in *Epílogo*'s last inserted story is different from the original in the published story and in the screenplay. The film's version, 'Cara de niño', has connotations associated with *film noir*. It brings to mind the title of a famous gangster film, *Baby Face Nelson* (1957), whose director, Don Siegel, figured in the pantheon of auteurs championed by *Cahiers du cinéma*.[11]

The influence of the Nouvelle Vague on the emergence in the late 1960s of the Barcelona School, in whose orbit Suárez began his career in cinema, was paramount.[12] Like their French mentors, the

[11]   Suárez had used the name Nelson for the protagonist of one of his novels, *De cuerpo presente*, described by Cercas as 'un irónico pastiche de las novelas y films de la serie negra' (1993: 198). The character in the novel has many similarities with the violent, elusive, psychopathic gangster of Siegel's film.

[12]   Suárez wrote the script of the film which is considered its starting point, *Fata Morgana* (1965), and his first films are included in every account of the movement's history. See the dossier 'Escuela de Barcelona' 1969. Despite Suárez's reluctance to identify himself with the more radical tendencies of the Barcelona School, *Ditirambo* (1967), *El extraño caso del Dr Fausto* (1969), as well as his short-length films *Ditirambo vela por nosotros* (1966) and *El horrible ser nunca visto* (1966), participate in the break with the neorealist aesthetics of the film-makers associated with the state-run film school (EOC), and also register the assimilation of the European vanguard which animated the Catalan movement. However, Suárez's films are more conservative on a formal level than those of his Catalan counterparts.

film-makers associated with the Catalan movement defined their cinema in opposition to a tradition of social realism, and opted for an independent, experimental cinema, with little commercial viability. The originality of their films lies in the incorporation of the world of publicity and fashion which had in Barcelona a strong tradition and a very competitive industry. Thus the Catalan movement added a look of cosmopolitan sophistication to the New Wave's camerawork and cultural eclecticism. Many elements in *Epílogo* conjure up the aesthetics of the Barcelona School, among them, the presence among the cast of a real-life fashion model in the role of Hamlet's mother, as well as of Charo López, who had featured in Suárez's first films, *Ditirambo* (1967) and *El extraño caso del Dr Fausto* (1969), and of Paco Rabal, who was a protagonist in one of the most renowned films of the movement, Jacinto Esteva's *Después del diluvio* (1968).

The film also engages with a current vogue for the thriller genre in Spanish novels and films where *noir* imagery was prevalent—in most cases having an underlying affinity with the American model of seedy violence and cynicism. The thriller became the vehicle for the portrayal of corruption and perversion, and the sexual explicitness characteristic of the genre made it popular because of its novelty. Furthermore, the choice of the *film noir* mode to frame the story acquires a new significance against the subsequent development of Suárez's career and many of his contemporaries. The fact that the genres associated with *noir* cinematography are perceived as entertainment rather than as art seems to indicate the dangers of a type of cinema which relies too much on the material of popular culture and is, therefore, susceptible to being absorbed into an irretrievable present associated with TV ephemera. At the same time, however, embodying as it does the golden age of genre film, *film noir* has become a favourite target for that postmodern form of pastiche which is the metageneric or nostalgia film. This trend derives from the self-consciousness that theorists of auteurism,

His mixture of narrative coherence and wry humour is reminiscent of the most humanistic tendency within the French Nouvelle Vague, with whom he also shared a fascination with Hitchcock's cinema and American *film noir*. The similarities and discrepancies between Suárez's style and that of the most representative film-makers of the Barcelona School are discussed in Hernández Ruiz 1991: 161–77. For a comparison between the styles of the Nouvelle Vague and the Barcelona School, see Riambau i Möller 1991.

with their emphasis on individual style, brought to practitioners of genre. Whereas, according to Jameson, 'the cult of the glossy image' in nostalgia films 'ratifies the triumph of all values of contemporary consumer society, of late capitalist consumption' (1992: 85), the effect of its visual enhancement signifies, paradoxically, a virtual return of the 'Benjaminian aura' to the movie screen.

By the logic of the film's recursive structure, the end-frame is identified with the present whereas the body of the film, with its different diegetic levels, is displaced to the past. This past, in turn, is associated with the 1960 generation, whose artistic practices integrated high modernism and mass culture in a complex relationship which is illustrated in this part of the film. François Truffaut's film *Jules et Jim* (1962) is unavoidably recalled in *Epílogo*'s *ménage à trois*, and the film also incorporates motifs such as the Double and the Innocent, two icons belonging to the movements—German expressionism and Italian neorealism, respectively—from which neomodern stylistics derive.[13] The recurrent neorealist figure of the innocent child, embodied in *Epílogo* by Ana's naive gaze, is in contrast, in a characteristically neomodern way, to its dystopian opposite in the knowing gaze of the young Hamlet. Likewise, the Double, a Romantic motif emblematic of expressionist cinema, loses its numinous quality in the Western bourgeois world of the Cold War, becoming a symbol of the conflict between economic and cultural forces. In *Epílogo*, doubling is a constant theme, particularly highlighted in the relationship between the two writers. The threat that the arrival of Ditirambo provokes in Rocabruno corresponds to what John Orr describes as 'the fear of being petrified into the fixed value of a commodity' (1993: 39). The film's last sequence of the TV screen with Rocabruno's voice-over conveys precisely this idea. The extratextual connotations that the presence of Paco Rabal, one of Spain's most international actors, in the role of Rocabruno brings to the film are associated with the European art cinema of the period between 1958 and 1978, which has been categorized as neomodern. The term designates a generation of auteurs, born out of the renaissance of national cinemas, whose films are character-

---

[13] Orr 1993. Orr devotes a chapter (pp. 35–58) precisely to these two figures, studying the way they are assimilated and transformed by neomodern cinema.

ized by a mixture of modernist techniques of dislocation and of romanticism tinged with irony and despair. This is a combination which finds its most representative expression in the French Nouvelle Vague which, in turn, embodied the spirit behind the May 1968 revolt, with its combination of cultural iconoclasm and socio-political utopianism. Rocabruno's affiliation to this movement is underlined in his remark 'La literatura está en el poder': a reworking of the 1968 slogan which expresses the disillusion of the 1970s.

It may seem unlikely to associate a movement so concerned with reality (*cinema vérité*) and identity (auteurism) with a medium whose parameters are ontological plurality and simulacra. However, the merging of life and art that this movement propounded has found its most appropriate site in television. One of the distinctive features of the medium's regime of representation is precisely the illusion it gives of an unmediated reality.

Epílogo's mise-en-scène places us in a context where the mass media, jazz, and pop iconography—a Roy Lichtenstein painting, an inflatable with the Michelin logo, an Italian comic, several Coca-Cola bottles in an empty fridge—are combined with literary quotations, *film noir*, and classical music, all contributing to the evocation of the eclectic neomodern spirit of the 1960s and 1970s. The heterogeneity of styles the film displays may at first recall modernist strategies. However, the variety of languages, citations, visual styles, verbal registers, and inserted genres juxtaposed and interwoven in the film are not unified on the single originating level which the modernist project sought. The television screen, the final frame of the film, carries with it the implication of an ontological plurality. Thus, *Epílogo* reflects the crisis of a conception of subjectivity, that of the unified subject associated with modernism and cinema, which is superseded by the decentred consumerist subject, associated with postmodernism and television.[14] The epilogue of the film's title is finally the epilogue of the whole neomodern mythology of opposition. Having lost its adversarial position, it is reduced to the series of clichés that Suárez's film parades, a part of the mass spectacle of postmodern culture.

[14] For the notion of television as the privileged model or metaphor for postmodern culture, see Jameson 1991: 69.

REFERENCES

Adorno, Theodor W. (1991*a*), 'The Schema of Mass Culture', in J. M. Bernstein (ed.), *The Culture Industry: Selected Essays on Mass Culture*, London: Routledge: 53–85.

—— (1991*b*), 'How to Look at Television', in J. M. Bernstein (ed.), *The Culture Industry: Selected Essays on Mass Culture*, London: Routledge: 136–53.

Altman, Rick (1986), 'Television/Sound', in Tania Modleski (ed.), *Studies in Entertainment: Critical Approaches to Mass Culture*, Bloomington: Indiana University Press: 39–55.

Ang, Ien (1985), *Watching Dallas: Soap Opera and the Melodramatic Imagination*. London: Methuen.

Benjamin, Walter (1992), 'The Work of Art in the Age of Mechanical Reproduction', in Hannah Arendt (ed.), *Illuminations*, trans. Harry Zohn, London: Fontana: 211–44.

Cercas, Javier (1993), *La obra literaria de Gonzalo Suárez*. Barcelona: Sirmio/Cuaderns Crema.

Ellis, John (1992), *Visible Fictions: Cinema, Television, Video*. London: Routledge.

Enzensberger, Hans Magnus (1974), 'Constituents of a Theory of the Media', in *The Consciousness Industry: On Literature, Politics and the Media*, New York: Seabury: 95–128.

'Escuela de Barcelona' (1969), *Film ideal*, 208: 36–125.

Gamman, Lorraine, and Marshment, Margaret (1988), *The Female Gaze: Women as Viewers of Popular Culture* (1988). London: Women's Press.

Hernández Ruiz, Javier (1991), *Gonzalo Suárez: un combate ganado con la ficción*. Alcalá de Henares: Festival de Cine de Alcala de Henares.

Horkheimer, Max, and Adorno, T. W. (1972), 'The Culture Industry: Enlightenment as Mass Deception', in *Dialectic of Enlightenment*, trans. John Cumming, New York: Herder & Herder: 120–67 (1st pub. 1947).

Jameson, Frederic (1979), 'Reification and Utopia in Mass Culture', *Social Text*, 1: 130–48.

—— (1991), *Postmodernism or The Cultural Logic of Capitalism*. Durham, NC: Duke University Press.

—— (1992), *Signatures of the Visible*. London: Routledge.

Jordan, Barry (1995), 'Redefining the Public Interest: Television in Spain Today', in Helen Graham and Jo Labanyi (eds.), *Spanish Cultural Studies: An Introduction*, Oxford: Oxford University Press: 361–9.

Metz, Christian (1982), *The Imaginary Signifier: Psychoanalysis and the Cinema*, trans. Celia Britton, A. Williams, B. Brewster, and A. Guzzetti. Bloomington: Indiana University Press (1st pub. 1977).

Mulvey, Laura (1975), 'Visual Pleasure and Narrative Cinema', *Screen*, 16/3: 6–18.

—— (1981), 'Afterthoughts on "Visual Pleasure and Narrative Cinema"', *Framework*, 6/15–17: 12–15.
Neale, Stephen (1992), *Genre*. London: BFI (1st pub. 1980).
Orr, John (1993), *Cinema and Modernity*. Cambridge: Polity Press.
Place, J. A., and Peterson, L. S. (1976), 'Some Visual Motifs of *Film Noir*', in Bill Nichols (ed.), *Movies and Methods*, i, Berkeley and Los Angeles: University of California Press: 325–38.
Riambau i Möller, Esteve (1991), 'De Victor Hugo a Mallarmé (con permiso de Godard): influencias de la Nouvelle Vague en la Escuela de Barcelona', in J. Romagera i Ramió et al. (eds.), *Las vanguardias artísticas en la historia del cine español*, Donostia: Euskadiko Filmategia: 393–411.
Stacey, Jackie (1988), 'Desperately Seeking Difference', in Lorraine Gamman and Margaret Marshment (eds.), *The Female Gaze: Women as Viewers of Popular Culture*, London: The Women's Press: 112–29.
Todorov, Tzvetan (1977), 'The Typology of Detective Fiction', in *The Poetics of Prose*, trans. Richard Howard, Oxford: Blackwell: 42–53.
Williams, Raymond (1990), *Television: Technology and Cultural Form*, 2nd edn. London: Routledge.

15

¿Qué he hecho yo para merecer esto?
(Almodóvar, 1984)

NÚRIA TRIANA-TORIBIO

¿QUÉ he hecho yo para merecer esto? is a story of the migrant rural poor, the urban dispossessed of Spain in the 1980s. Its characters live in the suburban Barrio de la Concepción, a horrid Madrilenian 1960s high-rise complex overlooking the M30. Gloria (Carmen Maura) is an overworked working-class housewife who cleans, washes, and cooks for her uncommunicative and abusive taxi-driver husband (Ángel de Andrés), two teenage sons (Juan Martínez and Miguel Ángel Herranz), and a mother-in-law (Chus Lampreave) who dresses in traditional black from head to toe. In order to supplement their income, Gloria cleans in a gym and other people's flats and to keep herself going she takes 'Minilip', which is in fact amphetamine. Her husband works all day and longs for the past he spent in Germany as the chauffeur (and lover) of a Nazi chanteuse, Frau Müller. Her children go to school sporadically; Toni (14) is a heroin pusher and Miguel (12) a male prostitute. The grandmother's dream is to go back to the village but in the meantime cakes and fizzy water and slot machines keep her happy. Gloria's neighbours are Cristal (Veronica Forqué) and Juani (Kitti Manver). Cristal is a prostitute who learns English and dreams of travelling to America. Juani is an embittered dressmaker, abandoned by her husband and with a daughter (Sonia Holimann) she treats with contempt; the girl retaliates using her paranormal powers.

Gloria has a particularly bad day: she sells her son to the dentist in payment for the boy's treatment and is refused amphetamine by a pharmacist, who adds insult to injury by calling her 'an addict'. Back home, in a jealous fit, she murders her husband with a ham bone and cooks the murder weapon (the police never discover she

For Josefina, Rosalind, and Kathy.

is the killer). Toni and the grandmother leave for the village and Gloria is left alone contemplating suicide. The return of Miguel brings her back from the brink.

¿Qué he hecho . . . ? displays such an array of political and social subtexts that it seems tailor-made for studying Spain after Franco: a modern industrial consumer society haunted by its rural past, the uneven economic growth of the 1960s that benefited some, a dog-eat-dog world built on the relics of a 'moral' nation, a community with its underclasses of poverty and exploitation of women's labour in the family, are some of the thematic possibilities. From aesthetic and cinematic angles, the film also offers several possibilities for analysis: it reproduces with verisimilitude ugly and *cutre* interiors and clothes, shot harshly[1] and from a tripod, suggesting a commitment to naturalistic representation. Yet it would be very difficult to use this film to illustrate political and social questions without making important qualifications and caveats. All the elements, therefore, seem to be there to read *¿Qué he hecho . . . ?* sociologically, as a semi-documentary, but the way Almodóvar processes the material (often associated with postmodern production in general[2]) resists such a reductive approach. It may be more productive to explore *¿Qué he hecho . . . ?*'s complicated relationship to Spanish cinematic history, and more precisely to its genres.

¿Qué he hecho . . . ? is a collage, a kind of pastiche, harnessing and mixing countless facets of Spanish society and culture and, like a prism, giving out different colours with each new angle. Such a collage exemplifies Almodóvar's characteristic compositional and representational strategy: a hybrid textual weave bearing the traces of earlier uses with little respect for the (traditional) historical and theoretical notion of genre as a discrete and taxonomically certain set of categories. As Jacques Derrida remarks in 'The Law of Genre', 'as soon as the word "genre" is sounded, as soon as it is heard, as soon as one attempts to conceive it, a limit is drawn. And when a limit is established, norms and interdictions are not far behind.'[3] It has traditionally followed from this, according to

[1] 'It had to be a very hard film', remarked Almodóvar, 'in which would become clear the ugliness of the environment in which these people live' (Vidal 1989: 95).
[2] Collage and pastiche, as Jameson argues (1988: 15), are the most significant practices in art today.
[3] Derrida 1980: 56. I am grateful to Peter Buse for his invaluable help and intellectual generosity.

Derrida, that genres must not be mixed, that to do so is aberrant to artistic production: 'as soon as genre announces itself, one must respect a norm, one must not cross a line of demarcation, one must not risk impurity, anomaly, or monstrosity' (1980: 57). And yet, in spite of this law, or indeed because of it, claims Derrida, genres inevitably mix; because as soon as a limit is introduced, the possibility of transgressing or crossing that limit must also arise. The films of Almodóvar simply confirm and embrace this possibility of generic transgression, merrily building monsters, Frankenstein-films which deliberately call attention to the stitches which hold them together.[4] In the case of *¿Qué he hecho . . . ?*, the mixture of genres is not unproblematic. The disparate generic elements do not necessarily link up seamlessly, but often clash. In fact, *¿Qué he hecho . . . ?* stages an unlikely encounter between the elements of melodrama, the horror genre from Hollywood and Spanish tradition, neorealism, surrealism, contemporary underground cinema, oppositional Spanish cinema, the subgenre of the 'sexy Spanish comedy', *folklóricas . . .*

The two main components of Almodóvar's collage are neorealism and surrealism, which are usually associated with oppositional directors, such as Buñuel, Saura, and Erice. As Paul Julian Smith would have it, in *¿Qué he hecho . . . ?* we find ourselves on a journey from 'straight neo-realism (the documentation of working-class life) to surrealism (the unmotivated irruption of the grotesque and extreme into the real) by way of an uneasy compromise between the two' (1994: 58). The treatment to which Almodóvar subjects such 'raw material' prevents *¿Qué he hecho . . . ?* from being simply an updated neorealist product: it 'rejects the ethical responsibility and commitment to social change of the neo-realist, but preserves and enhances their respectful attention to everyday detail of human lives' (Smith 1994: 59). Although I agree with Smith about the journey from neorealism to surrealism taken by the film, I feel there are many more stops along the route, as *¿Qué he hecho . . . ?* freely pillages and quotes from cinematic history. Apart from the many allusions to Hollywood melodrama which would be too lengthy to discuss here (Triana-Toribio 1994), the film alludes to a plurality of earlier filmic traditions through the

---

[4] For discussion of 'generic confusion' in other Almodóvar films see Smith 1992: 163–215.

presence of a number of oppositional directors and actors. For example, there is a reference to more experimental genres and styles conjured up by Gonzalo Suárez (member of the Barcelona School[5]) as the would-be biographer of Hitler. Jaime Chávarri's cameo as the well-hung exhibitionist alludes to yet another 'school' of Spanish cinema: that of the younger members of the auteur tradition, still politically committed to the rewriting of history. Actors such as the prolific Amparo Soler Leal (Patricia) evoke the oppositional cinema of the 1960s and 1970s and the later hegemonic style of the Socialist government of the 1980s (Smith 1996: 25). She held important roles throughout these decades, perhaps the most memorable as *La Varona* in Pilar Miró's *El crimen de Cuenca* (1979), while Emilio Gutiérrez Caba, who so often in his 1960s roles played the shy, inexperienced youth (even wearing short trousers in *La caza*), is here cast against the grain, as the psychiatrist dishing out sexual therapy. Kitti Manver (and, obviously, Carmen Maura) contributes to the collage references to the *comedia madrileña*, a movement in which both women became pivotal actors in films like *¿Qué hace una chica como tú en un sitio como éste?* (Fernando Colomo, 1978) and, in the case of Manver, *Opera prima* (Fernando Trueba, 1980). Both actors, as in the case of Gutiérrez Caba, are consistently associated with quite different, even contrary, roles from the ones they represent in *¿Qué he hecho . . . ?*

More important, and numerous, are the traces of genres which were less respectful of 'reality' and more interested in escapism. Notable among these are the commercial popular genres produced for the wider public under Franco with the aim of 'merely' providing entertainment. I am referring here to the tradition of Spanish melodrama and folkloric cinema which spans from the Republican years to the dictatorship as well as the identifiable presence of the discourses of the Sexy Spanish Comedy and the *subgénero de terror*. I will dedicate the bulk of my analysis to the presence of some elements from these genres and subgenres and their effects in *¿Qué he hecho . . . ?*

Decades of Marxian ideas of social and film analysis have seen

---

[5] The Barcelona School was an idiosyncratic movement of Catalan cinema which cultivated distinctive generic mixtures. For a discussion see Porter i Moix 1992: 284–5.

these genres (and any other cinema which was not openly politically committed, for that matter) as 'forced on Spaniards' by the
ideological machinery of the regime. For example, Fernando Lara
in 1975 identified the ideal (and perhaps future) function of cinema
in Spanish society as one of education for democracy and of
providing a window onto aspects of Spanish reality that the regime
had either neglected or repressed:

The heroes of the new cinema should be those who until now have been
excluded from cinema; that is to say, the proletarian masses will make use
of it as a means of expression of their problems, achievements and of the
reality in which they find themselves. (Lara 1975: 238).

This wishful thinking about the political role that cinema could
play in Spanish society is the ultimate consequence of the
Conversaciones de Salamanca spirit, carried on through the oppositional cinema, something that became the inspiration of many
directors in the pre- and early democratic years, namely Saura,
Erice, Camus, and Borau, all of whom continued to direct overtly
political films. Even critics abroad wanted Spanish cinema to take
on that messianic role and save Spain for democracy.[6] By the same
token, these critics identified commercial Spanish cinema solely
with the compliant attitudes of directors supportive of the regime
who, it was assumed, were cashing in on the ignorant public. The
logical conclusion which not only informs Lara's study but also lies
at the heart of much work on Spanish cinema of late Francoism
and early democracy was that once barriers were removed, these
masses would seize the opportunity to demand a hearing. Such critics assumed that a liberated public would be eager for political
discourse and, moreover, that the younger generations would join
in setting the records straight.

To the dismay of many a critic, the new generation turned out
to be more cynical and less political, screen-wise and experienced
in many cinematic languages and genres from Spain and abroad.
Also they were reacting to the 'hyper-politicization of culture' that

---

[6] Roger Mortimore writes: 'The Spanish cinema can do nothing more worth-
while than help the Spanish people to face the past honestly, to conquer their fear
of shibboleths, to slough off what Luis Carandell has aptly termed "baja calidad
humana" (low quality of life) endemic since 1939, evident in thousands of books
which represent a trampling on the truth appalling in its implications and which it
will take decades to eradicate' (Mortimore 1974: 202).

censorship had induced, treating lightly texts like *Raza* (Sáenz de Heredia, 1942) which the previous generation had seen as infuriatingly doctrinaire.[7] Furthermore, these new spectators no longer felt the need to criticize popular genres for their reactionary politics but rather reclaimed their right to pleasure. They saw the relevance of popular genres as being just entertainment.

¿Qué he hecho . . . ?, therefore, relies on audience familiarity with and enjoyment of all these discourses of and about Spanish cinema but also relies on having decontextualized past cinematic languages and reconstituted them free from their origins. For example, in its perspective on the city and the country we find a mixture of attitudes to match the various cinema genres. In the 1940s, the many films set in the countryside (a practice that had been established in the Republican years) helped to perpetuate the myth of 'a sanitized provincial world of pure spiritual and moral values, implicitly opposing the milieu of moral corruption, sexual promiscuity and heretical foreign ideas that was synonymous for the regime with urban culture' (D'Lugo 1991: 43).

During the mid- to late 1950s oppositional directors, inspired by neorealist commitment to social improvement, were offering alternative representations, either through demystification—by exposing the artificiality and hypocrisy of those rural communities, as in *¡Bienvenido Mr Marshall!* (García Berlanga, 1952) or *Calle mayor* (Bardem, 1956)—or through the portrayal of a dystopian countryside, the site of violence and backwardness.[8] Another way of undermining the myth was to 'rescue' Madrid, removing its teeth by presenting it as the dwelling of Capraesque lovable losers and honest human beings trying to make a living, characters with whom the public could emphathize, as in *La gran familia* (Fernando Palacios, 1962) or *Atraco a las tres* (Forqué, 1962). As time went on, Spanish film-houses were creating a meeting space for an increasingly urban audience. The younger film-goers from the provinces could look at Madrid in the films and then step out again into streets that, in most cases, resembled those of the film they had just seen. This was perhaps the greatest demystification of Madrid's corrupting powers. Furthermore, this growing culture of

---

[7] See Labanyi 1995: 214.
[8] This was particularly the case of the younger oppositional directors in the 1960s. See Kinder 1994: 136–96.

232 Núria Triana-Toribio

cinema-going produced audiences well versed in reading and deciphering multiple generic codes. Almodóvar sits on the fence, allowing all these generic discourses not only to coexist, but to interbreed. Thus, in ¿Qué he hecho . . . ? the rural idyll that is desired by some characters (Toni, for instance, who focuses on a healthier lifestyle and pleasurable activities such as fishing) is anachronistically utopian, and yet the city is the site of moral corruption and sexual promiscuity just as the regime's representation would have had it. However, in spite of this retrograde discourse on the city, the 'negative' elements are integrated and nonchalantly accepted by the characters.

The film's indiscriminate and levelling presentation of discourses can also be seen in the characterization. Gloria and Antonio could be *Esa pareja feliz* (Bardem–García Berlanga, 1951) revisited, with a grandmother who bears many traits of the Paco Martínez Soria character in Pedro Lazaga's complicit productions (see *La ciudad no es para mí* and *Abuelo 'Made in Spain'*, 1965 and 1969 respectively). The children evoke the streetwise manner of urchins such as Chirri (*Segundo López: aventurero urbano*, Ana Mariscal, 1952) or Pepote (*Mi tío Jacinto*, Ladislao Vajda, 1956), who knew how to survive in the hostile city, but the innocent aura that neorealism and escapist cinema often conferred on children is lacking here, particularly in the case of Miguel. Other genres contribute to the characterization of children: American and Spanish horror cinema (the most profitable genres in the 1970s) and more specifically Brian de Palma's *Carrie* (1976), as Almodóvar himself declares.[9] However, despite the obvious presence of horror references, Vanessa, with her long red hair and angelic face, still conjures up the traditions of the innocent, but sometimes naughty (certainly neither evil nor possessed), Marisol, Rocío Durcal, and so on, as her powers are put to the service of very useful causes (such as redecorating a kitchen). The stunted (and middle-class) children of the oppositional cinema seem to have been left out. Almodóvar's children have no time for being psychologically 'sorry for themselves' like the Anas, Luisitos, or Angélicas who had to recover from the serious traumas of witnessing a fratricidal war. If psychoanalytic interpretations are invoked they are soon shown to be at odds with the story

9 See Vidal 1989: 107.

for a very down-to-earth motive: these characters lack the money
to have traumas treated.

Qué bonitas son las canciones de mi época
(How lovely are the songs of my time)

The 'principle of contamination . . . law of impurity . . . parasitical
economy' inherent in the 'law of genre' is perhaps most discernible
in the soundtrack of *¿Qué he hecho . . . ?* (Derrida 1980: 59). What
we find in *¿Qué he hecho . . . ?* is the appropriation of two popular songs of an earlier epoch and their incorporation into a present-
day narrative. One of the songs, 'La bien pagá', is a very popular
tonadilla of the kind that used to be inserted diegetically into musical films, such as the Sara Montiel vehicles, or into *folklóricas*.
Although this song is of a genre normally performed by women, it
is here sung by Miguel de Molina. The other song, 'Nur nicht aus
liebe weinen', is a German song of the early 1940s performed by
Zarah Leander. Both songs and both performers carry out a variety of functions, cross a number of boundaries, and upset expectations that their presence, prima facie, would raise.

   To take these in turn, let us begin with the genre of the musical
itself. Even though *¿Qué he hecho . . . ?* does not stay for long
within the generic 'boundaries' of the musical cinema, these songs
are here accorded the centrality normally given to songs in musicals: action stops, songs take over, and dialogue is disrupted as
characters substitute song or dance instead. The first scenes are
played without dialogue, although there is some diegetic sound.
Two characters, a man and a woman, enter a shower, unsuccess-
fully attempt copulation and, as the woman (Gloria) leaves, wet,
humiliated, and unsatisfied, to pick up a kendo club and vent her
frustration, the only comment offered by the film is through the
words of a song: 'Nur nicht aus liebe weinen'. In its lyrics, love,
disenchantment, and frustration are linked. As the song is
presented as extra-diegetic, we are first led to assume that it is a
device for the characterization of Gloria, but soon the source of the
song changes, and becomes diegetic (a taxi driver is playing the
same song in his taxi and miming the lyrics as they travel through
Madrid), the song and what it connotes now becoming associated
with the man.

Zarah Leander conjures up an important presence in Almodóvar's mixture of genres: the melodramas of Douglas Sirk.[10] However, it is even more productive to consider the aspects of Spanish culture that Almodóvar was seeking to cover up with this choice of a 'Germanic theme'. In his interview with Núria Vidal, Almodóvar declares that he deliberately chose a foreign song from the 1940s to undermine the assumptions about music one might normally expect to associate with a taxi driver (working classes): one would perhaps expect Manolo Escobar, Marifé de Triana, or Juanita Reina.[11] This refusal to resort to clichéd representation, as well as undermining expectations, opens up the possibility to review a whole chapter of the economic history of Francoism: the emigration of many Spaniards to European countries in the 1960s to provide cheap labour. The film is thus reintroduced as a text within the neorealist boundaries, even though the song identifies the social and political problems without making them explicit.[12] Nevertheless, in his overdetermination to avoid serving up an *españolada*, he again falls prey to the 'law of genre': because, while setting a limit in his representation of the working classes, the possibility of transgressing or crossing that limit has indeed been provided. Soon the text will show how hard the law is: the second song ('La bien pagá') central to the narrative is, against his previously acknowledged intention, a popular folkloric song.

Both songs express the view that love is absent from the lives of the characters; however, the second one takes the theme further, adding that economic dependency plays a significant role in their relationships. This song, on the one hand, demystifies bourgeois, Catholic myths about the role of love in holding together couples and families; the families in the film manage to survive without the support of love. On the other, 'La bien pagá' indicates how the relationships are governed by money and the stratagems that the characters have to resort to in order to acquire it, bringing capitalism and exploitation to the fore. This proto-Marxist concern is thrown into question by the way in which the song is inserted into the

[10] Zarah Leander was the protagonist of melodramas that Detlef Sierck (Douglas Sirk) made in Germany 1936–7 before fleeing to Hollywood to make the films that so influenced Almodóvar. See Halliday 1972: 15–22.

[11] See Vidal 1989: 110–11.

[12] Paul Julian Smith observes how because of these practices the apolitical label ascribed to Almodóvar fails to define his films properly. See Smith 1994: 2.

narrative. Through montage, the song moves from being an extra-diegetic comment on Gloria's lack of sexual fulfilment with her husband, to providing an opportunity to insert the country's past into the diegesis of the film. We are plunged into a scene in which two characters are wearing clothes from an (undefined) earlier period as they mime 'La bien pagá'; this is initially disorienting, and it is only when the camera tracks back that we see it is only a television programme. As we discover that the source of the song is diegetic (the television is broadcasting it), we are able to associate it with the grandmother and her 'epoch'. She muses nostalgically on the songs of her day, pointing to a past which to her is more desirable than the present. This may be so, but her statement is qualified by its context; this is a past whose representation provides no clues for its definite location, since the clothes are too artificial (signalling fancy dress rather than period authenticity), and the decor, a pastiche of those of TVE *zarzuelas*, flaunts its construct-edness by including posters of Almodóvar's own films.[13] In this way, the sudden irruption into neorealism is disrupted by the combined effects of a background which evokes the director's origins as a punk-underground film-maker, and also low-budget escapist television productions.

In his interview with Vidal, Almodóvar gives another reason for the presence of this song: it appears in the film as an allusion to the Republican singer Miguel de Molina, who was persecuted and had to leave Spain (Vidal 1989: 114–15). The past is brought forward through the political resonances of Molina in a manner the oppo-sitional directors would have liked: rescuing neglected or forgotten left-wing figures. The context in which Molina is placed seems to belie this acknowledged interest in the singer's predicament. There is no intention of dealing with the past by judging it, or by sepa-rating the authentic from the artificial.

Music in Almodóvar is always central and its use bears traces of the different functions that music and songs have carried out in popu-lar culture and musical cinema. We can identify these functions by means of a Marxist understanding of popular music and the contes-tation that this understanding has had in recent theoretical work.

---

[13] In the 1960s and 1970s, TVE consistently broadcast many *zarzuelas* (popu-lar light opera close to the *españolada*) performed by well-known actors who could not sing and mimed the singing instead.

The power of music to work directly on emotions and feelings was the object of study of the Frankfurt neo-Marxist philosopher Theodor Adorno. A trained and accomplished musician himself, Adorno wrote several studies on the subject, but here I shall be referring to two in particular, namely 'On Popular Music' (1941) and a study he co-wrote with the composer Hanns Eisler, *Composing for the Films* (1981). This work analyses the function of music in cinema from the starting point of the general function of music in our society. The authors attribute to music the role of cementing relations between humans, of 'gluing society together'.[14] For them, music can achieve such a goal by virtue of its immateriality and its remoteness from the extreme pragmatism of the industrial world and bourgeois society. They relate how acoustic perception retains the characteristics found in the closed societies of the pre-industrial era (termed by them 'pre-industrial collectivism'), underlining their Marxist longing for a 'utopian' pre-capitalist past whose location in time is notably hazy. From Adorno's theories (as expressed not only here but in other studies of popular music), it emerges that music is capable as an art of touching an unconscious sense of community and bringing together individuals into a coherent mass.[15] From a neutral beginning Adorno and Eisler move on, as they put forward certain examples, to more dangerous assertions as they argue that the 'pre-industrial collectivism' that music evokes can be manipulated to create the feeling of unity which was needed, for example, by fascist regimes. Music can act upon individuals directly, favouring the creation of a group: a 'false collectivity'.[16] The conclusion that can be derived from Adorno and Eisler's arguments is conveniently twofold: when the music serves to unite the 'pre-industrial utopian communities' it is viewed positively. However, when it is put to the service of ideologies such as fascism, then it becomes 'the drug that it really is' (Adorno and Eisler 1981: 42). I have described these ideas at length because Marxism-informed attitudes to popular music are central to how some Spanish directors and critics have come to view the folkloric genre; also, because such theories

[14]   Eisler believed so much in this cementing potential that he composed workers' marches and revolutionary songs. As Claudia Gorbman points out (1987: 100), in doing this he was rejecting the intellectual isolation of modernists (like Schoenberg, under whom he studied).   [15]   See Adorno 1941.
[16]   See Adorno and Eisler 1981: 41.

identify the propagandistic role that can be ascribed to popular music, a possibility taken advantage of by the regime. Almodóvar as a Spaniard growing up under Francoism witnessed both strategies in the music that surrounded him, and as we have seen in *¿Qué he hecho . . . ?* he took a stance with regard to them that has determined an important part of his filmic representations.

It must be stressed that the seeds for either role for music had been planted before, during the previous century (Alvarez Junco 1995: 86). By the time Franco arrived much of Spain was already 'la España de charanga y pandereta' (Spain of bullfighters and flamenco dancers[17]) of which the poet Machado despaired.[18] Spain did not venture outside the existing core of popular folkloric traditions or accept much outside influence, and after the Civil War, under the *nacionales* dictatorship, idiosyncratic popular themes were encouraged by the necessity to create an ideal of difference, unity, and patriotism which would sustain the government's ideology and justify Spain's evolution, isolated from Europe by a right-wing dictatorship. It is undeniable that the hegemonic iconography of the regime was attained, to a certain extent, by making flamenco and Andalusian popular music and costume signifiers of 'Spanishness' and, moreover, by unifying Spain under that single imposed identity, which was further promoted in the years of developing tourism.

Nevertheless, the success and importance of the popular folkloric traditions cannot be attributed only to imposition and manipulation on the part of the regime. Andalusian songs and dances and the idea of 'Spanishness' that they convey had already been disseminated by the time folkloric cinema contributed to their reification among the population of the whole country.

---

[17] Not a literal translation.
[18] The term *españolada* defines the particular sensibility as well as the peculiar mode of representation in these films. The same term has been adopted by many critics to describe the musical comedies and melodramas themselves. Gubern explains the origins of the word and the genre in these terms: 'The *españolada* was, in fact, originally a French genre, born under Romanticism with works such as Mérimée's *Carmen* (1845), which cultivated the exoticism and local colour of an underdeveloped part of southern Europe. Napoleon III's marriage to Eugenia de Montijo (who was from Granada) gave this genre a renewed impulse, in order to create a propagandistic pro-Spanish atmosphere in France. This picturesque view was continued in both Spanish and French silent film' (Gubern 1989: 93). He goes on to describe how this type of cinema, basing itself on the precedent created by the silent cinema, was favoured by many directors of the 1940s and 1950s with a renewed emphasis. See also Gubern 1993: 12.

The commitment to 'authenticity' of some oppositional directors in the early years of democracy (and we can argue that in
some cases this commitment stretches into the present day) challenged the false images of local colour and custom produced by
the folkloric cinema. In other words, these 'progressive' directors
attempted to establish a sort of counter-folkloric tradition which
would substitute a 'true' authenticity for the supposedly 'false'
authenticity (mass culture) served up by the regime. In Adorno's
terms the regime's manipulation of popular folklore (through
folklóricas among other means) generated a false collectivity,
whereas Saura, Borau, and Molina (to name the best-known
directors) are attempting to recapture the illusory 'pre-industrial
collective'. We see examples of this 'authentic' folklore in Saura's
Andalusian trilogy (*Bodas de sangre*, 1981, *Carmen*, 1983, *El
amor brujo*, 1986).

Almodóvar, however, disrupts this opposition between false/true
authenticity and folklore not only in *¿Qué he hecho . . . ?* but in
most of his production. He continuously (and ironically) evokes the
non-authentic folkloric music and costumes as they appeared in the
folklóricas or in ways inspired by their mode of representation.
Thereby he poses a challenge to the political duty of representing
the 'authentic' masses of Spain. As we saw above, it was assumed
by the critics that the 'non-authentic' representations of Spain in
the popular texts would be challenged by the new generations and
that the masses would seize cinema to portray their 'reality'.
Almodóvar's popularity and the recent revival of the folkloric and
commercial music of the past seem to bear witness to a different
phenomenon: perhaps these tampered-with traditions are truly
embraced. These *folklóricas*, their songs, and their singers carried
out the important social function of 'gluing' and thus, to an extent,
healing a fragmented society, even if the glue was of the 'wrong'
kind. I suggest that it is necessary to emphasize the 'healing' effects
by putting these 'manipulations' of the folkloric genre into context,
because these explain not only Almodóvar's use of the genre but
also the positive reactions to these songs of characters like the
grandmother in *¿Qué he hecho . . . ?*

In his influential article 'Entertainment and Utopia', Richard
Dyer identifies the effectiveness with which forms of entertainment, especially those that involve music, make up for some of
society's deficiencies by providing a sense of 'what utopia would

feel like'.[19] The fragmentation of Spanish society was a reality that the Civil War made even more painfully obvious. The utopian solution proposed by the sharing of a core of popular music and customs was to establish a sense of togetherness, a sense of belonging, among people who had experienced a tragedy that involved one part of the country fighting another. The cinematic genres that were predominant during the immediate post-war years (historical and religious melodramas as well as *folklóricas*), in which overdetermination to indoctrinate can be more clearly identified, surely signal the conscious intentions of the Church and the regime apparatuses to encourage unity. It is often ignored that, in reality, such practice met with a desire on the part of much of the population to put the past behind them.[20] And indeed, once these films were launched they inevitably became part of the popular heritage. Acknowledging this (and building on it as a commercial strategy) is one of the achievements of Almodóvar and a factor largely responsible for his popularity in Spain. Moreover, as Almodóvar's appropriations serve to illustrate, these texts, whether regressive or progressive in their nature, can be read, pastiched, cut, and pasted into the most transgressive of uses.[21]

Almodóvar is the Spanish director who has received the most scholarly attention in the 1990s, something which has often meant that his work has been 'elevated' from the popular by foregrounding its 'art' components. However, this film in particular has offered a fair degree of resistance to this practice by crossing, transgressing, and mixing its contradictory components. What seems to render futile our attempts to 'rescue' the film for 'high art' is the principle that put together and levelled these discourses: a reluctance, on the part of the masses, to accept that their lot was to recover the past. Almodóvar's first strategy as a film-maker was to read the writing on the wall and make films that focus on the 'present' and the 'individual's' desire, and then laugh all the way to the bank.

---

[19] Dyer points out that a facile dismissal of the practices of entertainment as manipulatory is too simplistic and hardly reflects the true nature of texts. He proposes a new form of evaluation: 'The advantage of this analysis is that it does not offer some explanation of why entertainment works. It is not just left-overs from history, it is not just what show business, or "they", force on the rest of us, it is not simply the expression of eternal needs—it responds to real needs created by society' (Dyer 1992: 24).   [20] See de Blaye 1974: 377–9.

[21] For discussion of some of these uses see Smith 1992: 163–215

REFERENCES

Adorno, Theodor W. (1941), 'On Popular Music', *Studies in Philosophy and Social Science (Zeitschrift für Sozialforschung)*, 9: 17–48.

—— and Eisler, Hanns (1981), *El cine y la música*, trans. Fernando Montes. Madrid: Editorial Fundamentos.

Alvarez Junco, Juan (1995), 'Rural and Urban Popular Culture', in Helen Graham and Jo Labanyi (eds.), *Spanish Cultural Studies: An Introduction*, Oxford: Oxford University Press: 82–90.

de Blaye, Édouard (1974), *Franco and the Politics of Spain*. Harmondsworth: Penguin.

Derrida, Jacques (1980), 'The Law of Genre', trans. Avital Ronell, *Critical Inquiry*, 7/1 (autumn): 55–81.

D'Lugo, Marvin (1991), 'Almodóvar's City of Desire', *Quarterly Review of Film and Video*, 13: 47–65.

Dyer, Richard (1992), 'Entertainment and Utopia', in *Only Entertainment*, London: BFI.

Gorbman, Claudia (1987), *Unheard Melodies: Narrative Film Music*. London: BFI.

Gubern, Román (1989), '1930–1936', in Augusto M. Torres (ed.), *Cine español (1896–1988)*, Madrid: Ministerio de Cultura, Instituto de Cine (ICAA): 89–103.

Halliday, Jon (1972), 'Notes on Sirk's German Films', in Laura Mulvey and Jon Halliday (eds.), *Douglas Sirk*, Edinburgh: Edinburgh Film Festival: 15–22.

Jameson, Frederic (1988), 'Postmodernism and Consumer Society', in E. Ann Kaplan (ed.), *Postmodernism and its Discontents: Theories, Practices*, London: Verso: 13–29.

Kinder, Marsha (1994), *Blood Cinema: The Reconstruction of National Identity in Spain*. Berkeley and Los Angeles: University of California Press (1st pub. 1993).

Labanyi, Jo (1995), 'Censorship or the Fear of Mass Culture', in Helen Graham and Jo Labanyi (eds.), *Spanish Cultural Studies: An Introduction*, Oxford: Oxford University Press: 207–14.

Lara, Fernando (1975), 'El cine español ante una alternativa democrática', in Enrique Brasó et al. (eds.), *7 trabajos de base sobre el cine español*, Valencia: Fernando Torres: 221–43.

Moix, Terenci (1993), *Suspiros de España: la copla y el cine de nuestro recuerdo*, Barcelona: Plaza y Janés.

Mortimore, Roger (1974), 'Spain: Out of the Past', *Sight and Sound*, 43: 199–202.

Ponga, Paula (1993), *Carmen Maura*. Barcelona: Icaria Editorial SA.

Porter i Moix, Miquel (1992), *Història del cinema a Catalunya (1895–1990)*. Barcelona: Deparament de Cultura de la Generalitat de Catalunya.

Smith, Paul Julian (1992), *Laws of Desire: Questions of Homosexuality in Spanish Writing and Film 1960–1990*. Oxford: Oxford University Press.

—— (1994), *Desire Unlimited: The Cinema of Pedro Almodóvar*. London: Verso.

—— (1996), *Vision Machines: Cinema, Literature and Sexuality in Spain and Cuba, 1983–1993*. London: Verso.

Triana-Toribio, Núria (1994), 'Subculture and Popular Culture in the Films of Pedro Almodóvar', Ph.D. thesis, Newcastle upon Tyne.

Vidal, Núria (1989), *El cine de Pedro Almodóvar*. Madrid: ICAA.

16

La vida alegre (Colomo, 1986)

ROBIN FIDDIAN

LA *vida alegre* is the seventh full-length feature by Fernando Colomo, whose career as both a director and a producer is closely linked to the phenomenon of the *nueva comedia española* of the late 1970s and 1980s.[1] Having scripted and directed *Tigres de papel* in 1977, Colomo produced *Opera prima* for Fernando Trueba in 1980, and then resumed work directing films of his own including *Estoy en crisis* (1982) and *La línea del cielo* (1983), both of which manifest a clearly perceptible 'intención de humor'.[2] Turning predominantly on couple-based relationships, sexual liaisons, and marital infidelity, many of the films in the category of the *nueva comedia* were *comedias de costumbres* which paid considerable attention to the contemporary social and historical situation of the characters portrayed in them. An example is *Tigres de papel* (credited with being 'en el origen de las "nuevas comedias"') (Marinero and Marinero 1982: 40), which projected a story of unstable marital relations against the background of the run-up to the Spanish general election of June 1977.

In the case of *La vida alegre*, the setting is Spain in the mid-1980s, governed by a Socialist administration represented, in the diegesis, by Eduardo, the PSOE Ministro de Sanidad, whose main concerns throughout the film are his chances of re-election to office and the arranging of further opportunities for extramarital sex with his personal secretary, the bimbo Carolina. Set in a number of milieux in Madrid, *La vida alegre* offers a carnivalesque vision of

[1] On the *nueva comedia española*, see Hopewell 1988: 294–300.

[2] The comic basis of Colomo's vision is the subject of Manolo and Pachín Marinero's interview article (1982). The continuity of the director's style and concerns is demonstrated in *El efecto mariposa* of 1995, 'a comedia romántica' which is a joint Spanish, French, and British production starring María Barranco, Coque Malla, Rosa María Sarda, James Fleet, and Pete Sullivan.

sexual behaviour in a city that is in the grip of a collective euphoria and permissiveness alluded to in the title phrase and theme
song of the film: 'La vida alegre arrasa la ciudad | la vida alegre
batirá sin piedad.' Spreading like an epidemic, the euphoria
described in these lyrics affects indiscriminately 'ministros,
doctores, la gente corriente', 'llenando de envidia a los seres
decentes', and is a menace from which the musical refrain exclaims,
in mock terror, '¡Sálvese quien pueda!'

The vision of a sickness running rampant through the body
politic of Madrid and, by extension, Spain materializes most tangi-
bly in those sections of the narrative which are centred on a clinic
for drug-related and sexually transmitted diseases. This is the
workplace, in the first instance, of the film's leading female character, Ana (played by Verónica Forqué), who displays political inge-
nuity, humanitarian concern, and organizational efficiency as she
turns an under-funded, shambolic operation into a thriving centre
of public health care whose patients include prostitutes and their
punters, an unemployed drug addict suffering from hepatitis, a
practising homosexual cleric who is instructed to send his partner
along for a check-up, and, in one of the film's many ironic twists,
Ana's own husband Antonio. Played by his namesake Resines,
Antonio contracts an STD on a one-night stand with his boss's
secretary Carolina (Ana Obregón), and then passes it on to his
wife, who had previously given him a present of a cigarette-lighter
containing a condom and bearing the inscription 'I love you'.
Locked into a chain of venereal transmission which she soon
discovers includes the Minister of Health, his bodyguards, wife,
and others, Ana nonetheless remains the driving force behind the
activities of the clinic and stands out as the focal point of a concern
with social sickness that acquires its most graphic representation in
a poster hanging on the wall of her office, which reads boldly
'AIDS Metaphor and Reality'.

Through its hyperbolic metaphors, piquant ironies, and comic
extravagance, the narrative of *La vida alegre* explores important
issues of sexual politics that are rooted very firmly in the social
reality of democratic, 1980s Spain. It attests especially to the rise of
an unprecedented sexual freedom, exemplified in the film by the
patrons of the polysemously named gay club CU-EROS (suggestive, variously, of nudity, anality, eroticism, and vitality), and in the
lifestyle of a drop-out community centred on the home of Manolo,

244   Robin Fiddian

a gay man from Burgos. An equally important feature of the social order mirrored in the film is a concerted drive towards the redefinition of male and female gender roles in Spanish society of the time, with implications for the health and stability of the institutions of marriage and the family. In this latter respect, the dynamic relation between Ana, who seeks appointment to a permanent position at the clinic through the time-honoured system of 'oposiciones', and Antonio, who engineers a 'recomendación al revés' as a means to stymie her chances, is emblematic of a broader pattern of social and economic conflict in post-1970s Spain.

Of the many oppositions that are set up between characters in *La vida alegre*, that between Ana and Antonio possesses the widest and most pointed significance. Ana's roles as wife and mother are emphasized in the opening sequences of the film, along with her ambition to establish herself professionally and financially on an equal footing with her husband. Antonio's response, '¿No te das cuenta que esto puede perjudicar nuestra historia?', marks him out as a stick-in-the-mud who will do all he can to block her attempts at progress in the narrative. Along with Eduardo (Miguel Ángel Rellán), Antonio exemplifies the conservatism of old-fashioned Spanish macho men—as he and Eduardo laughably picture themselves—in the face of modern-day challenges to male dominance. And, like the leading men in a long line of classic film comedies stretching from Ernst Lubitsch to Woody Allen, their political sensibilities are indivisible from anxieties about gender and sexuality. Thus, for Eduardo and Antonio, a central preoccupation is the rise of 'el hombre nuevo' who, as exemplified on the squash court next to theirs, combines the physical attributes and sporting prowess of 'tíos cachas' with a 'new' sensitivity to women which threatens to win the day in the competition for heterosexual favours in post-Franco Spain. As Antonio explains in defeatist mood to his wife, 'El nuevo hombre. Eso es lo que os gusta . . . No puedo competir, no puedo competir . . . Sí, sí, es el que se lleva el gato al agua. Ya se acabó el masculinismo, la prepotencia, el falo . . . Ahora todo tira como suave, como ambiguo. Es lo que triunfa.' To drive the point home, Antonio's discomfort then materializes literally in a humiliating episode where he is required to bare his limp penis to Ana and her female assistant at the clinic and suffer the insertion into his urethra of a medical probe which causes him so much pain that he faints. The film thereby exposes the vulnerability of old-style Spanish phallocracy as it struggles to come to terms with the demands of a new domestic and social order—one already in place in other Western nations, where the 'fears and anxieties' experienced by some middle-class males whose wives belatedly take up a career are expressed in the following confession, made by a male citizen of the United States and recorded in the mid-1980s: 'I see myself being stripped of my masculine, dominant, father, success image. There it is. I have said it' (Fields 1987).

For many male spectators, the spectacle of a trouserless Antonio mocked and at the mercy of a medical probe will inevitably evoke feelings of embarrassment grounded, ultimately, in castration anxiety. However, *La vida alegre* rules out a sympathetic identification with the dominant male characters through various mechanisms of spectatorial engagement and control. First, there is the prevailing comic register of the film, which consistently deflates the pretensions of a character like Antonio (forever trying to impose himself as paterfamilias in a female household which remains largely beyond his control), ridicules him for addressing his boss and friend obsequiously as 'Sr. Ministro', and shows the backfiring of a whole series of stratagems which, devised to enhance Eduardo's political image, actually tarnish it beyond repair.

In addition, the film exhibits a rich vein of satire targeted exclusively on patriarchal institutions. As already noted, there is provision in its script for an STD-infected Minister of Health and a priest who leaves the clinic clutching a medical prescription; less light-heartedly, the narrative also features an unprincipled male journalist who lies about his mission at the clinic in order to steal a confidential record card, and a doctor appointed to the directorship of the centre who callously classifies the patients under his care as belonging to 'las tres pe's: putas, parientes, pobres'. Individually and as a group, these four males cast the institutions that they represent in sharply and incrementally unfavourable light.

As the characterizations of the journalist and doctor, in particular, indicate, *La vida alegre* operates a moral economy that pits good against bad in a binary scheme which also opposes male and female, and institutional and alternative lifestyles. Thus, while Antonio and Eduardo are spared some of the opprobrium heaped on the director of the clinic and the journalist, they are nevertheless stigmatized incurably by their association with authority and power. Epitomizing 'the suffocating decorum of official life and style',[3] the two men belong to the class of 'killjoys' identified by Harry Levin in his book on the theory of comedy: 'They cannot make a joke; they cannot take a joke; they cannot see the joke; they spoil the game' (1987: 38). From an ethical perspective, Antonio's involvement in the 'recomendación al revés' which is intended to destroy Ana's career prospects persists as a stain on his character over the remainder of the narrative; as far as Eduardo is concerned, the fact that he authorizes the underhand action requested by Antonio cannot easily be forgotten, even when, near the conclusion of the film, he announces that he is eloping with Carolina to Japan, seemingly abandoning the ranks of the killjoys for those of the playboys. There are simply too many lingering suspicions about Antonio and Eduardo's moral and professional integrity to allow either of them to emerge with much credit at the narrative's close.

Resolutely anti-patriarchal and anti-Establishment, *La vida alegre* reserves its sympathy and approval for other elements of the dramatis personae: principally, the prostitute Rosi, Manolo, the gay from Burgos, and, in a dominant role, Ana. Of these, Rosi is a flamboyant and gutsy character played—in the evocative description provided by Koro Castellano (1986)—by 'una Massiel insólita: traje de leopardo ajustado y minifaldero, altísimos zapatos de ante negro, zorros al cuello, purpurina en el escote y un penacho de mechas rubias en la coronilla. Resumiendo, Tina Turner en versión castiza'. As soon as she is diagnosed as suffering from a venereal infection, Rosi leaves her patch on a Madrid street-corner and becomes nanny to Ana and Antonio's two children, on whom she showers motherly affection and presents. It is noticeable that the film passes no judgement whatsoever on her choice of profession. Manolo, the gay from Burgos, personifies a wide range of virtues and is a supportive friend to Ana who places at her disposal a suite of rooms in his house where she can prepare herself for 'oposiciones'. Played most engagingly by Guillermo Montesinos, Manolo demonstrates his opposition to all forms of unfairness, intolerance, and moralistic narrow-mindedness in a series of episodes where, for example, he mobilizes a massive popular protest against the Ministry for its unjust treatment of Ana, and tells two prurient neighbours (Chus Lampreave and Rafaela Aparicio), who are permanently scandalized by the goings-on in his

---

[3]   The phrase derives from Stam 1989: 85.

flat, to mind their own business. His openness to other human beings is manifested most clearly in his tolerance of alternative forms of sexuality—namely the presence in his home of Olga, the transsexual—which further enhances his positive moral standing.

The greatest beneficiary in the moral economy of *La vida alegre* is Ana, who enjoys pride of place in the diegesis of the film. Through her attitudes and conduct she commands the sympathy, and indeed the admiration, of those around her, including Rosi, who remarks on her delicate and considerate professional manner, Carolina, who thinks that she is 'una tía fantástica', and numerous male patients and friends who appear captivated by her personality and moral integrity. Comparisons with other female characters in the story redound very much to Ana's advantage: she comes over as being less severe than Cata, her assistant at the clinic, more scrupulous than Carolina, and more serious and consequential than Elvira, the frivolous wife of Eduardo. In relation to most of the men in the film, she moves on an altogether higher moral plane, and radiates an aura which is, quite simply, exceptional.

The fact that Ana, rather than any of the male characters, is the principal motor of narrative change in *La vida alegre* has inevitable consequences for spectators of the film. We have seen how the principal male figures of authority are ridiculed and discredited, also how, in terms of their narrative function, they are relegated to the role of blockers and killjoys. For the male spectator of *La vida alegre*, deflected from identifying with Antonio except as a source of displeasure and deterrent example, Ana effectively assumes the function of narrative agency, while at the same time offering herself up in more conventional ways as an object to be looked at by the male gaze.[4] To the female spectator, she provides a means of indulging a 'fantasy of action'[5] and a point of reference for identification. So, as she negotiates a narrative of obstacles and setbacks, Ana carries with her the hopes of the spectators, who identify with her in her paradigmatic search for personal and professional fulfilment.

The casting of Verónica Forqué in the role of Ana is crucial in determining the viewers' response to the film. Selected for a role that is far more substantial and extensive than the parts played by

---

[4] I evoke here the seminal theories of Laura Mulvey (1975).
[5] Quoted from Laura Mulvey's follow-up essay of 1981 (Mulvey 1993).

her in films like *¿Qué he hecho yo para merecer esto?* and *Matador* of 1984 and 1985 respectively, Verónica Forqué takes maximum advantage of the opportunity to stamp her mark on the narrative of *La vida alegre*. The high-pitched voice heard in the opening sequence, when Ana receives a telephone-call at home informing her of the official announcement of the post in health care, is just one of the actress's trademarks, which serves at this moment in *La vida alegre* to convey a comic impression of juvenile hysteria that is soon superseded by more adult qualities of guile and determination. Within seconds of the end of the phone-call, that same voice expresses a firmness of purpose that effectively steamrollers a reluctant and slightly stuffy husband into assisting with the provision of equipment for the under-funded laboratory.

The wide-eyed look and pale complexion that distinguish Verónica Forqué from other actresses of her generation convey a number of emotional states and conditions. One of these is a vulnerability previously seen in her roles as the defenceless, sentimental maid Vito in *La guerra de papá* by Antonio Marcero (1977), and the doleful jilted secretary Silvia in *Sé infiel y no mires con quién* (Fernando Trueba, 1985)—roles which confirm Mary Gentile's observation on the likelihood of spectatorial identification 'if the character we are following seems vulnerable or endangered, or if the character clearly experiences an intense desire' (1985: 74). In *La vida alegre*, Forqué's reaction, as Ana, to the news that she has been passed over for the position as director of the clinic is reminiscent of the emotional states of Vito and Silvia, and elicits just such a response from the spectators of Colomo's film at this point.

Another quality that the actress projects is a personal warmth and sympathy conveyed almost exclusively by facial expression, as in certain scenes with patients at the clinic. In a comic register, her wide-eyed expression serves to paralyse an audience of prostitutes and punters who listen in stunned silence as she delivers a breathless warning about the life-threatening effects and symptoms of STDs. And lastly, there are aspects of homeliness and companionship in her persona which go well with her role as wife and mother in the film, as demonstrated in the final party-sequence at Manolo's house, where she makes up with Antonio and kisses him sweetly, rather than passionately, on the cheek. Through these and numerous other traits, Verónica Forqué determines the chemistry, and therefore the appeal, of entire swathes of the narrative of *La vida alegre*.

Yet, at the same time as we celebrate the achievements of Forqué as Ana (who announces to Antonio at the end of the film that she will shortly be taking up a new position in charge of the prevention of STDs in the national prison system), it is important to appreciate some of the extra-diegetical factors which limit Ana's contribution to the narrative and circumscribe her role as a wannabe career woman who, on the face of it, attains her goals. Some further consideration of questions of genre, involving a comparison of *La vida alegre* with an American film which provides a blueprint for the story of Ana and Antonio, promises to shed more light on Colomo's film in respect of its aesthetic workings and ideological implications.

As much as any other character in *La vida alegre*, Ana has to negotiate space for herself within the bounds and conventions of comedy, a genre premissed, in Harry Levin's words, 'on the persistence of types, as manifested in character, plot, and technical devices' (1987: 4). In addition to certain character-types that have already been identified, the matrix of comedy supplies *La vida alegre* with narrative incidents and motifs of an entirely conventional kind. These include sexual entanglements (the 'enredos' mentioned in the theme song of the film), ambiguous identities, cross-dressing, and a disguise trotted out in the episode where Eduardo tries to pass incognito at the CU-EROS club and only succeeds in bringing the ministry of which he is the representative into disrepute, by unnecessarily arousing suspicions about his sexuality. More problematically, the carnivalesque comedy of *La vida alegre* imposes a happy ending on the narrative, in which Ana at last achieves the professional recognition that is her due, and promptly forgives Antonio. Looked at from an ideological perspective, this is an outcome which is at best a trade-off and, more questionably, a concession made in continuing ignorance about Antonio's involvement in the 'recomendación al revés' that so undermined her chances in the first set of 'oposiciones'. In either case, the narrative exacts a price from Ana, restoring her to her place in the home while letting Antonio more or less off the hook.

Such resolutions are, of course, part of the stock-in-trade of comedy, as illustrated in both drama and film. An especially pertinent example from the history of cinema is *The Thrill of it All*, directed by Norman Jewison in 1963. In this Hollywood film, a wife, Beverly Boyer (Doris Day), disturbs the balance of her marriage to her obstetrician husband Gerald (James Garner) by taking a highly lucrative job advertising 'Happy Soap' on American television. Beverly's financial and professional ascendancy unsettles Gerald, and causes tensions and anxieties in the marriage which are finally resolved only by restoring the status quo ante of male mastery and female subordination. In formal terms, that resolution foreshadows the reconciliation of Ana and Antonio in *La vida alegre*, where an initial equilibrium is also upset and a new one established at the narrative's end.

In fact, Colomo's film may be seen as offering a variation on the narrative formula of *The Thrill of it All*, with attendant parallels in ideological content. Through its narrative, *The Thrill of it All* celebrates the ideology of the couple and the virtues of family life. The composite message of Jewison's film, as read by Bruce Babington and Peter Evans (1989: 199), is that women 'gravitate to domesticity' (this is shown most clearly in the way that the leading female character introduces herself at a dinner party, 'My name is Beverly Boyer, and I'm a housewife'); also, women valorize motherhood over all other activities (for the starry-eyed Mrs Frawley, 'There's nothing more fulfilling than having a baby'); and they are content to be admiring satellites of their husbands' achievements and lives (Beverly compliments Gerald, 'Oh, you are a great doctor').

The Jewison film also promotes a certain type of woman over another, as demonstrated in its preference for the immaculate Beverly (who dresses in white for dinner at the Frawleys) over the tainted blonde starlet 'Spot' Checker (who in some respects is a 1960s forerunner of Carolina in *La vida alegre*). At the same time, *The Thrill of it All* circumscribes the woman's freedom of movement, reining Beverly in when she pushes too hard against recognized boundaries; indeed, it goes so far as to punish her for allowing an 'asinine career' to distract her from 'wifely duties'. In the medical idiom which permeates the diegesis, the narrative gives Beverly Boyer a taste of her own medicine, as Gerald—raised to chivalric status in the final sequence where he arrives at the hospital on horseback just in time to deliver Mrs Frawley's baby— employs various strategies to make her feel jealous and guilty about neglecting husband and family.

The conservative drive of *The Thrill of it All* aligns it with other romantic comedies, largely associated with Doris Day, that were produced in Hollywood around the turn of the 1950s. In these works, which have been described by Babington and Evans as 'the conformist comedies of a conformist era' (1989: 197), narrative design and ideology conspired with generic convention to neutralize the threat of the independent woman. Yet, not even films of this type were so monolithic as to silence completely voices of resistance and reason impinging on them from the extra-diegetic world. In the case of *The Thrill of it All*, there are at least two moments in the narrative when a discourse of equal rights for women challenges the prevailing logic of patriarchy and achieves a victory of sorts. The first of these moments occurs when Gerald Boyer, who enjoys the respect, admiration, and gratitude of several parents whose babies he has delivered, tells Beverly categorically that 'There is no reason for you to work', and is immediately accused of inconsistency by his wife who reminds him that he has repeatedly encouraged her to take up hobbies and to pursue activities outside the home. Hearing Beverly's entreaty and assurance that she will not let her work 'interfere with my wifely duties', he admits to having been 'shot down by my own artillery'. A second moment of feminist potential occurs in a heated exchange when Beverly asks, 'What ever happened to my rights as a woman?' and Gerald replies, 'They grew and they grew until they suffocated my rights as a man.' This head-to-head conflict exposes Gerald's wounded pride along with several of his prejudices, as he berates his wife: 'You have finally succeeded in equating the delivery of a baby with the delivery of a commercial.' The animus of his remark is a sure sign that he is overreacting, and reveals an Achilles heel in the moral anatomy of the patriarchal system that he defends and represents.

The appearance of these two eruptions on the otherwise uniform surface of the narrative of *The Thrill of it All* betrays a fissure in the dominant ideology articulated in the film. From a comparative perspective, the tension thus highlighted helps to illuminate the implied sexual politics of *La vida alegre*. While clearly there are grounds for interpreting the narrative of Colomo's film as tending towards an ultimate restoration of harmony in keeping with the conventions of conformist comedy; and while it is also legitimate to view *La vida alegre* as being governed by a moral economy, personified in the character of Ana, which promotes entirely orthodox values of decency, fairness, and responsibility;

252   Robin Fiddian

there are nevertheless perceptible differences between Colomo's film and *The Thrill of it All* which mark *La vida alegre* out as being ideologically less constrained. Those differences have to do, largely, with historical setting: almost a quarter of a century separates Colomo's film from that of Jewison, during which time the Western capitalist world had undergone dramatic social and technological change, in Spain as much as in other countries from the early 1960s on. Differences in political culture also apply, especially as regards issues of gender affecting women and gays, which constitute the main focus of interest in Colomo's film. In aesthetic terms, the Bakhtinian and satirical impulses of *La vida alegre* are part of a genuinely subversive project, and create a very different tone and atmosphere from those found in *The Thrill of it All*. And, in spite of what has been said before, the narrative resolution of *La vida alegre* ultimately sets Colomo's film apart from its predecessor, by leaving an intriguing question mark hanging over the future operation of Ana and Antonio's partnership.

In relation to Jewison's film, these differences provide evidence of substantial development of its radical potential, with a proportional weakening of the conservative tendencies of a Hollywood subgenre that had flourished in the late 1950s and early 1960s. In the mid-1980s in Spain, Fernando Colomo marshals the considerable talents of Verónica Forqué, Antonio Resines, Guillermo Montesinos, and others and casts them into the crucible of the *nueva comedia* to show the obsolescence of institutionalized masculinism and to unsettle accepted stereotypes of gender at a fascinating moment of fluidity in the historical evolution of Spanish society.

REFERENCES

Babington, Bruce, and Evans, Peter (1989), *Affairs to Remember: The Hollywood Comedy of the Sexes*, Manchester: Manchester University Press.
Castellano, Koro (1986), 'El retorno de Massiel', *Fotogramas*, 1725 (Dec.): unpaginated.
Fields, Harvey J. (1987), 'On-the-Job-Training', in Edward Klein and Don Erickson (eds.), *About Men: Reflections on the Male Experience*, New York: Poseidon: 86–9.
Gentile, Mary (1985), *Film Feminisms: Theory and Practice*, London: Greenwood Press.

Hopewell, John (1988), *El cine español después de Franco 1973–1988*, Madrid: Arquero.

Levin, Harry (1987), *Playboys and Killjoys: An Essay in the Theory of Comedy*, New York: Oxford University Press.

Marinero, Manolo, and Marinero, Pachín (1982), 'Fernando Colomo: con más intención de humor', *Casablanca*, 23: 39–42.

Mulvey, Laura (1975), 'Visual Pleasure and Narrative Cinema', *Screen*, 16/3: 6–18.

—— (1993), 'Afterthoughts on Visual Pleasure', in Antony Easthope (ed.), *Contemporary Film Theory*, London: Longman (1st pub. 1981): 125–34.

Stam, Robert (1989), *Subversive Pleasures: Bakhtin, Cultural Criticism and Film*, Baltimore: Johns Hopkins University Press.

17

Las cosas del querer (Chávarri, 1989)

CHRIS PERRIAM

Synopsis

Las cosas del querer (Jaime Chávarri, 1989) tells the story of three musical variety performers, Pepita (stage name Dora) (Angela Molina), Mario (Manuel Bandera), and Juan (Ángel de Andrés López), brought together by chance at the end of the Civil War and building a career in the first years of the Franco era with shows based around popular Spanish songs, traditional and contemporary. Juan is Pepita's lover and Mario—who had served with Juan in the same Republican regiment—wishes he were Juan's. His politics, his visible homosexuality, and his rebuff of an aristocratic suitor, Gonzalo (Juan Gea), with a mother with friends in high places lead to Mario's being framed, beaten up by police agents, and told to leave Spain, which he does, thus completing the break-up of the trio which had already begun with an earlier falling out of Juan and Pepita.

Mario's Story

At the film's beginning and end, and twice briefly in reels two and four, the narration of the private lives of Mario, Pepita, and Juan, of their careers as performers, and of the construction of official and unofficial regimes of power in the wake of Nationalist victory is at one level a simple retrospective commentary by the solitary Mario. Covering these three aspects of the recent lives of the trio, this commentary is given voice-over (a sensual Andalusian accent emphasized) as he looks at his bruised face in the mirror and the reflecting window of his train compartment. As much as a simple device for clinching the tale in the double embrace of spectatorial foreknowledge and grim contrast, this is an open-ended address to a set of others absent in memory, projection, and imagination. First there is the absence of the Mario who once was; an absence marked by the bruising and defeat on a face soon to be revealed—in the main body of the film—as having been flawless and untroubled. Then there is the void of a future without the other two, the conversion of Spain into an uninhabitable space, and finally his own identity now emptied of knowledge of itself:

We'll never see each other again now, we all know that. I can't live in this bloody country. And I'm not leaving just because they're throwing me out, but because I don't know what to do about my life and about the two of you [looks in the mirror]. We've been together so much this past year, the three of us . . .

The next shift is to Juan—'You and I, Juan, knew each other from before'—and the main narrative begins at this crucial moment with a cut to the day that 'everything changed': a street under bombardment in a scene which is stagy—a few extras doubling up in classic streets-under-siege routines—but nonetheless acutely balanced, spatial limitations becoming a focusing rather than distracting factor. The monologue fades into the musical performance by a colourfully costumed Pepita (at first very much Angela Molina still) of the famous song 'Triniá'. Triniá, Trinidad, is a girl from Seville so 'pure and lovely' that a local painter gives up his habit of making copies of Murillo's and Rafael's Virgins in the art museum, preferring to watch and paint her instead in the gardens outside; he is broken-hearted when a rich American whisks her away. This is the first of a number of arrestingly tangential cross-references between diegesis and the micro-narratives of the songs which make up half the film. Mario's story is there, in a fragmentary, abstract way, in the pay-off lines (not in fact arrived at in the interrupted performance, but inevitably recalled by the audience) 'she fled from Spain, did Trinidad. | And to the unfinished picture | the painter said, | "You have made me so unhappy | Without you, what am I to do" ' Without Juan, without Pepita too, what indeed is Mario to do? This sharp, sentimental issue overlays the scenes of bombardment neatly, a generalized sense of loss overlapping a scene itself emblematic, for Spaniards, of rupture with the past.

In the street, explosions and deep-focus shots of fleeing figures and disruption are offset by a centrally placed, trembling, and strikingly out of place Pepita; close-ups reveal her lips, Juan's reaction at his first sight of her; eye-line shots establish the start of their story; Mario, in a passing truck, intersects the line of sight. A classic combination of historical event and personal relationships is achieved.

Generic Intertexts

The film moves in and out of several genres and pseudo-genres at once: it narrates war and its aftermath, a romantic triangle, an individual's decline and fall, love in a cold climate (here the drear early years of Franco's dictatorship), it flirts with a fledgling Hollywood subgenre—tales of the homosexual past—, it is show musical and folk musical, it is in the rich vein of 1970s and 1980s evocations of the 1940s and 1950s.

This latter tradition had started, in this period, with *Canciones para después de una guerra* (Basilio Patino, 1971), moving through Pedro Olea's *Pim, pam, pum . . . ¡fuego!* (1975) (also plotted around the world of entertainment, and a triangular rivalry), to, in different veins, Mario Camus's *La colmena* (1982), Víctor Erice's *El sur* (1983), and Vicente Aranda's *Si te dicen que caí* (1989). The depiction in *Las cosas* of the world of wartime entertainers also connected, in the following year, with Carlos Saura's *¡Ay Carmela!* (1990). There was, then, an audience already constructed and ready for this aspect of *Las cosas*. Moreover, the characters recall those of Chávarri's family-in-hard-times drama *Las bicicletas son para el verano* (1983) and help make convincing the portrait of Spaniards struggling to survive in the aftermath of war. Realistic and engaging in a manner proper to this historical subgenre too are the cameos of greed and compromise, and of the hypocrisy and ruthlessness of the winning side (although Llopis (1989: 9) considers the caricature approach to be a weakness). Pepita's mother Doña Carmen (Mari Carmen Ramírez) colludes in the effective prostitution of Pepita in the cause of her career. Gonzalo's mother the Marquesa (Ana Sainz) destroys Mario for his homosexuality by adducing the need to protect her own son from the effects of his; she is abetted by the judge Don Benito Campoverde (Rafael Alonso), who on the one hand at a post-performance party at the Marquesa's home has flirted clumsily but enthusiastically with one of the company of singers, Marisol Rentería (a brilliantly blowsy Eva León), but on the other storms out offended by Pepita's performance of a risqué song, 'El Tracatrá'.

The film, along with other queer affiliations, also has elements of gay fictionalized testimonial, depicting a specific *ambiente*, and reminding a late 1980s audience of Francoist persecution of homosexuals (Txoriburu 1990). The machinations against Mario, his framing, and especially the violent *film noir* sequence in the last reel involving long coats, deep shadows, raked angles, car headlights, and a remote location, are as effective rhetorically as they are visually—'Quién quiere dar una patada al maricón?' (who wants to get a kick at the queer?), shouts one of the attackers. José Arroyo (1997) has also suggested that the final scenes may be read as a dual critique of specific political oppression and generalized compulsory heterosexuality. Mario's boarding of a fully fired-up long-haul steam train at Madrid, its purposeful departure, and a long shot back down the platform in the opposite direction to the figures of Pepita and Juan retreating into a cloud of escaping steam to go back out into the night can—Arroyo suggests—be read in terms of a repudiation not only of the Spain left behind but obliquely of the destiny of the heterosexual couple too; this is a new start for the victimized but focal Mario—it gives him his story—but it is the start of a long and dismal haul for the other two, and for Spain.

La Copla

Most inescapably, though, this is a film in a long tradition of films and shows around the sometimes interchangeable musical forms of *la copla* and *la canción española*, the evocation of a typically yet legendary 'Spanish' world of gypsies, peasants, passion, wisdom, timelessness (Blas Vega 1996: 37–40; Moix 1993: 18–19; Pineda Novo 1991: 7–8). *Las cosas* begins, in the title sequence, with a dedication, white on black, to [Álvaro] Quintero, León [Manuel López 'El Maestro'] Quiroga, [Juan] Mostazo, and others 'who made *la canción española* possible', then a slow pan down towards a set on a proscenium stage and a representation of the Mosque at Córdoba. This apparent *mise-en-abîme*, centring on the 'deep' Spain of the south, romance, and nostalgia, settles the audience into the expectation of a directly mimetic homage to the tradition (an expectation disrupted by the increasingly obvious artificiality of the set and by a train whistle which bridges over into Mario's bleak night-time monologue).

The *copla* at its simplest is a song structured around the four-line unit: the special fascination of these films and shows, though, is with an Andalusian use and understanding of the form. Here *la copla* ('la copla andaluza') is a more complex, hybrid form, especially once taken up by poets at the beginning of the century, by Manuel Machado, and by Federico García Lorca. By the time of the Civil War it had become, along converging tracks of oral performance and a written tradition, a composite of torch-song, nostalgic evocation of lost customs and places, and an affirmation of deep identity centred on Andalusian popular cultures and forms of speech. The *canción española*, as its name implies ('Spanish song tradition'), might look further, or in different regions, and contain within it celebrations of present, always Spanish, glories, customs, beauties, loves, and dances. Unlike the *copla*, which is for solo or duo voices and does not imply (though often has) orchestration, the *canción española* implies more or less full staging, accompaniment, chorus, dancing. It is these two forms which are the main substance of the performances of the artistes known as the *folklóricas* starring in a vast corpus of films—its watershed being *El último cuplé* (Juan de Orduña, 1957)[1]–with their roots in a mix of cosmopolitan music hall, *zarzuela* (Spain's distinctive light operatic form with its emphasis on national, regional, and even neighbourhood customs), more or less popularized flamenco, and above all *la copla*.

The songs of Seville-born Rafael de León (1908–82), author of the lyrics of eight of *Las cosas*'s fourteen numbers, stand between the oral and the written and are quintessentially of the tradition of *la copla*. They are nearly all about intense, usually impossible, love and formed—continue to form—an important matrix for the sentimental life of a generation of listeners, audiences, and spectators, as Acosta Diaz et al. (1989: 13, 51–6, 62–4) and Vázquez Montalbán (1986) remind us. The sexual

---

[1] For a brief résumé of the tradition under its usual catch-all name of 'cine folklórico', see Blas Vega (1996: 45–52); also—for a much more revisionist account—Labanyi 1997.

politics are 'reactionary and patriarchal' with the female protagonist placed in positions of extreme inferiority (Acosta Díaz et
al. 1989: 53); their feelings and often their social status are
represented archetypically; their names are sometimes exclusively epithetical (La Parrala, La Lirio) (1989: 54–6, 60–4).
Terenci Moix (1993: 15) also notes the 'extreme conservatism'
of the *copla* in general but suggests, briefly, that there is an
admixture of 'suggestions of more progressive thinking'; León's
copla too, Acosta Díaz et al. argue (1989: 53), is radical in its
presentation of 'an exalted and violent world': 'by placing his
protagonists, his voices, on the margins of society and in exceptional situations Rafael de León is reflecting a morality far
removed from that promoted by Franco's regime.' Elements of
this potential radicalism are liberated in *Las cosas* by the indirect
intertextual traffic between its own and the songs' preoccupations, as also by the slant it puts on the romantic triangle, its
socio- and sexual-political subtexts, and by the sensuality of
Angela Molina's and Manuel Bandera's performances.

Conchita Piquer, Miguel de Molina, and the 1980s

It was generally supposed—such is the suggestive power of the
genre most evoked by this film—that it was closely based on two
key figures in the micro-history of *la copla*, Conchita Piquer
(1908–90) and one of a handful of male performers, Miguel de
Molina (1908–93), superstar in the heterosexual world (at least
that of the left) and 'an idol of 1940s queers' as the gay magazines
¿Entiendes? and *Gay Hotsa* reminded their readers when the film
came out (Cerveza 1990: 21). The famous story of his abduction
and severe beating by three men in a black car (suggesting official
involvement) and his decision to flee Spain would seem to be the
source for Mario's own tale of victimization (Blas Vega 1996:
73–4; Román 1993: 148–51).[2] However, biographical readings of
the film were played down, with producer Luis Sanz suggesting
that there was only a coincidental similarity between Mario and

---

[2] Molina spent the war in Valencia and his return to the mainstream in Madrid
and Barcelona was difficult and short-lived: in the early years of the new regime his
friendships, politics, and homosexuality were not in his favour. He settled, eventually, in Buenos Aires (the setting for the sequel *Las cosas del querer II*, 1995).

Miguel de Molina, or between Pepita and Concha Piquer.[3] The second claim is the easier to understand: the memory of Piquer herself is barely discernible either in the physical appearance or the singing of Angela Molina, despite the latter's personal familiarity with the genre,[4] though it is strongly inscribed in the audience's expectations and in the soundtrack itself ('La Triniá', for example, was one of her most famous numbers). Further, Pepita is a Republican sympathizer with no solo career: Piquer, on the other hand, had an independent and international career and was known (and admired) as a staunch if disrespectful and iconoclastic right-winger.[5] What Angela Molina brings is her own stardom, the aura—the intertextual construct—of her appearances on screen and in print to date, her then recent sensual performance in the title role of Bigas Luna's *Lola* (1986) in one part of the spectators' imaginations, and in another her more gently radiant performance as Rosa in Manolo Gutiérrez Aragón's *La mitad del cielo* (1986). It is a construct which all but eclipses 'La Piquer' and her time.

Manuel Bandera, however, comes with no immediate star context. When the names Antonio Banderas and Imanol Arias—originally to take the roles of Mario and Juan—faded away as production hit repeated delays Sanz finally discovered for the role of Mario Málaga-born Bandera, almost a complete unknown in the film world, with a background in physical education and dance. Three sets of iconography at once attached themselves to his figure: that of the history of *la copla*, that of the leading man, and (overlapping with both and coming out of the 1940s as well as the 1980s) that of gay icon. His novelty appeal (and an ability to sing) came with stunning good looks which were widely noted on the opening night: *Panorama* (Madrid) considered him the true star of the evening, mobbed by female fans

<hr />

[3] Sanz denied in a pre-release interview that the film was a 'biography' of Molina, 'although . . . his personality attracts me a lot' (Muñoz 1988). The reclusive Miguel de Molina himself saw enough parallels to be upset by the release of the film (Román 1993: 152).

[4] Her father was another great folkloric artist, Antonio de Molina (1928–92): 'It's all hugely familiar to me . . . an exciting rediscovery' (Ponga 1989: 113).

[5] Piquer was nearly refused entry into Mexico in October 1946 for her Francoist sympathies and was rumoured to have been accused by Miguel de Molina of having been instrumental in his downfall and eventual exile (Román 1993: 135); however, there were picturesque anecdotes of her disdain for authority, and she turned down in 1962 the award of the Lazo de Isabel la Católica (on the grounds that everyone else had one too) (1993: 139).

and almost stopping the traffic on the Gran vía (like the stars of the *folklóricas* in the old days) ('Manuel Bandera' 1989: 112–13); *Ya* suggested with unusual astuteness that 'Manuel Bandera, who plays the ambiguous Mario, has become a real star. He has the sort of body which pleases men and women alike and nowadays that can prove a good selling point' (Villacastín 1989). Indeed, one more audience needs to be borne in mind as we consider this film, the modern gay audience. Its avatars are there in the film, at Mario's performances: giggling knowingly when cut to during the Madrid first night speech by a pompous journalist hailing Pepita and Mario as 'this sublime couple . . . who represent the purest spirit of the youth of this our country Spain, full of glory, peace, and future promise as she is'; calling out ecstatically and throwing flowers when he performs 'Te lo juro yo' in Seville; even the pretty policeman soon to entrap him is seen, in a brief shot, to be moved by his beauty in this performance. Manuel Bandera is obvious material for gay icon status, though not through the gradual route, retraced by Stacey (1991) in relation to women, of identification with roles played and lifestyles publicized— although some 'identificatory practices' (153–7) might easily be imagined across a swathe of Spanish homosexual subcultures: songs sung, poses struck, hats bought—but instead along a fast-track of novelty value, looks, and musical affiliation. As Juan Vicente Aliaga has observed, there is anyway a history of identification among 'certain sectors of the male homosexual population' with the dilemmas of the female protagonists of the *coplas* which by way of 'hints and codes' have served as a 'refuge' for the expression of passion and desire for men (1997: 28). There is also a more specifically imposed identificatory practice in Bandera's intense performance of Miguel de Molina's key number, 'Te lo juro yo', and in the mimetic wearing of Molina's favoured costume of voluminous polka-dot shirt, wide-brimmed hat, and scandalously tight trousers—a get-up which, backed by the classic Molina poses, is at its most striking in the performance of the film's title song (the first performed) and in 'La bien pagá' (the last) another Miguel de Molina trademark.[6]

---

[6] For a beautifully staged portrait of Molina in his polka-dot shirt, tilted hat, and neckerchief—'one of his favourite pictures'—see Román 1993: unnumbered plate [14] between pp. 160 and 161 (also reproduced in Blas Vega 1996: 70). The plate on the page opposite shows, by contrast, an effete, dandified Molina in a tight waistcoat. Molina performs 'Te lo juro yo' on *Miguel de Molina en vivo*, vols. 2–3, EFEN Records (Seville, 1993) CD111001, track 14.

'La bien pagá'

'La bien pagá' and 'Te lo juro yo'—unlike 'Las cosas del querer', which is a light little number marvelling at love's quirky ability to overcome differences in character and origin—are firmly embedded in the plot and motivation. The main theme of 'La bien pagá'—disillusionment with a relationship based, the singer realizes, on material interests—though not directly applicable to the relationship between Mario and Pepita, does have strong echoes of recent events when performed by him. Pepita, pushed by her mother, has allowed herself to be seduced into the world of the movies by way of seedy producer Don Servando (Santiago Ramos), and has had the requisite casting-couch (actually dressing-room) session with him: Juan, confronting the two women, has accused her mother of being an 'alcahueta' (procuress), thus acknowledging what has long been an open secret (Pepita's entrée into the world of variety was similarly arranged); Pepita he has called 'puta' (whore), reinforcing his earlier use of the term in reaction to her behaviour at Gonzalo's party. Along one axis she is the addressee of Mario's singing, up in a box in the theatre, and Mario the proxy for the embittered Juan, sitting in the audience: a mix of shot/reverse shot pivoted on Mario and free-floating reaction shots (of her welling tears and Juan's deepening scowls) makes the pattern clear. Mario, however, may also be heard singing of his own story in these words, though again at a different angle from the narrative of the song. He too has moved on, having brushed off Gonzalo and his world of proffered cocaine and gold watches. Ringing out inevitably too are audience responses to the narrative structure and expectations from *copla* and melodramatic traditions alike which dictate that, of all the characters, Mario is the one who will have to pay for the way he is—that is the very destiny and fascination of the singer in the *copla* tradition.

There are, finally, further and more complex directions for the song to take in the imagination of the hearer, in lines which gain a belated resonance in the tense enclosure which is Mario's desire for Juan and Juan's fear of it. At its centre is an explanation to the woman left behind that this is no betrayal—the singer has met another who 'didn't fall into my arms | she gave me just one kiss, | the only kiss | I've had and never paid for'. In a sharply choreographed scene in the train compartment minutes before the end of the film, in which close camerawork and tight shifts of position ring the changes of trios and duos in the farewell scene, Juan gives Mario a single kiss. For Mario this kiss might well be the first and only truly disinterested kiss of his erotic career, so based on rapid exchanges of pleasures, favours, and bodies has it been. It is the shadow of the kiss that Juan has been denying him all along.

The Odd Man Out

For Juan suffers from a complex that the late 1980s Spanish audience would be familiar with (the women in their fifties and sixties through experience; the younger audience through culture too): fear of intimacy because of fear of the feminine because of insecurity about his masculinity (Kaufman 1994; Kimmel 1994). He fears contact with Mario's shirtless body as they remove uniforms on demobilizing after the war, hesitating to hug him, then converting the hug into that curious, cautious, two-handed lower-back patting which connotes camaraderie. Sharing a room together—with Mario just out of prison for refusing to sing the Falangist hymn when picked up by a street patrol—Mario's bare torso is again problematic for Juan. The camera lingers on its textures and musculature lit and striated by moon- and street-light through bars in a high window (some dozing art-film-goer might wake with a start and believe themselves watching Genet's *Un chant d'amour*). Mario is shown hands behind tilted head, big eyes in medium close-up, languid:

Mario [wistfully] You're the one who's always loved me the most.
Juan: [gruffly] Yes, but in my own way.
Mario: [ruefully] Of course, in your own way.

As his relationships with Pepita progresses and becomes problematic, Juan is increasingly disconcerted by the rerouting of the usual energies of the triangle of friendship: on top of the whole unmanly situation of being in thrall to the mother-in-law with whom the couple are forced to live, his best friend fails him by being unapproachable because of his (perceived) desire for physical love, and by not being there for Juan, according to the practices of homosociality as suggested by Sedgwick (1985: 21–7), as a sexual rival with whom to sympathize and paradoxically bond, excluding the woman emotionally, or using her as a vehicle for man-to-man negotiations of power and desire. Fearing the potentially unmasculine in his relationship with Mario as much as the woman in Pepita he has nowhere to turn. Since 'men [must] prove their manhood in the eyes of other men' in 'homosocial enactment' (Kimmel 1994: 127, 129) Juan finds himself poorly placed, whether at the piano and on show or in life and on guard against the inappropriate. Having to act as accompanist, being implicated in the world of music and dance—in the first half of the century at least, dangerous, sensual, ambiguous, unmanly (Studlar 1993), and even revisionary of conventional masculinity (Cohan 1993: 46–8, 64)—and having to bear some outrageously misdirected looks and words from Mario in rehearsal, only increases his instability. Ángel de Andrés López has a nicely limited range of scowls in this regard. A key scene is the rehearsal of the intense 'To lo juro yo', a confession of undying love by a singer whose lover has left him for (several) other men. For the last verse Mario turns, eyes brimming, toward Juan; at the end of the performance he is clapped ironically by the secretly watching Gonzalo, which means an escalation for Juan from scowling to storming off. He is unable to confront so many overlaid structures of dependency and control (within the song, between Mario and himself, and between Gonzalo and Mario) or so close a brush with sadomasochistic intensity as comes in the third verse:

> Lead me down streets
> of bitterness and gall . . .
> take a fistful of sand
> and throw it in my eyes
> kill me with sorrows
> if you must, but love me.

As well as being troubled over Mario, Juan is ill at ease with what Pepita does with her body: her performance of 'El Tracatrá' at Gonzalo's party provokes one of his several outbursts (the most poignant of which is his staggering, possibly sobbing, flight from Mario on the beach at Cadiz on the last night of their last run together, when Mario playfully wrestles him into submission and attempts—suddenly serious—to kiss him). The song is a minor highlight of the film in which Angela Molina (her star presence, not for the only time, eclipsing the character of Pepita) is a glitteringly earthy raconteur of an erotic adventure at first tactile and finally plain rhythmic—'and then he started tra, tra, tra-tra-tra'. Her spirited hip touching and thrusting is a grim turning point for the trio, though. It activates internalized, institutionalized homophobia in Don Benito who leaves warning Gonzalo that Mario is bad company and is to blame (obscurely) for the immorality affecting the party. When the Marquesa seeks revenge for Mario's frustration of Gonzalo's erotic intentions, Don Benito can make his judgement in the context of Mario's having been suspect all along, in line with homophobic expectation.[7] For Juan what is activated is unfocused and perhaps conflicted jealousy (it is with Mario that Pepita dances and sings the pay-off lines: who knows whom Juan is most jealous of) and her alleged indecency becomes a pretext for an outburst of rage against his lack of control over Pepita and her body (and her mother's excess of control over it).

Just the Three of Us

After the later row over Pepita's film career Juan again storms out of the building, this time followed by a tearful Pepita. Mario beckons her across the street and the emotional divide, bundling them all into a horse-drawn carriage (no fringe), ushering in a new set of generic expectations. He notes how things are fine when it is 'just the three of us', they jog along medium close-up in a line on the seat with night-time Seville as their mobile backdrop, the gruff old driver makes mention (in heavy Andalusian) of the threat of a storm which has now passed, and suggests as a good place for a late drink a bar called Paraíso (Paradise). But none of these cues for a song are taken up. Instead some new variations on the old triangular theme are made available here through Mario's homosexuality. Adopting a familiar trope from present-day popular culture (and life)—the gay man who helps his women friends sustain their relationships with men[8]—the film is able to make Mario break the asymmetrical pattern by reconciling not excluding.

---

[7] For instances of homophobic assumptions in the Tribunal Supremo (roughly equivalent to the High Court) in the Franco years, see Pérez Cánovas 1996: 18–25.

[8] Archetypically in Armistead Maupin's *Tales of the City* series.

It is its quiet subversion of a conventional romantic situation, its making a triangle out of three not quite straight lines, that gives the film a specifically post-1970s interest; just as its self-aware approach to the world of *la canción española* argues in its favour both for the older audiences who appreciate a detailed re-creation of the songs and the circumstances of their performance, and for the Almodóvar generation who might take a more camp view of all the staginess, the masquerade, the melodrama. Llopis (1989: 9) objects that the film

seems to be unaware of how such affairs function in real life, does not take into account even the most rudimentary psychology (or indeed the psychology of the period: the characters are too 'modern'), and resolves issues with a flick of the—one might say limp—fingers.

But it is in its 'modern' approach in part that the film is a success. That there are such easy resolutions as Llopis implies is questionable: the issues arising out of Mario's early monologue—incompleteness, absence, uncertainty of identity—have touched upon and been inflected by the content of the songs performed, and have informed and been revealed in several micro-histories of oppression and repression (even if the film has the grace to discharge its audience of the absolute obligation of engaging with these issues and missing out on the songs and costumes).

Although Chávarri himself recognized it as one of his films *por encargo*, made to order (Monterde 1989: 77)—this is a film which could not pretend to be innocent of the lure of the market, is strongly led by genre, and whose lead roles show few signs of being directed as such—the director's own aesthetic should perhaps be allowed to make a shadowy appearance in conclusion. Not the Chávarri of *Los viajes escolares* (1973) and *El río de oro* (1986) with their explorations of family dynamics, history, and memory. More the imagination behind *A un dios desconocido* (1977), a film structured principally around interlocking patterns of three-way relationships (as was the Super-8 *Ginebra en los infiernos*, made in 1968–70).[9] Its stage magician protagonist—a gay man in his fifties scarred by nostalgia, alienation, and a vicarious obsession with Lorca—enacts as part of his performance, to melancholy piano

[9] For a synopsis and excellent extended analysis of this film and of Chávarri's early career see Marías (1977).

accompaniment ('I Dream of Jeannie with the Light Brown Hair'), a mock resurrection of a 'dead' assistant. Loss, impossible desire, emotional entanglement, and the paraphernalia of performance; magic and nostalgia; a queer intense melancholia: all these emerge in *Las cosas* too, as vital counterpoints to the glamour and the musicality. Like a folk musical it lets memory—in the songs but also in the street scenes—'[colour] every corner of the world' and create the 'intermediary space' where history, myth, and traditional commingle (Altman 1989: 272–3) here creating an unproblematic 'Spain'; but it simultaneously disrupts this through its critiques, wry and direct, of social and sexual regimes. Like a show musical it offers the fascination of the illusion of seeing behind the stage, into the wings (Altman 1989: 206–7), but also—exploiting the aesthetic of *la copla*—into an intense and much less glitzy world of lack, the death of illusions, and precariousness. A world which, especially in its emphasis on performance, fascinates us as post-modern spectators, creatures of a culture more than fifty years on from the day Juan and Mario and Pepita exchanged their first three-way glances at a double moment of transition into years of hunger, or days of glamour.

REFERENCES

Acosta Díaz, Josefa, Gómez Lara, Manuel, and Jiménez Barrientos, Jorge (eds.) (1989), *Poemas y canciones de Rafael de León*. Seville: Ediciones Alfar.

Aliaga, Juan Vicente (1997), 'Cómo hemos cambiado', in Juan Vicente Aliaga and José Miguel Cortés (eds.), *Identidad y diferencia: sobre la cultura gay en España*, Barcelona: Egales: 19–107.

Altman, Rick (1989), *The American Film Musical*. Bloomington: Indiana University Press (1st pub. 1987).

Arroyo, José (1997), 'Imagining a Queer Country: Gay Identity in the Contemporary Spanish Folklore Film'. Unpublished paper given at Queering the Nation, conference organized by the University of Warwick Lesbian and Gay Studies Group and Humanities Research Centre, University of Warwick, May.

Blas Vega, José (1996), *La canción española (de la Caramba a Isabel Pantoja)*. Barcelona: Taller el Búcaro.

Cerveza, Tita (pseud.) (1990), 'Algunos chismes sobre Miguel de Molina', *Gay Hotsa* (Mar.): 21 (1st pub. 1989–90).

Cohan, Steven (1993), ' "Feminizing" the Song-and-Dance Man: Fred

Astaire and the Spectacle of Masculinity in the Hollywood Musical', in Steven Cohan and Ina Rae Hark (eds.), *Screening the Male: Exploring Masculinities in Hollywood Cinema*, London: Routledge 46–69.

Kaufman, Michael (1994), 'Men, Feminism, and Men's Contradictory Experience of Power', in Harry Brod and Michael Kaufman (eds.), *Theorizing Masculinities*, Thousand Oaks, Calif.: Sage: 142–63.

Kimmel, Michael (1994), 'Masculinity as Homophobia: Fear, Shame and Silence in the Construction of Gender Identity', in Harry Brod and Michael Kaufman (eds.), *Theorizing Masculinities*, Thousand Oaks, Calif.: Sage: 119–41.

Labanyi, Jo (1997), 'Race, Gender and Disavowal in Spanish Cinema of the Early Franco Period: The Missionary Film and the Folkloric Musical', *Screen*, 38/3 (autumn), 215–31.

Llopis, Silvia (1989), '*Las cosas del querer*', *Diario 16 (Guía de Madrid)* (6 Oct.): 9.

'Manuel Bandera encendió la nostalgia de las folclóricas' (1989), *Panorama* (16 Oct.): 112–13.

Marías, Miguel (1977), 'El cine desencantado de Jaime Chávarri', *Dirigido por* (Dec.): 44–56.

Moix, Terenci (1993), *Suspiros de España: la copla y el cine de nuestro recuerdo*. Barcelona: Plaza y Janés.

Monterde, José Enrique (1989), '*Las cosas del querer* por Jaime Chávarri', *Dirigido por* (Nov.): 77–8.

Muñoz, Diego (1988), 'Primera película de Angela Molina como cantante', *La vanguardia* (20 Nov.): 67.

Pérez Cánovas, Nicolás (1996), *Homosexualidad, homosexuales, y uniones homosexuales en el derecho español*. Granada: Editorial Comares.

Pineda Novo, Daniel (1991), *Las folklóricas y el cine*. Huelva: Festival de Cine Iberoamericano/Productora Andaluza de Programas.

Ponga, Paula (1989), 'El cine español que veremos: últimos rodajes', *Fotogramas* (Feb.): 112–13.

Román Fernández, Manuel (1993), *Memoria de la copla: la canción española de Conchita Piquer a Isabel Pantoja*. Madrid: Alianza.

Sedgwick, Eve Kosofsky (1985), *Between Men: English Literature and Male Homosocial Desire*. New York: Columbia University Press.

Stacey, Jackie (1991), 'Feminine Fascinations: Forms of Identification in Star–Audience Relations', in Christine Gledhill (ed.), *Stardom: Industry of Desire*, London: Routledge: 141–63.

Studlar, Gaylin (1993), 'Valentino, "Optic Intoxication", and Dance Madness', in Steven Cohan and Ina Rae Hark (eds.), *Screening the Male: Exploring Masculinities in Hollywood Cinema*, London: Routledge: 23–45.

Txoriburu (pseud.) (1990), '*Las cosas del querer*', *Gay Hotsa* (Mar.): 20.

Vázquez Montalbán, Manuel (1986), *Crónica sentimental de España*. Madrid: Espasa Calpe.

Villacastín, Rosa (1989), 'Ha nacido una estrella: Manuel Bandera', *Ya* (15 Oct.): 38.

18

Motherland: Space, Femininity, and Spanishness in *Jamón jamón* (Bigas Luna, 1992)

CELESTINO DELEYTO

JAMÓN jamón (1992) was the first and commercially most successful film of Bigas Luna's 'Trilogía Ibérica', followed the next year by *Huevos de oro* and, finally, *La teta y la luna* (1995).[1] The three films provide different but interconnected views of contemporary Spain: *Jamón jamón* is set in a rural area of Aragón; the central and longest part of the action of *Huevos de oro* takes place among the sky-scrapers of Benidorm, Spain's most popular tourist resort on the Mediterranean; and the story of *La teta y la luna* is situated in a little village in the autonomous region of Catalonia. The films are, therefore, more consciously than, for example, those of Pedro Almodóvar, explicit attempts to present a cultural tapestry of Spain in the last decade of the twentieth century. In all three cases, the main emphasis is on gender relationships and sexuality. The central protagonists of both *Huevos de oro* and *La teta y la luna* are males whose sexual fantasies are variously incorporated into the narrative. Although narrative centrality is more evenly shared between the six central characters of *Jamón jamón*, critical attention has tended to concentrate on the ideologically suspect display of 'machismo' through the character of Raúl (Javier Bardem).[2] This, along with the popularity

I wish to thank Linda Williams for permission to use unpublished material, Leandro Martínez, Carmelo Romeo, and Monica Stacconi for their help with the bibliography, and Chantal Cornut-Gentille, Constanza del Río, and Anita La Cruz for their valuable suggestions.

    [1] This trilogy format seems to have pleased the director, since his next two films are *Bambola* (1996) and *La camarera del Titanic* (1998), the first two entries in a new trilogy on women.

    [2] Leslie Felperin Sherman summarizes this position in her review of *Huevos de oro*: 'For some, *Jamón, jamón* was flawed by its seemingly unproblematic celebration of Hispanic male potency' (1994: 45).

attained by Bardem, a popularity which was then confirmed by his roles in *Huevos de oro*, in Imanol Uribe's extremely successful *Días contados* (1994) and in Almodóvar's *Carne trémula* (1997), may have obscured the narrative and ideological importance of the film's female characters.

For this reason, I will concentrate on these three characters and, in the final part of the chapter, on the ways in which their representation interacts with the film's construction of a discourse of contemporary Spanishness through gender stereotypes. The link between the discourses of gender, female sexuality, and Spanishness is provided by the film's spectacular and complex use of filmic and real space, which will also be taken into consideration.

When *Jamón jamón* first came out, Spanish critics agreed on the importance of the film's location: the visually spectacular region of Los Monegros, a large expanse of grey hills and arid land situated in the proximity of Aragón's capital, Zaragoza. The geographical reference is relevant not only because it is the area chosen to represent what various reviewers have aptly described as 'la España profunda', 'la España de puticlubs, de jubilados, de carretera y polvo, . . . la idiosincrática España de ajo arriero y tortilla de patatas con cebolla' (Freixas 1992: 36)—a different kind of Spain from the common stereotypes of the south and the Mediterranean coast—but also because of the cultural and filmic history of the region as representative of a certain kind of Spanishness. Although many other Spanish films have been set in Aragón, the one film that immediately comes to mind in connection with this region is Florián Rey's *Nobleza baturra* (1935), a film that eulogized the qualities of honesty, frankness, and uprightness stereotypically associated with people from the region and contained in the term 'baturro'.

Critics and reviewers also rushed to find explicit 'high cultural' references in *Jamón jamón*, such as Goya, Lorca, Valle-Inclán, surrealism, and Buñuel, among others. The film no doubt attempts to incorporate earlier texts in order to put forward a certain idea of Spain that will be more appealing abroad than, for example, the one encapsulated in 'jamón serrano' and 'tortilla de patatas'. Yet connections with other, less prestigious texts, like *Nobleza baturra*, have been overlooked. Rey's film was immensely popular in Spain and launched its protagonist, Imperio Argentina, into stardom.[3]

---

[3] For a detailed account of this film and its importance in the history of Spanish cinema, see Sánchez Vidal 1991: 187–214.

The film's heroine, Pilar, becomes a representative of the quintessential virtues of the Spanish race. According to Marvin D'Lugo, she encapsulates what Spanish people came to see as 'folkloric authenticity' (1991: 176). Moreover, Zaragoza, through the prominence of its famous temple, El Pilar, is presented as the centre of 'la Hispanidad', the cultural space designed in the twentieth century to bring Spain back together with its old colonies in Latin America.[4] The film starts with a series of shots of the region, emphasizing the fertility of the landscape and its open spaces. The first scene, a musical number spectacularly filmed, shows Pilar singing as she happily participates in the communal harvest. The emphasis is on a sense of community with nature, with the wheat gently swaying in the breeze and flocks of sheep peacefully moving across green fields.[5] It is in this context that the love story between Pilar and Sebastián (Juan de Orduña), a humble shepherd who works for her father, develops. Although pre-Franco, the film fits Peter Evans's description of the Francoist film tradition that 'denigrated urban culture while celebrating a folkloric, sanitised Spain, innocent of sexuality, communism and foreign influence' (1996: 21).[6]

The implication that this idealized perception of Spain, which existed only in the conservative discourses of the dictatorship, was totally at odds with the 'real' Spain is part of the discourse of *Jamón jamón*. To the impossibly idyllic Aragón of the beginning of *Nobleza baturra*, Bigas Luna opposes a more immediately recognizable landscape of the region. The exuberant vegetation and clear skies of the older film are replaced by dusty roads and arid land. The sheep, which are central not only as part of the bucolic atmosphere of *Nobleza baturra* but also as part of its plot, have now been replaced by pigs and will only be introduced in the final shot in a blatantly unmotivated way. Instead of happy peasants and carefree shepherds, the first human figures we see are two idle young men practising bullfighting in an otherwise empty landscape. By going back to the same region of the country and presenting it in such a

---

    [4] According to Sánchez Vidal, the film was very popular not only in Spain but in most Latin American countries (1991: 199).

    [5] Philip Strick finds a reference to Buñuel in the flock that appears in the final shot of *Jamón, jamón* (1993: 58), but nobody has connected these sheep to their very important presence in *Nobleza baturra*.

    [6] On Rey's conservative ideology and his relations with Nazi Germany, see Sánchez Vidal 1991: *passim*, esp. 228–40. A later, equally popular film, in this same tradition is *Surcos* (José Antonio Nieves Conde, 1951).

dramatically different way, the film is speaking to the 'folkloric' tradition of Spanish cinema and calling the knowing spectator's attention to its own, radically different, representation of Spanish culture.

Jamón jamón establishes its visual ironic mode from the first shot. The film's credits are superimposed on a black screen with white dots that seems to represent a starry night, but, as the camera pans down, we discover that the dots are little holes in an old Osborne brandy road advertisement featuring a black bull. The camera, placed behind the figure of the bull, stops its descending movement when it reaches the animal's genital region, on which is now superimposed the director's credit. Any native spectator will immediately recognize the advertisement as a decades-old regular feature on Spanish roads. What is different is the perspective, from behind the figure, rather than from the road and, of course, the deliberate concentration on the genitals. Beyond them, the final part of the shot shows a road in the midst of a dusty, grey Monegros landscape, routinely travelled by massive, impersonal lorries. The 'new' perspective on Spain provided by the film is, therefore, announced through the manipulation of point of view and the use of space. At the same time, the shot also declares that this new perspective is inevitably and spectacularly gendered . . . and oversexed.

The broad saturnalian comedy of the opening shot is maintained in the next sequence of shots with the intentionally obscene concentration on Raúl's crotch and conspicuously erect penis under his flimsy shorts as he practises bullfighting with a friend and, again, in the following scene, as the camera tracks along a line of young men, wearing onlytight underpants, posing for a male underwear advert. Bigas Luna explains his enthusiasm for Los Monegros in the following way: 'es un mar de tierra, donde la aridez hace que todos los elementos destaquen' (in Alegre 1991: 10). In the opening sequences it is the bull advertisement and the young men's genitals that stand out in the midst of this arid sea of land. Later on, other obvious symbols of masculinity, like the motorbike or the underpants advertisement, will add to the list. Yet these all-too-obvious displays of excessive masculinity should not obscure the centrality of the landscape itself, a landscape which, in this as in other texts, is coded as feminine. Speaking about the place of the US land in *High Sierra* (Raoul Walsh, 1940), Constanza del

Río has argued that 'it is America, a mythic past rural America whose body Roy traverses with pleasure, that stands to signify the silenced Mother, a dying sign of the pre-Oedipal phase: Motherland' (1992: 112). In *Jamón jamón*, as in Lorca's tragedies, the dry land also stands for motherhood and is associated in various ways with the film's three female characters: Silvia (Penélope Cruz), who is pregnant, her mother Carmen (Anna Galiena), and Conchita (Stefania Sandrelli). Los Monegros is the space in which a family melodrama of good and bad motherhood is developed but the place is also, in its impressive visual barrenness, the most powerful symbol of motherhood and of its violent desires.

The film underlines its attitude to the representation of characters in both the publicity notes and the final credits. Rather than by their names, the characters are introduced by means of short definitions. Thus, Silvia is 'la hija de puta', Carmen 'la puta madre', and Conchita 'la madre puta'. Clearly, this strategy seeks to consider the characters not so much as individuals but as stereotypes, as symbols of certain kinds of Spanishness.[7] Our recognition of the characters, therefore, is closely connected with the types they are supposed to represent.[8] We are less interested in their individual predicaments than in the stereotypes with which they are associated. At the same time, since these characters tend to respond to ready-made clichés, impressed upon the spectator through actor performance, immediately recognizable habits and attitudes, and frequent use of contemporary linguistic mannerisms, we tend to distance ourselves from them as individuals and our sympathies or antipathies are directed, instead, towards what they represent. I will be arguing that the three female characters can best be seen in this light, both as universal representations of motherhood and as signifying a certain idea of Spain.

Initially, the definitions of the female characters are meant as problematizations of the moral connotations of both the institutions of motherhood and prostitution. In interview, Bigas Luna insists on his admiration for prostitutes:

El término puta no tiene nada de peyorativo, todo lo contrario. Yo a las mujeres más queridas las llamo putas, empezando por mi propia madre.

---

[7] Strick rightly notes that the Spanish specificity of the stereotypes is problematic (1993: 58).

[8] On the concept of recognition, as one of three levels of spectatorial engagement with a film's characters, see Murray Smith (1995: 75).

Eres una puta maravillosa, le digo. Lo mejor del mundo, las putas y las madres. Y una puta que sea madre, o una madre que sea puta, ya es lo máximo. Por eso cuando algo nos gusta mucho decimos que está de puta madre. (in Alegre 1991: 11)

This ideal association between mother and prostitute is, as Bigas Luna's words confirm, clearly a male fantasy, a fantasy that becomes pivotal in the film's narrative line. Carmen is the good prostitute, who lives and would die for her children. In addition, when her services are required by José Luis (Jordi Molla), she also performs the role of the desired mother, as we suspect she did in the past with his father Manuel (Juan Diego). She encapsulates the director's fantasy of the ideal mother/prostitute, nurturing, protective, and forever sexually available. She embodies the most positive characteristics of the two central female stereotypes of our culture without any of the negative aspects associated with either of them. In the film, she gives men shelter and protection from the oppression of the bad mother. Carmen, in spite of social appearances, is the prototypical heroine of such maternal Hollywood melodramas as *Imitation of Life* (John M. Stahl, 1934), *Stella Dallas* (King Vidor, 1937), or *To Each his Own* (Mitchell Leisen, 1946).[9] Not much is revealed about her past, but we infer that, after leaving or being left by her violent lorry-driver husband, she became a prostitute in order to support her three daughters. Evidently a foreigner, she has settled in the region, and owns the brothel and the very humble house in which she lives. Anna Galiena, although born in Rome, is an itinerant actress, whose first screen success was the French film *Le Mari de la coiffeuse* (Patrice Leconte, 1990). She has worked as a theatre actress in New York and has regularly made films in Italy, France, and Spain. Her 'Europeanness' is used

[9] In spite of the importance of the figure of the mother in Spanish culture, there is no equivalent genre to the maternal melodrama in Spanish cinema. There have obviously been examples of melodramas in which the relationship between mothers and children is central, like some of Marisol's films, but, in general, the figure of the father is predominant, as is the case in such popular films as Fernando Palacio's *La gran familia* (1962) and *La familia y uno más* (1965). We can also note, within the tradition of art film, the narrative 'repression' of the mother in Erice's *El espíritu de la colmena* (1973) and *El sur* (1983) or her outright demonization in José Luis Borau's *Furtivos* (1975). A more recent example of maternal melodrama of sorts is Agustín Díaz Yanes's *Nadie hablará de nosotras cuando hayamos muerto* (1995). The impact of the mother figure of this film, played by Pilar Bardem, with audiences and critics may be proof of the relative scarcity of such narratives in Spanish cinema.

thematically to depict the outsider who has now become the moral centre of the region. The beauty of the desert land also works as a metaphor for the downtrodden prostitute who retains a kind of moral beauty in spite of her worn body, her poverty, and her gloomy future. She is the film's 'puta madre', the Kleinian 'good mother', or, in Bigas Luna's own words, 'el gran coño' (Agulló 1992: 4). She is also the social outcast whom the film saves from received morality in exchange for her permanent availability as prostitute and mother or as mother/prostitute.

Silvia is the main character and the spectator's main point of reference in the story. It is mostly through her that we perceive the other characters and for her that the spectacle of both powerful and weak masculinity is staged. In generic terms, she is initially presented as the modernized suffering heroine of classical melodrama, whose social class prevents her marrying José Luis. Both physically and narratively, she appears to be a mirror image of her mother, but she is also easily comparable to such heroines of classical melodrama as Tess in Thomas Hardy's *Tess of the d'Urbervilles* (1891) or Anna (Lillian Gish) in D. W. Griffith's *Way Down East* (1920), whose virtue is threatened because of their social class. Peter Brooks has argued that, in such stories, the link between virtue and innocence is embodied, at the outset, in a setting—a garden or a rural home—which he terms the 'space of innocence' (1984: 29). In a recent elaboration of this concept, Linda Williams (forthcoming) argues that the melodramatic happy ending depends on the extent to which the characters can, at the end, return in a real or metaphorical form to this space of innocence. For this reason, melodrama is suffused with a nostalgia for the lost innocence associated with the rural and the maternal and is structured around the increasing awareness of this loss. In *Jamón jamón*, the old region of Los Monegros, and, more specifically, the spot on the hill behind the figure of the bull, where we first see Silvia and José Luis together, represent this space of innocence. This space is associated, on the one hand, with the socially acceptable institution of marriage through the symbolic engagement ring (really the tab of a drink can) that José Luis gives Silvia as a promise of marriage. On the other hand, this space associates both characters with the mother and with infant sexuality when José Luis sucks her breasts.

The main point of departure from classical versions of the genre comes about when Silvia succumbs to Raúl's advances and falls in love with him. Although the film is explicitly placing itself on the side of sexual passion against social convention through her change of heart, narratively, it is her involvement with Raúl, along with Conchita's jealousy, that brings about the final duel between the two young men and José Luis's death. Silvia's generic positioning becomes more and more problematic as the film develops and her desire for Raúl increases. The melodrama of submissive and unyielding virtue cannot contain her sexual desire and, for this reason, it is partially abandoned as she comes closer to a different female stereotype in Western culture: the mysterious woman whose sexuality, when unleashed, wreaks havoc in society and provokes the death of 'innocent' men. The film's definition of her seems now to refer less to the biological link with her mother than to the more usual—and pejorative—meaning of the expression. As 'la hija de puta', she becomes more closely associated with Conchita, the bad mother, than with Carmen, the good prostitute.

In her analysis of the iconography of the myth of Pandora, Laura Mulvey uses Kristeva's concept of the abject in order to qualify the nature of the contents of Pandora's box, a 'phantasmagoric topography [that] has haunted representations of femininity across the ages' (1996: 63). She further describes the surface of the box:

The surface is like a beautiful carapace, an exquisite mask. But it is vulnerable. It threatens to crack, hinting that through the cracks might seep whatever the 'stuff' might be that it is supposed to conceal and hold in check. (1996: 63).

This 'stuff' inside is the abject, the term that Kristeva employs to describe the consequences in adult life of the experience of lack felt at the discovery of sexual difference. The symbolization, the 'naming' of the abject is an attempt to incorporate into language, into the symbolic, what has been lost. The paradox with Pandora's box, as with the abject, is that they both contain a horror that we keep wanting to see. In Kristeva's view, this produces an eroticization of abjection, one which, like abjection itself, is related to the repressed maternal body:

But devotees of the abject, she as well as he, do not cease looking, within what flows from the other's 'innermost being,' for the desirable and terrifying, nourishing and murderous, fascinating and abject inside of the maternal body. (1982: 54)

One of the most frequent criticisms of *Jamón jamón* in Spain was its superficiality, its inability to go beyond a beautifully packaged product of easy consumption. In this sense, the conscious use of flat stereotypes instead of complex, contradictory characters contributes to the overall feeling of an alarming lack of depth (Freixas 1992: 34–7). Yet, this obsession with surfaces, this fetishization of the exterior, may be seen as just a thin veil that hides the urge to behold the 'stuff seeping from the inside': the maternal abject. As Silvia's infatuation with Raúl progresses and her sexual 'voracity' comes to the fore, the spectator's attitude changes not only towards the characters but also towards the 'seventh character', the landscape of Los Monegros, which gradually loses its initial inert quality and working-class deprivation to threaten eruption, like a volcano that has been inactive for centuries. The 'lava' struggling to break free from under the spectacular surface is the maternal abject 'stuff', the uncontrollable passion of the mother.

It may seem far-fetched to associate this meaning of the landscape with Silvia, who, in many senses, remains the 'virtuous' heroine of melodrama right to the last scene, yet it is precisely this façade of an innocent young girl that allows the film to imbue her with conscious meanings of transgressive sexuality. Penélope Cruz was 16 when *Jamón jamón* was made and this was the part that launched her career as a film star, yet, since then, she has often complained that she was not ready for this role and her experience in the film scarred her psychologically.[10] This proves that the choice of a young, untrained actress was deliberate on the part of the film-maker. The excesses of masculinity, both the excessive potency of Raúl and the excessive emasculation of José Luis, exist as functions of Silvia's (and Conchita's) sexuality. Male sexuality is, therefore, the packaged product that the film is trying to sell and, within the film's diegesis, Silvia is one of the prospective customers.

Conchita is the other one. Unlike Silvia, she does not change in the course of the film, yet her increasing centrality as the action progresses allows the spectator a certain degree of understanding towards her predicament. From the beginning she is Carmen's opposite, la 'madre puta', the castrating mother whose dominating

---

[10]   Interview with Ángel Casas, *Tal cual*, TVE2, 5 Nov. 1996.

role in the family has all but erased her husband, while her barely disguised incestuous desire for her son has also seriously curtailed his 'natural' development towards normative masculinity—as one of his friends says in Luna's typically coarse way, 'Sansón, polla de maricón.'[11] Although, at first sight she disapproves of José Luis's wedding to Silvia on the grounds of their class differences, the film always makes it clear that she is simply jealous of the competition. When she asks Raúl to stop seeing Silvia, after having herself hired him precisely to seduce the young girl, her unabating sexual appetite is emphasized once again. Silvia's desires in the final section of the story are only a pale reflection of Conchita's constant threat to patriarchal institutions through her sexuality.

Stefania Sandrelli was an apt choice for this part.[12] A European sex symbol of the 1960s and 1970s, she hit immediate fame at the age of 15 through her part as false *ingénue* in *Divorzio all'italiana* (Pietro Germi, 1962). Defined in an encyclopedia as 'an instinctive actress with a natural capacity to project both innocence and sensuality' (Katz 1994: 1198), she herself agrees with this image when she remembers her personality in Germi's film as 'a force of nature' and a 'quindicenne scatenata' (an unbridled teenager) (in Faldini and Fofi 1979: 114–15). She subsequently established her international reputation as a European star in films like *Seddotta e abbandonata* (Pietro Germi, 1966), *Brancaleone alle crociate* (Mario Monicelli, 1970), and Bertolucci's *Il conformista* (1969) and *Novecento* (1976), and played the part of a sexually active mother who not only participates willingly in her husband's sexual fantasies but also steals her ultra-conservative daughter's boyfriend in the erotic comedy *La chiave* (Tinto Brass, 1983). Conchita's role as the sensual mother, whose social position is constantly overridden by her instincts, is, therefore, a compilation of the most salient features of her persona. As opposed to Galiena, the good mother, Sandrelli represents the two aspects of what Barbara Creed has termed the monstrous-feminine of horror films: the phallic woman, who has replaced men as head of both family and business, and the archaic mother who, like the mother in Kristeva's 'abject', threatens to reabsorb the male child into the all-encompassing womb, the

---

[11] Sansón, an obvious reference to the biblical story, is also the commercial name of the underpants made at his parents' factory.

[12] She, however, only got the part of Conchita after Laura Antonelli turned it down (Montero 1991: 38).

traditional *vagina dentata*, thus erasing his hard-earned sense of identity. For Creed, the ideological project of the popular horror film is a form of defilement rite: the purification of the abject (1993: 71) and of its cultural representation in patriarchy: woman's power to create new life. Clearly not a horror film, *Jamón jamón*, however, has in Conchita its own feminine monstrous figure, through whom the male spectator is allowed to face, in however distanced a way, his ambivalent attitude oscillating between attraction/repulsion towards patriarchal representations of the mother. As in Creed's archaic mother, her inordinate sexual desire has turned her husband into a taciturn outsider, deprived her son of the traditional masculine will to make his own decisions, and, in the course of the film, will even inhibit Raúl, the sexual wonderboy, who, before long, is turned into another, if more ambiguous, submissive son who will fight to the death with José Luis for full possession of the mother. In this scenario, the spectator is enabled to demonize the figure of the bad mother, 'la madre puta', and what she represents, while increasingly feeling attracted towards her unashamed display of overpossessive motherhood and incestuous sexuality.

Possessive and destructive motherhood is all triumphant at the end of the film, in the final tableau, which, apart from pairing the characters off in three heterosexual couples, brings the two mothers visually together for the first time: after José Luis's death, both Carmen and Conchita sit on the barren land, holding the two fighting sons in motherly poses, like two modern-day *pietà*. Carmen, the ideal good mother image, to whom José Luis is finally reunited after his death, and Conchita, the all-encompassing archaic mother, pressing the wild son Raúl to her chest, finally look remarkably like each other, both occupying the central position in the landscape. Slightly off centre, the 'odd couple', Manuel and Silvia, stand together, a relationship which remains unexplained. As the bolero 'Házmelo otra vez' is heard in the background, a lengthy tracking shot nervously scans the scene of the tragedy, moving past the cars, hams, and people and finally enveloping them all and emphasizing once again the grey stillness of Los Monegros, the apparently passive space of the tragedy that has finally engulfed all its children. We now realize, or at least intuitively apprehend, that Carmen's ideal mother image was not enough, that Bigas Luna's 'gran coño' is not complete without the more abject aspects of the female organ, here spectacularly encapsulated in Conchita.[13]

Conchita and Carmen, then, represent the two opposite poles of the motherland: good and bad, mother and prostitute, rich and poor, compliant and transgressive, space of innocence and space of abjection, with Silvia moving between the two. They are the two universal feminine stereotypes adapted to the specific requirements of the motherland of Los Monegros and, as such, the film's central symbols of 'la España profunda'. Even though the other characters also represent, as we have seen, different aspects of contemporary Spain, Carmen and Conchita are more central than the rest because of their close relation to the land and because their double dimension as mothers and prostitutes encapsulates the film's most powerful obsessions, the hidden secret underneath the shiny surface.

In his study of the films of Carlos Saura, D'Lugo analyses some of the traditional myths of Spanishness, which in the films of Saura and other 'progressive' Spanish film-makers are intensely scrutinized and often debunked (1991: 7, 28). In his Iberian trilogy, Bigas Luna also examines various myths of traditional and contemporary Spain but his perspective is less obviously critical and sometimes openly celebratory. It would seem that part of the ideological strategy of the film consists in rescuing those myths by transferring them into a discourse of 'uncensored' modern sexuality. The old myths are then invested with a new prestige that makes them and the national culture they stand for attractive to both Spanish and foreign audiences. The reference to and reversal of some of the meanings of *Nobleza baturra* is part of this operation, as is the parodic allusion to such Lorquian tragedies of blood and honour as *Bodas de sangre*. One of the myths that the film engages with is that of traditional Spanish masculinity. In the film, apart from the more obvious displays of masculine sexual potency, this exploration is carried out through the use of bullfighting and the reference to Goya in the final scene. For D'Lugo, bullfighting has been viewed as the emblem of the most reactionary aspects of Spanish culture, a mixture of excessive individuality and 'machismo' (1991:

[13] One of the most spectacular shots of the film is a close-up of a woman's red lips. These lips, however, belong to Carmen, the good mother. This can be read as one more gesture on the part of the film to recuperate and 'sanitize' meanings associated with prostitution through this character.

34). The prominence of the Osborne bull is an ambivalent reference both to the lasting popularity of 'la fiesta nacional' in contemporary Spain and to its cultural crisis: the already half-broken testicles of the bull are finally torn off by José Luis when he and Silvia split up. Yet rather than concentrate on the maimed cardboard figure we now follow Silvia, who uses the severed parts as protection from the rain as she runs to meet and have passionate sex with Raúl. Therefore, while José Luis attempts to destroy the myth, Silvia ironically rescues it by underlining its association with Raúl's sexuality. Through this strategy, the film is reluctant to let go of all the connotations of the myth and prefers to recontextualize it in a more appealing way.

Sánchez Vidal, however, sees the tradition of bullfighting in a different way. For him, since bullfighters were, and in many cases still are, of very humble origins, their success is an illustration of the historical loss of centrality of the aristocracy in favour of the popular classes. For him, bullfights are a symbol of the 'promiscuidad interclasista que penetra tantos aspectos de la vida española' (1990: 75). In this story of a competition between a rich boy and a poor boy, Raúl's use of bullfighting as part of his sexuality is made to contrast with the massive repression of the wealthy middle classes of which José Luis is a pitiful product. A similar value can be ascribed to the reference to Goya's *Pelea a garrotazos*, a painting which not only attempts to 'debunk the exotic and picturesque renditions of Spanish folk customs' (D'Lugo 1991: 50) but also points to the irreconcilable coexistence of the higher and lower classes in the Aragonese painter (Sánchez Vidal 1990: 94). In the context of the film, the scene of the ham fight is turned into the tragic denouement of a polygonal story of intertwined jealousy and infidelity, one which points to the negative consequences of excessive masculinity, but one which, in its reference to Goya, reframes the myth of Spanish machismo in a culturally prestigious environment of progressive class critique.

In narrative and visual terms, however, the two representatives of masculinity are defeated at the end of the film and it is the two desiring and suffering mothers, along with the symbolic motherland, that occupy the most prominent position. Neither the noisy displays of masculine sexuality nor the insistent celebration of Spanish food are placed at the centre of the text. It is, as has been argued in this chapter, motherhood with its meanings of desire and separation, dread and envy, guarantor of and threat to subjectivity, that encloses the film's most powerful meanings. The final question to be asked is, therefore, in what sense is this powerful and all-encompassing motherhood coded as carrying a specific idea of Spanish culture? What is the film saying about Spain through the characters and the geographic space with which they are associated? The immediate paradox is that the two mothers, Carmen and Conchita, who most powerfully dominate in this space of essential Spanishness, are . . . Italian. I have already suggested that Anna Galiena's dimension as an 'international actress' contributes to her narrative function by presenting her as a woman of unknown past who has come from abroad to embrace the culture of which she has now become a representative. Her foreign accent but very articulate use of Spanish make her position narratively coherent. The case of Stefania Sandrelli is different. Conchita is not a foreigner but a Spanish woman, who speaks with a Spanish accent (Sandrelli has been dubbed) and has no diegetic connections outside Spain. No effort has been made to justify the actress's nationality. Sandrelli's star persona, however, does not only signify 'erotic myth' but also, through her association with Bertolucci, Scola, and others, prestigious European art cinema. Her presence serves to incorporate *Jamón jamón* within that tradition and, more importantly, to present Spanish culture as part of a European tradition. Conchita represents the Spanish motherland but Sandrelli is European and culturally on the same level as the other artistic references with which the film is sprinkled. In other words, through the presence of Anna Galiena but, above all, Stefania Sandrelli, the film is seeking international recognition for contemporary Spain by suggesting that what is essentially Spanish is also essentially European, that the Pyrenees have lost their symbolic meaning as a cultural barrier. For D'Lugo, the level of political and cultural maturity achieved by Spanish democracy by the end of the 1980s 'made it increasingly less fashionable for artists to harp on the historical differences that had traditionally separated the dominant cultural and intellectual spirit of Spain from that of the rest of Europe' (1991: 225). This erasure of historical differences, which is perceived as compatible with the celebration of easily recognizable local symbols, is part of the film's discourse of Spanishness and a central ingredient of the cultural anxieties of contemporary Spanish cinema. In a different sense, the simultaneously flaunted and effaced transnational hybridity of Conchita's character can be metaphorically connected with her excessive display of voracious motherhood throughout the narrative: just as the external image of the mother hides a cluster of unconscious patriarchal monsters, the attractive international 'Spanishness' of the character turns out to be no more than the Mulveyan 'beautiful carapace', the fetishized surface that, for all its fashionable posturing, hides the same old ghosts of the past. The film's nagging attempts to modernize the past, like its attempts to recuperate traditional forms of masculinity for a postmodern discourse of liberated sexuality, fail to erase the most obvious real consequences of its fantasized anxieties.

REFERENCES

Agulló, Xavier (1992), 'Entrevista con Bigas Luna', El periódico, La gente (13 Sept.): 3–4.
Alegre, Luis (1991), 'Pasiones bajo el sol de Los Monegros', El periódico, La gente (10 Nov.): 10–11.
Brooks, Peter (1984), The Melodramatic Imagination: Balzac, Henry James, Melodrama, and the Mode of Excess. New York: Columbia University Press (1st pub. 1976).
Creed, Barbara (1993), The Monstrous-Feminine: Film, Feminism, Psychoanalysis. London: Routledge.
del Río, Constanza (1992), 'High Sierra: Going Back Home', in Celestino Deleyto (ed.), Flashbacks: Re-reading the Classical Hollywood Cinema, Zaragoza: Servicio de Publicaciones: 97–119.
D'Lugo, Marvin (1991), The Films of Carlos Saura: The Practice of Seeing. Princeton: Princeton University Press.
Evans, Peter William (1996), Women on the Verge of a Nervous Breakdown. London: BFI.
Faldini, Franca, and Fofi, Goffredo (comps.) (1979), L'avventurosa storia del cinema italiano. Milan: Feltrinelli.
Felperin Sherman, Leslie (1994), 'Huevos de oro', Sight and Sound, 4/7 (July): 45.
Freixas, Ramón (1992), 'Jamón Jamón', Dirigido, 205 (Sept.): 34–7.
Katz, Ephraim (1994), The Film Encyclopaedia. New York: HarperCollins.
Kristeva, Julia (1982), Powers of Horror: An Essay in Abjection, trans. Leon S. Roudiez. New York: Columbia University Press (1st pub. 1980).
Montero, Manuel (1991), 'Bigas Luna rodará en Los Monegros', El periódico (24 Aug.): 38.

Mulvey, Laura (1996), *Fetishism and Curiosity*. London: BFI.

Sánchez Vidal, Agustín (1990), *Sol y sombra*. Barcelona: Planeta.

—— (1991), *El cine de Florián Rey*. Zaragoza: Caja de Ahorros de la Inmaculada.

Smith, Murray (1995), *Engaging Characters: Fiction, Emotion, and the Cinema*. Oxford: Clarendon Press.

Strick, Philip (1993), '*Jamón, jamón*', *Sight and Sound*, 3/6 (June): 57–8.

Williams, Linda (forthcoming), *Melodramas in Black and White: American Racial Melodrama from Uncle Tom to O. J. Simpson*. Princeton: Princeton University Press.

19

Promiscuity, Pleasure, and Girl Power: Fernando Trueba's *Belle Époque* (1992)

BARRY JORDAN

Introduction

In an industry normally characterized by almost permanent crisis, *Belle Époque* was undoubtedly one of the major Spanish film success stories of the early 1990s.[1] At the Seventh Annual Goya Awards (held on 13 March 1993), sponsored by Spain's own Film Academy, Trueba's stylish, period sex comedy virtually swept the board, picking up nine out of twenty-three prizes, including those for best film, best director, best actress (Ariadna Gil), best supporting actor (Fernando Fernán Gómez), and best screenplay (involving Rafael Azcona and José Luis García Sánchez, as well as Trueba himself) (UK Press Book (Apr. 1994): 3–4; *Cine & Teleforme* (Apr. 1993): 52). Apart from representing Spain at various international

---

[1] By most objective measures (e.g. numbers of films produced or in production, ticket sales, spectator numbers, foreign sales), the period 1992–4 was a critical one for the Spanish film industry. Having herself introduced a film policy in the mid-1980s which had failed to halt the industry's decline, no less a figure than Pilar Miró, ex-director general of ICAA, asserted in 1992 that the Spanish cinema was finished (*El mundo*, 16 Aug. 1992). By contrast, amidst deepening crisis, Spain was still able to produce a clutch of quality, international art-house hits such as Bigas Luna's *Jamón jamón* (1992), Julio Medem's *Vacas* (1991), Pedro Olea's *El maestro de esgrima* (1992), Alex de la Iglesia's *Acción mutante* (1993), as well as Trueba's *Belle Époque*. This was so because, as Paul Smith rightly argues, to a greater or lesser extent, all these hits 'benefited from the frame of legibility that Almodóvar had offered foreign audiences, who now expected stylish eroticism and zany humour from Spain' (1994: 138). While one cannot overestimate Almodóvar's positive contribution to raising the profile of Spanish cinema abroad, regrettably, having opened the gate for others, he was still lacking major critical recognition in his own country (Smith 1994: 139). Meanwhile, with the Oscar award and all the attendant hype this created, Fernando Trueba was to become Spain's national and international directorial success of the 1990s, challenging Almodóvar's pre-eminence as the country's premier film-maker.

film festivals (Berlin, Toronto, and the Gramado Festival, Brazil), and rather more significantly, *Belle Époque* was also nominated for an Academy Award for best non-English-language film for 1993 (preferred over a much weaker Spanish candidate, Berlanga's disappointing *Todos a la cárcel*, 1993).[2] To everyone's utter amazement, Trueba's light-hearted, nostalgic, romantic comedy triumphed over stiff art-house competition to win the coveted title.[3] The award was arguably crucial in consolidating Trueba's uneven career, which up to that moment had enjoyed only a limited degree of international success.[4] The Oscar also gave him the exposure, the platform, and

[2] Hitherto, the international success of Spanish films at this level had been rather meagre. Despite fourteen Spanish nominations since 1956 (when the prize was first introduced), including directors such as Almodóvar, Armiñán, Bardem, Berlanga, Saura, and Buñuel, Spain's last major Oscar success in this category (excluding Buñuel's *Le Charme discret de la bourgeoisie* (1972), entered as a French film) had been José Luis Garci's rather lachrymose, sentimental comedy *Volver a empezar* (1982). Its heightened international profile promised much in the early 1980s for Spanish movies abroad but yielded little in the way of market opportunities. As Peter Besas points out (1985: 239–43), *Volver a empezar* was not a high-grossing film in Spain and made little money abroad. Nor did it please the critics, who objected to its whingeing tone and over-American look. Indeed, despite the Oscar, Garci found it almost impossible to find a producer and financial backing for his subsequent project *Sesión continua* (1984). Twelve years later, at the Oscar ceremony which concerns us (March 1994), an event dominated by Spielberg's *Schindler's List*, Jane Campion's *The Piano*, and Tom Hanks's outstanding performance in *Philadelphia*, *Belle Époque* was arguably small beer by comparison. Yet, after overcoming the main competition, represented by Chen Kaige's impressive, art-house movie *Farewell my Concubine* (1992), the Spanish entrant was finally awarded the Oscar for best non-English-language film. It may be worth recalling, given that the directors are frequently compared, that Almodóvar did not cast his Academy vote in favour of Trueba's nomination.

[3] Trueba himself was clearly taken aback, astonished that the Chinese entrant had not won. Cast members, such as Jorge Sanz, were equally amazed yet delighted: 'Es cojonudo para todos los que hicimos la película y una oportunidad impresionante de que se vea nuestro cine' (see *El país*, 23 Mar. 1994 and *El mundo*, 23 Mar. 1994). Also, the manner of Trueba's acceptance of the Academy's accolade was surprising. Unable to ascribe his good fortune to divine providence, in which he confessed little faith, his acceptance speech recalled his spiritual indebtedness to more earthly filmic deities: 'Quisiera agradecérselo a Dios pero sólo creo en Billy Wilder; por lo tanto, gracias a Billy Wilder' (*El mundo*, 23 Mar. 1994). Curiously, until then, Wilder had never heard of Trueba, yet, after hearing himself deified on national television, the veteran Hollywood director congratulated the Spaniard by telephone the following day and thanked him for the free publicity.

[4] After the national success of his first feature, the 'boy meets girl' comedy *Opera prima* (1980), Trueba's next two projects *Mientras el cuerpo aguante* (1982) and *Sal Gorda* (1983) were rather less well received. A breakthrough came with *Sé infiel y no mires con quien* (1985), inaugurating his collaboration with Andrés Vicente Gómez as producer. This was followed by *El año de las luces* (1986), winner

the professional cachet he needed to embark on the much bigger-
budget, Hollywood-based, screwball comedy *Two Much* (1995).[5]
On a wider plane, the award also provided a much-needed boost to
the Spanish film industry, reaffirming Spain's ability to make good-
quality products and helping to enhance the commercial possibilities
of Spanish feature films abroad.[6]

of the Silver Bear, Berlin, 1986, sister film to *Belle Époque* and the first to gain serious international plaudits. Then in 1989, Trueba attempted a formula movie, the
international co-production *El sueño del mono loco* (1989), a perverse rereading of
the Peter Pan story starring an up-and-coming Jeff Goldblum. Despite its five Goya
awards, the film did poorly at the Spanish box office and not much better abroad
(see Kinder 1993: 417–22).

    5 Made entirely in the USA, with a largely American cast (including Daryl
Hannah, Melanie Griffith, Danny Aiello as well as the newly consecrated modern
Valentino, Antonio Banderas) and with absolutely no reference to Spain whatsoever,
the film has been remarkably successful in Spain though a critical and commercial
flop virtually everywhere else. The reasons for this paradoxical and divided reception are intriguing. As regards the film's reception in Spain, its success clearly relates
in part to Trueba's high profile in his country (after the worldwide acclaim lavished
on *Belle Époque*), his enhanced standing for having 'made it' in Hollywood, as well
as his use of rising 'megastar' Banderas, one of Spain's favourite sons. Aside from
this solitary factor, there is also the fact that Spanish audiences are long-standing,
indeed avid (and rather uncritical), consumers of American comedies and high
production values, especially where the thematics are largely fantasy and make-
believe (*Fotogramas*, 1827 (Jan. 1996): 7). On the other hand, the format adopted
by *Two Much* is that of a 1940s screwball comedy, with touches of bedroom farce,
i.e. an old-fashioned, arguably outdated format, which Trueba fails to modernize
successfully. And while the film's look is glossy and sophisticated, its American stars
(Melanie Griffith, Daryl Hannah) are no longer premier league actors. However,
Banderas (who plays an exploitative, sexist character) was probably still not well
known enough among international audiences to carry the film by himself.
Moreover, on its UK release, *Two Much* was showcased in only one cinema before
going to video, a sign perhaps that non-Hispanic audiences did not find Trueba's
visual or verbal gags sharp, witty, or amusing enough. Intriguingly, as happened
with his choice of *Belle Époque* after the mixed fortunes of *El sueño del mono loco*,
for his next project, Trueba returns to a recognizably 'Spanish' theme, though with
an international outlook, in *La niña de tus ojos*. Scripted by the ever-reliable Rafael
Azcona, this is another period piece drawing upon a little-known agreement made
between Hitler and Franco in 1938 to produce a number of films jointly. Trueba's
story recreates the journey of a Spanish film crew to Berlin and their adventures in
the Nazi capital, including an apocryphal love affair between Dr Goebbels and
Imperio Argentina.
    6 Enrique Balmaseda, director of Spain's Film Institute (ICAA) in the early
1990s, saw Trueba's Oscar success as a crucial example of penetration into the
American market, opening up potential opportunities. Likewise, Trueba himself was
convinced that the Oscar would not only raise his own personal standing and career
prospects but also provide greater market opportunities for Spanish films in the vast
USA market: 'El Oscar no es una culminación, es sólo un arma promocional que
puede abrir puertas' (*El mundo*, 23 Mar. 1994). Amidst all the hype and euphoria,

The critical and commercial success of Trueba's period feature and its appeal to international audiences depended in large part on its unconditional celebration of a certain Hispanic/Mediterranean sensibility, a *joie de vivre* predicated on an anti-authoritarian, libertarian philosophy of friendship and free love, unconstrained by political or moral taboos. Indeed, *Belle Époque* presents a luminous, feel-good fantasy in which sexual promiscuity and experimentation attract no moral censure, no negative costs, no downside. In order to develop this libertarian ethic, Trueba sets about destabilizing class, gender, and sexual boundaries. This results in a significant decentring of identities in the film, an unfixing of sex and gender roles and much boundary confusion, all of which has the effect of bringing female identity and desire to the forefront. In the following pages, my aim is to explore a number of aspects relating to the ways in which Trueba attempts to realize and sustain this seemingly pro-feminist, libertarian fantasy. In no particular order of priority, I will briefly consider: the functioning of the gaze, the destabilization of male identities, the roles of transvestism and the masquerade, as well as issues of matriarchy and adolescent development. To round off the discussion, I will also turn briefly to the question of Trueba's nostalgic vision of the past and, in the light of the movie's critical reception, some of the implications of Trueba's apparently amoral, freewheeling, postmodern view of interpersonal relationships.

Desiring Eyes

Over the last two or three decades, in much psychoanalytical and film theory, particularly those aspects influenced by Lacan, it has been generally assumed that the gaze is implicitly gendered, i.e. the woman is generally regarded as a non-looker, as absent, as the subject of the look.[7] Representation, it is argued, tends to be carried out along mainly male lines of sight and such specular activity simply reinforces the dominance of a male, sado-voyeuristic gaze in

Carlos Saura, Oscar nominee in his time, struck a more cautious note by arguing that this particular Oscar category was little more than a concession to 'third', i.e. marginal countries, though such awards could be very useful for promotional reasons (*Cambio 16*, 4 Apr. 1994).

[7] See Lacan 1977.

Western culture.[8] In short, images of women in film are created mainly as fetishized objects for male scopophilic desire.[9] According to Laura Mulvey, this has the effect of strengthening the connection between the visible male body and invisible, male, specular mastery.[10] Extrapolating from this general theoretical paradigm and with regard to the function of 'looking' in *Belle Époque*, I would like to argue that, while certainly active and desiring, the male gaze within the movie is by no means dominant or commanding and that the male (as well as the female) body also functions as an object of fetishistic attention. Moreover, female characters in the film achieve a degree of visibility as active gazing subjects which seems to contradict notional male mastery of the visual field and the ability to define that field. This is so, for example, in the sense that the central quartet of young sisters in the film, whose libidinal desires drive the narrative, become active, uninhibited 'lookers' and their combined gazes in fact transform the young male lead, Fernando (Jorge Sanz), into an appropriable eroticized object or spectacle. However, rather than pose the metaphorical threat of castration of the male (by way of a powerful returning gaze in the manner, for example, of Freud's Medusa's head (1955: 273–4)), the female gaze in *Belle Époque* signals a degree of complementarity and mutual reflexivity with that of the male. We can see this process at work in the psycho-sexual dynamics of looking at the beginning and end of the film.

After escaping arrest by the two Civil Guards, the young army deserter Fernando (still wearing one handcuff and fearful of being implicated in what appears to be a double murder) stumbles upon a brothel in the forest (suggestive of an enchanted, fairy-tale scenario) where he seeks refuge. And in a deliberate parody of the Freudian primal scene, the eyes of the innocent bugle boy become transfixed on a bout of vigorous sexual coupling through an open window.[11] However, our young hero's desire to transcend his feverish infantile voyeurism and become an active sexual subject in his own right is thwarted and delayed. His initial plan is to stay the night at the brothel as a client and hopefully evade the inevitable investigation into the deaths of the Civil Guards. But, almost in the

---

[8]   See Irigaray 1984: 120–33; also Kaplan 1983; de Lauretis 1984.
[9]   See Douane 1982.
[10]   Mulvey 1975, and her 'Afterthoughts' on this influential piece (1981).
[11]   See Rycroft 1968: 123–4.

manner of a Buñuelian plot, Fernando is destined not to enjoy any of the carnal delights on offer. Moreover, La Polonia (María Galiana), the madame of the house, in a bold instance of female scopophilia, declares her strong specular interest in this young innocent. Her libidinous look reverses dominant male lines of sight and casts Fernando in the traditional female role as erotic sex object but now lined up for female desire. Indeed, she marks him out as a 'chico guapo' and even as a possible consort for her hard-working daughter, the formidable Encarna. Right at the beginning of the movie, then, traditional masculine and feminine roles begin to be redefined, by way of a strong, libidinous female gaze, which complements that of the male and redefines young Fernando as erotic spectacle. Other obvious examples of this reversal of specular privileges involve the initial meeting between the four sisters and Fernando, which begins at the station, as the youngster is about to make his first departure. The other main instance occurs at the end of the movie, with the final departure, as the characters go their separate ways.

In the first instance, in an early scene in which Fernando's libidinal male gaze (already in evidence at the brothel) is repeated, he catches sight of Manolo's four young daughters as they alight from the Madrid train: Luz (Penélope Cruz), Clara (Miriam Díaz Aroca), Violeta (Ariadna Gil), and Rocío (Maribel Verdú). He is so smitten and aroused by the spectacle of the four attractive young sisters that he decides to suspend his departure and return to Manolo's mansion in an opportunist quest for sex and romance. In the scene, through Fernando's relatively innocent eyes, the females are still regarded as erotic objects for male voyeuristic pleasure. At the same time, conditioned by his Jesuit upbringing, Fernando also assumes that the four sisters will follow conventional patterns of female behaviour and adopt the self-sacrificing, virginal, dutiful values and mores of traditional, backward Spain. However, on first contact with the sisters at the country house, Fernando is confronted with a rather different situation. Indeed, far from appearing demure, domesticated, and self-effacing, the sisters are shown as strong-willed, self-confident, and independent-minded. And when Fernando looks at them, they deal effortlessly with his presence, behave with a total lack of inhibition, and are able to function as active gazing subjects in their own right, in pursuit of their own pleasures and emotional fulfilment. Immature, naive, on the run, Trueba's young picaresque hero is variously specularized by the sisters as erotic object and transformed into a vehicle through which they will all eventually realize their fantasies. And by the end of the film, with the second departure, the privileged gaze of desire, initially dominated by Fernando (married to Luz), has now been appropriated visibly by the three older sisters. As they board the train for Madrid, it is they who nostalgically gaze on Fernando as erotic object and source of their pleasure, in a mixed gesture of friendship and desire; it is now they who have gained visibility and power as active gazing subjects.[12]

Destablizing Male Identities

In the opening scene of the film, through the stereotyped pantomimic figures of the Civil Guards (Juan José Otegui and Jesús Bonilla), Trueba presents us with a comical father–son relationship fatally undermined by the son-in-law's absurd, homicidal dedication to discipline. This murderous, macho outlook arguably corresponds to Trueba's own view of traditional patriarchal (and Francoist) Spain: dogmatic, repressive, violent, incapable of dealing with intellectual argument or allowing people to live their lives freely. Belle Époque proposes a radically alternative, libertarian social and family model for Spain, in part represented by a far more benign and successful father–son rela-

[12] The working title for the film was Las cuñadas (sisters-in-law, denoting a clear focus on the four sisters with whom the young male lead has incestuous relations, one by one). The UK Press Book also confirms Trueba's intention to establish his female protagonists as strong, active subjects in the pursuit of pleasure. For example, in interview, Trueba declared: 'Women love the film in Spain because Belle Époque does not present them as passive objects of leisure but as active seekers of pleasure.' The early title was changed to Belle Époque for reasons mainly to do with marketing the movie and exploiting a more evocative, international label, which would transcend linguistic frontiers and express to a wider audience the spirit and outlook of the film. The title also had other obvious resonances: it referred to Fernando's sojourn at the country house and his sentimental education. It also referred not only to the transitional months before the declaration of the Second Spanish Republic, but to the whole five-year experiment in democratic politics before the outbreak of the Civil War in Spain in July 1936. The title also evoked a certain golden age of freedom, happiness, joy, and experimentation, associated with Trueba's fantasy version of Republican Spain.

tionship, symbolized by Fernando and Manolo (Fernando Fernán-Gómez).[13]

Manolo is the lonely, elderly, liberal-Republican intellectual, painter, freethinker, sceptic, and *bon viveur*. He is the relaxed, non-judgemental father figure, who rescues Fernando, takes him under his wing, and—despite initial reservations—creates the conditions for his sexual education. Manolo also has a wife (an opera singer, on tour) and four attractive young daughters but, interestingly, no sons. (The film hints subtly at Manolo's desire for male friendship but also for a son, in order to continue patrilinear descent, and it is Fernando who is soon co-opted into fulfilling this role.) At the same time, through his domestic skills, mainly culinary, Fernando rapidly assumes the roles of cook, domestic servant, and companion, roles centred on nurturing activities and coded as feminine. Here, Trueba draws our attention to the paradoxical and the 'other' in the make-up of individual male subjectivities and identities, to the viability and legitimacy of the 'counter-stereotype', i.e. the feminized man. In return for shelter, protection, and the prospect of romance, and in a spirit of friendship and mutual respect, Fernando is quite amenable to adopting a supportive, domesticated role, despite initial equivocations. However, in an early scene, when Manolo suggests they occupy the same bed, Fernando initially draws back, fearful that the old man might be homosexual: '¿No será Vd maricón?' he asks. Manolo calmly explains to the youngster that he is not gay: 'De maricón nada. Fuera de mi mujer, completamente impotente.'

As in his earlier film *El año de las luces* (1986), Trueba once again employs the figure of the enlightened intellectual to guide the youngster's sexual education. And as before, the older man also represents male sexual impotence, adopting the role of bystander and voyeur, though one who is nonetheless happy to live his sexual and patrilinear fantasies through his adoptive, stand-in son, Fernando. Here, also, Trueba presents the spectator with a positive image of male friendship and support between the generations, based on genuine understanding and sharing, with no coercion either way. Interestingly, while presenting Manolo and Fernando as

---

[13] Trueba argues that the story is based on biographical fact, i.e. his own experience of getting to know Manolo Huete and his four daughters, one of whom, Christina, he finally married.

an attractive role model for a father–son relationship in which sharing is paramount, the initial bedroom scene also obliquely raises the matter of homosexuality as a possible identity and sexual option, and thus evokes—in a metaphorical sense—the taboo of (male) incest. Here, Trueba might have conceivably allowed Fernando the chance of exploring an alternative gay identity, yet the matter is broached fleetingly only to be rapidly closed down, with Manolo's declaration of impotence and his reassurance that he does not constitute a threat to heterosexual norms. (Curiously, in a film ostensibly committed to the delights of alternative sexualities, the lack of other gay male relationships, real or staged, might well indicate a possible blind spot on Trueba's part or conceivably a hint of homophobia.)

Compared to the strong, self-confident, liberated female characters, the leading male protagonists of *Belle Époque*, as noted above, are presented as benign, accommodating, non-macho, and sensitive, playing secondary, supporting roles. And in contrast to that of their female counterparts, male behaviour is also characterized by self-control and repression. Indeed, most of the expressions of male sensuality and desire tend to be overridden by a streak of masochistic self-denial. Manolo is the advocate of a freewheeling intellectual and sexual libertarianism yet he is unable to engage in any form of sexual activity himself until his wife's return from abroad. It is not made clear whether this self-denial is a result of a commitment to a concept of enduring marital fidelity (which would contradict his outlook) or the consequence of some other condition. Whatever the origins of his restraint, Manolo's sexuality is determined and regulated by his wife. In effect, as noted above, he represents a form of male impotence; his sexual activity remains suspended in the face of female mastery. He is thus more than happy to allow his adoptive son Fernando to stand in for him and see his frustrated desires and nostalgia for male virility achieved through the youngster with his own daughters. Manolo is thus a mere spectator on the scenes of desire of others, and only fleetingly (when Amalia arrives) is allowed to function as an active sexual subject in his own right.

The ridiculous young Carlist bigot Juanito (Gabino Diego), Rocío's fiancé, is also sexually neutered, subject to a domineering, castrating mother, Doña Asun (Chus Lampreave), who has repressed and infantilized him. In line with tradition, he is denied the opportunity to consummate his relationship with Rocío until after their marriage. Yet he is driven mad with sexual desire and on several occasions vows to recant his religion, renounce his family, and abandon his reactionary politics; he even becomes a Republican supporter simply in order to gain access to Rocío's bed. However, in his case, sexual fulfilment appears to be indefinitely deferred, unlike that of his fiancée, who enjoys the delights of pre-marital sex courtesy of Fernando.

As regards the priest, Don Luis (Agustín González) is the foul-mouthed, irascible, liberal figure (created by Rafael Azcona, Trueba's co-writer) who embodies many of the ideological contradictions of 1930s Spain. He is described by Doña Asun as 'hereje y masón' and by Juanito as a disgrace to his calling. Yet he is a warm, friendly, benign member of the Catholic clergy, with liberal social attitudes, and is generous (to the extent of raising the wages of his sexton, who promptly turns to anarchism and burns down the church). Don Luis also has a monstrous appetite for good living, especially for good food, cooked so appetizingly by Fernando. By his dress, i.e. by being a man in a skirt, Don Luis is to some extent already 'feminized'; and by his very vocation, he is also neutered, having renounced sexual activity in the name of the Church. Apart from food and drink, he derives his pleasures from flouting Catholic conventions and wrestling with heterodox ideas and philosophical speculation. In this connection, Manolo cannot understand the priest's curious fascination with Unamuno, 'poeta no un pensador', whose writings he blames for having addled the priest's ability to reason. For Don Luis, the pleasures of the flesh are thus both deferred and denied and in the end, by committing suicide, the priest enacts the ultimate form of denial. Yet, he is clearly Trueba's preferred version of a Catholic priest, easy-going, open, liberal, and tolerant.[14]

[14] At the end of the film, the priest is found hanging in the church with a copy of Unamuno's *El sentimiento trágico de la vida* in his hand, indicating perhaps his inability to live with contradiction. Miguel de Unamuno was one of Spain's fore-most Catholic philosophers who lost his religious faith. Unamuno's work focused on the contradiction between a humanist conception of God as man-created and man-centred and a separate, theological, abstract God, out of reach of man's knowl-edge. What may have been troubling Don Luis is that, according to Unamuno, a belief in God is faced with insurmountable difficulties. Unamuno is no atheist or agnostic, but finds it impossible to know a God who is more than a projection of man's own self-consciousness. In other words, being unable to know and thus believe in God means that life is a constant desire for certainty that cannot be met; hence the 'tragic sense of life'. See Longhurst 1994: 37–45.

Finally, and briefly returning to Fernando, we find in him a contradictory mixture of a Catholic seminary upbringing and agnostic attitudes. He proclaims Republican political sympathies (yet observes the strictures of army discipline—he is unable to burn his uniform). Above all, he displays a soft, nurturing outlook. It is precisely this domesticated, feminized persona which the four sisters (as well as the male characters) find extremely attractive and with which they can experiment in order to satisfy their differing requirements. Indeed, Fernando is the medium through which the young women can project their desires, lacks, and longings, and give vent to their libidinal energy. In the end, Trueba's heroines occupy the more dominant, self-motivating roles, with the male characters playing secondary, supportive parts, engaged in servicing and accommodating female desire. With this inversion of gender roles, *Belle Époque* thus acts as a stage for a powerfully attractive erotic fantasy, one which reverses traditional gender and power relations. And in order to allow the film's female dissidents to respond fully to their unconscious libidinal drives, Trueba stylishly puts masculine identity into temporary disarray and crisis. This can be seen at its most acute and amusing in the now famous cross-dressing scene.

Transvestism and the Masquerade

Towards the middle of the movie, a sceptical Manolo criticizes the local mayor for organizing a fiesta while momentous political change is beginning to sweep the country. Yet, despite its diversionary function in relation to Republican politics, the Carlist fiesta is a key scene in the development of the film's sexual politics. This carnivalesque, cross-dressing sequence establishes the fantasy scenario of the masquerade, where reversals of dress, behaviour, and sexual identities are openly put on display and the resulting pleasures (visual and sexual) hungrily consumed.

Even before the fiesta, in a bout of good-humoured horseplay in the attic, the four sisters 're-dress' Fernando for the party; it is they who choose his outfit and thus define what role he will play for the evening. At the same time, by appropriating his army uniform, Violeta assumes Fernando's male, 'soldier boy' identity, the equivocal authority this confers, his identity as protagonist in

Republican politics (i.e. his role in the rising at Cuatro Vientos—
the story of which he narrates at dinner), as well as the pleasures
she herself derives from the act of transvestism. For Violeta, this is
not simply a disguise. She genuinely wants to be male, not a mere
parody of a male figure; nor does she simply want to don a mask
for an evening and then cast it aside; in fact, she wants maleness for
real. With Violeta, then, gender boundaries collapse totally, thus
opening the way to desire and pleasure. Fernando, for his part, is
decked out as a French maid, a classic guise, long employed to titil-
late male sexual fantasies in music halls, burlesque, brothel, etc. In
a sense, Fernando is transformed into a sexualized female stereotype, a whorish figure normally intended for male specularization
(this reverses the opening scene in the brothel, where Fernando
wished to be the subject not the object of whorish desire). Now he
himself is the object of male visual contemplation, fantasy, and
lesbian consumption, a positioning he accepts, with reasonably
good humour, though this fluctuates. Before joining the party,
Violeta reinforces Fernando's feminization by applying a further
layer of thick red lipstick. The latter is again a classic sign of feminine masquerade and more conventionally a sign of female sexual
relations with the male; and having 'feminized' her prey, Violeta
feels greatly aroused by the spectacle: '¡Qué guapa estás!' she
remarks to a quizzical Fernando. She then pushes him/her onto the
dance floor and embarks on the dance which traditionally symbol-
izes male potency and the culture of the brothel: the tango (inci-
dentally outlawed by the Catholic Church and thus socially taboo),
where she plays the lead role and Fernando the subordinate female
partner.

At this point, Fernando's willingness to collude in the masquerade comes to a temporary halt. Though not quite in total disarray,
his sense of masculine identity is put under severe strain, as he
fends off the threat of metaphorical castration by leaving the
dance floor to find Dutch courage in copious amounts of anis.
However, so convincing is his drag image that it attracts other
male admirers, whom Violeta violently assaults and sees off, in a
parodic role-play reversal of the jealous boyfriend. Paradoxically,
such muscular macho behaviour evokes Fernando's admiration.
One parody follows another, as Violeta then simulates the
Cinderella story (where Fernando loses the shoe, which is picked
up and replaced by Violeta). The whole scene then culminates in a

dramatic explosion of sexual coupling in the hayloft. What is striking about the scene, but also totally consistent with the rest of the sequence, is Violeta's systematic maintenance of control over the whole love-making process: she is on top, she controls the pace of undressing, she controls the moment of penetration and never once allows Fernando to touch or kiss her and thus refocus her as erotic object. At the moment of climax, she appropriates Fernando's bugle as an obvious phallic object and signals her victory/success/pleasure with an audible blast of the horn.

The transvestism/cross-dressing scene at the fiesta certainly merits more detailed attention than can be given here. It stands as a provocation to traditional gender roles and appears to subvert (while curiously affirming) the notion of the specularized female figure as victim. As noted earlier, the model of the dominant male gaze which specularizes the passive female object is at once reversed (Violeta, the masculinized female, prohibits the assertion of male identity and achieves her own pleasures, through drag, by acting manly) and yet reinforced (though male, Fernando still plays the role of passive female object to Violeta's gaze and thus confirms traditional power relations). At the same time, the scene is clearly intended to appeal to the female spectator, providing a fantasy of role reversal and lesbian desire, with the female in full control. And since Fernando is allowed the pleasure of being dominated by Violeta, the scene also reveals to the male spectator (hetero- and homosexual) the pleasures to be derived from operating in drag and role-playing alternative sexualities, even though those roles may involve male subordination to female desire. A further part of the scene's appeal has to do with the fact that both males and females are allowed to dress up and licensed to dramatize their sexual desires. In the controlled conditions of the carnival/dance, rather than signalling fragmentation and division, the purpose of this masquerade is to allow both males and females to engage in alternative fantasies of wholeness, to occupy fully desired roles and experiment with new possibilities. And here, Violeta, the veterinary doctor and thus supposed master of animal instincts and behaviour, sets out to subdue and transform Fernando, who is reduced to a pantomimic figure. Violeta's goal is to override her own biological make-up and sexually master/tame the young male animal (facilitated by his appearing in drag). Here, the female masquerade is used by Trueba to signal a powerful form of female pleasure and to acknowledge the need for fantasy in both female and male sexual lives. Both the sequence and indeed the film as a whole thus offer a utopian stage for the performance of more flexible, and fluid gender identities, with a clear emphasis on female desire and mastery.

Matriarchy

The figure of the matriarch in contemporary Spanish film has been widely represented. During the 1970s and into the 1980s, we find numerous incarnations, as in Saura's *Ana y los lobos* (1972) and *Mamá cumple cien años* (1979), Borau's *Furtivos* (1975), Bardem's *Siete días de enero* (1977), Gutiérrez Aragón's *Camada negra* (1977) and *Demonios en el jardín* (1982), and Camus's *La casa de Bernarda Alba* (1987). Leaving aside the non-phallic figure of the Mother Superior in Almodóvar's lesbian convent comedy *Entre Tinieblas* (1983), what most of these representations broadly had in common was a negative view of the matriarch as tyrannical and repressive, occupying the authoritarian, patriarchal role normally assumed by the traditional Hispanic male. Moreover, the matriarchal figure was used as a political allegory of despotism and dictatorship. As Paul Smith indicates, Spanish matriarchs have been figures through whom mainly male writers (including Lorca) and film-makers have projected their fears and horrors of dictatorship, authoritarianism, and fascism (1996). Marsha Kinder also notes how these female figures were often exaggerated into phallic, castrating mothers, who stunted, perverted, and traumatized their male offspring in the process of usurping traditional male authority. Highly effective in political terms, such representations attached very negative connotations to the image of strong, purposeful women (Kinder 1993: 197–277).

More recently, in the 1990s, filmic matriarchs have become far more benign and positive; their power and standing have less to do with authoritarian attitudes and the repression of sexual activity than with the advice, support, and protective influence they exert, as in Fernando Fernán Gómez's *El mar y el tiempo* (1991). If the omnipotent, sexless, castrating matriarchs of the 1970s and early 1980s were constructed in terms of their relations with their sons, the influence of the more benign figures of the 1990s is usually focused on their daughters and granddaughters, as in Gutiérrez Aragón's *La mitad del cielo* (1986), Díaz Yanes's *Nadie hablará de nosotras cuando hayamos muerto* (1995), Almodóvar's *Tacones lejanos* (1991), and indeed Trueba's *Belle Époque* (1992). In *La mitad del cielo*, for example, the grandmother protects her daughter from male exploitation and even after death exerts a protective influence over her granddaughter; in *Nadie hablará . . .* , Doña Julia persuades her daughter-in-law Gloria to take control of her life and resume her education; in *Tacones lejanos*, Becky is prepared to take on board her daughter's guilt in order to protect her from the consequences of killing her husband; and in *Belle Époque*, Amalia returns home to visit her four daughters and dispense benign wisdom and advice on how they might arrange their emotional lives.

Interestingly, if we compare Trueba and Almodóvar, we find that Trueba's Amalia, very much like Becky in *Tacones lejanos*, is an example of the absent matriarch, who has abandoned her offspring (and husband) in order to pursue a singing career in the New World, and this includes (literally) taking a lover (Danglard, who is her manager). In *Tacones lejanos*, however, the act of maternal abandonment leaves daughter Rebeca traumatized, pulled between the desire for maternal presence and the counter-desire for revenge for always being subordinate to and humbled by her mother's talents and wishes. *Tacones lejanos* is thus a film in which maternal abandonment of the daughter leads to trauma and smouldering resentment. In *Belle Époque*, by contrast, we are given no origins, no flashbacks, no material to establish family and childhood background. Indeed, Trueba makes no attempt to delve into the childhood pasts of the four sisters, nor does he attempt to exploit childhood trauma as a basis for melodrama. Remarkably, the sisters appear trauma free. They seem relatively stable, happy, and self-confident, without harbouring any serious childhood resentments, despite the fact that Luz is often bossed about by her elder sisters. They form part of a liberated family unit, i.e. they live in Madrid and work in various occupations. They are also fully aware of the unorthodox arrangements between their father and mother and seem prepared to accept them. Relations between parents and offspring appear to be based on love, friendship, and mutual support. The children have clearly separated successfully from the mother figure and are able to lead independent lives, even though they have in common a lack of emotional and sexual fulfilment.

Belle Époque thus focuses on the light-hearted incestuous rivalry of the four young sisters for one young man; the film also charts a much more tenuous rivalry between the two older men for the same wife/mother figure, Amalia. But unlike *Tacones lejanos*, in Trueba's enclosed, rural paradise we find no camp melodrama, no murder of the lover shared by mother and daughter, little or no rivalry; indeed, rather than suffer any form of retribution, the errant mother is welcomed back with open arms, by daughters and cuckolded husband alike. It seems she can enjoy her career, her lover, her husband, and her children, according to her own needs and timetable, and all at the same time; in short, she can have her cake and eat it. Moreover, in the glorious scene of the mother's return, the song (a flop in Latin America but one which relates to the film narrative, the setting, the country house, and the acquisition of new identities) is a bonding rather than a divisive element. Rather than a route to trauma and memories of unstable relations between adults and children as in *Tacones*, the song is a reinforcement, it helps bring the family back together; and indeed the reunion of mother and daughters is warm, soft, intimate, though fleeting. Above all, on Amalia's return, there is no guilt, no need to confess, and no punishment, since there is no surprise at Dangland, Amalia's manager/lover. Manolo accepts his rival's position, though demands from his wife his brief annual sexual encounter. No guilt, no serious male rivalry, no injurious female rivalry. Everyone gets to fulfil their wishes. In the fantasy offered by *Belle Époque*, therefore, the family may be fragmentary, but it is not riven by power struggles, jealousies, and bitter rivalries, as in Almodóvar's arguably more complex and troubling tale.

Yet like Almodóvar's Becky, in Amalia we find a maternal figure who is passionate, self-confident, in control, and unprepared to set aside her desires in deference to patriarchal norms. It is as if in *Belle Époque* Trueba were signalling to us a recipe for family relations in the 1990s, a situation where nothing is off limits, where anything can be said, and where the family is not a locus of discord, conflict, and trauma, but a place of openness, sharing, and uninhibited pleasure. Also, relations between the sexes are not predicated on a repressive theatricalization of desire, where females defer to and feign respect for traditional male values. Trueba's heroines can in fact stop acting and express themselves directly without feeling guilty. *Belle Époque* thus contradicts all Francoist, traditionalist precepts based on a repressive, self-sacrificing maternity and demonstrates how an acceptance of uninhibited sexual experimentation and flexible attitudes overcome domestic strife and repression. Also, if Trueba's rural utopia represents an apparent refusal of history, his affirmation of a libertarian sexual outlook clearly resonates with Spain's political culture of the 1980s and 1990s and the dictatorship to which it stands so resolutely opposed.

History and Nostalgia

On the surface, *Belle Époque* is a period piece. However, it is not an historical film in the same sense as Miró's *El crimen de Cuenca* (1979) or Camus's *Los santos inocentes* (1984). Unlike the latter directors, Trueba was not particularly concerned with historical accuracy or veracity, in setting the record straight or in restaging events which have been ignored, misunderstood, or deliberately silenced. So while he sets his film against the period running from the attempted Republican rising of December 1930 (the failed Jaca military plot; the rising at Cuatro Vientos airbase near Madrid, etc.) to the elections of 12 April 1931 and the installation of the provisional Republican government on 14 April 1931, this is little more than a backcloth. Occasionally, snippets of historical detail are woven into the narrative and even foregrounded, as in the case of the news reaching Manolo's house of the Monarchist attempts to rig the April 1931 elections. However, such concessions to real historical events are rather tangential when we realize that the broad historical context of Primo de Rivera's *dictablanda* (1923–30), Primo's fall from grace, his replacement by General Berenguer and Admiral Aznar (during 1930–1), plus the role of the monarch, Alfonso XIII, in legitimizing the dictatorship, are hardly touched upon. As Trueba himself has declared: 'I'm not crazy about period movies, but sometimes I like to escape from the present. This was the case with *Belle Époque*. We chose this short period of agitation and freedom in Spain's history because it was perfect background for Fernando's story. But it is just background, I hate historical movies. I don't want to give anybody history lessons' (UK Press Book, Apr. 1994).

Indeed, what Trueba seems to do is to take the transition period before the inauguration of the historical Second Republic and transform it into a popular, enclosed, mythical space, an interregnum or parenthesis which presents and prefigures the Republican period as one of unalloyed joy, happiness, and freedom. In other words, Trueba conjures up a scenario where he displays a powerful NOSTALGIA for a Republican Spain that never was, but might have been, an invented republic whose citizens had the freedom to enjoy a multitude of possibilities, moral, cultural, sexual, etc. Sadly, so his scenario suggests, this paradise on earth was cruelly suppressed, after a Civil War, by a fascist military regime which replaced democratic freedoms and the pleasures of the flesh with the police state, repression, and traditionalist Catholic dogma and self-denial. Trueba's republic is a far cry from the real, historical republic of well-meaning but ineffective reformers, economic upheaval, and social crisis. Yet, his filmic version—however hopelessly romantic and stereotypical—still manages to capture some of the desires, hopes, and aspirations which undoubtedly inspired and underpinned the reformist and revolutionary trends in Spain in the 1930s. Though not totally romanticized (note the deaths which open and close the film), *Belle Époque* remains a largely uncritical, indulgent celebration of a mythic libertarian, Republican Spain. The film is particularly wide of the historical mark in its depiction of personal and sexual relations, presenting Manolo's country residence as almost an anarchist paradise predicated on mutual tolerance and respect, free love, and good food. This is precisely the sort of vacuous stereotypical—though no less appealing—imagery which was exploited and demonized by the Spanish right as the insidious creation of Jews, Masons, communists, and Moscow.

Trueba's version of 1930s Spain, I would argue, has been transfigured by the social and moral revolutions that have come afterwards. It is an example of what we might call the colonization of the past by the present. In fact, the rural paradise depicted in the film is a composite, a mixture of 1960s hippy culture, the cult of 'make love not war', plus generous helpings of 1970s *apertura*, pre-Aids freedoms of the transition period, 1970s and 1980s feminism, as well as gender bending and a postmodern taste for blurring political, moral, and sexual boundaries. It is the 'anything goes' society. All this is then projected back onto the Spain of the 1930s, producing a luminous, attractively optimistic, joyous view of life, where freedoms (political and sexual) are bestowed not earned, where one need not work, where all the bills appear to be paid, and where we need only find the energy to enjoy ourselves in indulging our various appetites. In short, it is the Never Never Land of Peter Pan or Aladdin's Cave, an imaginary childhood paradise. And this is perhaps one of the keys to the film's success internationally. By transfiguring the complex, troubled, historical Spanish republic of the 1930s into an oasis of freedom, pleasure, and uninhibited sexual experimentation, Trueba assigns a universality to *Belle Époque* which is highly attractive to the spectator just as it is highly misleading historically. The Spain of *Belle Époque* is not a recognizable 1930s Spain (as in Saura's more sober *¡Ay Carmela!*, 1990) but a myth, a joyous one which we all wish had been the case.

Adolescent Development/Sexual Initiation

Interviewed after his Oscar success, Trueba indicated that 'Tal vez todas mis películas tratan sobre crecer' (*Cambio 16* (4 Apr. 1994): 24). Like its sister movie *El año de las luces*, *Belle Époque* foregrounds adolescent emotional and sexual development. It explores the delights and disasters of growing up within the context of the 'amistades incestuosas' generated between the young deserter Fernando and Manolo's four desirable daughters. At the same time, the film touches upon the nature and value of male friendship between the old Republican painter and the young neophyte. Like the odd job man in *El año de las luces*, Manolo is the intellectual, man of letters, the source of knowledge, learning, and wisdom, to whom Fernando refers/defers for advice and counsel about women and the world. In his turn, as we have seen, Fernando brings to the male relationship the domestic skills he has acquired in the seminary, skills which are coded as feminine. And in return for his domestic prowess and housekeeping acumen, the 'feminized' Fernando not only learns the value of friendship from an enlightened father figure; he is also allowed by the patriarch the freedom to seek his own initiation into love, sex, and romance by being courted by the four sisters in turn. In other words, as adopted son/stand-in male offspring, he is invited to transgress the (imaginary) taboo of incest while at the same time exploited as feel-good therapy/sexual initiation by the four sisters. However, having led a very sheltered existence before stumbling upon this rural paradise, Fernando is initially unskilled in the *ars amatoria*. Also, from his Catholic background, he observes the traditionalist maxim that, like it or not, consummated sex must automatically lead to love and marriage. His old-fashioned attitudes are rapidly disabused by Manolo's daughters and, rather than take the lead in romance and dominate the scene of courtship, Fernando is the one who is dominated. Indeed, as we have seen, conventional male–female power relations are reversed, with Fernando becoming the object rather than the subject of the battle of the sexes. Moreover, gender roles and sexual identities are blurred and transgressed, as Fernando submits to female direction and dictates. In the case of Violeta and the scenes involving transvestism, the boundaries of Fernando's male identity are virtually dissolved, as he re-enacts the role of the subjected female, a performance which vaguely hints at (staged) rape. Within the context of the rural oasis, where all manner of desires can be catered for, it seems, Fernando learns tolerance, the pleasures of being dominated, respect for other sexual and lifestyle choices, and that sexual difference, not patriarchal dominance, is the norm. All of which raises the question of the limits of freedom and happiness in the sexual domain, as in other areas, and how to make wise, non-oppressive choices. It becomes clear that, despite the lay marriage of Fernando and Luz, the film advocates a strongly libertarian, anti-Catholic relativism. As the play of gazes at the end of film suggests, neither Fernando nor the three elder sisters are able to purge their underlying desire for difference and unregulated desire. Whether Trueba is advocating an outlook which sets any boundaries or controls against the irresponsible indulgence of the appetites is an issue which is open to debate.

Reception/The Moral Maze

Reviews of *Belle Époque*, particularly in the Spanish press and well before the film's Oscar success, were on the whole very encouraging. Among the more established critics, Ángel Fernández Santos, in *El país*, was particularly effusive. Traditionally hostile to Almodóvar, Fernández Santos found in Trueba the epitome of a quality, mainstream, commercial director. He remarked on Trueba's 'maestría absoluta' as a film-maker, his remarkable execution of an excellent script, and the film as a turning point in Spanish cinema production (*El país*, 13 Dec. 1992). José Luis Guarner, in *La vanguardia*, and usually more sympathetic to Almodóvar, acknowledged Trueba's obvious debts to Renoir's *Une partie de campagne* (1936) and Wilder's *Some Like It Hot* (1959). He was also mightily impressed by a film which successfully combined adolescent loss of innocence, nostalgia for a mythical Republican past, a deeply Spanish sensibility, and a determination to take risks (creating scenes such as the Carlist fiesta, the transvestite tango, and Amalia's song) (*La vanguardia*, 12 Dec. 1992). When it came to the Oscars, other Spanish reviewers and commentators reporting on the film's award were uniformly positive and enthusiastic, all supporting the home team.[15] Among the few dissenting Spanish voices, only the critic of *Woman* magazine warned its more sensitive female readers to beware a 'película subversiva' and its 'absoluta relajación moral' which offered the unwary spectator no alternative to the film's vexatious moral relativism (*Woman* (Barcelona), 1 Apr. 1994). The reviewer was particularly concerned by the film's ability to induce spectatorial collusion in its anti-authoritarian message and create sympathy for a type of sexual promiscuity which attracted no moral or social censure. Elsewhere, the moral tone of certain reactions was even more alarmist. In the Philippines, for example, the film was regarded by the official censorship board (MTRCB) as 'una absurda y obscena comedia sexual que se basa en la burla de la libertad y la religión católica' (*El periódico* (Barcelona), 10 June 1994). In the USA, opening in commercial cinemas rather than being released through the usual art-house channels (the fate of most European films), *Belle Époque* was widely regarded as the comedy of the year, light, sexy, entertaining, an exuberant, natural celebration of friendship and sex, uncomplicated by social and moral taboos (*New York Times*, *Miami Herald*, *Newsday*). However, while Michael Medved, critic of the *New York Post*, discovered in *Belle Époque* yet another trivial, escapist exploration of a supposed Mediterranean sensibility, Janet Maslin of the *New York Times* found Trueba's alleged superficiality giving way to more challenging hidden philosophical and moral depths.[16]

[15] See also *Diario 16* (30 Aug. 1992); *El siglo* (14 Dec. 1996); *Reseña* (Jan. 1993); *Cambio 16* (4 Apr. 1994); *El mundo* (23 Apr. 1994); *El país* 23 Mar. 1994).
[16] See, for example, the summary of American critical opinion in *El mundo*, 3 Mar. 1994. A point worth developing perhaps is that, at a time when Almodóvar

Alongside the Philippine censors, as noted above, one or two American critics and the odd Spanish commentator argued that *Belle Époque*'s exuberant celebration of casual sex without complications was problematic. It was said that the film operated within a moral vacuum and that despite the filmic closure of marriage (followed by the female gaze of desire as the girls depart the station), notions of commitment and personal and social responsibility were absent. Trueba himself also noted: 'Me dio . . . satisfacción que la crítica reaccionaria la pusiera mal. Todo lo que sea ofender al puritanismo me parece bien' (*El mundo*, 23 Mar. 1994). But what seems to have impressed American audiences in particular about this free, tolerant, positive, optimistic microcosm depicted in the film was its unconditional, uninhibited celebration of sex and unregulated desire, indeed promiscuity and pleasure, with no thoughts of guilt, with no regard to the consequences. In the film, sexual relations are set within the frame of sharing, tolerance, and friendship and appear completely normalized. The lack of an explicit moral framework (beyond a vague 'clima libertario republicano') allows desire to flourish and sexual promiscuity to appear as the natural outcome of healthy emotional/sexual drives.

The movie tries to sell us the delights of paradox and foregrounds the unregulated side of human desire as perfectly legitimate, indeed necessary to healthy living. This is because Trueba regards self-control, discipline, denial, etc., taken to extremes (as in the case of the Civil Guards), as negative behavioural traits which can only lead to frustration, madness, and death. By contrast, the spectator is made to feel that casual sex, promiscuity, and the joys of partying are fundamentally life-affirming and that to set limits or to suppress such urges would be authoritarian. The only limits Trueba appears to place on sexual behaviour are those negotiated between tolerant, understanding friends and relations.

Belle Époque is thus an optimistic, feel-good movie, an allegory for the 1990s of a libertarian political order, which celebrates an

---

was virtually Spain's only recognizable international star director, the sort of recognition conferred by success at the Oscars still eluded him and went to a director seen by some as far more mainstream, conservative, and unwilling to take too many risks in content, style, and generic experimentation. Indeed, among academic critics, one of Almodóvar's more unconditional admirers referred to Trueba's film, rather disparagingly as a 'slight period comedy, extravagantly praised by critics often hostile to Almodóvar' (Smith 1994: 139).

imagined Hispanic family model (matriarchal, non-hierarchical, loving and sharing, but fragmented) and particularly foregrounds female desire. It reveals a faith in human nature to put pleasure above pain and repression and, by doing so, to achieve a healthy, positive, sexual and social education. There is no tangible down-side attendant on the philosophy of pleasure which Trueba espouses. The comedy argues for non-oppressive sexualities, cultural and political freedoms, reversal of gender hierarchies, bringing the marginal to the centre. Rules, boundaries, and oppressive social conventions are erased; libidinal energies are allowed to run free. The film revels in fluid, unbridled desire, in having fun, in being kids again, and while it is mainly an entertainment, it argues for desublimation as a mode of resistance in social and political terms. Also, according to some recent research in the UK, the film would seem to have prefigured changes taking place in the sexual behaviour of at least some young women in the late 1990s: 'We are confident, sexual women and if others can't understand that, tough,' remarked Sara and Louise, commenting on a remarkable holiday spree of casual sex (*Sunday Times*, 27 July 1997). It seems that, for increasing numbers of young women, the restraints that pregnancy, Aids, and other diseases might have placed on sexual promiscuity have dissolved and that sex is now increasingly separated from any moral context of partnership or sharing. With its focus on girl power and their pleasures, Trueba's nostalgic sexual fantasy might well be an even more desirable provocation now than it was in the early 1990s. Indeed, the film's unabashed (hetero-sexual) moral relativism seems in rather than out of step with changing public attitudes and values. Of course, a few more years down the line, Trueba's heroines for whom deregulated desire and recreational sex is great fun may find that their pastime has its dangers. For the moment, it seems, the party continues.

REFERENCES

Besas, Peter (1985), *Behind the Spanish Lens: Spanish Cinema under Fascism and Democracy*. Denver: Arden Press.
de Lauretis, Teresa (1984), *Alice Doesn't: Feminism, Semiotics, Cinema*. Bloomington: Indiana University Press.
Douane, Mary Ann (1982), 'Film and Masquerade: Theorizing the Female Spectator', *Screen*, 23: 74–7.

Freud, Sigmund (1955), 'Medusa's Head', in *The Complete Psychological Works of Sigmund Freud*, ed. and trans. James Strachey, xviii, London: Hogarth Press.

Irigaray, Luce (1984), *Speculum of the Other Woman*, trans. Gillian C. Gill. New York: Cornell University Press.

Kaplan, E. Ann (1983), *Women and Film: Both Sides of the Camera*. New York: Methuen.

Kinder, Marsha (1993), *Blood Cinema: The Reconstruction of National Identity in Spain*. Berkeley and Los Angeles: University of California Press.

Lacan, Jacques (1977), *The Four Fundamental Concepts of Psychoanalysis*, trans. Alan Sheridan. London: Hogarth Press and Institute of Psychoanalysis.

Longhurst, Alex (1994), 'Miguel de Unamuno and European Existentialism', *Donaire*, 2 (May): 37–45.

Mulvey, Laura (1975), 'Visual Pleasure and Narrative Cinema', *Screen*, 16/3: 6–18.

—— (1981), 'Afterthoughts on "Visual Pleasure and Narrative Cinema"', *Framework*, 6/15–17: 12–15.

Rycroft, Charles (1968), *A Critical Dictionary of Psychoanalysis*. London: Penguin.

Smith, Paul Julian (1994), *Desire Unlimited: The Cinema of Pedro Almodóvar*. London: Verso.

—— (1996), 'García Lorca/Almodóvar: Gender, Nationality and the Limits of the Visible', in Paul Julian Smith, *Vision Machines: Cinema, Literature and Sexuality in Spain and Cuba 1983–93*, London: Verso: 17–36.

20

Julio Medem's *Vacas* (1991): Historicizing the Forest

ISABEL C. SANTAOLALLA

The moss and the various seats in the house were the only ones which did not know how to speak; all the rest, both animals and things, could speak. Those who possessed the power of speech wanted to teach those who didn't; but it happened that all lost speech, all forgot how to speak.

(Basque legend)

When the 30-year-old Julio Medem decided to put his medical career and psychiatric training on standby and embark on a creative adventure called *Vacas* (1991), he could hardly anticipate the immediate critical and box-office success the film would enjoy both in Spain and abroad. The film received over twenty international awards, its director was hailed by many as a new promise of Spanish cinema, and his name linked to those of a number of other young directors and actors, referred to as 'the new crop of Spanish cinema', whose 'young flesh and fresh blood' were making 'the miracle' of Spanish cinema in the 1990s possible (Cristóbal 1994: 20–3; Castellano and Costa 1995: 16).[1] For others, however, Medem had to be placed within a different framework: that of Basque—as distinct from Spanish—cinema. Having emerged at a time when the growth of the post-democracy, subsidized *cine*

---

[1] Other directors forming part of this so-called *relevo generacional* (generational takeover) included Juanma Bajo Ulloa, Enrique Urbizu, Chus Gutiérrez, Mariano Barroso, Gracia Querejeta, Ángel Fernández Arnero, Álex de la Iglesia, and Manuel Huerga, among others. Their films were populated by a cohort of young new faces: Javier Bardem, Carmelo Gómez, Ruth Gabriel, Jordi Mollà, Candela Peña, Penélope Cruz, Cristina Marcos, Ana Álvarez, Pere Ponce, Karra Elejalde, Silke, Achero Mañas, and many others.

autonómico (regional cinemas)[2] of the 1980s seemed, like the decade, to be reaching an end, Medem and other young directors born in the Basque Country—such as Urbizu, Bajo Ulloa, de la Iglesia, and Calparsoro—were greeted as the new generation supposedly destined to carry the flame of Basque cinema forward into the new millennium. But perhaps resenting this pressure to be 'representative', these young directors have almost systematically rejected such a label, and, largely discarding the mimetic style of historical and political discourse of their predecessors, have pursued, instead, less predictable formal and thematic interests. Films as varied as *Todo por la pasta* (1991), *Alas de mariposa* (1991), *Acción mutante* (1993), *Salto al vacío* (1995), to mention only a few, are testimony to their directors' refusal to follow trodden paths.

Admittedly, for all its many formal and stylistic innovations, Medem's first film shared many features—setting, action, and the occasional documentary quality—with earlier Basque films.[3] And yet, it also contained too many questions, too many disruptive views on land and identity to make any attempt at attaching patronymic labels to film and director unproblematic. Besides, if *Vacas* already anticipated the tension between conflicting impulses for belonging to and escaping from inbred territories, his next two films—*La ardilla roja* (1993) and *Tierra* (1995)—as well as offscreen comments, have more than confirmed his uncomfortable relationship with prescriptive notions of identity.

Medem's films invariably feature individuals trying to escape from constraints of various kinds—(home)land, tradition, gender, sex, subjectivity—in narratives where the motif of the 'journey' features prominently. Thus, in *Vacas*, two transgressive couples in two successive generations decide to abandon the claustrophobic atmosphere of their Guipuzcoan valley and flee to America and France respectively. *La ardilla roja* begins with a young woman's

---

[2] In reality, this amounted to no more than a Catalan and Basque cinema, the rest of the autonomies having lacked the money, the political will, or both to create and maintain an industry. For their part, both Catalonia and the Basque Country seemed to have found in the cinematic medium a good vehicle for their claims of independence and distinctive national identity: politics, history, language, characterological or sociological features have often been foregrounded and made to reflect ethnic or cultural idiosyncrasy.

[3] Xon de Ros (1997) considers the film within this context.

(Emma Suárez) crisis of memory caused by a motorbike accident. Having witnessed this incident, J. (Nancho Novo) decides to persuade her that she is his girlfriend and that her name is Lisa, creating a whole new identity for her and taking her away from San Sebastián to a Riojan campsite. Lisa—whose real name is Sofía and whose amnesia turns out to be a mere pretence—will eventually undertake a further journey, away from both psychotic husband and false boyfriend, leading to the Madrid zoo, where J. will eventually join her. Finally, *Tierra* also features a displaced protagonist, Ángel Bengoechea (Carmelo Gómez), on a quest for meaning in a foreign land, a dry wine-growing region, where his divided self becomes simultaneously attracted to the maternal Ángela (Emma Suárez) and to the oversexed Mari (Silke). Unable to choose, Ángel decides to leave on his own, but is eventually joined by Mari, and the two of them head for Castellón.

In a sense, the journeys undertaken by all these characters can be read as the fictional parallels of Medem's own creative quest. His choice of settings for the films seems to distance him progressively from his homeland: from the Basque-Navarran forests of *Vacas*, down to the Riojan countryside for *La ardilla roja*, to the Aragonese parched vineyards in *Tierra*, and, in his latest *Los amantes del círculo polar*, to the edge of the globe. Considering the extent to which nationalistic feelings are tied to territorial claims, it is no wonder some see this trajectory as proof of Medem's refusal to engage with the reality of the Basque Country. And yet, this view overlooks the fact that, despite the impression given by their surface *mises-en-scène*, these films have a strong emotional and metaphorical bond with it—an affiliation, however, not exempt from difficulty or even angst.[4] Like Trojan horses, Medem's constructs conceal hidden forces raging with turmoil and dissidence, ready to unsettle complacent notions of individual and national identity.

In his fictional worlds little is stable or whole: the physical and the psychological criss-cross, reality and fantasy blend, nature and artifice imitate each other. The films are open-ended processes in which one-dimensional or essentialist notions of identity and subjectivity are ruthlessly exposed: in *Vacas* successive generations of male characters lose their individuality as the same actor

---

[4] I have dealt with this aspect in more depth in Santaolalla 1998.

performs all the various roles; in *La ardilla roja* the female protagonist has two different names and life-stories; in *Tierra*, the male
character's split conscience actually materializes in two identical
bodies. And if, separately, each of Medem's films reveals that identity is, at best, a fragile construct, a panoramic view of the trilogy
further complicates the picture: his choice of Carmelo Gómez,
Emma Suárez, and Karra Elejalde in prominent roles in all three
films effectively—if perhaps not intentionally—leads to further
identity confusion, giving the impression that all three narratives
and their characters form some kind of integrated continuum.

Metaphysical and psychological questions run parallel to—and
are inseparable from—material realities in Medem's films: inner
landscapes are inextricably linked to outer ones, and thought
processes take place not at the expense of, but, rather, *from* and
through earthy substance. Even the titles of the films highlight this
telluric approach, as do the stories themselves, and a visual style
which delights alternatively in the physicality of ground-level,
earth-bound shots of grass or lice underneath the earth, and in
abstraction, allowing the camera to soar up into the sky, or to
record characters' daydreams and visions. As Medem once
explained in a TV programme:

I usually like to create situations which can incorporate various worlds at
the same time. I often like to use a very real, very immediate and recognizable photography, adjusting myself to the rules of reality as it is known
and shared by all of us. But I am also interested in contrasting this reality
with another one, with another space which looks like this reality but
which is not, which has not yet been made and which is somehow
connected to it; and sometimes I want to narrate the trajectory from one
world to the other. (Medem 1994)

The connections with surrealism are as evident here as they are in
the films' recurrent linking of seeming opposites (inner and outer,
waking and dreaming), their use of the eye as a threshold, or the
inscription of the viewer's look in the text itself.[5] The director has
often been criticized for the films' self-conscious style, wild imagin-
ings, and unexplained breaches of realism. And yet, his somewhat
fantastic worlds—like those of his much-admired precursors
Buñuel, Saura, or Erice—conjure up recognizable historical and

---

    [5] For an interesting study of the text as a threshold, as a boundary or a cross-
ing, see Caws 1981.

social orders, in a sort of film equivalent of political allegories by Swift or Gracián. In this sense, of Medem's films, *Vacas* is perhaps the one which, in connection with Basque realities, has seemed most congenial to *roman-à-clef* readings. It is also a film which examines the literal and the metaphorical meanings of 'reality', and explores the links between space and identity. All of this turns it into a challenging text, worthy of examination from a perspective which takes into consideration its position inside *and* outside discourses of Basqueness.

The action of *Vacas* unravels in a small Guipuzcoan valley over a sixty-year period, from the 1875 Second Carlist War to the 1936 Civil War. Framed by these two large-scale fraternal confrontations, the film recounts the story of the enduring rivalry over three generations between two local families, the Irigibels and the Mendiluces. The feud, which in the former generation revolves around Manuel Irigibel (Carmelo Gómez) and Carmelo Mendiluce's (Manolo Uranga) woodcutting contests, is interrupted by the death of the latter at war. Manuel, for his part, manages to survive by feigning death, covering his face with his rival's blood. As the cart in which his body is being carried away under a pile of other corpses crosses the forest, he drags himself off it and falls onto the ground, suddenly becoming aware of the overpowering gaze of a white cow, whose eye Manuel's and the camera's look penetrate, thus moving the action thirty years on. He now appears as an aged man (Txema Blasco) surrounded by his son Ignacio (Carmelo Gómez), the latter's wife, and their three daughters. The narrative foregrounds the close partnership between Manuel Irigibel and his youngest granddaughter Cristina (Ana Sánchez as a child, and Emma Suárez later), as well as the very special relationship they both have with the natural world of forest and cows. In the nearby *caserío* (Basque rural house) live Carmelo Mendiluce's widow and their two children, Juan (Manolo Uranga) and Catalina (Ana Torrent). The inherited family feud is exacerbated in the younger generation: not only does Ignacio Irigibel beat Juan Mendiluce in a woodcutting contest, but he also sleeps with his sister Catalina, who eventually gives birth to an illegitimate son, Peru (Miguel Ángel García as a child, and Carmelo Gómez as a young man). When Peru grows up he is often found in the company of his half-grandfather Manuel and half-sister Cristina, to whom he becomes very attached. When some time later Catalina and Ignacio decide to emigrate to America, they take Peru with them, leaving Ignacio's lawful family behind. Cristina and Peru's relationship continues through correspondence until, in the summer of 1936, the latter—who has by now married in the United States and is the father of a child—returns to the valley as a war newspaper photographer. Upon reunion, Peru and Cristina decide to emigrate to France, in search of a new life as a couple in more open, unconfined spaces, thus re-enacting the journey that their father undertook some twenty years before.

Obviously, a mere episodic account of events like this can by no means convey the full significance of *Vacas*. Just as important as the three generations of humans who succeed each other are the two *caseríos*, the valley, and the forest that they all inhabit, and which Carles Gusi's photography and Medem's shooting and editing turn into meaningful, almost animated protagonists. If environment has often been figured as the generator and preserver of identity in much of the cinema produced in the Basque Country,[6] in this film it acquires a function only paralleled by that of the three generations of cows which witness human actions—La Txargorri, La Pupille, and La Blanca—and which the title of the film highlights. The forest, the cows, and the women are all engaged in the eternal cycle of regeneration, and, interconnected through eyes and orifices, treasure within them an inexhaustible life-*potential*. Men, for their part, hold the *power*—either literally, or with their more symbolic phallic instruments like the gun and the axe—to cut into and ignite forest and women.

The film relies on an extraordinary blend of different layers of experience and perception. Here, factual and symbolic substance contribute to the formation of a multifaceted and labyrinthine reality, an effect which owes much to a dual structure which makes events in the story rest upon two different kinds of frame simultaneously: a historical one, formed by a number of precise dates and clues indicating the passing of time (1875; thirty years later: spring 1905; ten years later; summer 1936); and a legendary one, conjured up by the four intertitles which open up the respective chapters (I. *The Coward Woodcutter*; II. *The Axes*; III. *The Burning Hole*; IV. *War in the Forest*).

The fact that there is no match between chapter transition and

---

[6] See, for instance, Zunzunegui 1986.

CHAPTER	DATE	IRIGIBELS		MENDILUCES
I. The Coward Woodcutter	1875	Manuel survives through blood of	→← ⟲	Carmelo (killed)
	+30 years	Manuel, Ignacio, and family	→←	Juan+Catalina
II. The Axes		Ignacio fights and beats	→←	Juan
		Ignacio has sex with	⟲	Catalina
III. The Burning Hole		Ignacio and family+new calf		
	+10 years			Juan, Catalina+new Peru
		Ignacio escapes with	⟲	Catalina+Peru
IV. War in the Forest	1936	Cristina in valley		Peru abroad
		Cristina has sex with Ilegorri's son		Peru married in USA Peru arrives in valley
		Cristina escapes with	⟲	Peru

→ ← confrontation
⟲ conciliation

chronological transition is worth noting: thus, for instance, the first chapter incorporates events occurring over a period of thirty years (half of the total of the story-time), whereas no passage of time is perceptible either at the start of or over the second chapter. Thus myth and history run parallel and occasionally intersect, but they are ruled by a different logic: myth-related episodes have a life of their own, independent—but not far—from history-linked incidents. Although the inexorable progression of history is economically conjured up by the changes in guns, uniforms, and by the gradual introduction of horses, cameras, and cars, its course is less linear than one would expect. In the self-contained, claustrophobic world of the film—some characters move in and out of the limits of the forest and the *caserios* but the camera never does—myth and history overlap: centuries and wars succeed one another, characters die but the same actors 'reincarnate' them in other characters, and the landscape remains unchanged in its surrealist blend of the ordinary and the fantastic. It is almost as if the valley, the forest, and their inhabitants were occupying the motionless centre of a rotating wheel: history here takes a rather curved and spiralling trajectory, trapped as it is in a centripetal force which moves around but never fully abandons the centre.

Thus, clearly distant from systems of thought which conceive of history and myth as opposites, the world of *Vacas* evokes instead a unifying approach to reality, very much in tune, for instance, with the one described by Andrés Ortiz-Osés in the introduction to his recent essay on Basque mythology:

Reality would be in a middle point, from which any time—past, present, future—is, has been and will be simultaneously the *same and different*, according to the post-Nietzschean law of the eternal return of the same differencially. (author's emphasis; Ortiz-Osés 1996: 19)

Although the notions of sameness and difference involve here a particular type of cosmogony/ontology, these are also key concepts in any process of identity-formation. In a thought-provoking piece entitled 'Sobre la identidad vasca (ensayo de identidad dinámica)', Julio Caro Baroja draws attention to the etymological connection between *identidad* (identity) and *idéntico* (identical), in order to contend that, as is the case with an individual's identity—one remains 'the same' regardless of the many transformations that take place during one's life—a nation's identity is necessarily informed and affected by the dynamics of change (1986: 25–6). He then retrieves the notion of historical cycle (from German historians of the turn of the century, from ethnologists like Frobenius and Graebner, and, further back, from Gianbattista Vico) in order to account for the element of *variability within the identical* that he considers intrinsic to any notion of identity. Thus, Basque identity is to be seen not as a fixed given, but as a construct which has been constantly reshaped by the changing circumstances of the various cycles through which the Basque Country has gone. Of the eight cycles into which Caro Baroja divides its history, the seventh is clearly relevant to this discussion of *Vacas*: this cycle, the author claims, stretched from the end of the Second Carlist War (1876) to the beginning of the Civil War of 1936, and was marked by 'contradictory signs', and by the fact that the Basque countryside lost much of its centrality (1986: 38–9).

Rather surprisingly, both the chronological frame and the thematic concerns of Medem's film perfectly match Caro Baroja's cyclical division and overall perception of history. The film's dual structure (historical *and* legendary) very effectively creates the impression that the setting and the action not only occupy a specific moment in history, but also bear the traces of the previous cycles which have preceded that moment. Although by the time in which the action of *Vacas* takes place the communities inhabiting the ancient valley and forest are living under an essentially patriarchal regime based on confrontation and violence, those immemorial natural spaces still store the more integrating, regenerative energy which, in Basque mythology, is associated with the female Earth Goddess, Mari. Thus the film manages to evoke both the original pre-Indo-European matriarchal structures of Basque civilization and the later Indo-European patriarchal norms which merged with and eventually overruled them.

In Basque myths and legends, the categories of *adur* and *indar* seem to superimpose on the bipartite scheme corresponding to potential (matriarchal-feminine-moon-Mother goddess) and power (patriarchal-masculine-sun-masculine numina). (Ortiz-Osés 1996: 41)

Vacas abounds in symbols which evoke the various attributes which Basque mythology ascribes to the feminine principle *adur*: matriarchal-feminine potential, agrarian canon, self-contained energy, and binding. These same associations, of course, can be traced in many other imaginary systems. Cows, for instance, have since remote times been associated with the earth and the moon, and have also been seen as a symbol of the primeval mother. Jung treats them, like all animals, as a symbol of the unconscious (Cirlot 1982: 455). For its part, the forest, being a space where, protected and secluded by vegetation, life generates and grows freely, is also related to the maternal principle, as well as to the world of the unconscious (Cirlot 1982: 102). All these meanings are regularly stressed in *Vacas*, usually through a series of formal strategies— close-ups, lighting, eerie score—which foreground or accentuate specific objects or spaces. Within the forest, the tree-stump to which Manuel refers as the *agujero encendido* deserves special attention: first the tree, like any other form of vegetation, is a symbol of interconnectedness, its roots giving access to the mystic interior of the earth; but secondly, this rugged opening also clearly represents the female sexual organ, that inscrutable threshold to the depths of life. The ambiguous nature of the *agujero encendido*, as well as the simultaneous fascination and dread it arouses, feeds into a long tradition of representations of the feminine. Its 'devouring' nature, in particular, links it to the motif of the 'monstrous-feminine' which Barbara Creed (1993) has related to the image of the castrating—rather than castrated—mother. In *Vacas*, this motif clearly takes on a further political dimension, evoking the idea of the Basque Country—the *mother*land—as insatiable devourer of its offspring.

To all these symbols of femininity—particularly of its reproductive potential—the film counterposes one single object, the axe, which with its obvious phallic significance represents values attached to the concept *indar*: patriarchal-masculine power, physical energy, opening, or cutting (Ortiz-Osés 1996: 42-4). While clearly related to Basque cultural lore, these various symbols have a much wider significance: they re-enact that eternal dynamics of differentiation *and* unification between the feminine and the masculine. Thus, although on the surface *Vacas* seems to be dramatizing the rivalry between two local families, it is also—in a coded way—narrativizing the struggles inherent in gender division. Various characters in *Vacas*—especially, but not exclusively, the women—suffer the effects of a system which has replaced the binding impulses of the feminine with more dichotomizing masculine practices. Both men and women struggle to perform within a patriarchal system which expects its men to construct their identity through a double dynamics of differentiation (gender and kinship), and which requires its women to help 'reproduce' that pattern. Unable to bear the pressure, some seek alternative psychological, bodily, and physical spaces.

This is the case for most of the male characters in the film, most noticeably Manuel Irigibel. The film actually starts when Manuel discovers his inability to respond to expectations placed on him: being the most famous *aizkolari* in the valley, his overrated masculinity fails him at the war front. The death of his rival, however, allows Manuel to live on: when, as the cart crosses the forest, his head—stained with the blood of the Mendiluces— emerges from within a heap of human flesh, Manuel is symbolically reborn to a new self, a self which he can no longer relate to male prowess or blood pride. As he lifts his head from the ground, his face—white bulging eyes standing out against mud and blood- stained skin—recalls the white, red, and black masks used in the regenerative carnivalesque rituals in Basque folklore, supposedly capable of 'transferrals, inversions and multiple investments of Nature's vital energy' (Ortiz-Osés 1996: 101). Benefiting, then, from the magical power of metamorphosis, Manuel penetrates the cow's eye and, through it, its womb-like protective and transfor- mative space. When thanks to a thirty-year narrative ellipsis he emerges from it, both his age and his state—he is taken to be mentally disturbed—allow him to occupy a marginal space, free now from the demands of normative masculinity. Manuel remains, however, a traumatized individual: he is not whole and compact anymore but irredeemably fragmented—as a number of close-ups of his broken leg tied up with pieces of wood and a rope symboli- cally denote.[7] Like his body, his scarred subjectivity is also still haunted by the ghosts of a past that he tries to exorcize through a series of fetishistic humanoid effigies which he equips with axes and scythes—even crowning one of them with his old Carlist

---

[7] Manuel's method of keeping his leg in place recalls, again, traditional Basque remedies (against hernia, for instance) that consist of making the sufferer go through the open fissure of a tree and then tying the tree up in order to cause the symbolic suture of the wound—a ritual in which the tie represents *adur* (the feminine princi- ple) and the fissure *indar* (the masculine one) (Ortiz-Osés 1996: 43). This is, then, another of the ways in which Manuel seeks identification with the feminine princi- ple.

beret—thus distancing himself from, and hoping to gain control over, his masculinity-related anxieties.

Manuel establishes new allegiances now: his identification with cows, the forest, and its holes implies a search for new spaces, for new ways of looking at things. But, unlike his granddaughter Cristina—who 'naturally' forms part of the integrated female sphere (she is so intimately identified with cows, for instance, that when her grandfather is painting La Txargorri, Cristina takes its place and models for him)—Manuel's position requires some mediating strategies which, in fact, both bridge and foreground that distance: his perception of the 'reality' around him is thus negotiated either *through* painting, or through the eye of the cow and the 'eye' of the camera. Manuel occupies a space of in-betweenness, indebted as he is to two bloods and two genders. He is the madman who remains marginal to the logic of the ruling system: when the world of normality and consciousness is sick, only abnormality and the unconscious can heal. Manuel's delirious remarks and behaviour, like those of the buffoon, question and expose the perverse hegemonic order.

Like Manuel, his grandson Peru is also caught between conflicting allegiances. Being the fruit of the adulterous union between an Irigibel and a Mendiluce, Peru—even more literally than Manuel—carries the blood of both families within himself. As he grows up, he shows total disregard for the masculine world represented by his woodcutting uncle and father, and instead opts for the less patriarchal partnership formed by Manuel and Cristina. Peru rejects the masculine symbol of the axe and, as his career as a photographer indicates, also inherits his grandfather's attraction for those artificial 'eyes' which can mediate and open up reality. To a certain extent, Peru seems to be a representative of what Ortiz-Osés calls 'fratriarcal hero': an androgynous mediator who assimilates within himself the *animus* and the *anima*, the patriarchal and the matriarchal (1996: 25). In his performance as Peru, Carmelo Gómez effectively tones down part of the in-built stout, manly bearing which is much more on display in his role as Ignacio. And yet, for all his positive mediating qualities, even Peru remains at least partially influenced by the 'grand narratives' of manhood. Peru's declaration to Cristina towards the end of the film—'Cristina. Voy a dar mi vida por ti'—suggests that the structures which constitute our subjectivity have a stronger hold on us than we may think. Although Cristina's reply seems at first to accept Peru's offer—'¡Qué bien!'—the more mundane concerns which actually come with it—'¡En este caballo hay comida! ¡Con el hambre que tengo!'—expose the grandiloquence and meaninglessness of Peru's discourse.

The decision taken at the end of the film by Cristina and Peru to leave the forest on a horse has perhaps understandably led to readings of *Vacas* as a narrative about the loss of Paradise or the end of a civilization: when the Francoist troops reach the forest in 1936, the sexual and regenerative energy of the forest is replaced by chaos and death, with the mythical cows fleeing when confronted with the outsiders' horses, and the two young characters having to leave their homeland. Openly political interpretations might want to see the outsiders' (Spanish) intrusion in the small Guipuzcoan valley (Euskadi) as the cause of its destruction. But crude readings of this kind are pre-empted by the film in a number of ways. Some are merely anecdotal—like the fact, for instance, that Juan Mendiluce himself is involved in the killing of other *paisanos* (countrymen) in that terrible final scene—but others clearly structural. By featuring a second military conflict in this last chapter, the narrative links the ending with the beginning, thus recalling the fact that fratricidal instincts were already present then. Moreover, as well as a literal battleground, the valley has since the start been the arena for another internal conflict: the feud between the two families seems to be printed on the region's identity from times immemorial. As the woodcutting contest which takes place between Ignacio Irigibel and Juan Mendiluce in the second chapter ends, its symbolic association with the initial armed conflict is brought home by a high-angle shot which shows Manuel and Cristina flanked by a wastage of trunks and woodcuttings, as if walking along a trench, while Manuel wonders regretfully: 'And all this destruction, why?'

Vacas relies on a combination of strategies which—in keeping with Caro Baroja's conception of history and identity—highlight both repetition *and* change. It is significant, however, that in the former, as in the latter, change does not necessarily imply 'evolution'. As Peru and Cristina jump on the horse and leave the visual frame of the camera, there is no indication that the end of this cycle will bring forth the beginning of a more perfected stage. In fact, by retaining their voices in the foreground and making the camera move towards the hole in the tree-stump and penetrate it, the film implicitly suggests that they are after all staying here, that there may be no real way out of this claustrophobic spatial and temporal cycle. In this rather bleak reading, Peru and Cristina's incestuous relationship could be seen to reinforce the endogamous and ultimately constraining dynamics which rule life in the valley.

More positively, however, it could be argued that this final step towards the further blurring of boundaries between the Irigibels and the Mendiluces consummates the film's ongoing efforts to expose the ultimate ineffectiveness of systems which rely on axioms of difference and exclusion. In *Vacas*, thematic, structural, and stylistic features work together to knock down physical and psychological barriers, eliminate distinctions, and thus put into question the categories of 'sameness' and 'difference'. The reappearance of actors in different roles, the blending of the real and the fantastic, the combination of objective and subjective point-of-view shots, the lack of coincidence between chapter and temporal transition, the duplication of processes of mental alienation (Manuel Irigibel and Juan Mendiluce), as well as of incests (only attempted between Juan and Catalina, but fulfilled between Peru and Cristina), among other things, place into question those structures—psychological, philosophical, *and political*—which attempt to define identity through ironclad notions of difference.

The film argues that when identity relies excessively on difference and exclusion, the result is death and destruction. When the parameters of sameness and difference are applied in rigid intransigent ways, when normative notions of identity impose themselves on more fluid alternatives, when external aggression imposes itself on internal consonance, the most destructive forces of Nature are unleashed. *Vacas* cannot unproblematically envisage the natural world as a Green-World: the forest in *Vacas* is far from representing that utopian world which—as theorized by Northrop Frye (1973)— offers relief from the pressures of the city. It is not depicted either— as in some Spanish films of the Francoist period—as a metaphorical space proposing an alternative to dictatorial oppression. The forest here partly shares, in its ambivalence, the rather disturbing aspects of the forest in *Furtivos* (1975): it is a space where reliance on the world of instincts does not necessarily guarantee contentment.[8]

---

[8] The maternal principle retains much more positive connotations in *Vacas* than in *Furtivos*, where the figure of Martina is to a great extent figured as the sickly victim-and-executor of all the evils of ideology.

As well as the dialectics of *adur–indar* innate in Nature, the forest in this little Guipuzcoan valley contains within itself the fortunate and the ill fated. Medem is making a film in 1992, a time when perhaps the discontents of the Basque Country cannot any more be blamed exclusively on the intrusive agency of an Other. *Vacas* suggests that the roots of conflict have always been and perhaps always will be there. And yet, the film's insistence on the inexhaustible regenerative properties of the land—its various holes guaranteeing successive literal and metaphorical rebirths—carries with it the more hopeful possibility of reversal and change. After all, the fact that the film actually ends with images of the *agujero encendido* and the cow seems to imply that, even though violence, death, and expatriation are on the agenda now, the potential for inclusion and regeneration still permeates the land.

REFERENCES

Caro Baroja, Julio (1986), *El laberinto vasco*. Madrid: Sarpe.
Castellano, Koro, and Costa, Jordi (1995), 'La nueva cosecha', *El país semanal* (5 Mar.): 16–27.
Caws, Mary Ann (1981), *The Eye in the Text: Essays on Perception, Mannerist to Modern*. Princeton: Princeton University Press.
Cirlot, Juan Eduardo (1982), *Diccionario de símbolos*. Barcelona: Labor.
Creed, Barbara (1993), *The Monstrous-Feminine: Film, Feminism, Psychoanalysis*. London: Routledge.
Cristóbal, Ramiro (1994), 'Cine español: las últimas estrellas', *Cambio 16* (Oct.): 20–3.
de Ros, Xon (1997), '*Vacas* and Basque Cinema: The Making of a Tradition', *Journal of the Institute of Romance Studies*, 5: 225–34.
Frye, Northrop (1973), *Anatomy of Criticism: Four Essays*. Princeton: Princeton University Press (1st pub. 1959).
Medem, Julio (1994), in *Creadores de hoy*, TVE.
Ortiz-Osés, Andrés (1996), *La Diosa Madre: Interpretación desde la mitología vasca*. Madrid: Editorial Trotta.
Santaolalla, Isabel C. (1998), 'Far from Home, Close to Desire: Julio Medem's Landscapes', *Bulletin of Hispanic Studies*, 75: 331–8.
Zunzunegui, Santos (1986), *El cine en el País Vasco: la aventura de una cinematografía periférica*. Murcia: Filmoteca Regional de Murcia. Colección Imagen.

21

The Eroteticism of *Nadie hablará de nosotras cuando hayamos muerto* (Díaz Yanes, 1995)

BERNARD P. E. BENTLEY

FROM present discussions and current film reviews, a 'gripping' film is frequently defined as one which contains much action, usually in sequences that have been rapidly edited, now more easily achieved with digitized editing, from a mosaic of different shots more often filmed with a steadycam camera closely tracking the characters portrayed. *Nadie hablará de nosotras cuando hayamos muerto* certainly reflects all these elements. It is packed with action and filmed with a constantly moving camera. Close shooting of the subjects, often framing out the tops of heads and cutting below the shoulders, as well as sharp editing, soon establishes itself as a norm, which lends medium and long shots particular significance. The plot, concisely stated, presents a prostitute who witnesses in Mexico the murder of two undercover narcotics agents from the USA; she is repatriated back to Spain carrying an address book with information concerning the whereabouts of laundered drugs profits which she attempts to get for herself, unaware that there is a contract on her life. The film is scripted by Augustín Díaz Yanes and is the first that he has directed. Because of circumstances and funding difficulties, he also involved himself and friends in the production (Aguinaga 1997: 13). There were other production difficulties to be faced: the Mexican sequences were introduced to satisfy the Mexican co-producers, but a number then had to be reset back in Spain due to the 1995 socio-political turmoils in Mexico (Aguinaga 1997: 16). The film came out in Spain on 6 October 1995, winning eight prizes at the subsequent Goya distribution.[1] It was released in

---

[1] Best picture, best new director, best leading actress (Victoria Abril), best supporting actress (Pilar Bardem), best script, best music (Bernardo Bonezzi), best

326 Bernard P. E. Bentley

Mexico and France in 1996. The World Wide Web announced that a number of festivals would be showing the film to anglophone and other audiences throughout 1997.[2] The actual film script was published in 1996.[3] The film stars the established Victoria Abril who was also the protagonist of Díaz Yanes's first three scripts; four films frequently described with reference to Scorsese with touches of Tarantino (Torres 1994: *passim*), whose influence Díaz Yanes has never denied (e.g. Fonseca 1996: 115–17, 144). For those who are not yet familiar with Díaz Yanes's cinema, he is part of the new generation establishing itself in the 1990s (Saura 1997: esp. 108–9). He had previously co-scripted *Belmonte* with Juan Sebastián and Enrique Bollaín, the biopic directed by Juan Sebastián Bollaín and released in 1995. This was a move away from his previous thrillers, since he had already scripted *Demasiado corazón* (1992) and *A solas contigo* (1990), both directed by Eduardo Campo, and *Bâton rouge* (1988), co-scripted with and directed by Rafael Moleón.

I would argue that the success of a film depends on factors other than action and rapid editing from multiple shots with a steadycam camera, although *Nadie hablará . . .* does reflect all these features.

production manager (José Luis Escolar), best editor (José Salcedo). Also awarded prizes at other festivals were Federico Luppi for best actor (Premios Ondas and San Jordi), Francisco Femenía for best photography (San Sebastián); in New York (1996) the film was rewarded as best first picture, Federico Luppi as best actor, Pilar Bardem and Daniel Jiménez Cacho as best supporting actors. The excellent performance by Ana Ofelia Murgia should also be noted.

  [2] It is interesting and pertinent to the argument outlined below that, in spite of the prizes mentioned above, a number of francophone reviews accessed on the WWW are far from positive in their evaluation of this film. For instance Antoine Duplan: 'D'un coup de corne, un toro transforme un matador en légume—c'est comme ça que ça se passe en Espagne. Gloria, la presque veuve du torero, émigre au Mexique où elle sombre dans l'alcoolisme et la prostitution. Suite à une fusillade entre stups yankees et bandidos, la belle déchue entre en possession du carnet de comptes de l'organisation. Elle retourne à Madrid retrouver son mari comateux et sa belle-mère digne dans la douleur. Elle tente de cambrioler les blanchisseurs d'argent sale, ce qui s'avère dangereux. Hésitant entre le second degré d'un Tarantino, le kitsche d'un Almodovar et le réalisme social, ce film louvoie entre vulgarité et incohérence. Blême, bouffie de larmes, Victoria Abril incarne passionnément Gloria. Ce navet valait-il la peine de se défigurer et de s'avilir pareillement?' (http://webdo.ch/cineweb/personne_parlera.html); or http://www.dtr.fr/lyoncap/anciens/32cine.html; or *Cahiers du cinéma*, 500 (Mar. 1996): 127.
  [3] The film script is published by the *Revista viridiana* (1996, no. 16) and is in its details different from the released film. Changes were made during the shooting and editing of the film (Fonseca 1996: 124–30, esp. 128). All quotations are from the film itself as recorded from Canal+, followed by a page reference to the script (*RV*) with an asterisk* when there is a difference.

For some spectators it might be the story-line itself and/or the actor(s), or for a more reflective audience the implicit themes and ideas. There is, however, another factor which engages more than the spectators' visual connection with the screen or their ideological sympathies, and which arouses an implicit anticipation, at times increased by an explicit mental curiosity, arising from the images seen and/or the soundtrack heard. This is the principle of erotetic narration introduced by Noël Carroll in his book *Mystifying Movies* (1988: 170–81). Carroll's pragmatic approach is a persuasive explanation for the compulsion to watch a film, because it is so clear and simple (1988: 180–1). One good reason for trying out his suggestions on a Spanish film of whose existence he is probably unaware is that it allows us to test an alternative approach to contemporary critical and theoretical trends (see for instance the useful anthology compiled by Easthope (1993) and the lucid account by Gaut (1997)). Carroll establishes his premises on cognitive psychology rather than ambiguous and at times conflicting psychoanalytic or ideological theories (1988: 212–13, 226–34). Although Carroll applies his principle specifically to popular cinema (e.g. 1988: 170, 175–6, 199), his suggestions should not be restricted to 'movies' because they can also be observed in more artistic and intellectual films. Not only do 'pictorial representation, erotetic narration and variable framing' go a long way to explain 'the power of movies—their capacity to evoke unrivalled widespread and intense response' (1988: 212), but the erotetic narrative principle can also help understand more complex films such as *Nadie hablará* . . . , and is in fact a very useful complementary heuristic tool, although not exclusive (1988: 230–3), to analyse film narrative. Surprisingly the erotetic principle has not really received the attention it deserves in the film criticism I have come across. Carroll's comments rank with the obvious *perogrulladas* that command respect; like Racine's statement that tragedy need not involve gore and violence but 'il suffit que l'action en soit grande . . . et que tout s'y ressente de cette tristesse majestueuse qui fait tout le plaisir de la tragédie . . . toujours simple' (preface to *Bérénice*, Racine 1950–2). It seems to me that directors who do not exploit or intuit the erotetic principle do so at their peril.[4]

---

4 An attempt will be made to discuss the film from this erotetic perspective without revealing the answers to all the questions, so that those reading the account before viewing the film for themselves may still enjoy the experience of the erotetic narrative.

Carroll elaborates his principle on the basis of Pudovkin's
(1960) precepts of film-making (Carroll 1988: 170). In a nutshell:
'A movie will portray a sequence of scenes or events . . . the relation of earlier scenes and events in a film narrative to later scenes
and events can be generally understood on the model of the relation of a question to an answer . . . Earlier narrative scenes raise or
intimate questions, issues, or possibilities, that are answered or
actualised by later scenes' (1988: 171–2). Consequently 'most
movies are animated by macro-questions which organize the large
movements of the bulk of the significant action in the film and the
micro-questions are generally hierarchically subordinate to the
macro-questions' (1988: 179). Carroll goes on to qualify that this
question and answer process, the erotetic narrative, is usually experienced subconsciously by the spectator and at times manifested
as an expectation (1988: 172–3, 206). The image puzzles the spectators in such a way that they want or need to discover the explanation which is then presented in a subsequent sequence, shot, or
image, and which in turn raises another puzzle or question. In fact
a blank screen with a soundtrack can also raise a number of questions. The narration proceeds with this *encadenamiento* until the
plot is finally resolved and closed (1988: 178, but see 212–13 for
Carroll's own caveat), thus keeping the spectators gripped by the
narration, fixed to the screen, and glued to their seats.

Carroll's erotetic principles might be a clearer way of expressing
and articulating Díaz Yanes's own comments on film narrative:

no me refiero ahora a la creación de la historia, si no a la realización de la
película. Es contar la historia con elipsis brutales, comprendiendo lo que
debe quedar fuera. Las elipsis mueven la película. En ese sentido, lo que no
se cuenta es más importante que lo que se cuenta, porque son las llaves que
abren la imaginación del público, su participación. Me estoy explicando
fatal. (Matjí 1997: 27)

Joaquín Oristrell's reply, although focusing on the scriptwriter(s),
also has implications for the spectator:

Escribir para el cine es un asunto de hacer las preguntas correctas y esa
fórmula que hemos encontrado, que no es fórmula ninguna fuera de discu-
tir cuatro personas sobre la misma cosa, se basa en eso. Hacer preguntas y
encontrar las respuestas adecuadas. Si las preguntas son buenas, el resul-
tado también lo será. Como todos, este oficio consiste en conocer las
preguntas que hay que hacer. (Matjí 1977: 27)

In films these questions are present on various levels and any number of cinematographic techniques is used to embed them in the image or soundtrack. They can be identified on a macro-level, directing the plot and linking sequences as well as informing those sequences (Carroll 1988: 178–9), but they are more often experienced at the micro-levels of *mise-en-scène*, shots, frames, and even individual freeze-frames. In all cases these questions maintain the spectators' interest and, when consciously formulated, may even lead to a better understanding of the film viewed. Examples of each will be examined below.

Because thrillers depend on suspense or mystery they, by definition, continuously raise questions as to what is to happen next. Thrillers are in fact structured on erotetic principles, even if their scriptwriters have not seen the word before, otherwise there would be no suspense or mystery (Bordwell and Thompson 1990: 64–6). The narrative builds up gradually to provide the answers to a few basic macro-questions which are seen to direct the plot. Once identified these macro-questions are usually very simple and, however different, the answers are usually interrelated (Carroll 1988: 178). This is good dramatic practice. In the case of *Nadie hablará* . . . these macro-questions can be reduced to three: Will Gloria be able to use the drug dealers' address book to her advantage? Will the Mexican gangsters catch up with her? Will she overcome her alcoholism and poverty? It may not, however, always be possible to identify the macro-questions on first viewing, because there are so many other questions to distract the spectator, both linking sequences and within sequences themselves. Carroll suggests that it is easier to identify macro-questions once the film has been viewed and even, sometimes, to work backwards from the end in order not to get sidetracked by the many micro-questions (1988: 254–5 n. 43).[5] In this film there are another two macro-questions which emerge, concerning the Argentine gunman Eduardo, and which might be described as organizing a subplot. Will Eduardo fulfil his contract and will his daughter survive? For most of the film Gloria will be unaware of this contract on her life, providing a further source of suspense for the whole film (Branigan 1992: 74–5).

Before giving examples of how the erotetic principle can link

---

5 Some readers may here recall their experience of Golden Age Spanish drama, and Alexander Parker's principle of dramatic causality: 'The tracing back of the events that constitute the climax of a play to their first cause' (1970: 699).

sequences,[6] it is pertinent at this stage to comment on the way the film has been structured and edited, because it demonstrates how Gloria's and Eduardo's narratives are interwoven. The editor, José Salcedo, and his contribution have been acknowledged by Díaz Yanes as crucial (Fonseca 1996: 124–30), and comparing the film with the script shows how the latter has been pruned and simplified for the better (n. 3). The film can be divided into three almost equal movements of thirty minutes each, with a credit sequence and an epilogue to suggest a possible answer to the final question.[7] The first half-hour establishes the situation, as Gloria witnesses a double murder and acquires an address book, and it leads to the confirmation of the Mexican threat as Eduardo learns that she has returned to Madrid when he acquires a photograph of the Bar Ramiro, located on the ground floor of Gloria's building. In the second thirty minutes Gloria uses the information contained in the address book to carry out what turns out to be a carefully prepared but poorly rehearsed break-in, concluding with the intensification of the threat to her person as Eduardo, now in Madrid, first makes contact with the bar in the photograph. The third half-hour presents Gloria's unexpected second attempt to get her hands on the laundered money, and goes on to answer the five macro-questions to conclude the thriller. The two lives are at first separate but, as stated, they are also related and interwoven in the second half-hour, since the action of one has repercussions on the other and will merge for one sequence in the third section. They are therefore persuasively presented by cross-cuts through parallel montage.[8] It

---

[6] *Sequence*: film criticism uses this term in so many different ways, at times synonymous to scene, that it will here be defined according to Monaco as 'A basic unit of film construction consisting of one or more scenes that form a natural unit' (1981: 452; see also 189), and a *scene* as 'A complete unit of film narration. A series of shots (or single shot) that take place in a single location and that deal with a single action' (1981: 451).

[7] A tripartite structure is perhaps too frequently used to suggest a parallel with the three movements of the bullfight, however neatly this observation fits in with the present interpretation.

[8] *Parallel montage*, as an editing technique to present different sequences or scenes in different locations with different characters, is here distinguished from *alternate montage* which presents simultaneous actions or events. In this film it is not possible to ascertain that the Gloria/Madrid and Eduardo/Mexico sequences take place simultaneously although this may be the case in some instances. Following Bordwell and Monaco, montage and editing are taken as synonymous terms representing a different perspective on the process (Bordwell and Thompson 1990: 410; Monaco 1981: 183–4, 442).

is not difficult to appreciate how such a structure can continuously raise questions. In the first sequence Gloria and Eduardo are involved in a chance encounter, and they both go their own way as Eduardo escapes with his colleague whilst Gloria is found by the police holding Eduardo's dying victim. Here begins the parallel montage. The first cross-cuts involving Eduardo are very brief, all referring to his daughter, but always overshadowed by Gloria's progress narrated in much longer sequences and thus raising more questions. In these early parallel sequences it is therefore the events in Madrid that dominate the spectators' attention. The Mexican sequences inform the spectators of a threat that Gloria does not perceive whilst at the same time filling in Eduardo's more personal concerns. Eduardo's sequences are expanded from the moment he arrives in Madrid, as from the end of the second half-hour of the film, to become an immediate threat for Gloria. With each section the cross-cutting of the parallel montage becomes more rapid and regular, increasing the pace and intensity of the narrative, until the events merge as Eduardo catches up with Gloria and all but one of the macro-questions are answered.

So far we have come up with the description of an average 'movie', popular cinema, with an active, even aggressive, female protagonist who is not spared violence and disfigurement, and with a twist in the ending.[9] To use this film as a model case to illustrate the principles of the erotetic narrative is perhaps not the most persuasive example, because we are dealing with a thriller.[10] Notwithstanding, the erotetic principle as discussed by Carroll is also evident at the level of individual sequences and scenes, and the first sequence of this film can serve as an example.[11] It is set in the office corner of a warehouse where each event depicted comes as a surprise since the credit sequence has provided no context from

---

[9] Here with the reshuffling and deconstruction of male/female and active/passive binaries the film could be discussed with reference to contemporary feminist perspectives that no longer accept the simple polarities (see Humm 1997: 23–5, for a recent and lucid update).

[10] This film, however, was chosen out of concern for the whole volume so that the book would be as representative of Spanish cinema as possible, introducing its great variety to anglophone readers.

[11] This sequence is preceded by the credit sequence in a bullring, which introduces a different set of micro-questions and, as will be discussed below, is peripheral to the plot but of thematic importance, filling in Gloria's background as well as her psychological profile.

which to anticipate any development. Each action raises the question of what is going to happen next. Are the dollar bills really false? Are the undercover agents really working for themselves? Who will shoot first? Will anyone be killed? etc. . . . Gloria witnesses the shoot-out between two parties and is advised to retrieve the drug dealers' address book if she wants to make her fortune. A Spanish-speaking audience, with its cinema experience, will have identified Victoria Abril and Federico Luppi, the two main actors, and will expect a plot that will almost certainly oppose or join the victimized witness, Gloria, and the Argentine gunman, Eduardo. This is an extreme illustration of how 'in narrative construction the viewer goes massively beyond what is given, by using her background knowledge to construct a story out of exiguous clues' (Gaut 1995: 12). Other spectators, not familiar with the actors, will not be able to anticipate or restrict the possibilities so easily. There is a series of shots which oppose Gloria in high-angle shots holding a gun on Eduardo, seen in low-angle reverse shots helping his partner Evaristo. These angles establish power statements about relationships (Monaco 1981: 161, and his caveat). The shots, angles, and editing would lead those who are unable to identify the main actors to anticipate the demise of one of them, or at least to ask a leading question. They will have to wait until both undercover agents are shot to rule out their participation and to experience the forthcoming clues which will help them eliminate any number of potential plots. At the end of the sequence the immediate question is what will happen when the Mexican police find the only witness with a body? How will she be involved in the narrative? At this stage this question is more pressing than whether she is able to keep the address book, which is bracketed off and disappears from the frame as soon as it has been referred to (Carroll 1988: 202). The question concerning Gloria's arrest is answered two sequences later when Gloria is repatriated and the spectators are left to wonder whether a new life awaits in Madrid, apparently well out of reach of the Mexican gangsters. The spectators need to wait for another six sequences, some twelve minutes, to discover that she does have the address book, and its importance for the plot will gradually emerge in the following sequences.

The erotetic principle is even more obvious of course at the end of scenes or sequences, providing the spectators with a good reason to stay in their seats. What is going to happen next? The question helps to link the sequences and scenes even if there is no eye-line, graphic, or other match to observe. As just stated, the first sequence concludes with the immediate question: will either Gloria or Eduardo get away? But consider the first contact with the furrier *Americana*, one of the outlets for the laundered drug money. This is an example of how successive scenes can build up numerous questions which are only answered some time later, so only a few questions will be mentioned as examples of what Carroll describes as the 'question/answer structure' and for which he identifies six types of scene (1988: 174–5). Because of her nervous behaviour and cheap clothes, out of place in such an expensive shop, a large mastiff is allowed to intimidate Gloria, who leaves in a hurry. This is an establishing scene for a succession of scenes that will keep on accumulating questions. What was she doing in the shop? What is going to happen next, as the manageress locks the door of the shop and, through its glass, watches Gloria disappear across the street? The front of the shop seen through venetian blinds then comes on the screen, we do not know how much later, perhaps immediately since Gloria is wearing the same clothes. As the camera moves back it includes the back of Gloria's head in the left of the frame. A reverse shot through the same venetian blinds, from outside, shows her at a table in the bar eating *pipas* as she observes the shop across the road. She is repeating a telephone number provided by a brief reverse shot of the shop across the road with a small hoarding, which is actually dwarfed by the sign of the shop's name below it. These facts are actually overshadowed by the following longer creationistic scene evoking Gloria's alcoholic problem, emphasized by one of the few moments of non-diegetic music in the film. In an example of the soundtrack raising questions, one also wonders why she should come so slowly out of her trance to the sustained sound of a pneumatic drill carrying out roadworks which have so far been held out of the frame. This shot is taken through a window, or glass door, without venetian blinds, and is also sustained for longer than expected. Why this should be will be justified much later as the answers are withheld until reaching what Carroll calls the fulfilling scene (1988: 252–3 n. 38), when Gloria starts to break into the shop, and only some of the preceding questions are answered. But the scene which immediately follows, with a jump cut to a tracking medium shot of Doña Julia chatting as she walks arm in arm with her friend Doña Esperanza, confirms many of the answers to even earlier questions raised by the narrative. Carroll calls this an answering scene (1988: 174), and the spectators are told that Gloria has only just returned to Madrid; that Doña Julia is her mother-in-law; that nothing good can come or be expected of Gloria, but Doña Julia is fond of her; that Gloria says she has stopped drinking; that the flat in which Doña Julia lives belongs to Gloria and her husband but that it is Doña Julia who has been paying the mortgage for the last three years and looking after Gloria's husband. Dialogue and language, as exemplified by this scene, are the most direct way of conveying questions and answers (Carroll 1988: 206); but as most of my examples imply the image is a more persuasive, although not exclusive, medium of information in films (Carroll 1988: 205). Sometimes image and language can be seen in opposition and thus generate more questions (Humm 1997: 56–7), as in the sequence on the Mexican ranch where Eduardo is told to go to Madrid to find the prostitute. The information received concerning Gloria's situation is however again overshadowed, this time by the McGuffin, of which there are a number in this film, of Doña Esperanza's forthcoming marriage. Immediately, and with another jump cut, Gloria is seen passing behind three young women waiting to cross the street. Why does Gloria come back and wait so close behind them? Why does she rush off in another direction when they eventually cross the street? Non-diegetic music is then heard as one of the young women shouts that her wallet has been stolen. The music announces that a first climax in these sustaining question scenes has been reached, although more are to follow. The next scene is an overhead shot of a toilet-seat where Gloria's hands are going through a wallet. Why do the identity card and a family photo appear to be more impor-tant to her than the money? This strange behaviour is explained some sequences later in another fulfilling scene that also starts another line of enquiry, as we see Gloria proceeding with her preparations which turn out to be for the break-in into the furrier's strong room. As Carroll explains, the spectator sometimes has 'to leapfrog, so to speak, in order to connect question scenes with their answer' (1988: 253 n. 40).

The erotetic principle also works well at the level of *mise-en-scène*. Many thrillers have failed, and been relegated to very late night or early morning broadcasts on television, precisely because they rely on poorly constructed suspense or mystery and do not consistently raise enough questions at every level of the narration. One effective example of how the *mise-en-scène* can be exploited is Gloria's first break-in, a succession of disasters. Erotetically speaking the spectators keep asking themselves a number of questions in rapid succession. What is Gloria doing? Will she drill in the right spot? Will she get it on her second attempt? Will she find any money? Will she get herself and the full bag back up through the hole in the ceiling? Will she get herself through the hole? Will she get away from the gangster rushing up the stairs? The camera follows Gloria rushing out of the flat to go downstairs, and in her hurry she leaves the door open on the right of the frame. She hears sounds coming up the stairs, and the reverse shot following her inquisitive gaze confirms that the gangster is rushing up to the landing. Gloria is not to be seen. Where has she gone? The gangster reaches the landing and storms through the open door of the flat. Is Gloria caught? Will she get beaten up or killed? No; Gloria re-enters the frame from the left, on the side opposite the door, and creeps down the stairs. She had hidden on the stairs to the second floor on the left of the frame. Up to now the *mise-en-scène* had not required the spectator to consider the left-hand side of the landing as relevant for the narrative. With the conspiracy of the *mise-en-scène* and the frame, both the gangster and the spectators formulated the same question and all came up with the wrong answer! Gloria's movements had been edited and bracketed off (Carroll 1988: 202).

It is all these questions which, on the micro-level, keep the spectator interested, intrigued, and watching. But when one looks at a film in even more detail, the erotetic principle is seen to be present at the level of the shots themselves. One example will have to suffice. At the beginning of the first sequence in the warehouse all sorts of questions are raised by the slow close-up travelling shot of the table-top. The spectators' attention is first focused on a small glass being picked up (some may be able to deduce it is probably full of tequila), then a radio broadcasting a football commentary, followed by two bottles of beer, a mobile phone, pizza remains, another small glass, an ashtray, bundles of dollar bills in an attaché case which are picked up by a hand before the frame is expanded to include a face and then a second face (the first time the spectators are shown Federico Luppi). This is a good example of indexing (Carroll 1988: 201–2), which Díaz Yanes has explored to his own erotetic advantage. The conventions of so-called classical film narrative techniques lead the spectators to consider each one of these detailed objects as significant, but since there are so many it is the last one which eventually takes semantic precedence in this shot. In fact these bundles of US dollars, which get the narrative moving, prove to be less important to the whole film than the small glasses and the beer bottles, because of Gloria's alcoholism, or the mobile phone without which Eduardo is rarely seen. These objects become metonyms for Gloria and Eduardo.

The erotetic principle can also be seen exploited at the level of the frame on its own. As mentioned above, in the first sequence the all-important address book disappears from the frame once it has been referred to, and the spectators forget their initial questions in order to focus on others that appear more pressing, until the address book returns to raise more questions. Another example will be presented. The relevance of the credit sequence presenting the nervous bullfighters getting ready to enter the ring gradually establishes itself as the narrative unfolds. This is an example of deferred reading, so frequent in films, which is another way of expressing the question/answer structure. Gradually the credit sequence is linked to Gloria's husband who, throughout the film, lies on his bed in a coma. This is established when Gloria returns to Madrid. She is tracked by the camera to a flat and met by one who will later be identified as her mother-in-law. The only verbal exchange is a muted: '¿Juan?', answered after a long pause by 'Donde tú lo dejaste' (*RV* 19–20*). At this stage the spectators wonder who is this elderly lady, not happy at seeing Gloria, and to whom does the flat belong? Why is the *mise-en-scène*, the close camerawork and lighting, showing a dark and cramped flat? Why is the frame constantly fragmented by doors and straight lines? All these are reminding the informed spectator of that other flat inhabited by another Gloria.[12] As these questions are raised, Gloria is panned by the camera anxiously entering another room in deep focus and going round what turns out to be a bed. There is a light from the window to the left of the frame, the first bright light seen

---

[12] Eleven years apart, in another genre and exploiting different conventions, there is much in common in the implicit social comments of *Nadie hablará . . .* and Almodóvar's 1984 *¿Qué he hecho yo para merecer esto?* (Smith 1994: 51–62).

in this sequence. Gloria's face is in the centre beside the framed black-and-white photo of a bullfighter on the same level as her face because of the tilt of the camera, but in the three-dimensional world represented the photo is actually behind her on the wall. Beside the photograph on the right of the frame there is a drip bottle on a stand which is actually in the foreground. The frame at this point presents a puzzling image which raises many questions, but it actually encapsulates the situation (*RV* 20, sec. 11). The frame is slowly expanded as the camera tilts down to follow Gloria's gaze to include her arm and then her hand gently touching the lips of the man in bed connected to the drip. This is an example of how 'variable framing' and indexing (Carroll 1988: 201–4; Bordwell refers to this as 'mobile framing', Bordwell and Thompson 1990: 181–94) direct the spectators' attention either to formulate or to answer a question. 'The importance of variable framing for movies is the potential it affords for assuring the audience attends to everything that is *relevant*, and that it does so automatically, so to speak' (Carroll 1988: 206). Gloria's injured husband, who has been in a coma for the previous three years, must be the bullfighter of the credit sequence—no other construction is justified (Gaut 1995: 114–15), and later snippets of dialogue confirm this.

According to Carroll it is not just the framing of a shot that can supply micro-questions. An individual freeze-frame from a scene can also perform this task and supply a number of pertinent questions, like the zoom into a freeze-frame on Doña Julia's calendar indicating 6 April. These freeze-frames can also answer questions. The scene discussed in the above paragraph was preceded by Gloria's arrival in Madrid. This is indicated erotetically by a jump cut and short freeze-frame of the outside of the bullring De las Ventas in an imposing low-angle tilt-up, then we see her through a bus window waking up and staring at the building, its reflection conspicuous on the glass of the window (*RV* 19, sec. 8). This is another of the few scenes with non-diegetic music to link with the preceding sequence: the music started seconds previously as a Mexican customs officer stamped 'REPATRIADA' (*RV* 18) in Gloria's passport. The Madrid bullring disappears as the bus moves off, cross-cut to another bus arriving. The camera follows Gloria off the second bus to a similar low-angle tilt-up but rarely used long shot of high-rise buildings on the outskirts of Madrid (*RV* 19, sec.

8A). The camera includes then slowly scales down on the first view of the Bar Ramiro (Carroll 1988: 200–2), whose significance can only be anticipated erotetically as she pauses in front of it. Another persuasive example can be quoted from the end of the second half-hour once Eduardo and Oswaldo have arrived in Madrid. The sequence begins with a brief freeze-frame close-up of a finger pointing to the Bar Ramiro's number in the telephone directory. Eduardo then dials the number and, just before he is answered, church bells are heard. Phone in hand, Eduardo moves to the window which frames a totally different world: the dome of a church that dwarfs his figure. He slowly lowers the telephone without replying (*RV* 50, sec. 45). This complicates further the macro-question: will Eduardo fulfil his contract? An up-to-now meaningless prop in Eduardo's hand, a Bible, is explained and used: Is Eduardo acquiring a conscience or becoming superstitious? Does he take the intrusion of the church bell as a divine warning? A subsequent conversation with an ex-Nationalist priest suggests this growing possibility and a more complex psychology for the hired gunman. As Carroll explains, 'the devices of visual narration, if not the original source of the questions, help make those questions salient' (1988: 206).

Only two minutes long, the bullfighting credit sequence has been consistently referred to as a perplexing preface, and therefore raises many questions once the narrative is introduced by the intertitle 'MEXICO D.F. 3 AÑOS DESPUES' (*RV* 9*). There is only the voice-over of the one who will turn out to be the protagonist answering the phone to link the two sequences, another example of erotetic sound. The script makes it clear that the bullfighting sequence is seen on television (*RV* 16, 9), but the film ensures that the image is much more ambiguous and puzzling. The filmic frame, which could have included the frame of a television, leaves no clue for this interpretation and thus raises more questions. As the first sequence unfolds, the spectators gradually realize that the credit sequence had nothing to contribute to the first sequence. The questions raised by the credit sequence may even be forgotten or just leave a vague trace which is then picked up some twelve minutes later when Gloria returns to Madrid, as described in the preceding paragraph. Subsequent and gradual references then build up an answer, suggesting she left to avoid her responsibilities, perhaps traumatized by her husband's accident and wanting to make a fresh start. Hence repatriation to Spain represents her failure as she endeavours to make another start.[13] Once the whole film has been viewed, and in the context of other images, when the question is asked again, the credit sequence can be understood as an integral part of the film's texture. The bullfighting elements, the connotations of the man's world and *machista* values, through the visual link and high angle of the bullring's red bricks matching those of the high-rise flat (*RV* 19, sec. 8 and 8A), are rich in cultural and social reference to the patriarchal values of the Franco years which have been exploited in many other films (Kinder 1993: 99–100). The implications and consequences of these values and policies are intimated in the fate of its circumstantial victims: be they a guilt-laden priest, Juan the bullfighter, Doña Julia the former tortured communist, or Gloria forced into prostitution and finding relief in alcohol—according to her friend the Mexican prostitute 'No es una profesional, y no más trabaja para beber' (*RV* 29*). It is the desire to crawl out of her poverty which motivates Gloria in her various endeavours throughout the narrative: be it prostitution, robbery, finding a job, or sitting her school-leaving certificate. Only within the limitations of the first option is she shown to be relatively successful, although the upbeat ending allows the constructed possibility of success in the last two options (Gaut 1995: 19–22). As Gloria likes to quote, 'Los pobres son príncipes que tienen que reconquistar su reino' (*RV* 31). Her impatient attempts are contrasted to the resigned Doña Julia, who belongs to the older generation that has been emotionally scarred and physically tortured by the executors of Francoist ideology and who espouses with dignity the work ethic, by giving private classes and baking, in order to scratch a living and pay the mortgage. This link to the years of dictatorship is further manifest through Doña Julia's occasional reminiscences, justified within the narrative since they give Gloria the courage to stand up to Oswaldo, and by the presence of Doña Julia's friends, who actually strengthen Gloria's characterization. Eduardo's behaviour and his conversation with the priest also link the spectators back to the Civil War and earlier, suggesting a parallel between the wartime executioners and the gangsters of today, with little difference between the patriarchal and *machista* values.

---

[13] Díaz Yanes himself has justified the bullfighting elements as personal and autobiographical memories (Fonseca 1996: 138–9).

But the first question arising from the film might very well come from the title itself which, by its unusual length, is also very puzzling: *Nadie hablará de nosotras cuando hayamos muerto*. What can it be referring to? Titles are usually brief and often provide an initial previewing clue, just as a knowledge of the actors will provide other clues, to the macro-questions offered by the narrative. This one does not at first sight do so. In the first sequence the audience is reminded of the long title by the Mexican-American detective dying in Gloria's arms who inverts the title: 'Mi madre está muerta y si tú no te acuerdas, nadie se va a acordar de mí. Me llamo Many Robaina. You got that? Many . . .' (*RV* 17*), and Gloria uses his name when she holds up the furrier. At the end Doña Julia takes leave of Gloria with 'Acuérdate de mí' (*RV* 86) and repeats in her letter 'Acuérdate de nosotros' (*RV* 88). The length of the title also draws linguistic attention to itself. The 'nosotras' marks the gender and focuses on the characters. This is not evident in the English: *Nobody Will Speak of Us When We Are Dead*, or in German, Italian, or Danish for instance, where the pronoun is not marked for gender. In French the gender signal is transferred to the concluding past participle, *Personne ne parlera de nous quand nous serons mortes*, focusing on the result rather than the protagonists themselves. The questions raised linger on once the film has finished and it is only later, upon reflection, looking for coherent and satisfying explanations, that some suggestions may occur.

Most of the women in this film do not die, but they are presented as marginalized or as victims of patriarchal values. There is one woman who at first can only be described as close to Eduardo, although the script immediately refers to her unequivocally as his wife (*RV* 18), but whom the film, changing the script, identifies as his daughter the second time she is on screen. Celia is first seen lying on the kitchen floor, an appropriate female space within a patriarchal setting, and appears to be dead, in a brief twenty seconds shot between the police finding Gloria in the warehouse and her repatriation. After Gloria's return to Madrid there is an equally brief hospital sequence where the audience learns that Celia is not dead but suffering from unidentified internal bleeding. This information is partly obscured by the more important fact for the plot that the spectators now discover the identity of Eduardo's boss as he is asked to find the prostitute from the warehouse. Furthermore, during most of the sequence,

the hospital bed is presented in such a way that the other characters in the room mask its occupier. Of course the whole is
constructed in such a way as to raise successive micro-questions,
not least about the identity and relationships of those present in
the room. In the last half-hour of the film Eduardo is told that the
bleeding was caused by a surgical needle left in her body during a
previous operation. Celia is presented as a victim of the experts'
inattention (Humm 1997: 68–70), but within the context of this
particular answering scene the information cannot be trusted or
her life taken for granted. There is also the Mexican prostitute
intimidated by Eduardo when he first traces Gloria. She sells her
body and her friends, because her situation only allows her money
or violence. Women are also collectively presented as vulnerable
and exploited in the film, for instance the scene of the 'señoritas
vestidas de rojo' in the male preserve of the stadium. The presentation of women as commodities is epitomized by the film's focus
on prostitution, clearly marked when Gloria applies for the post
of receptionist. Although these sequences are not crucial to the
plot, they are examples of men exploiting their position over
women, and they do raise many micro-questions which can all
lead the spectators to consider the wider context as well as enrich
Gloria's characterization.

The film also presents strong women. Doña Julia may be seen as
a strong character for most of the film. She finds strength in her
resignation and fortitude, and she comforts Gloria, inspiring her
with the internal strength to face up to her misfortunes by retelling
how she used her voice to save herself (Humm 1997: 57; Kinder
1993: 255–7), but her walking stick and symbol of authority is not
that big and she actually needs it to hobble around.[14] The partial
lighting and shadows, a constant feature of this film, are particularly conspicuous when presenting her face, and this also raises
questions in the spectator's mind, suggesting a character that is
more complex and not fully known or understood. The film will
gradually fill in her psychological profile, and warned by this

[14] The walking stick, in various sizes and shapes, is often used as a symbol or
metonym of authority and power normally, but not always, associated with patriarchal values; contrast for instance its various presentations in *La mitad del cielo*
(Manuel Gutiérrez Aragón, 1986), *La casa de Bernarda Alba* (Mario Camus, 1987),
or *Alas de mariposa* (Juanma Bajo Ulloa, 1991) (Bentley 1995: 263–5): three films
I would have gladly used as examples of the erotetic narrative.

erotetic lighting the spectators will be more receptive to the clues offered later on. Associated with Doña Julia is La Pasionaria, Dolores Ibárruri, who died in 1989 and therefore before the film is set, always present in the background through the framed photograph in her bedroom. Here is another strong woman who has also suffered for her beliefs and lived to see the recognition and legalization of her party by the Spanish state. Doña Julia's two friends who come to her dinner party, prepared by Gloria at considerable expense and thus strengthening the bond between the daughter- and mother-in-law, also belong to this group of survivors. Doña Amelia, the head of the drug-dealing organization, is a powerful woman who is still coquettish enough to dye her hair jet black. She has made it to the top of a male organization and stays there by outwitting men at their own games. The ambivalence of the gender power stakes in this film is also exemplified by María Luisa, who orders her bodyguard around, but when Eduardo and Oswaldo arrive in Madrid she is pushed into a more servile relationship to male authority: cooking, washing, and ironing for them, accepting orders, and making no decisions. These female characters, together with Gloria the active female protagonist who is not lacking in aggression or courage to survive in a man's world, even when handicapped by partial illiteracy and an alcohol problem, present a more complex and still vulnerable image of womanhood in 1990s cinema (Humm 1997: 31).

At this stage, any reader who has seen the film may wonder why so little mention has been made so far of Doña Julia, because in screen time she receives more attention than Eduardo, and her participation raises just as many, if not more, questions than his involvement. This is due to the fact that the macro-questions, which were our starting point, do not give her a central position within the plot and there was a definite attempt to be selective in order to allow those who have not yet seen the film some of the pleasures of the erotetic narrative. An awareness of the erotetic principle allows the spectators to appreciate the importance and relevance of Doña Julia to the film. Although, for the plot of the film as a thriller, Doña Julia is marginal, thematically, viewing the film as a statement about women in their specific social context, the micro-questions raised allow the spectator to appreciate that she is as important as her daughter-in-law who finally takes a stand against *machista* attitudes when, for instance, Gloria holds her own against the impatient car owner.[15] In fact the film can be viewed as the story of two women, presented through the actions of the younger one and her relationship to her mother-in-law. Both are victims of circumstances: deprived of their husbands, they have to survive in a patriarchal and violent society. Both are strongly bonded, and not just by the comatose bullfighter, son and husband; for as Doña Esperanza informs the spectators of Doña Julia: 'Tú siempre has tenido debilidad por esta chica' (*RV* 28). Due to the focalization of the camera (Deleyto 1991), the daughter-in-law is seen physically, and perhaps emotionally, to suffer more than Doña Julia. The spectator is positioned on Gloria's side (Deleyto 1991), and within the film she does not form any relationships except with her mother-in-law. This emphasizes the transference of emotions and a bonding of situations which lead the spectator to consider both women, through their different reactions but similar frustrations, to be dealing with the same problem. By presenting the two women as victims of violence and torture, parallels are also established in the spectator's mind between the forces of Franco's law and order and the Mexican gangsters, both influencing in very different ways individual behaviours and perceptions. This is the answer to the more problematic questions raised by the narrative. Both women are victims of tragic circumstances. There is sadness in the fact that after so much frustration and suffering, one of them is to be thought so insignificant as to be forgotten. It is the tragedy in the situation of these two widows, and that of many other women, which leads us back to Racine and 'cette tristesse majestueuse . . . toujours simple'. There is a difference in that the actions of the nobility that moved seventeenth-century audiences have been replaced by the action thrillers of contemporary spectators. There is gore and violence in *Nadie hablará de nosotras* . . . but this goes with the genre and is also part of the film's implicit social comments within its Spanish context.[16] There is tragedy in the emotions, suffering, and frustrations the two women are seen

---

[15] This sequence actually concludes the film in the script (*RV* 90–1), see Fonseca 1996: 125–7.

[16] The violence in this film is actually very limited in screen time and, unlike a Scorsese or Tarantino film, only a few people are involved; but when present it might be considered excessive by some sensibilities because it is so personal, albeit with potent socio-political implications (Kinder 1993: chs. 4–5, esp. 137–40; and 1996: 11–13).

to experience. If the feeling of tragedy has been generated, the spectators are left at the end to construct their own conclusion as to whether Doña Julia's sacrifice and Gloria's optimism will be justified (Fonseca 1996: 125–6). This question, which is raised by the ending, is not answered by the film. Like the reference to bullfighting this is an excellent example of what Berys Gaut identified as 'discretionary construction' which some films ask their spectators to perform (1995: 19–22).

According to Carroll: 'Unlike those of real life, the actions observed in movies have a level of intelligibility, due to the role they play in the erotetic system of questions and answers. Because of the question/answer structure, the audience is left with the impression that it has learned everything important to know concerning the action depicted' (1988: 180; see also 205). But, as we have seen, when this principle stops being automatic and becomes a conscious process it provides a positive analytical tool to understand what emerges as a complex and fascinating film, in spite of being, or rather because it is, a thriller. An awareness of the erotetic principle also allows the spectators to avoid the confusion experienced by some who have not followed up some of the basic questions raised by the narrative.[17] In this film, Art has ensured that the women cannot be forgotten. An awareness of the erotetic principle not only allows the creation of a spectacle that will grip its spectators to watch a popular film, or movie, with satisfaction, but it may also help spectators understand what Carroll keeps defining as an Art Film (e.g. 1988: 170, 180, 199–200, 208 ff.).

The erotetic principle is an extremely useful heuristic device, so obvious that one wonders why it took so long to be formulated and why so little use has been made of it in film criticism. But perhaps the last word should go to Díaz Yanes: 'tengo que saber lo que voy a contar. Que siempre es una idea con fuerza. En el caso de *Nadie hablará* . . . esa idea era una mujer en paro. Los problemas de una mujer en paro. La metáfora, que es un poco cursi, era María Magdalena pecadora. Y a partir de ahí ya empiezo a construir la película' (Fonseca 1996: 100).

---

[17] See n. 2 for examples of the confusion that can arise, and consult Marsha Kinder's illuminating commentary on *Bilbao* (1978, José Luis Bigas Luna), which is actually describing the erotetic principle without using the word (1993: 268–70).

REFERENCES

Aguinaga, Atocha (1997), 'Lo que hay que tener', *Revista academia*, 19: 8–20.

Allinson, Mark (1997), 'Not Matadors, Not Natural Born Killers: Violence in Three Films by Young Spanish Directors', *Bulletin of Hispanic Studies* (Liverpool), 74/4: 315–30.

Bentley, Bernard P. E. (1995), 'The Credit Sequence of *La mitad del cielo* (1986)', *Forum for Modern Language Studies*, 31/3: 259–73.

Bordwell, David, and Thompson, Kirstin (1990), *Film Art: An Introduction*, 3rd rev. edn. New York: McGraw-Hill.

Branigan, Edward (1992), *Narrative Comprehension and Film*. London: Routledge.

Carroll, Noël (1988), *Mystifying Movies: Fads and Fallacies in Contemporary Film Theory*. New York: Columbia University Press.

Deleyto, Celestino (1991), 'Focalisation in Film Narrative', *Atlantis*, 13/1.2: 159–77 (also reprinted in Susana Onega and José Ángel García Landa (eds.), *Narratology: An Introduction*, Harlow: Longman, 1996: 217–33).

Díaz Yanes, Agustín (1996), *Nadie hablará de nosotras cuando hayamos muerto*, *Revista Viridiana*, 16: 9–91.

Easthope, Anthony (1993), *Contemporary Film Theory*. London: Longman.

Fonseca, Mercedes (1996), 'Una tarde de cine: tres generaciones de Directores-Guionistas', *Revista viridiana*, 16: 94–158.

Gaut, Berys (1995), 'Making Sense of Films: Neoformalism and its Limits', *Forum for Modern Language Studies*, 31: 8–23.

—— (1997), 'Analytic Philosophy of Film: History, Issues, Prospects', *Philosophical Books*, 38/3: 145–56.

Humm, Maggie (1997), *Feminism and Film*. Edinburgh: Edinburgh University Press.

Kinder, Marsha (1993), *Blood Cinema: The Reconstruction of National Identity in Spain*. Berkeley and Los Angeles: University of California Press.

—— (1996), 'Sangre española', *Revista academia*, 13: 11–13.

Matjí, Manolo (1997), 'Sacar algo de la nada', *Revista academia*, 19: 24–9.

Monaco, James (1981), *How to Read a Film: The Art, Technology, Language, History, and Theory of Film and Media*, rev. edn. New York: Oxford University Press.

Parker, Alexander A. (1970), 'The Spanish Drama of the Golden Age: A Method of Analysis and Interpretation', in Eric Bentley (ed.), *The Great Playwrights Introduced by Eric Bentley*, New York: Double Day: 679–707.

Pudovkin, Vsevolod I. (1960), *Film Techniques and Film Acting*, ed. and trans. Ivor Montagu. New York: Grove Press.

Racine, Jean-Baptiste (1950–2), *Œuvres complètes*, 2 vols., ed. R. Picard. Paris: Gallimard.

Saura, Antonio (1997), 'El nuevo cine español', *Revista viridiana*, 15: 103–17.

Smith, Paul J. (1994), *Desire Unlimited: The Cinema of Pedro Almodóvar*. London: Verso.

Torres, Augusto M. (1994), *Diccionario del cine español*. Madrid: Espasa Calpe.

Index